YOU DECIDE! 2007

Current Debates in American Politics

JOHN T. ROURKE
University of Connecticut

PEARSON
Longman

New York Boston San Francisco
London Toronto Sydney Tokyo Singapore Madrid
Mexico City Munich Paris Cape Town Hong Kong Montreal

Editor in Chief: Eric Stano
Senior Marketing Manager: Elizabeth Fogarty
Production Cordinator: Scarlett Lindsay
Project Coordination and Electronic Page Makeup: Lorraine Patsco
Cover Design Manager: John Callahan
Manufacturing Buyer: Roy L. Pickering, Jr.
Cover image courtesy of Getty Images, Inc.
Printer and Binder: R.R. Donnelley/Crawfordsville
Cover Printer: Phoenix Color Corporation

Library of Congress Cataloging-in-Publication Data

Rourke, John T., 1945-
You decide! 2007 : current debates in American politics / John T. Rourke.
— 4th ed.
p. cm.
1. Political planning—United States. 2. United States—Politics and government. I. Title.
JK468.P64R67 2007
320.60973—dc22

2006035192

Visit us at www.ablongman.com

ISBN 0-321-43016-6

1 2 3 4 5 6 7 8 9 10–DOC–09 08 07 06

CONTENTS

Filibustering Federal Court Nominees: Protecting the Minority
ADVOCATE: Harry F. Byrd, U.S. Senator (D-WV)
SOURCE: *Congressional Record,* March 1, 2005
Also suitable for chapters on Constitution, Congress

15. STATE AND LOCAL GOVERNMENT 230

TAKING PROPERTY BY EMINENT DOMAIN FOR ECONOMIC DEVELOPMENT: SERVING THE PUBLIC GOOD *OR* ABUSING OF GOVERNMENT POWER?

Taking Property by Eminent Domain for Economic Development: Serving the Public Good
ADVOCATE: Jeffrey Finkle, President And Chief Executive Office, International Economic Development Council
SOURCE: Testimony during hearings on "Protecting Property Rights After *Kelo,*" before the U.S. House of Representatives, Committee on Energy And Commerce Committee, Subcommittee on Commerce, Trade, and Consumer Protection, October 19, 2005

Taking Property by Eminent Domain for Economic Development: Abuse of Government Power
ADVOCATE: Michael D. Ramsey, Professor, School of Law, University of San Diego
SOURCE: Testimony during hearings on "Protecting Property Rights After *Kelo,*" before the U.S. House of Representatives, Committee on Energy And Commerce Committee, Subcommittee on Commerce, Trade, and Consumer Protection, October 19, 2005
Also suitable for chapters on Constitution, Courts, Economic Policy

16. BUDGETARY POLICY 244

A LINE-ITEM VETO FOR THE PRESIDENT: PRUDENT WAY TO RESTRAIN SPENDING *OR* UNWISE GRANT OF POWER?

A Line-Item Veto for the President: Prudent Way to Restrain Spending
ADVOCATE: Paul Ryan, U.S. Representative (R-WI)
SOURCE: Testimony during hearings on "The Constitution and the Line-Item Veto," U.S. House of Representatives, Committee on the Judiciary, Subcommittee on the Constitution, April 27, 2006

A Line-Item Veto for the President: Unwise Grant of Power
ADVOCATE: Cristina Martin Firvida, Senior Counsel, National Women's Law Center
SOURCE: Testimony during hearings on "The Constitution and the Line Item Veto," U.S. House of Representatives, Judiciary Committee, Subcommittee on the Constitution, April 27, 2006
Also suitable for chapters on Constitution, President, Congress

EXTENDED CONTENTS

WEB ISSUES

The following topics are available on the Web at:
http://www.ablongman.com/YouDecide/

22. PROPORTIONAL REPRESENTATION

ADVANCE OF DEMOCRACY *OR* DESTABILIZING IDEA?

Proportional Representation: Advance of Democracy

ADVOCATE: Theodore S. Arrington, Professor, Department of Political Science, University of North Carolina at Charlotte

SOURCE: Testimony during hearings on "H.R. 1173/States' Choice of Voting Systems Act" before the U.S. House of Representatives Committee on the Judiciary, Subcommittee on the Constitution, September 23, 1999

Proportional Representation: Destabilizing Idea

ADVOCATE: Abigail Thernstrom, Senior Fellow, Manhattan Institute

SOURCE: Testimony during hearings on "H.R. 1173/States' Choice of Voting Systems Act," before the U.S. House of Representatives Committee on the Judiciary, Subcommittee on the Constitution, September 23, 1999

Suitable for chapters on Elections, Congress

23. REGULATING "SOFT MONEY" IN ELECTIONS

NECESSARY REFORM *OR* OPPRESSIVE RESTRICTION?

Regulating "Soft Money" in Elections: Needed Reform

ADVOCATE: Michael J. Malbin Executive Director of the Campaign Finance Institute and Professor, Department of Political Science, State University of New York at Albany

SOURCE: Testimony during hearings on "S.271, a Bill Which Reforms The Regulatory And Reporting Structure Of Organizations Registered Under Section 527 of the Internal Revenue Code" before the U.S. Senate, Committee on Rules and Administration, March 8, 2005

Regulating "Soft Money" in Elections: Oppressive Restriction

ADVOCATE: Robert F. Bauer, Chair, Political Law Group, Perkins Coie, LLP, Washington, DC

SOURCE: Testimony during hearings on the "Regulation of 527 Organizations," before the House of Representatives, Committee on Administration, April 20, 2005

Suitable for chapters on Civil Liberties, Elections, Interest Groups

PREFACE

To the Students

This book is founded on two firm convictions. The first is that each of you who reads this book is profoundly affected by politics, probably in more ways than you know. The second "truth" is that it is important that everyone be attentive to and active in politics.

POLITICS AFFECTS YOU

The outcome of many of the 19 debates in this printed volume and the 5 supplemental debates on the Web will impact your life directly. If you play college sports, for example, the controversy over Title IX in **Debate 13** has and will help determine what teams and athletic scholarship support are available at your school. Similarly, the issue of affirmative action in **Debate 18** may influence your admission to graduate school, if that is the course you take. It is also college-age students who are most likely to be sent to and to die in wars. There has not been a military draft since the Vietnam War era, and U.S. casualties in wars have been relatively light since then. But in that war, 61% of the more than the 58,000 Americans killed were between the ages of 17 and 21. Now, after many years, there is renewed talk about a draft, in part because the U.S. military is having trouble meeting its recruitment goals amid its ongoing involvement in Iraq, featured in **Debate 19**.

Freedom of religion is one of Americans' most cherished rights and is protected by the First Amendment. But the application of the First Amendment is something of a double-edged sword. There is widespread agreement that people should have the right to whatever religious belief they may hold. What is controversial and presented in **Debate 4** is whether even such traditional references to God, such as the words "under God" in the Pledge of Allegiance violate the separation of church and state principle in the First Amendment.

PAY ATTENTION TO THE POLICY PROCESS

Process may seem less interesting than policy to many people, but you do not have to study politics very long to learn that *who* decides something very often determines *what* the policy will be. Process does not always determine which policy is adopted, but plays a large role. Therefore, there are a number of debates in this volume whose outcome does not directly affect a specific policy, but which could have a profound impact on the policy process. For example **Debate 2** on Federalism may seem abstract, but one of the cases on which the debate turns involved whether or not California could legalize the use for medical reasons marijuana grown and distributed entirely within the state. Washington opposed the California measure and claimed that it could regulate the drug under the interstate commerce clause, and the Supreme Court had to decide the issue in a case about the division of power between the Washington, D.C. and the state governments in the federal system. **Debate 21** also addresses federalism, and one advocate proposes to diminish the traditional power of the states to determine marriage law by amending the Constitution to bar marriages between homosexuals. **Debate 12** focuses on the authority of the president as commander in chief and chief executive officer. The particular issue is the electronic surveillance of communications going out of and coming into the United States that President George W. Bush authorized the National Security Agency to carry out against suspected terrorists without getting permission from the courts. A former top

White House official contends the searches violated the Constitution and statutory law and that Bush should be censured. A second advocate argues the president's actions were both legal and wise. **Debate 16** also addresses presidential power. The debate explores how power is allocated between the president and Congress in the process by which the government spends money. In the debate, one advocate suggests that the president be given more power by allowing him to cut specific items out of appropriations bills enacted by Congress. A second advocate argues giving this power to the president is an unwarranted transfer of power from one branch of government to another.

Policy is also a reflection, in part, of who serves, and Debates 9, 10, and 11 all focus on that issue. The Democrats have now lost two presidential elections in a row and are—at the time when this edition went to press—a minority in both Houses of Congress, and **Debate 9** takes up whether the Democrats have the best chance of reversing their losing streak by making Senator Hilary Rodham Clinton (D-NY) their presidential nominee in 2008. Those who serve must, of course, come to office as the result of elections with little or no fraud, and the advocates featured in **Debate 10** differ over whether increasing the amount and type of identification required to register and vote is a worthwhile reform or an unnecessary step that will only serve to decrease turnout. Both advocates in **Debate 11** argue they want to give you more choice as to who will represent you in Congress. One advocate says the way to do that is to limit the term of federal legislators so that there will be regular turnover. The other advocate replies that doing so will limit your ability to be represented for many terms by an effective legislator whom you support. **Debate 22** takes up changing to a proportional representation system of elections. If adopted that would loosen, if not break the seeming stranglehold that the Republicans and Democrats have on who gets elected. Indeed, such a change might end the tradition of the United States being a two-party system.

YOU CAN AND SHOULD AFFECT POLITICS

The second thing that this volume preaches is that you can and should take part in politics. One prerequisite for good participation is good information. Much of that comes through the news media. Focusing on a instance in which one reporter was sent to jail in 2005 for refusing to disclose a confidential source to a grand jury, **Debate 7** asks whether journalists should be able to shield sources even in a criminal case.

Some debates may influence your ability to be active. Some people criticize those Americans who feel a strong tie to the land of their heritage and who favor U.S. policies that favor that land. Whether doing so is misplaced allegiance or an all-American tradition is taken up in **Debate 8** on ethnic lobbying. The debate focuses on those who lobby for U.S. support of Israel. Another line of criticism is leveled at those who take it upon themselves to volunteer to supplement the government efforts to cut down on the flow of illegal immigrants into the Untied States. The advocates in **Debate 6** differ on whether such volunteers are laudable patriots or dangerous vigilantes.

Debate 23 about campaign finance reform also addresses participation. Those who argue that there should be strict limits on how much people and organizations can spend to support or oppose a candidate for office claim that the impact of money on politics makes a mockery of the idea that all citizens should have an equal say. Opponents rejoin that the proposed restriction violates their freedom of speech. Perhaps more than any other issue, **Debate 20** relates to the idea that would most radically change participation in this country. That is instituting direct democracy by allowing the people as a whole to make law directly through processes called initiatives and referendums.

STATE AND LOCAL GOVERNMENTS ARE IMPORTANT TOO

The federal government is just one of the more that 80,000 different governments in the United States. Each of the state and local governments has the power to pass laws, establish regulations, and tax and spend. For example, state and local governments now spend over $2 trillion a year. One power exercised by state and local is eminent domain, the ability to take property from private individuals for public use. Relating to an instance where property was taken by New London, Connecticut, and turned over to private developers, **Debate 16** takes up the issue of what "public use" means and how far eminent domain should go.

THERE ARE OFTEN MORE THAN TWO SIDES TO A QUESTION

Often public policy questions are put in terms of "pro and con," "favor or oppose," or some other such stark choice. This approach is sometimes called a Manichean approach, a reference to Manicheanism, a religion founded by the Persian prophet Mani (c. 216–276). It taught "dualism," the idea the universe is divided into opposite, struggling, and equally powerful realities, light (good) and darkness (evil).

The view here is that many policy issues are more a matter of degree, and the opinion of people is better represented as a place along a range of possibilities rather than an up or down Manichean choice. Numerous debates herein are like that. For example, surveys of the American people over abortion, the subject of **Debate 3**, find that only a small minority of people is staunchly pro-choice or pro-life. The majority have a nuanced view that, on the one hand, supports women being able to terminate their pregnancies but that, on the other hand, reflects reservations based on timing and circumstances. Opinion is also something like that about the death penalty, the focus of **Debate 17**. A large majority of Americans favor it, but surveys also show that people are troubled by a range of possible injustices such as the relationship of wealth to the ability to mount a top notch defense, the ability to execute people for crimes committed while a juvenile, and claims of racial injustice.

Yet another emotional topic on which most people are unwilling to give a categorical yes or no answer is whether it is justified to torture terrorists. One advocate argues that doing so is always abhorrent, but another advocate contends that torture is sometimes justified. In light of the recent controversy over the Bush administration's refusal to classify captured terrorists as prisoners of war and its willingness to tolerate more forceful interrogations, the issue of torture is not an abstract question but a real policy debate.

MANY ISSUES HAVE MULTIPLE ASPECTS

Often political issues are sort of like Matryoshkas, the Russian nested dolls in which each comes apart many times, each time revealing an ever-smaller doll inside. **Debate 1** is about "the right to bear arms." At its most specific, the issue is whether individuals have such a right. But deciding that involves larger question of how to decide what those who wrote the Second Amendment meant. That matter, in turn, takes us to an even larger debate about whether we should follow the literal intent of those who wrote constitutional language, most of which is more than two centuries old, or apply the language of the Constitution within the context of the 21st century. In much the same way, **Debate 14**, on the use by the minority party in the Senate of filibusters (the practice of unlimited speeches on a topic) to block the president's judicial nominees. The topic has some specific and historical aspects, such what the phrase "advice and consent" of the Senate means. There is also specific constitutional controversy over whether a filibuster is permissible as a way for a minority of senators to block the judicial nominees of the president. Because the maneuver is usually based on the nominee's ideology (such as his or her stance on abortion), Debate 14 additionally includes the degree to which ideology and partisan politics should play a role in the confirmation or rejection of judges by the Senate. A larger and related question is whether filibusters to block the majority will on legislation, and other matters before the Senate, is acceptable constitutionally or democratically.

The discussion in **Debate 5** over whether productive, law-abiding illegal immigrants who have been in the United States for an extended time should be given a way to achieve U.S. citizenship is also multifaceted. There is a wide range of economic and social consequences. Do these immigrants take jobs from Americans or supply needed workers to fill jobs that the country needs but are left partly unfilled by American workers? Are illegal immigrants a drain on social services or an important source of taxes to support those programs? Should these people be considered criminal who have entered the country illegally or are they really economic refugees simply trying to support themselves and their families?

SOME CONCLUDING THOUGHTS

The points with which we began are important enough to reiterate. Whether you care about politics or not, it affects you every day in many ways. As the legendary heavyweight boxer Joe Louis put it after knocking out Billy Conn, a more agile but less powerful opponent, in their 1941 championship fight, "You can run, but you can't hide."

Simply paying attention is a good start, but action is even better. Everyone should be politically active, at least to the level of voting. Doing so is in your self-interest because decisions made by the federal, state, and local governments in the U.S. political system provide each of us with both tangible benefits (such as roads and schools) and intangible benefits (such as civil liberties and security). Also, for good or ill, the government takes things away from each of us (such as taxes) and restricts our actions (such as speed limits). It is also the case in politics, as the old saying goes, that squeaky wheels get the grease. Those who participate actively are more likely to be influential. Those who do not, and young adults are by far the age group least likely to even vote, are cosigned to grumbling impotently on the sideline.

As an absolute last thought (really!), let me encourage you to contact me with questions or comments. My e-mail address is john.rourke@uconn.edu. Compliments are always great, but if you disagree with anything I have written or my choice of topics and readings, or have a suggestion for the next edition, let me know.

To the Faculty

Having plied the podium, so to speak, for three decades, I have some well-formed ideas of what a good reader should do. It is from that perspective that I have organized this reader to work for the students who read it and the faculty members who adopt it for use in their classes. Below is what I look for in a reader and how I have constructed this one to meet those standards.

PROVOKE CLASS DISCUSSION

The classes I have enjoyed the most over the years have been the ones that have been the liveliest, with students participating enthusiastically in a give and take among themselves and with me. Many of the debates herein have been selected to engender such participation in your classes by focusing on hot-button topics that provoke heated debate even among those who are not heavily involved in politics and who do not have a lot of background on the topic. The very first topic, gun laws, in Debate 1, is just such a subject. More than once I have had students get into spirited exchanges over the "right to bear arms," so I though it would be a great debate to open the volume. Just a few of the other hot-button topics are abortion (Debate 3), potential citizenship for illegal/undocumented immigrants (Debate 5), the impact of Title IX on college athletics (Debate 13), and the death penalty (Debate 17). I hope they rev up your classes as much as they have energized mine.

Another point about class discussion that I point out in the Preface section "To the students" is that while the debate titles imply two sides, many policy topics are not a Manichean choice between yes and no. Instead, I have tried to include many issues on which opinion ranges along a scale. From that perspective, I often urge students to try to formulate a policy that can gain majority support if not a consensus. You will also find that many of the issues herein are multifaceted, and I try to point that out to the students. For instance, the debate about gun control is more than about weapons, it is also about how we interpret and apply the Constitution.

BE CURRENT

An important factor in engaging the students is being current. Debating Franklin Roosevelt's court-packing scheme has importance, but it is not as likely to interest students as to the acceptability of the Senate Democrats' current practice of sometimes filibustering President Bush's judicial nominees. Therefore, I vigorously update each edition. Even though *You Decide* appears annually, over 40% of the topics in *You Decide 2007* are wholly new or are revised from *You Decide 2006*. Additionally, some of the readings in the carry-over debates are new.

PROVIDE A GOOD RANGE OF TOPICS

I always look for a reader that "covers the waterfront" and have tried to put together this reader to do that. There are numerous debates on specific policy issues and others on process. All the major institutions are covered in one or more debates, and there are also debates touching on such "input" elements as parties, campaigns, interest groups, and the media. The primary focus of the reader is on the national government, but federalism also receives attention in Debates 2 and 20. State and local government issues are taken up in Debate 15 on eminent domain. I have also included several debates that are at the intersection of domestic and foreign affairs, including Debate 8 (the acceptability of ethnic groups of Americans lobbying the U.S. government for policies that favor the country of their heritage), Debate 19 (the U.S. presence in Iraq) and Debate 24 (torturing terrorists).

My sense of a good range of topics also has meant balancing hot-button topics with others that, while they will draw less of an emotional response, are important to debate because they give insight about how the system works and might work differently. For example, Debate 21 relates to the hot-button topic of gay marriage, but as noted, its more basic point is federalism. Hopefully the debate will get students to think of the federal system, which my experience tells me they mostly take as an unchanging given. Another example is the idea presented in Debate 23 of going from a single-member, plurality electoral system to a proportional representation system.

GIVE THE STUDENTS SOME BACKGROUND FOR THE READING

Readers that work well provide the students with some background material that is located just before the reading. This debate volume follows that scheme. There is a two-page introduction to each debate that establishes the context of the debate. As part of this setup, each introduction provides the students with several "points to ponder" as they read the debates.

Moreover, the introductions do more than just address the topic per se. Instead they try to connect it to the chapter of the text for which it is designed. For example, the introduction to Debate 14 on the tensions between President Bush and the Senate Democrats over judicial nominations begins with the power of the judiciary in the American system and how that makes judicial appointments such a high-stakes issue.

PROVIDE FOLLOW-UP POSSIBILITIES

One of the rewards of our profession is seeing students get excited about a field that intrigues us, and the reader provides a "continuing debate" section after each of the two readings. This section has three parts. **What Is New** provides an update of what has occurred since the date(s) of the two articles. **Where to Find More** points students to places to explore the topic further. I have particularly emphasized resources that can be accessed on the Internet on the theory that students are more likely to pursue a topic if they can do so via computer than by walking to the library. Needless to say, I think libraries are great and students should have to use them, so there are also numerous references to books and academic journals. Finally, the continuing debate section has a **What More to Do** part. This segment presents topics for discussion, suggests projects (like finding out how well your school is doing by Title IX standards), and advises how to get active on a topic.

FIT WITH THE COURSE

I favor readers that fit the course I am teaching. I prefer a book with readings that supplement all or most of the major topics on my syllabus and that also allows me to spread the reading out so that is evenly distributed throughout the semester. To that end, this book is organized to parallel the outline of the major introduction to American politics texts in use today. For those who favor the foundations-politics-institutions-policy approach, the table of contents of this volume should match almost exactly with their text and syllabus. For those who use a foundations-institutions-politics-policy scheme, a little, but not much, adjustment will synchronize the debates herein with your plans. Moreover to help with that, I have labeled each debate in the Table of Contents with the syllabus topic that fits with the debate. Additionally, for the 20 debates in the printed edition, I have indicated alternative syllabus topic for each, and I have also made suggestions about how each of the six debates on the Web might fit with various text chapters and syllabus topics.

FLEXIBILITY

While there is a fair amount of similarity in the organization of the major introduction to American politics texts, I suspect that the syllabi of faculty members are a good deal more individualistic. With that in mind, I have provided flexibility in the reader. First, there are 19 debates in the printed edition, each which is related to a topic, but each of which has suggestions in the table of contents for alternative assignment. Then there are five additional readings on the Longman Web site associated with *You Decide!* Each of these also has multiple uses and my suggestions about how to work each one into your syllabus. Thus, you can use all 24 debates or many fewer; you can substitute some on the Web for some in the printed edition; you can follow the order in the book fairly closely with most texts or you can rearrange the order at will. As the Burger King slogan goes, "Have it Your Way!"

As a final note, let me solicit your feedback. Every text and reader that anticipates future editions should be a work in progress. *You Decide* certainly is. Of course I will be pleased to hear about the things you like, but I and the next edition of the text will surely benefit more from hearing how I could have done better and what topics (and/or readings) would be good in the next edition. Thanks!

DEBATE 1

CONSTITUTION

GUNS, SAFETY, AND THE CONSTITUTION'S MEANING: Individual Right *or* Subject to Regulation?

INDIVIDUAL RIGHT

ADVOCATE: Robert A. Levy, Senior Fellow in Constitutional Studies, Cato Institute

SOURCE: Testimony during hearings on "Oversight Hearing on the District of Columbia's Gun Control Laws," before the U.S. House of Representatives, Committee on Government Reform, June 28, 2005

SUBJECT TO REGULATION

ADVOCATE: Daniel A. Farber, Henry J. Fletcher Professor of Law and Associate Dean of Faculty and Research, University of Minnesota

SOURCE: "Disarmed by Time: The Second Amendment and the Failure of Originalism," *Chicago-Kent Law Review*, 2000

In the early days of World War II, British Prime Minister Winston S. Churchill famously described the Soviet Union as a "riddle wrapped in a mystery inside an enigma." Had he been commenting on the current debate in the United States over gun control, Churchill might have used the same words to describe it.

The riddle, so to speak, is the meaning of the words of the Second Amendment to the U.S. Constitution: "A well regulated Militia, being necessary to the security of a free State, the right of the people to keep and bear Arms, shall not be infringed." Ask yourself, for example, Does "people" mean individuals, or does it refer to the collective citizenry, as in "We the people"?

The mystery is what, if anything, the framers of the U.S. Constitution and the Bill of Rights intended the amendment to accomplish. Scholars disagree mightily about this issue.

The enigma is whether the lawmakers of the late 1700s would argue that 21st century Americans should be bound by the literal meaning of words written more than 200 years ago, or should interpret them in the light of modern circumstances.

We might look to the courts to unravel these issues, but they have not been crystal clear. Generally, they have upheld the authority of government to regulate the ownership of weapons, but the Supreme Court has never ruled directly on the essence of the Second Amendment. To date, the most important case has been *United States v. Miller* (1939), in which the Supreme Court upheld a provision of the National Firearms Act (1934) requiring registration of sawed-off shotguns. The majority opinion held that "in the absence of any evidence...that possession [of a sawed-off] shotgun...has some reasonable relationship to...a well-regulated militia, we cannot say that the Second Amendment guarantees the right to keep and bear such an instrument." Notice that the opinion neither denies nor affirms a right to bear arms. It only rules that sawed-off shotguns are not protected, leaving it unclear if other weapons might be.

Most recently, gun control opponents were buoyed by the decision of the Fifth U.S. Circuit Court of Appeals in *United States v. Emerson* (2001). The majority opinion construed the word "people" in the Second Amendment to mean individuals, and said that the clause, "necessary to a well regulated militia," served merely to explain why individuals had the right to keep and bear arms. Still, it was a mixed case, because the judges also upheld the specific federal law that barred Timothy Emerson from owning a firearm based on his history of domestic violence. When the Supreme Court declined to hear Emerson's appeal, as it does in most cases, the major constitutional issues were left largely unresolved. In essence, no Supreme Court decision, including *Miller*, has definitively ruled either that there is an unrestricted right of individuals to keep and bear arms or that government has the unchecked authority to regulate, or even abolish, gun ownership and use.

What would you decide? Considering weapons is one way to start thinking about these policy and constitutional issues. There can be no doubt that weapons have changed. Flintlock pistols and rifles were the personal firearms when the amendment was written in 1789. Today's weapons have much faster firing rates and higher muzzle velocities and, therefore, vastly greater killing power than did their forerunners.

The presence and role of weapons in America is another piece of the puzzle. The latest data indicate that approximately 4.9 million firearms (including 1.7 million handguns) are manufactured or imported for the domestic U.S. market annually. In all, there are about 200 million privately and legally owned firearms in the United States, about 30% of which are handguns. Between 40% and 50% of all households have a legal gun. The uncertain but significant number of illegal weapons adds to these totals.

As for the yearly use of firearms, most are either never fired or are used for target shooting or hunting. But statistics also show that over 29,000 people died in the United States in 2004 as a result of a gunshot. Most (58%) were suicides. Another 37% were homicides, 3% were accidents, 1.5% were the result of police actions, and 0.5% were instances of self-defense by individuals. Of all homicides, 66% were by firearms, and they were also involved in over 300,000 other crimes in the United States during 2004.

POINTS TO PONDER

- The most specific debate is about gun control policy and whether widespread gun ownership provides greater or less safety. Given your views on this issue, would you vote for a bill in Congress to ban the manufacture, importation, sale, and possession of all handguns?
- At a second level, the debate is about the specifics of the Second Amendment and the intent of those who drafted and ratified it. What do the two advocates claim that those who wrote the language of the Second Amendment intended it to mean?
- The third, most general, and most important dispute is over whether the Constitution is a fixed document whose meaning should be derived by "strict construction" of its words and the original intention of those who wrote it, or whether the Constitution is a "living document" that it should be interpreted in light of modern realities. What is your view? Should we be bound in the first decade of the 21st century by what people meant in the last decade of the 19th century when the Second Amendment was added to the Constitution?

Guns, Safety, and the Constitution's Meaning: Individual Right

ROBERT A. LEVY

This afternoon, I testify in support of the principles underlying H.R. 1288, The District of Columbia Personal Protection Act, which would repeal the District's ban on handguns and make other changes to the city's gun control laws. Although I support the underlying principles, I am nevertheless opposed to enactment of the legislation at this time. Essentially, I believe that advocates of gun owners' rights will be better served if *Parker v. District of Columbia*, a Second Amendment challenge to the D.C. handgun ban, is first resolved by the U.S. Court of Appeals for the District of Columbia Circuit, then presented to the U.S. Supreme Court for final review. Of course, *Parker* will be dismissed as moot if the challenged law is repealed.

My reasons for preferring the judicial route before proceeding with legislation are elaborated in Part IV below, "What Role Should Congress Play in Securing Second Amendment Rights?" First, however, some background in Part I, "Does the Second Amendment Secure an Individual or Collective Right?" That is followed by Part II, "Does the Second Amendment Apply to the District of Columbia?" Then Part III, "How Can District Residents Best Secure Their Second Amendment Rights?"

I. DOES THE SECOND AMENDMENT SECURE AN INDIVIDUAL OR COLLECTIVE RIGHT?

A question that has perplexed legal scholars for decades goes like this: Does the right to keep and bear arms belong to us as individuals, or does it belong to us collectively as members of a militia? The answer has now been documented in an extended and scholarly staff memorandum opinion prepared for the Attorney General and released to the public last year. The memorandum opinion concluded that "The Second Amendment secures a right of individuals generally, not a right of States or a right restricted to persons serving in militias."

I concur. The main clause of the Second Amendment ("the right of the people to keep and bear Arms, shall not be infringed") secures the right. The subordinate clause ("A well regulated Militia, being necessary to the security of a free State") justifies the right. Properly understood, the militia clause helps explain why we have a right to bear arms. A well-regulated militia is a sufficient but not necessary condition to the exercise of that right. Imagine if the Second Amendment said, "A well-educated Electorate, being necessary to self-governance in a free state, the right of the people to keep and read Books shall not be infringed." Surely, no one would suggest that only registered voters (i.e., members of the electorate) would have a right to read. Yet that is precisely the effect if the Second Amendment is interpreted to apply only to members of a militia.

If the Second Amendment truly meant what the collective rights advocates propose, then the text would read, "A well regulated Militia being necessary to the security of a free State, the right of the states [or the state militias] to keep and bear arms shall not be infringed." But the Second Amendment, like the First and Fourth Amendments, refers explicitly to "the right of the people." Consider the placement of the amendment within the Bill of Rights, the part of the Constitution that deals exclusively with the rights of individuals. There can be no doubt that First Amendment rights like speech and religion belong to us as individuals. Similarly, Fourth Amendment protections against unreasonable searches are individual rights. In the context of the Second Amendment, we secure "the right of the people" by guaranteeing the right of each person. Second Amendment protections were not intended for the state but for each individual against the state—a deterrent to government tyranny. Here's how Ninth Circuit judge Alex Kozinski put it [in his opinion in *Unites States v. Stewart* (2003)]:

> The institution of slavery required a class of people who lacked the means to resist.... All too many of the... great tragedies of history—Stalin's atrocities, the killing fields of Cambodia, the Holocaust—were perpetrated by armed troops against unarmed populations.

Maybe the threat of tyrannical government is less today than it was when our republic was experiencing its birth pangs. But incompetence by the state in defending its citizens is a greater threat. The demand for police to defend us increases in proportion to our inability to defend ourselves. That's why disarmed societies tend to become police states. Witness law abiding inner city residents, disarmed by gun control, begging for police protection against drug gangs—despite the terrible violations of civil liberties that such protection entails (e.g., curfews, anti-loitering laws, civil asset forfeiture, non-consensual searches of public housing, and even video surveillance of residents in high crime areas). An unarmed citizenry creates the conditions that lead to tyranny. The right to bear arms is thus preventive; it reduces the demand for a police state. When people are incapable of protecting themselves, they become either victims of the criminals or dependents of the state.

What do the courts have to say? In a 2001 Texas case, *United States v. Emerson*, the Fifth Circuit [of the U.S. Court of Appeals] held that the Constitution "protects the right of individuals, including those not then actually a member of any militia... to privately possess and bear their own firearms... suitable as personal individual weapons." That constitutional right is not absolute, said the court. For example, killers do not have a constitutional right to possess weapons of mass destruction. Some persons and some weapons may be restricted. Indeed, the Fifth Circuit held that Emerson's Second Amendment rights could be temporarily curtailed because there was reason to believe he posed a threat to his estranged wife. And the Tenth Circuit, in *United States v. Haney* [2004], ruled that machine guns were not the type of weapon protected by the Second Amendment. The Supreme Court declined to review either case.

The high Court has not decided a Second Amendment case since *United States v. Miller* in 1939. On that occasion, the challenged statute required registration of machine guns, sawed off rifles, sawed off shotguns, and silencers. First, said the Court, "militia" means all males physically capable of acting in concert for the common defense. That suggested a right belonging to all of us, as individuals. But the Court also held that the right extended only to weapons rationally related to a militia—not the sawed off shotgun questioned in *Miller*. That mixed ruling has puzzled legal scholars for more than six decades. If military use is the decisive test, then citizens can possess rocket launchers and missiles. Obviously, that is not what the Court had in mind. Indeed, anti-gun advocates, who regularly cite *Miller* with approval, would be apoplectic if the Court's military-use doctrine were logically extended.

Because *Miller* is so murky, it can only be interpreted narrowly, allowing restrictions on weapons, like machine guns and silencers, with slight value to law abiding citizens, and high value to criminals. In other words, *Miller* applies to the type of weapon, not to the question whether the Second Amendment protects individuals or members of a militia. That's the conclusion the Fifth Circuit reached in Emerson. It found that *Miller* upheld neither the individual rights model of the Second Amendment nor the collective rights model. *Miller* simply decided that the weapons at issue were not protected.

Enter former U.S. Attorney General John Ashcroft [2001–2005]. First, in a letter to the National Rifle Association, he reaffirmed a long-held opinion that all law-abiding citizens have an individual right to keep and bear arms. Ashcroft's letter was supported by 18 state attorneys general, including six Democrats, then followed by two Justice Department briefs, filed with the Supreme Court in the *Haney* and *Emerson* cases. For the first time, the federal government argued against the collective rights position in formal court papers.

Despite Ashcroft's view of the Second Amendment, the Justice Department declared that both *Emerson* and *Haney* were correctly decided. In *Emerson*, the restriction on persons subject to a domestic violence restraining order was a permissible exception to Second Amendment protection. And in *Haney*, the ban on machine guns applied to a type of weapon uniquely susceptible to criminal misuse.

Many legal scholars are now taking that same position. Harvard's Alan Dershowitz, a former ACLU [American Civil Liberties Union] board member, says he "hates" guns and wants the Second Amendment repealed. But he condemns "foolish liberals who are trying to read the Second Amendment out of the Constitution by claiming it's not an individual right.... They're courting disaster by encouraging others to use the same means to eliminate portions of the Constitution they don't like." Harvard's Laurence Tribe, another respected liberal scholar, and Yale professor Akhil Amar acknowledge that there is an individual right to keep and bear arms, albeit limited by "reasonable regulation in the interest of public safety." In that respect, Tribe and Amar agree with the *Emerson* court and with Ashcroft on two fundamental issues: First, the Second Amendment confirms an individual rather than a collective right. Second, that right is not absolute; it is subject to regulation. To the extent there is disagreement, it hinges on what constitutes permissible regulation—i.e., where to draw the line.

To reinforce the views of Dershowitz, Tribe, Amar, and Ashcroft, let me comment briefly on a few of the underlying constitutional points.

- Three provisions limit the states' power over the militia. Article I, section 8, grants Congress the power to "organiz[e], arm[], and disciplin[e], the militia." Article I, section 10, says that "No state shall, without the consent of Congress,...keep troops in time of peace." Article II, section 2, declares the "President shall be Commander in Chief...of the Militia of the several States." Given those three provisions, how could the Second Amendment secure a state's right to arm the militia? No one argued then or argues now that the Second Amendment repealed all three earlier provisions.

- Consider the Supreme Court's pronouncement in *Miller*: "When called for service [in an organized militia] these men were expected to appear bearing arms supplied by themselves." If militia members were to arm themselves, the Second Amendment could not refer to states arming militias. Furthermore, if the *Miller* Court thought the Second Amendment merely enabled states to arm their militias, the Court would have dismissed the case on standing grounds. The plaintiff, *Miller*, was not a state and therefore had no standing to sue. The Court would never have reached the question whether a sawed off shotgun had military utility.

- Multiple provisions in the Bill of Rights refer to the right "of the people." In a 1990 case, *United States v. Verdugo-Urquidez*, the Court said, "'the people' protected by the Fourth Amendment, and by the First and Second Amendments, and to whom rights and powers are reserved in the Ninth and Tenth Amendments, refers to a class of persons who are part of a national community or have otherwise developed sufficient connection with this country to be considered part of that community." That statement contains no mention or even suggestion of a collective right

- What about the militia clause? That syntax was not unusual for the times. For example, the free press clause of the 1842 Rhode Island Constitution stated: "The liberty of the press being essential to the security of freedom in a state, any person may publish his sentiments of any subject." That provision surely does not mean that the right to publish protects only the press. It protects "any person"; and one reason among others that it protects any person is that a free press is essential to a free society.

- In the Militia Act of 1792, militia is defined as "every free able-bodied white male citizen...who is or shall be of the age of 18 years, and under the age of 45 years." That definition is expanded in the Modern Militia Act (1956–58) to read "all able-bodied males at least 17 years of age and...under 45 yrs of age [and] female citizens...who are members of the National Guard." The Act goes on to state that "the classes of the militia are (1) the organized militia, which consists of the National Guard and the Naval Militia; and (2) the unorganized militia, which consists of [all other members]." Ninth Circuit judge Andrew J. Kleinfeld wrote [in a dissenting opinion in *Silveira v. Lockyer* (2003) that the "militia is like the jury pool, consisting of 'the people,' limited, like the jury pool, to those capable of performing the service."

- Next, consider this historical context: Anti-federalists wanted three major changes prior to ratifying the Constitution: (1) include a Bill of Rights, (2) give states, not the federal government, power to arm the militia, and (3) eliminate federal power to maintain a standing army. Here was the federalist response, addressing those demands in reverse order: (1) Don't worry about the federal government maintaining a standing army; the federal militia power will obviate that need. (2) Don't worry about federal control over the militia; armed individuals will obviate those concerns. And (3) to ensure that individuals have a right to be armed, we will include such a provision in a Bill of Rights. So the federalist position depended on the people being armed. Clearly, the addition of the Second Amendment could not have been intended to eliminate that right. The Second Amendment's prefatory clause was the federalists' way of pacifying anti-federalists without limiting the power of the federal government to maintain a standing army or increasing the states' power over the militia.

- Here's a parallel view of that history, interpreting the term "well-regulated." In its 18th century context, well-regulated did not mean heavily regulated, but rather properly, not overly regulated. Looked at in that manner, the Second Amendment ensured that militias would not be improperly regulated—even weakened—by disarming the citizens who would be their members. The Framers feared and distrusted standing armies; so they provided for a militia (all able-bodied males above the age of 17) as a counterweight. But the framers also realized, in granting Congress near-plenary power over the militia, that a select, armed subset—like today's National Guard—could be equivalent to a standing army. So they wisely crafted the Second Amendment to forbid Congress from disarming other citizens, thereby ensuring a "well-regulated" militia.

For those of us eagerly awaiting a Supreme Court pronouncement on the Second Amendment, for the first time in 66 years, the Constitution is on our side....

That said, there is a legitimate and important reason for Congress to step aside until *Parker v. District of Columbia* is resolved. The *Parker* lawsuit was filed by upstanding D.C. residents who want to be able to defend themselves and their families in their own homes. *Parker* is now pending before the U.S. Court of Appeals for the D.C. Circuit. If H.R. 1288 is enacted, the lawsuit will be dismissed as moot. After all, plaintiffs cannot challenge a law that no longer exists.

Otherwise, *Parker* could well be headed to the Supreme Court; and that is where it belongs. The citizens of this country deserve a foursquare pronouncement from the nation's highest court about the real meaning of the Second Amendment for all Americans—not just the residents of D.C. Presently, because the Supreme Court has not resolved its view of the Second Amendment, the right to keep and bear arms under state law extends only as far as each state's constitution or statutes permit. That's unacceptable. A disputable Second Amendment right without a legally enforceable federal remedy is, in some states, no right at all.

Although the rights of D.C. residents can be secured by either legislation or litigation, a narrow bill aimed at the D.C. Code will do only part of the job. The bill could be repealed by the next anti-gun Congress. And more important, the bill will have no effect outside of the District. That means, of course, the bill will have negligible impact on gun owners' rights when contrasted with an unambiguous proclamation, applicable across the nation, from the U.S. Supreme Court.

If the Court should mistakenly hold that the Second Amendment provides a collective rather than an individual right, that would be the time for the legislative branch to ensure that D.C. residents have more protection than the judicial branch was willing to recognize. Until then, congressional action is premature.

Guns, Safety, and the Constitution's Meaning: Subject to Regulation

DANIEL A. FARBER

INTRODUCTION

[The prevailing] wisdom [is that] the Second Amendment is little more than a footnote to Militia Clauses of the Constitution, themselves virtually irrelevant to today's military. But this conventional view has been challenged by revisionist scholars [who] contend that the framers had a far more sweeping vision of the right "to keep and bear Arms." In their view, the Constitution protects the individual's right to own guns for self-defense, hunting, and resistance to tyranny. These scholars find no room for uncertainty about the historical meaning of constitutional language. "The Second Amendment," we are told by one scholar, "is thus not mysterious. Nor is it equivocal. Least of all is it opaque." The meaning of the "right to bear arms," says another, "seems no longer open to dispute," and "an intellectually viable response...has yet to be made."

The revisionists' confidence about the original understanding is the foundation for their reinterpretation of the Second Amendment. Yet, the appropriate role of original intent in constitutional law has been debated for the past two decades. That debate should, if nothing else, caution against this sense of certainty about the implications of historical materials for present-day constitutional issues such as gun control....

Reading the historical record on the right to bear arms turns out to be a difficult exercise, full of perplexities. And even if we had a definitive answer that turned out to favor the revisionists, the claim that original intent should always trump contemporary legislative decisions is itself problematic....

Thus, history cannot provide the kind of unshakable foundation for gun rights that some scholars have sought. Indeed, there is something profoundly amiss about the notion that the Constitution's meaning today should be settled first and foremost by a trip to the archives. The effort to apply this notion to an issue as contemporary and hotly contested as gun control only serves to underline the fundamental peculiarity of the originalist approach to constitutional law.

Given the deep flaws in originalism, its continuing appeal may seem mysterious. For its more sophisticated adherents, it may appeal as a value-neutral method of decision and as a solution to the countermajoritarian difficulty—perhaps a solution they would admit to be flawed, yet better than the alternatives. These arguments are ultimately unsatisfactory.

For less sophisticated adherents, however, originalism may have another, more visceral appeal. It harkens back to an earlier, purer age, when today's petty political concerns and squalid politicians were replaced with great statesmen devoted to high principle. This implicit appeal to a nobler, more heroic past may have particular resonance in the context of the Second Amendment, where it brings to mind visions of minutemen and frontier lawmen valiantly defending justice and freedom with their guns. These mythic versions of the past, however, can only obscure the all-too-real issues facing our society today. Being inspired by myth is healthy; being ruled by it is unsafe.

[There are] doubts [about] whether originalism provides a workable methodology for judges in deciding Second Amendment cases. Originalism requires them to make difficult historical judgments with little training in doing so; it gives no guidance about how concretely or abstractly to define the original understanding or about how to distinguish the framers' understanding of the text from their expectations about its implementation; and it leaves open the difficult problem of when to relinquish original understandings in favor of precedent or tradition. Furthermore, as practiced today, originalism may not even correspond with the methods used by the framers themselves to understand the text. Consequently, the so-called "original understanding" may not reflect the understanding of the original framers of how the provision would be applied under new circumstances. In short, with the best will in the world, judges who practice originalism will find themselves in vast disagreement over the meaning of the Second Amendment. Thus, if originalism is intended to constrain judges, it is a failure.

But even apart from these difficulties of implementation, the question remains whether we would want to implement originalism even if we could. The Second Amendment is a good illustration of why we should not want to be bound by the original understanding. Originalists claim that only originalism can reconcile judicial review with majority rule and make the Supreme Court something other than a super-legislature. But in reality, the Justices do not need to give up their bar memberships and join the American Historical Society in order to do their jobs properly. The conventional methods of constitutional law are completely legitimate and adequate to the task at hand. Originalism's greatest failing—in contrast to the conventional process of Common-law decision—is its inability to confront historical change. We should reject the originalist's invitation to ignore all of the history that has transpired since 1790 when we interpret the Constitution.

The Second Amendment once again provides an apt illustration of the defects of originalism. If the original understanding is to constrain judicial discretion, it must be possible to ascertain that understanding in a reasonably indisputable way. But, it is not even possible to give a clear-cut definition of what constitutes the original "understanding," as opposed to the original "expectation" or the original "applications" associated with a constitutional provision. And having cleared that hurdle, formidable difficulties confront the originalist judge, including a historical record that combines enormous volume with frustrating holes in key places, a complex intellectual and social context, and a host of interpretative disputes. If we do not trust judges to correctly interpret and apply their own precedents—a skill which they were supposedly taught in law school and have practiced throughout their professional lives—it is hard to see why we should trust them to interpret and apply a mass of eighteenth-century archival documents.

FIDELITY AND CHANGE

Originalism is an effort to fix the meaning of the Constitution once and for all at its birth. But there is an opposing view, one most eloquently expressed by Justice [Oliver Wendell] Holmes:

> [W]hen we are dealing with words that also are a constituent act, like the Constitution of the United States, we must realize that they have called into life a being the development of which could not have been foreseen completely by the most gifted of its begetters. It

> was enough for them to realize or to hope that they had created an organism; it has taken a century and has cost their successors much sweat and blood to prove that they created a nation. The case before us must be considered in the light of our whole experience and not in that of what was said a hundred years ago.

The Second Amendment is among the provisions of the Constitution that seem most to call out for Holmes's approach—for the historical changes relating to the right to bear arms have been far-reaching indeed.

Some of those changes relate directly to the two subjects of the Second Amendment: firearms and the militia. There is first of all the disappearance of the kind of militia contemplated by the framers. As [legal scholar] Akhil Amar explains, perhaps with some regret:

> [T]he legal and social structure on which the amendment is built no longer exists. The Founders' juries—grand, petit, and civil—are still around today, but the Founders' militia is not. America is not Switzerland. Voters no longer muster for militia practice in the town square.

Another relevant change is the development of professional police departments, which limit the need for individuals and groups to engage in self-help. Because these changes, unanticipated by the framers, undermined the asserted original purpose of the Second Amendment, its application today becomes problematic.

Apart from these changes relating directly to the Second Amendment's subject matter, broad changes in the constitutional landscape are also relevant. One watershed is the Civil War, which undermines the insurrectionist argument that armed revolt is a constitutionally sanctioned check on federal power.…

Perhaps there may be those who reject the validity of the decision at Appomattox even today. What cannot be disputed as a lesson of the Civil War, however, is that insurrection is not an acceptable practical check on the federal government. Quite apart from the question of whether insurgents could defeat a modern army, the Civil War suggests that the costs of exercising this option would simply be unbearable: if a similar percentage of the current population died during such an insurgency today, we would be talking about five million deaths. Brave talk about insurrection is one thing; "paying the butcher's bill" is quite another. Perhaps the framers can be forgiven for failing to appreciate this reality; it is harder to excuse similar romanticism today.

The Civil War also transformed our concept of the relationship between the state and federal government. The Second Amendment, at least if revisionist scholars are to be believed, was based on the threat a powerful national government posed to liberty. But one effect of the Civil War was to cement the federal government's role as a guarantor of liberty. Since the time of the Fourteenth Amendment, rather than state and local communities being seen as bulwarks of freedom against the federal leviathan, the federal government has been pressed into service to defend liberty. The Fourteenth Amendment arose in part out of a sense of the obligation of the federal government to protect the rights of its citizens, by force if necessary, whether the threat came from a foreign nation or a state or local government.

Thus, rather than entrusting liberty to the "locals," the Fourteenth Amendment calls into play federal judicial and legislative power to ensure that the states respect individual rights. This realignment of the federal government as friend rather than threat to liberty underlies much of our modern Supreme

Court jurisprudence and a plethora of twentieth-century civil rights legislation. This fundamental reassessment of the relationship between federal power and liberty would make independent state and local militias as much a threat to liberty as a protector.

If the insurrectionist argument is at odds with the lessons of the Civil War, the self-defense argument for constitutional protection clashes with the modern regulatory state. It is a commonplace that the New Deal [beginning in 1933] was a "watershed" in the development of the regulatory state, enough so to lead one prominent theorist to build a whole theory of constitutional interpretation around this shift. But the New Deal was only the beginning. In the 1960s and 1970s came a new wave of legislation covering matters such as consumer protection, discrimination law, and the environment. As a result, we live in a world where citizens routinely rely on the federal government rather than self-help to protect them against a host of threats.

Today, we expect federal protection against everything from potentially dangerous traces of pesticides in our foods to unwanted sexual overtures in the workplace. In this context, the notion that the government cannot protect us from the dangers of firearms seems like an odd relic of an earlier laissez-faire period. Indeed, it seems peculiar at best to say that the government can constitutionally protect us from one kind of hostile environment—coworkers displaying lewd pictures—but not from a more dramatic kind of hostile environment—neighbors carrying Uzis.

The point here is not that the Second Amendment is an anachronistic text that ought to be ignored, or that its interpretation should necessarily be narrowed in light of these later developments. It is not even that these later developments are fundamentally correct. What is wrong with originalism is that it seeks to block judges from even considering these later developments, which on their face seem so clearly relevant to the legitimacy of federal gun control efforts. But try as they may, it seems unlikely that judges can avoid being influenced by these realities.

CONCLUSION

What do we learn about originalism from the Second Amendment debate? What do we learn about the Second Amendment from the originalism debate?

One set of lessons relates to constitutional interpretation. The Second Amendment shows how the standard academic criticisms of originalism are not just academic quibbles: they identify real and troubling flaws. The debate about the Second Amendment vividly illustrates critical problems with originalism:

- The historical record concerning the right to bear arms is difficult for non-historians such as judges to evaluate, requiring a high level of historical expertise to evaluate the credibility and import of the evidence.
- Originalism might not accurately reflect the way in which contemporary readers understood the document; in particular, it may underestimate their willingness to contemplate limiting the "right to bear arms" clause in light of the purpose clause.
- The original understanding of the Second Amendment can be defined at different levels of generality, and the interpretation will depend on the choice of level as well as on how we distinguish the original "understanding" from mere original "expectations."
- Originalism, to be a realistic option, must acknowledge stare decisis, yet it does not provide us with clear guidance about whether the current Second Amendment case law should stand.

- Although originalism claims simply to be enforcing the will of "We the People," the Second Amendment shows how originalism can undermine majority rule.
- Because of the difficulties judges would face in basing their decisions on purely historical grounds, originalism would not eliminate the role of personal values in judging.
- Originalism forces us to ignore the ways our world has changed since the eighteenth century: the Civil War and its aftermath have cut the ground away from the notion of insurrection as a protection of liberty against federal power; and the New Deal and *its* aftermath have created a world in which we customarily turn to the regulatory state rather than to self-help to protect ourselves from threats.

It would, in short, be a serious mistake for judges to use originalism as their recipe for interpreting the Second Amendment or other ambiguous constitutional language. The fact that the arguments against this approach are familiar does not make them any less damaging.

At a more fundamental level, however, the lesson is not simply that originalists are wrong about how judges should read the Constitution. More importantly, they are wrong about the nature of the Constitution itself. In general, disputed constitutional provisions cannot simply be applied on the basis of whatever examples were discussed at the time, and so it is natural for originalists to attempt, instead, to reconstruct the theories underlying those provisions. This effort to theorize constitutional provisions is quite evident with the Second Amendment originalists we have discussed, but it is equally clear in the efforts of other originalists to find in the original understanding some unified theory of executive power or of federalism. But to look for an underlying theory is to misconceive the nature of the constitutional enterprise. Unlike physics, law does not lend itself to a "standard model" or a grand unified theory.

While the framers were indeed "concerned with such fundamental questions as the nature of representation and executive power," they were also engaged in "a cumulative process of bargaining and compromise in which a rigid adherence to principle yielded to the pragmatic tests of reaching agreement and building coalitions." In short, they were doing their best to create a viable set of democratic institutions, a task that required the utmost attention to both principle and pragmatism. Their task was not to agree on a theory but to create the basis for a working democracy. We hardly do justice to the spirit of their undertaking if we treat the resulting document as *their* Constitution alone rather than being ours as well. The last thing they would want would be for us to be ruled by false certainties about their intentions. Unfortunately, that is an invitation we have received all too often with respect to the Second Amendment.

THE CONTINUING DEBATE: Guns, Safety, and the Constitution's Meaning

What Is New

Advocates and opponents of gun control have both had victories in recent years. Advocates were heartened by several court cases in 2004. The Supreme Court in effect upheld a restrictive California gun law by refusing to hear a challenge to it, and a Federal District Court rejected a suit brought by the National Rifle Association challenging the constitutionality of a Washington, D.C. municipal law limiting gun ownership. But also in 2004, Congress let lapse a 10-year-old ban that barred weapons from having muzzle-flash suppressors, large capacity ammunition magazines, and other characteristics commonly associated with military assault weapons. Anti–gun control forces won a further victory in 2005 when Congress enacted legislation barring most civil suits against most firearms makers for the use of their products in crimes and other instances where victims were killed or wounded.

Where to Find More

For data, laws, and related information on firearms go to the U.S. Bureau of Alcohol, Tobacco and Firearms Web site www.atf.treas.gov/pub/#Firearms. The most recent data on firearms deaths in the United States is available from the U.S. Public Health Service's Centers for Disease Control Web site at: www.cdc.gov/nchs/fastats/homicide.htm.

For policy advocacy, turn to the Web sites of two of the major opposing interest groups. The anti–gun control forces are represented by the National Rifle Association's Web site at www.nra.org. For the opposing view, the URL www.bradycampaign.org/ will take you to the Website of the pro–gun control Brady Campaign to Prevent Violence (named after James Brady, a former White House press secretary who was shot in the head and disabled during the assassination attempt on President Ronald Reagan on March 30, 1981). For a rebuke of both camps, read John Casteen, "Ditching the Rubric on Gun Control," *Virginia Quarterly Review* (Fall 2004).

For more on the politics of gun control, read Nicholas J. Johnson, "The Constitutional Politics Of Gun Control," *Brooklyn Law Review* (2005). Several articles on various aspects of the issue are presented by the Fordham Law *Review* (2004) in a symposium issue on "The Second Amendment and the Future of Gun Regulation: Historical, Legal, Policy, and Cultural Perspectives."

What More to Do

One constant suggestion for this and every debate in this book is to get involved no matter which side you are on. The issue is important, and you can make a difference if you try. Also keep the larger constitutional questions in your mind as you read other debates in this book. Like this debate, some will involve questions about the meaning of words or phrases, such as "due process of law" in the Fourteenth Amendment. Other debates will also include the ongoing dispute over strict construction versus contemporary interpretation of the Constitution by the courts. Perhaps before any of this, though, think about and discuss with others the policy and constitutional issues presented in this debate. Then, as this book's title urges, You Decide!

DEBATE 2

FEDERALISM

FEDERAL REGULATION OF MEDICAL MARIJUANA: Appropriate National Power *or* Usurpation of State Authority?

APPROPRIATE NATIONAL POWER

Advocate: John Paul Stevens III, Associate Justice, U.S. Supreme Court
Source: Opinion in *Gonzales v. Raich*, June 6, 2005

USURPATION OF STATE AUTHORITY

Advocate: Sandra Day O'Connor, Associate Justice, U.S. Supreme Court
Source: Opinion in *Gonzales v. Raich*, June 6, 2005

Students are commonly taught that one way the delegates to the Constitutional Convention of 1787 in Philadelphia sought to safeguard democracy was by creating a federal system that divides powers between the central government and the states. The true story is more complex than that, but James Madison, the "father of the Constitution," did argue in the *Federalist Papers* (No. 45), "The powers delegated by the proposed Constitution to the Federal Government, are few and defined. Those which are to remain in the State Governments are numerous and indefinite."

Whatever anyone thought or intended, the Constitution is very imprecise about the boundaries between the authority of Washington and that of the state capitals. As a result, the division of powers has been the subject of legal, political, and even physical struggle ever since. It has not, however, been an even contest. Since 1789 authority has generally flowed away from the states and toward the central government.

One reason for this shift is the congressional use and judicial view of the Constitution's interstate commerce clause. Located in Article I, section 8, it gives Congress the authority "to regulate commerce...among the several states." For many years, the Supreme Court usually rejected attempts by Congress to use the interstate commerce clause to assert national control over an area traditionally within the realm of the states. But beginning in the 1930s, the court became more willing to allow the expansion of federal power under the interstate commerce clause. During the 1960s and beyond, the Supreme Court also usually upheld federal civil rights laws' use of the commerce clause to attack discrimination. In *Heart of Atlanta Motel v. United States* (1964), the Supreme Court upheld federal action against the motel's restaurant, Ollie's Barbecue, which only served white people. The court ruled that even though Ollie's only served local people, it was subject to federal regulation because some of the food it served originated outside of Georgia. Scholar Richard S. Randall (*American Constitutional Development*, 2002) has termed such use of the interstate commerce clause a constitutional "revolution" that "transformed the commerce power into an almost unlimited federal grant" of authority.

Something of a counter-revolution occurred, however. The Supreme Court under Chief Justice William Rehnquist (1986–2005) made several decisions rejecting federal laws enacted under the logic of the commerce clause. This counter-trend brings us to the debate here. Throughout most of history, there was limited federal power to regulate drugs because many of them are produced, distributed, and used locally, and thus fell within the purview of the states.

This changed in 1970 when Congress issued a "finding" that drugs travel in and impacted interstate commerce and enacted the Controlled Substances Act (CSA). It regulated the production, distribution, and possession of five classes of "controlled substances." Of these all those listed in Schedule 1, including 42 opiates, 22 opium derivatives, and 17 hallucinogenic substances (including marijuana) were banned outright.

The specific debate here involves federal authority to regulate "medical marijuana." Many physicians believe that marijuana can be medically useful, especially in easing pain and other side effects of cancer. Based on this belief, a 1996 referendum (see Debate 21) in California approved the "Compassionate Use Act" permitting the use of marijuana on a doctor's recommendation. Patients could either grow their own or obtain the drug from a "caregiver" (grower) within the state. Ten other states enacted similar laws. In 2002, federal agents seized medical marijuana being used by several Californians, including Angel Raich, who was using marijuana to treat brain tumor symptoms. Raich sued the U.S. Attorney General. The District Court found against Raich, but the Ninth Circuit of the Court of Appeals ruled that locally gown and used marijuana was not involved in commerce and, therefore, federal regulation was unconstitutional. The Bush administration appealed to the Supreme Court, which brings us to the readings by Justices John Paul Stevens and Sandra Day O'Connor presenting their perpectives about whether or not regulation represented an abuse of federal authority by overextending the meaning of the interstate commerce clause.

POINTS TO PONDER

- Separate your views on the main point of this debate, federal authority, and the second point, medical marijuana. You can, for instance, believe that on the constitutional level, the growth of federal authority is positive and also believe that on the policy level, medical marijuana should be legal.
- As you read, think about how well Madison's portrayal of the federal government's powers as "few and defined" and those of the states as "numerous and indefinite" corresponds to federalism's current reality. Is the change or lack of change positive or regrettable?
- Not too far below the surface of some critics' position on federalism is the view that it is an outdated system. The argument is that the United States has become a single country economically and socially and, therefore, should also be a unified politically. The defenders of federalism argue that it still, as it did in 1789, protects freedom, promotes diversity, and permits policy experimentation. What do you think? Does federalism make sense any more?

Federal Regulation of Medical Marijuana: Appropriate National Power

JOHN PAUL STEVENS, III

California is one of at least nine states that authorize the use of marijuana for medicinal purposes. The question presented in this case is whether the power vested in Congress by Article I, §8, of the Constitution "[t]o make all Laws which shall be necessary and proper for carrying into Execution" its authority to "regulate Commerce with foreign Nations, and among the several States" includes the power to prohibit the local cultivation and use of marijuana in compliance with California law.

I

California has been a pioneer in the regulation of marijuana. In 1913, California was one of the first states to prohibit the sale and possession of marijuana, and at the end of the century, California became the first state to authorize limited use of the drug for medicinal purposes. In 1996, California voters passed Proposition 215, now codified as the Compassionate Use Act of 1996. The proposition was designed to ensure that "seriously ill" residents of the state have access to marijuana for medical purposes, and to encourage federal and state governments to take steps towards ensuring the safe and affordable distribution of the drug to patients in need. The act creates an exemption from criminal prosecution for physicians, as well as for patients and primary caregivers who possess or cultivate marijuana for medicinal purposes with the recommendation or approval of a physician. A "primary caregiver" is a person who has consistently assumed responsibility for the housing, health, or safety of the patient.

Respondents [those charged with violating the law] Angel Raich and Diane Monson are California residents who suffer from a variety of serious medical conditions and have sought to avail themselves of medical marijuana pursuant to the terms of the Compassionate Use Act. They are being treated by licensed, board-certified family practitioners, who have concluded, after prescribing a host of conventional medicines to treat respondents' conditions and to alleviate their associated symptoms, that marijuana is the only drug available that provides effective treatment. Both women have been using marijuana as a medication for several years pursuant to their doctors' recommendation, and both rely heavily on cannabis to function on a daily basis. Indeed, Raich's physician believes that forgoing cannabis treatments would certainly cause Raich excruciating pain and could very well prove fatal.

Respondent Monson cultivates her own marijuana, and ingests the drug in a variety of ways including smoking and using a vaporizer. Respondent Raich, by contrast, is unable to cultivate her own, and thus relies on two caregivers, litigating as "John Does," to provide her with locally grown marijuana at no charge. These caregivers also process the cannabis into hashish or keif, and Raich herself processes some of the marijuana into oils, balms, and foods for consumption.

On August 15, 2002, county deputy sheriffs and agents from the federal Drug Enforcement Administration (DEA) came to Monson's home. After a thorough investigation, the county officials concluded that her use of marijuana was entirely lawful as a matter of California law. Nevertheless, after a 3-hour standoff, the federal agents seized and destroyed all six of her cannabis plants.

Respondents thereafter brought this action against the Attorney General of the United States and the head of the DEA seeking injunctive and declaratory relief prohibiting the enforcement of the federal Controlled Substances Act (CSA) to the extent it prevents them from possessing, obtaining, or manufacturing cannabis for their personal medical use. In their complaint and supporting affidavits, Raich and Monson described the severity of their afflictions, their repeatedly futile attempts to obtain relief with conventional medications, and the opinions of their doctors concerning their need to use marijuana. Respondents claimed that enforcing the CSA against them would violate the Commerce Clause, the Due Process Clause of the Fifth Amendment, the Ninth and Tenth Amendments of the Constitution, and the doctrine of medical necessity.

The District Court denied respondents' motion for a preliminary injunction [in 2003]. Although the court found that the federal enforcement interests "wane[d]" when compared to the harm that California residents would suffer if denied access to medically necessary marijuana, it concluded that respondents could not demonstrate a likelihood of success on the merits of their legal claims.

A divided panel of the Court of Appeals for the Ninth Circuit [later in 2003] reversed and ordered the District Court to enter a preliminary injunction [to block federal action]. The [appellate] court found that respondents had "demonstrated a strong likelihood of success on their claim that, as applied to them, the CSA is an unconstitutional exercise of Congress' Commerce Clause authority." The Court of Appeals distinguished prior Circuit cases upholding the CSA in the face of Commerce Clause challenges by focusing on what it deemed to be the "*separate and distinct class of activities*" at issue in this case: "the intrastate, noncommercial cultivation and possession of cannabis for personal medical purposes as recommended by a patient's physician pursuant to valid California state law." The court found the latter class of activities "different in kind from drug trafficking" because interposing a physician's recommendation raises different health and safety concerns, and because "this limited use is clearly distinct from the broader illicit drug market—as well as any broader commercial market for medicinal marijuana—insofar as the medicinal marijuana at issue in this case is not intended for, nor does it enter, the stream of commerce."

...[This] case is made difficult by respondents' strong arguments that they will suffer irreparable harm because, despite a congressional finding to the contrary, marijuana does have valid therapeutic purposes. [A congressional finding is a statement within a law of what Congress believes is a fact related to the purpose of the law.] The question before us, however, is not whether it is wise to enforce the statute in these circumstances; rather, it is whether Congress' power to regulate interstate markets for medicinal substances encompasses the portions of those markets that are supplied with drugs produced and consumed locally. Well-settled law controls our answer. The CSA is a valid exercise of federal power, even as applied to the troubling facts of this case.

II

Shortly after taking office in 1969, President Nixon declared a national "war on drugs." As the first campaign of that war, Congress set out to enact legislation that would consolidate various drug laws on the books into a comprehensive statute, provide meaningful regulation over legitimate sources of drugs to prevent diversion into illegal channels, and strengthen law enforcement tools against the traffic in illicit drugs. That effort culminated in the passage of the Comprehensive Drug Abuse Prevention and Control Act of 1970.

This was not, however, Congress' first attempt to regulate the national market in drugs. Rather, as early as 1906 Congress enacted federal legislation imposing labeling regulations on medications and prohibiting the manufacture or shipment of any adulterated or misbranded drug traveling in interstate commerce. Aside from these labeling restrictions, most domestic drug regulations prior to 1970 generally came in the guise of revenue laws, with the Department of the Treasury serving as the federal government's primary enforcer. For example, the primary drug control law, before being repealed by the passage of the CSA, was the Harrison Narcotics Act of 1914. The Harrison Act sought to exert control over the possession and sale of narcotics, specifically cocaine and opiates, by requiring producers, distributors, and purchasers to register with the federal government, by assessing taxes against parties so registered, and by regulating the issuance of prescriptions.

Marijuana itself was not significantly regulated by the federal government until 1937 when accounts of marijuana's addictive qualities and physiological effects, paired with dissatisfaction with enforcement efforts at state and local levels, prompted Congress to pass the Marihuana Tax Act...(repealed 1970). Like the Harrison Act, the Marihuana Tax Act did not outlaw the possession or sale of marijuana outright. Rather, it imposed registration and reporting requirements for all individuals importing, producing, selling, or dealing in marijuana, and required the payment of annual taxes in addition to transfer taxes whenever the drug changed hands. Moreover, doctors wishing to prescribe marijuana for medical purposes were required to comply with rather burdensome administrative requirements. Noncompliance exposed traffickers to severe federal penalties, whereas compliance would often subject them to prosecution under state law. Thus, while the Marihuana Tax Act did not declare the drug illegal *per se*, the onerous administrative requirements, the prohibitively expensive taxes, and the risks attendant on compliance practically curtailed the marijuana trade.

Then in 1970, after declaration of the national "war on drugs," federal drug policy underwent a significant transformation. A number of noteworthy events precipitated this policy shift. First, in *Leary* v. *United States,* (1969), this Court held certain provisions of the Marihuana Tax Act and other narcotics legislation unconstitutional. Second, at the end of his term, President Johnson fundamentally reorganized the federal drug control agencies. The Bureau of Narcotics, then housed in the Department of Treasury, merged with the Bureau of Drug Abuse Control, then housed in the Department of Health, Education, and Welfare (HEW), to create the Bureau of Narcotics and Dangerous Drugs, currently housed in the Department of Justice. Finally, prompted by a perceived need to consolidate the growing number of piecemeal drug laws and to enhance federal drug enforcement powers, Congress enacted the Comprehensive Drug Abuse Prevention and Control Act.

Title II of that Act, the CSA, repealed most of the earlier antidrug laws in favor of a comprehensive regime to combat the international and interstate traffic in illicit drugs. The main objectives of the CSA were to conquer drug abuse and to control the legitimate and illegitimate traffic in controlled substances. Congress was particularly concerned with the need to prevent the diversion of drugs from legitimate to illicit channels.

To effectuate these goals, Congress devised a closed regulatory system making it unlawful to manufacture, distribute, dispense, or possess any controlled substance except in a manner authorized by the CSA. The CSA categorizes all controlled substances into five schedules. The drugs are grouped together based on their accepted medical uses, the potential for abuse, and their psychological and physical effects on the body. Each schedule is associated with a distinct set of controls regarding the manufacture, distribution, and use of the substances listed therein. The CSA and its implementing regulations set forth strict requirements regarding registration, labeling and packaging, production quotas, drug security, and recordkeeping.

In enacting the CSA, Congress classified marijuana as a Schedule I drug. This preliminary classification was based, in part, on the recommendation of the Assistant Secretary of HEW "that marihuana be retained within schedule I at least until the completion of certain studies now underway." Schedule I drugs are categorized [by the law] as such because of their high potential for abuse, lack of any accepted medical use, and absence of any accepted safety for use in medically supervised treatment. These three factors, in varying gradations, are also used to categorize drugs in the other four schedules. For example, Schedule II substances also have a high potential for abuse which may lead to severe psychological or physical dependence, but unlike Schedule I drugs, they have a currently accepted medical use. By classifying marijuana as a Schedule I drug, as opposed to listing it on a lesser schedule, the manufacture, distribution, or possession of marijuana became a criminal offense, with the sole exception being use of the drug as part of a Food and Drug Administration preapproved research study.

The CSA provides for the periodic updating of schedules and delegates authority to the Attorney General, after consultation with the Secretary of Health and Human Services, to add, remove, or transfer substances to, from, or between schedules. Despite considerable efforts to reschedule marijuana, it remains a Schedule I drug.

III

Respondents in this case do not dispute that passage of the CSA, as part of the Comprehensive Drug Abuse Prevention and Control Act, was well within Congress' commerce power. Nor do they contend that any provision or section of the CSA amounts to an unconstitutional exercise of congressional authority. Rather, respondents' challenge is actually quite limited; they argue that the CSA's categorical prohibition of the manufacture and possession of marijuana as applied to the intrastate manufacture and possession of marijuana for medical purposes pursuant to California law exceeds Congress' authority under the Commerce Clause.

In assessing the validity of congressional regulation, none of our Commerce Clause cases can be viewed in isolation.... Our understanding of the reach of the Commerce Clause, as well as Congress' assertion of authority [under the cause] has evolved over time. The Commerce Clause emerged as the Framers' response to the central problem giving rise to the Constitution itself: the absence of any federal commerce power under the Articles of Confederation. For the first century of our history, the primary use of the Clause was to preclude the kind of discriminatory state legislation [against the products of other states] that had once been permissible. Then, in response to rapid industrial development and an increasingly interdependent national economy, Congress "ushered in a new era of federal regulation under the commerce power," beginning with the enactment of the Interstate Commerce Act in 1887.

Cases decided during that "new era," which now spans more than a century, have identified three general categories of regulation in which Congress is authorized to engage under its commerce power. First, Congress can regulate the channels of interstate commerce. Second, Congress has authority to regulate and protect the instrumentalities of interstate commerce, and persons or things in interstate commerce. Third, Congress has the power to regulate activities that substantially affect interstate commerce. Only the third category is implicated in the case at hand.

Our case law firmly establishes Congress' power to regulate purely local activities that are part of an economic "class of activities" that have a substantial effect on interstate commerce.... We [the justices] have never required Congress to legislate with scientific exactitude. When Congress decides that the "'total incidence'" of a practice poses a threat to a national market, it may regulate the entire class. In this vein, we have reiterated [in an earlier case] that when "a general regulatory statute bears a substantial relation to commerce, the [importance or lack of importance of the] character of individual instances arising under that statute is of no consequence."

...Thus establishes that Congress can regulate purely intrastate activity that is not itself "commercial," in that it is not produced for sale, if it concludes that failure to regulate that class of activity would undercut the regulation of the interstate market in that commodity....

[In] this case...respondents are cultivating, for home consumption, a fungible commodity for which there is an established, albeit illegal, interstate market. ...[and] a primary purpose of the CSA is to control the supply and demand of controlled substances in both lawful and unlawful drug markets.... [Therefore], Congress had a rational basis for concluding that leaving home-consumed marijuana outside federal control would similarly affect price and market conditions.

More concretely,... [a] concern making it appropriate to include marijuana grown for home consumption in the CSA is the likelihood that the high demand in the interstate market will draw such marijuana into that market.... The diversion of homegrown marijuana tends to frustrate the federal interest in eliminating commercial transactions in the interstate market in their entirety. In both cases, the regulation is squarely within Congress' commerce power because production of the commodity meant for home consumption, [including] marijuana, has a substantial effect on supply and demand in the national market for that commodity....

Findings in the introductory sections of the CSA explain why Congress deemed it appropriate to encompass local activities within the scope of the CSA. The submissions of the parties and the numerous *amici* [supporting arguments submitted to the court by interested parties or "friends"] all seem to agree that...a national and international market for marijuana [exists]. ...Respondents nonetheless insist that the CSA cannot be constitutionally applied to their activities because Congress did not make a specific finding that the intrastate cultivation and possession of marijuana for medical purposes based on the recommendation of a physician would substantially affect the larger interstate marijuana market. Be that as it may, we have never required Congress to make particularized findings in order to legislate, absent a special concern such as the protection of free speech. While congressional findings are certainly helpful in reviewing the substance of a congressional statutory scheme, particularly when the connection to commerce is not self-evident, and while we will consider congressional findings in our analysis when they are available, the absence of particularized findings does not call into question Congress' authority to legislate.

In assessing the scope of Congress' authority under the Commerce Clause, we stress that the task before us is a modest one. We need not determine whether respondents' activities, taken in the aggregate, substantially affect interstate commerce in fact, but only whether a "rational basis" exists for so concluding. Given the enforcement difficulties that attend distinguishing between marijuana cultivated locally and marijuana grown elsewhere, and concerns about diversion into illicit channels, we have no difficulty concluding that Congress had a rational basis for believing that failure to regulate the intrastate manufacture and possession of marijuana would leave a gaping hole in the CSA. Thus..., Congress was acting well within its authority to "make all Laws which shall be necessary and proper" to "regulate Commerce...among the several States." That the regulation ensnares some purely intrastate activity is of no moment. As we have done many times before, we refuse to excise individual components of that larger scheme.

IV

...The activities regulated by the CSA are quintessentially economic. "Economics" [according to a dictionary] refers to "the production, distribution, and consumption of commodities." The CSA is a statute that regulates the production, distribution, and consumption of commodities for which there is an established, and lucrative, interstate market. Prohibiting the intrastate possession or manufacture of an article of commerce is a rational (and commonly utilized) means of regulating commerce in that product. Such prohibitions include specific decisions requiring that a drug be withdrawn from the market as a result of the failure to comply with regulatory requirements as well as decisions excluding Schedule I drugs entirely from the market. Because the CSA is a statute that directly regulates economic, commercial activity, our opinion in *Morrison* casts no doubt on its constitutionality.

The Court of Appeals was able to conclude otherwise only by isolating a "separate and distinct" class of activities that it held to be beyond the reach of federal power, defined as "the intrastate, noncommercial cultivation, possession and use of marijuana for personal medical purposes on the advice of a physician and in accordance with state law." The court characterized this class as "different in kind from drug trafficking." The differences between the members of a class so defined and the principal traffickers in Schedule I substances might be sufficient to justify a policy decision exempting the narrower class from the coverage of the CSA. The question, however, is whether Congress' contrary policy judgment, *i.e.*, its decision to include this narrower "class of activities" within the larger regulatory scheme, was constitutionally deficient. We have no difficulty concluding that Congress acted rationally in determining that none of the characteristics making up the purported class, whether viewed individually or in the aggregate, compelled an exemption from the CSA; rather, the subdivided class of activities defined by the Court of Appeals was an essential part of the larger regulatory scheme.

First, the fact that marijuana is used "for personal medical purposes on the advice of a physician" cannot itself serve as a distinguishing factor. The CSA designates marijuana as contraband for *any* purpose; in fact, by characterizing marijuana as a Schedule I drug, Congress expressly found that the drug has no acceptable medical uses. Moreover, the CSA is a comprehensive regulatory regime specifically designed to regulate which controlled substances can be utilized for medicinal purposes, and in what manner. Indeed, most of the substances classified in the CSA "have a useful and legitimate medical purpose." Thus, even if respondents are correct that marijuana does have accepted medical uses and thus should be redesignated as a lesser schedule drug, the CSA would still impose controls beyond what is required by California law. The CSA requires manufacturers, physicians, pharmacies, and other handlers of controlled substances to comply with statutory and regulatory provisions mandating registration with the DEA, compliance with specific production quotas, security controls to guard against diversion, recordkeeping and reporting obligations, and prescription requirements. Furthermore, the dispensing of new drugs, even when doctors approve their use, must await federal approval. Accordingly, the mere fact that marijuana—like virtually every other controlled substance regulated by the CSA—is used for medicinal purposes cannot possibly serve to distinguish it from the core activities regulated by the CSA.

More fundamentally, if [it is true, as has been contended,] the personal cultivation, possession, and use of marijuana for medicinal purposes is beyond the "outer limits" of Congress' Commerce Clause authority, it must also be true that such personal use of marijuana (or any other homegrown drug) for recreational purposes is also beyond those "outer limits," whether or not a state elects to authorize or even regulate such use....One need not have a degree in economics to understand why a nationwide exemption for the vast quantity of marijuana (or other drugs) locally cultivated for personal use (which presumably would include use by friends, neighbors, and family members) may have a substantial impact on the interstate market for this extraordinarily popular substance. The congressional judgment that an exemption for such a significant segment of the total market would undermine the orderly enforcement of the entire regulatory scheme is entitled to a strong presumption of validity. Indeed, that judgment is not only rational, but "visible to the naked eye" under any commonsense appraisal of the probable consequences of such an open-ended exemption.

Second, limiting the activity to marijuana possession and cultivation "in accordance with state law" cannot serve to place respondents' activities beyond congressional reach. The Supremacy Clause [in the U.S. Constitution] unambiguously provides that if there is any conflict between federal and state law, federal law shall prevail. It is beyond peradventure that federal power over commerce [prevails]...Just as state acquiescence to federal regulation cannot expand the bounds of the Commerce Clause, so too state action cannot circumscribe Congress' plenary commerce power.

Respondents acknowledge this proposition, but nonetheless contend that their activities were not "an essential part of a larger regulatory scheme" because they had been "isolated by the State of California, and [are] policed by the State of California," and thus remain "entirely separated from the market." The notion that California law has surgically excised a discrete activity that is hermetically sealed off from the larger interstate marijuana market is a dubious proposition, and, more importantly, one that Congress could have rationally rejected.

Indeed, that the California exemptions will have a significant impact on both the supply and demand sides of the market for marijuana is...is readily apparent. The exemption for physicians provides them with an economic incentive to grant their patients permission to use the drug. In contrast to most prescriptions for legal drugs, which limit the dosage and duration of the usage, under California law the doctor's permission to recommend marijuana use is open-ended. The authority to grant permission whenever the doctor determines that a patient is afflicted [according to the California law] with "any other illness for which marijuana provides relief" is broad enough to allow even the most scrupulous doctor to conclude that some recreational uses would be therapeutic. And our cases have taught us that there are some unscrupulous physicians who overprescribe when it is sufficiently profitable to do so.

The exemption for cultivation by patients and caregivers can only increase the supply of marijuana in the California market. The likelihood that all such production will promptly terminate when patients recover or will precisely match the patients' medical needs during their convalescence seems remote; whereas the danger that excesses will satisfy some of the admittedly enormous demand for recreational use seems obvious. Moreover, that the national and international narcotics trade has thrived in the face of vigorous criminal enforcement efforts suggests that no small number of unscrupulous people will make use of the California exemptions to serve their commercial ends whenever it is feasible to do so. Taking into account the fact that California is only one of at least nine states to have authorized the medical use of marijuana, Congress could have rationally concluded that the aggregate impact on the national market of all the transactions exempted from federal supervision is unquestionably substantial....

V

We...do note...the presence of...[an] avenue of relief....[The CSA] authorizes procedures for the reclassification of Schedule I drugs. But perhaps even more important than these legal avenues is the democratic process, in which the voices of voters allied with these respondents may one day be heard in the halls of Congress. Under the present state of the law, however, the judgment of the Court of Appeals must be vacated.

controlled Substances Act

CSA deemed nec. + proper, so = constitutional

deemed marijuana sched. 1 drug, no med. use, can be abused.

Economic = Interstate, so unconstitutional

Federal Regulation of Medical Marijuana: Usurpation of State Authority

SANDRA DAY O'CONNOR

We enforce the "outer limits" of Congress' Commerce Clause authority not for their own sake, but to protect historic spheres of state sovereignty from excessive federal encroachment and thereby to maintain the distribution of power fundamental to our federalist system of government. One of federalism's chief virtues, of course, is that it promotes innovation by allowing for the possibility that [according to the often quoted words of Justice Louis D. Brandeis in 1932], "a single courageous State may, if its citizens choose, serve as a laboratory; and try novel social and economic experiments without risk to the rest of the country."

This case exemplifies the role of states as laboratories. The states' core police powers have always included authority to define criminal law and to protect the health, safety, and welfare of their citizens. Exercising those powers, California (by ballot initiative and then by legislative codification) has come to its own conclusion about the difficult and sensitive question of whether marijuana should be available to relieve severe pain and suffering. Today [in the decision written by Justice John Paul Stevens, III] the Court sanctions an application of the federal Controlled Substances Act that extinguishes that experiment, without any proof that the personal cultivation, possession, and use of marijuana for medicinal purposes, if economic activity in the first place, has a substantial effect on interstate commerce and is therefore an appropriate subject of federal regulation. In so doing, the Court announces a rule that gives Congress a perverse incentive to legislate broadly pursuant to the Commerce Clause—nestling questionable assertions of its authority into comprehensive regulatory schemes—rather than with precision....

I

What is the relevant conduct subject to Commerce Clause analysis in this case? The Court takes its cues from Congress, applying the above considerations to the activity regulated by the Controlled Substances Act (CSA) in general. The Court's decision rests on two facts about the CSA: (1) Congress chose to enact a single statute providing a comprehensive prohibition on the production, distribution, and possession of all controlled substances, and (2) Congress did not distinguish between various forms of intrastate noncommercial cultivation, possession, and use of marijuana. Today's decision suggests that the federal regulation of local activity is immune to Commerce Clause challenge because Congress chose to act with an ambitious, all-encompassing statute, rather than piecemeal. In my view, allowing Congress to set the terms of the constitutional debate in this way, *i.e.*, by packaging regulation of local activity in broader schemes, is tantamount to removing meaningful limits on the Commerce Clause.

The Court, [in the opinion written by Justice Stevens, argues that]...the CSA is "a lengthy and detailed statute creating a comprehensive framework for regulating the production, distribution, and possession of five classes of 'controlled substances.'" Thus, according to the Court,...the local activity that the CSA targets (in this case cultivation and possession of marijuana for personal medicinal use) cannot be separated from the general drug control scheme of which it is a part.

Today's decision allows Congress to regulate intrastate activity without check, so long as there is some implication by legislative design that regulating intrastate activity is essential (and the Court appears to equate "essential" with "necessary") to the interstate regulatory scheme.... The Court appears to reason that the placement of local activity in a comprehensive scheme confirms that it is essential to that scheme.... Furthermore, today's decision suggests we would readily sustain a congressional decision to attach the regulation of intrastate activity to a pre-existing comprehensive (or even not-so-comprehensive) scheme. If so, the Court invites increased federal regulation of local activity even if, as it suggests, Congress would not enact a *new* interstate scheme exclusively for the sake of reaching intrastate activity.

I cannot agree...[with the constitutionality of] such evasive or overbroad legislative strategies or that the constitutionality of federal regulation depends on superficial and formalistic distinctions. Likewise I did not understand our discussion of the role of courts in enforcing outer limits of the Commerce Clause for the sake of maintaining the federalist balance our Constitution requires as a signal to Congress to enact legislation that is more extensive and more intrusive into the domain of state power. If the Court always defers to Congress as it does today, little may be left to the notion of enumerated powers.

The hard work for courts, then, is to identify objective markers for confining the analysis in Commerce Clause cases. Here, respondents challenge the constitutionality of the CSA as applied to them and those similarly situated. I agree with the Court that we must look beyond respondents' own activities. Otherwise, individual litigants could always exempt themselves from Commerce Clause regulation merely by pointing to the obvious—that their personal activities do not have a substantial effect on interstate commerce. The task is to identify a mode of analysis that allows Congress to regulate more than nothing (by declining to reduce each case to its litigants) and less than everything (by declining to let Congress set the terms of analysis). The analysis may not be the same in every case, for it depends on the regulatory scheme at issue and the federalism concerns implicated.

A number of objective markers are available to confine the scope of constitutional review here. Both federal and state legislation—including the CSA itself, the California Compassionate Use Act, and other state medical marijuana legislation—recognize that medical and nonmedical (*i.e.*, recreational) uses of drugs are realistically distinct and can be segregated, and regulate them differently. Respondents challenge only the application of the CSA to medicinal use of marijuana. Moreover, because fundamental structural concerns about dual sovereignty [federal and state independent authority] animate our Commerce Clause cases, it is relevant that this case involves the interplay of federal and state regulation in areas of criminal law and social policy, where [according to earlier court decisions,] "States lay claim by right of history and expertise"...[Moreover, as found by the Court in another case,] "State autonomy is a relevant factor in assessing the means by which Congress exercises its powers" under the Commerce Clause. California, like other states, has drawn on its reserved powers to distinguish the regulation of medicinal marijuana. To ascertain whether Congress' encroachment is constitutionally justified in this case, then, I would focus here on the personal cultivation, possession, and use of marijuana for medicinal purposes.

Having thus defined the relevant conduct, we must determine whether, under our precedents, the conduct is economic and, in the aggregate, substantially affects interstate commerce. Even if intrastate cultivation and possession of marijuana for one's own medicinal use can properly be characterized as economic, and I question whether it can, it has not been shown that such activity substantially affects interstate commerce. Similarly, it is neither self-evident nor demonstrated that regulating such activity is necessary to the interstate drug control scheme.

The Court's definition of economic activity is breathtaking. It defines as economic any activity involving the production, distribution, and consumption of commodities. And it appears to reason that when an interstate market for a commodity exists, regulating the intrastate manufacture or possession of that commodity is constitutional either because that intrastate activity is itself economic, or because regulating it is a rational part of regulating its market. Putting to one side the problem endemic to the Court's opinion—the shift in focus from the activity at issue in this case to the entirety of what the CSA regulates. The Court's definition of economic activity for purposes of Commerce Clause jurisprudence threatens to sweep all of productive human activity into federal regulatory reach.

The Court uses a dictionary definition of economics to skirt the real problem of drawing a meaningful line between "what is national and what is local." It will not do to say that Congress may regulate noncommercial activity simply because it may have an effect on the demand for commercial goods, or because the noncommercial endeavor can, in some sense, substitute for commercial activity. Most commercial goods or services have some sort of privately producible analogue. Home care substitutes for daycare. Charades games substitute for movie tickets. Backyard or windowsill gardening substitutes for going to the supermarket. To draw the line wherever private activity affects the demand for market goods is to draw no line at all, and to declare everything economic. We have already rejected the result that would follow—a federal police power.

In [earlier cases], we suggested that economic activity usually relates directly to commercial activity. The homegrown cultivation and personal possession and use of marijuana for medicinal purposes has no apparent commercial character. Everyone agrees that the marijuana at issue in this case was never in the stream of commerce, and neither were the supplies for growing it. (Marijuana is highly unusual among the substances subject to the CSA in that it can be cultivated without any materials that have traveled in interstate commerce.) Possession is not itself commercial activity. And respondents have not come into possession by means of any commercial transaction; they have simply grown, in their own homes, marijuana for their own use, without acquiring, buying, selling, or bartering a thing of value....

Even assuming that economic activity is at issue in this case, the [federal] government has made no showing in fact that the possession and use of homegrown marijuana for medical purposes, in California or elsewhere, has a substantial effect on interstate commerce. Similarly, the [federal] government has not shown that regulating such activity is necessary to an interstate regulatory scheme. Whatever the specific theory of "substantial effects" at issue (*i.e.*, whether the activity substantially affects interstate commerce, whether its regulation is necessary to an interstate regulatory scheme, or both), a concern for dual sovereignty requires that Congress' excursion into the traditional domain of states be justified.

That is why characterizing this as a case about the Necessary and Proper Clause does not change the analysis significantly. Congress must exercise its authority under the Necessary and Proper Clause in a manner consistent with basic constitutional principles. Congress cannot use its authority under the Clause to contravene the principle of state sovereignty embodied in the Tenth Amendment. Likewise, that authority must be used in a manner consistent with the notion of enumerated powers—a structural principle that is as much part of the Constitution as the Tenth Amendment's explicit textual command. Accordingly, something more than mere assertion is required when Congress purports to have power over local activity whose connection to an intrastate market is not self-evident. Otherwise, the Necessary and Proper Clause will always be a back door for unconstitutional federal regulation.

There is simply no evidence that homegrown medicinal marijuana users constitute, in the aggregate, a sizable enough class to have a discernible, let alone substantial, impact on the national illicit drug market—or otherwise to threaten the CSA regime. Explicit evidence is helpful when substantial effect is not "visible to the naked eye." And here, in part because common sense suggests that medical marijuana users may be limited in number and that California's Compassionate Use Act and similar state legislation may well isolate activities relating to medicinal marijuana from the illicit market, the effect of those activities on interstate drug traffic is not self-evidently substantial....

The Court [in Justice Steven's opinion] refers to a series of declarations in the introduction to the CSA saying that (1) local distribution and possession of controlled substances causes "swelling" in interstate traffic; (2) local production and distribution cannot be distinguished from interstate production and distribution; (3) federal control over intrastate incidents "is essential to effective control" over interstate drug trafficking....[These clauses] amount to nothing more than a legislative insistence that the regulation of controlled substances must be absolute. They are asserted without any supporting evidence—descriptive, statistical, or otherwise....

In particular, the CSA's introductory declarations are too vague and unspecific to demonstrate that the federal statutory scheme will be undermined if Congress cannot exert power over individuals like respondents. The declarations are not even specific to marijuana. (Facts about substantial effects may be developed in litigation to compensate for the inadequacy of Congress' findings; in part because this case comes to us from the grant of a preliminary injunction, there has been no such development.) Because here California, like other states, has carved out a limited class of activity for distinct regulation, the inadequacy of the CSA's findings is especially glaring. The California Compassionate Use Act exempts from other state drug laws patients and their caregivers "who posses[s] or cultivat[e] marijuana for the *personal* medical purposes of the patient upon the written or oral recommendation of a physician" to treat a list of serious medical conditions. The Act specifies that it should not be construed to supersede legislation prohibiting persons from engaging in acts dangerous to others, or to condone the diversion of marijuana for nonmedical purposes. To promote the Act's operation and to facilitate law enforcement, California recently enacted an identification card system for qualified patients. We generally assume states enforce their laws and have no reason to think otherwise here.

The [federal] government has not overcome empirical doubt that the number of Californians engaged in personal cultivation, possession, and use of medical marijuana, or the amount of marijuana they produce, is enough to threaten the federal regime. Nor has it shown that Compassionate Use Act marijuana users have been or are realistically likely to be responsible for the drug's seeping into the market in a significant way. The [federal] government does cite one estimate that there were over 100,000 Compassionate Use Act users in California in 2004, but does not explain, in terms of proportions, what their presence means for the national illicit drug market. [A study by the U.S.] General Accounting Office, Marijuana: Early Experience with Four States' Laws That Allow Use for Medical Purposes" (2002) [found that] in four California counties before the identification card system was enacted, voluntarily registered medical marijuana patients were less than 0.5 percent of the population; in Alaska, Hawaii, and Oregon, statewide medical marijuana registrants represented less than 0.05 percent of the states' populations. It also provides anecdotal evidence about the CSA's enforcement. The Court also offers some arguments about the effect of the Compassionate Use Act on the national market. It says that the California statute might be vulnerable to exploitation by unscrupulous physicians, that Compassionate Use Act patients may overproduce, and that the history of the narcotics trade shows the difficulty of cordoning off any drug use from the rest of the market. These arguments are plausible; if borne out in fact they could justify prosecuting Compassionate Use Act patients under the federal CSA. But, without substantiation, they add little to the CSA's conclusory statements about diversion, essentiality, and market effect. Piling assertion upon assertion does not, in my view, satisfy the substantiality test.

III

We would do well to recall how [in *Federalist* No. 45] James Madison, the father of the Constitution, described our system of joint sovereignty to the people of New York: "The powers delegated by the proposed constitution to the federal government are few and defined. Those which are to remain in the state governments are numerous and indefinite.... The powers reserved to the several states will extend to all the objects which, in the ordinary course of affairs, concern the lives, liberties, and properties of the people, and the internal order, improvement, and prosperity of the state."

Relying on Congress' abstract assertions, the Court has endorsed making it a federal crime to grow small amounts of marijuana in one's own home for one's own medicinal use. This overreaching stifles an express choice by some states, concerned for the lives and liberties of their people, to regulate medical marijuana differently. If I were a California citizen, I would not have voted for the medical marijuana ballot initiative; if I were a California legislator I would not have supported the Compassionate Use Act. But whatever the wisdom of California's experiment with medical marijuana, the federalism principles that have driven our Commerce Clause cases require that room for experiment be protected in this case. For these reasons I dissent.

Not interstate commerce, state sovereignty
states = each a lab, can do as wish

THE CONTINUING DEBATE: Federal Regulation of Medical Marijuana

What Is New

One June 6, 2005, the Supreme Court handed down its decision in *Gonzales v. Raich.* By a 6 to 3 vote, the court reversed the ruling of the Court of Appeals and held that the federal government could regulate marijuana under the interstate commerce clause. The decision applies to California and, by extension, to all other states permitting the use of medical marijuana. In one of the last cases over which he presided before his death in September, Chief Justice Rehnquist, who had often sided with the states, did so again and dissented along with Justice O'Connor and Justice Clarence Thomas. On the day of the decision, John P. Walters, President George Bush's director of national drug control policy, proclaimed, "Today's decision marks the end of medical marijuana as a political issue." Walters was almost certainly wrong. Seven months after the *Raich* decision, Rhode Island became the eleventh state to legalize medical marijuana, and proposals to legalize the drug are pending in several other states. Moreover, 72% of Americans support the use of medical marijuana, and the effort to get Congress to change federal law or to get the Justice Department to reconsider its stance are ongoing.

Where to Find More

For an entertaining view of the history of non-medical drug control, read "The History of the Non-Medical Use of Drugs in the United States" a speech to the California Judges Association 1995 annual conference at www.druglibrary.org/schaffer/History/whiteb1.htm. An authoritative review, "Workshop of the Medical Utility of Marijuana," sponsored by the National Institute for Health is available at www.nih.gov/news/medmarijuana/MedicalMarijuana.htm. Also worthwhile is Lawrence O. Gostin, "Medical Marijuana, American Federalism, and the Supreme Court," *JAMA: Journal of the American Medical Association* (2005). For the views of a group favoring the use of medical marijuana, go to the Web site of the Drug Policy Alliance at www.drugpolicy.org/marijuana/medical/. The view of an anti-use organization, the U.S. Drug Enforcement Administration, in its report, "Exposing the Myth of Smoked Medical Marijuana: The Facts" is at www.usdoj.gov/dea/ongoing/marijuana.html.

What More to Do

Analyze the positions of those in your class on this subject by dividing them into four groups according to each person's view of whether or not the expansive view of the commerce clause is acceptable or not and whether or not medical marijuana should be legalized. How many people have a constitutional position and a policy position that, in this case, are at odds with one another? Another project is to pick a different policy area that you think should not be subject to federal law under your concept of how federalism should work. Spend a little time finding out if there are federal laws governing that policy area. A group or an entire class can do this project together, with each person taking a different policy area.

DEBATE 3

CIVIL RIGHTS

EVALUATING THE "RIGHT TO AN ABORTION" DECISION IN *ROE V. WADE*:

Positive Impact *or* Negative Impact?

POSITIVE IMPACT

ADVOCATE: R. Alta Charo, Professor of Law and Bioethics; Associate Dean for Research and Faculty Development, University of Wisconsin Law School

SOURCE: Testimony during hearings on "The Consequences of *Roe v. Wade* and *Doe v. Bolton*," U.S. Senate Committee on the Judiciary, Subcommittee on the Constitution, Civil Rights and Property Rights June 23, 2005

NEGATIVE IMPACT

ADVOCATE: Teresa Collett, Professor of Law, University of St. Thomas School of Law, Minneapolis, Minnesota

SOURCE: Testimony during hearings on "The Consequences of *Roe v. Wade* and *Doe v. Bolton*," U.S. Senate Committee on the Judiciary, Subcommittee on the Constitution, Civil Rights and Property Rights June 23, 2005

January 22, 1973, was a pivotal day in one of the most contentious legal and social debates in U.S. history. On that date the U.S. Supreme Court handed down its decision in *Roe v. Wade*. By a 7–2 vote, the justices, in effect, invalidated state restrictions on the ability of women to medically abort their pregnancies. At that time, four states permitted abortion "on demand" (for any reason), 15 allowed abortions if continuing the pregnancy endangered a woman's health, and 31 banned abortions unless the woman's life was endangered.

The court based its decision on a "right to privacy." In the majority opinion, Justice Harry Blackmun conceded, "the Constitution does not explicitly mention any right of privacy." Nevertheless, he continued, "The Constitution recognizes that rights exist beyond those specified in that document...this right of privacy...is broad enough to encompass a woman's decision whether or not to terminate her pregnancy."

Supporters of *Roe v. Wade* often claim it secured the right of women to have to an abortion and to control their bodies. However, Blackmun said otherwise. In his words, "Some argue that the woman's right is absolute and that she is entitled to terminate her pregnancy at whatever time, in whatever way, and for whatever reason she alone chooses. With this we [justices] do not agree." Blackmun continued, "The privacy right...cannot be said to be absolute," and he indicated, "It is not clear to us [the justices] that the claim...that one has an unlimited right to do with one's body as one pleases bears a close relationship to the right of privacy."

Thus, instead of unrestricted right, the court outlined a limited right with different standards for each trimester of a normal pregnancy. In Blackmun's words, during the first trimester, "the abortion decision...must be left to the medical judgment of the pregnant woman's attending physician." Abortion could only be regulated during the second trimester in "ways that are reasonably related to maternal health." And during the third trimester, a state "may, if it chooses, regulate, and even proscribe, abortion except where it is necessary...for the preservation of the life or health of the mother."

The Court's decision changed the law, but the debate continues. Indeed, it is hard for many of those who differ on abortion to discuss the subject calmly. They do not even agree on what the fundamental issue is. Abortion rights advocates view the issue as about a woman's right to choose and thus label themselves "pro-choice." Foes of abortion say they are "pro-life" based on their view that human life begins at conception—or at least much sooner than the beginning of the third trimester.

Since *Roe v. Wade*, those oppose abortions altogether or who want to limit them have made numerous attempts to overturn the decision by amending the Constitution. They have also sought to pass state or federal laws that regulate abortion within the parameters set down by the Supreme Court in *Roe v. Wade* and subsequent court decisions.

As the readings that follow by R. Alta Charo and Teresa Collett demonstrate, passions about the abortion issue have not abated in the more than 30 years since the *Roe v. Wade* decision. During the 108th Congress (2003–2005) alone, dozens of bills related to abortion were introduced in the House and Senate. For example, in 2003 congress enacted a ban on an abortion procedure termed "intact dilation and extraction" (D&X), also commonly called "partial-birth abortions" by anti-abortion advocates.

Public opinion is has been very divided on abortion since *Roe v. Wade* in 1973. Soon after that decision, one poll found 47% in favor of the ruling, 44% opposed, and 9% unsure. A poll taken in 2005 just a month before the congressional hearings from which the readings that follow were drawn revealed similar opinion, with, on average, 48% of respondents saying they were "pro-choice," 44% being "pro-life," and 10% unsure.

POINTS TO PONDER

- The *Roe v. Wade* decision generally allows states to bar abortions during the third trimester of pregnancy because the fetus is considered "viable," that is, it could survive outside the womb. Are "viability" and "life" synonymous?
- If advances in medicine make it possible for fetuses to usually become viable earlier and earlier into pregnancy, would you favor generally banning abortions earlier to meet the existing viability time?
- In addition to abortion, Justice Blackmun's declaration in the *Roe v. Wade* decision that people to not have an unlimited right to do whatever they want with their body affects issues like suicide, assisted or not. Do you agree with the court on this matter?

Evaluating the "Right to an Abortion" Decision in *Roe v. Wade*: Positive Impact

R. ALTA CHARO

Roe v. Wade's broad vision of the right to privacy is our constitutional bulwark against legislation mandating a Chinese-style one-child policy; governmental eugenics policies that penalize parents who choose to have a child with disabilities; state prohibitions on home-schooling our children; forcible intubation of competent but terminally ill patients; and the issuance of a state-approved list of permissible forms of sexual intercourse between husband and wife. If we reject the core holding of *Roe v. Wade* that some activities are too intimate and some family matters too personal to be the subject of governmental intrusion, then we also reject any significant limit on the power of the government to dictate not only our personal morality but also the way we choose to live, to marry, and to raise our children.

Roe v. Wade is at the core of American jurisprudence, and its multiple strands of reasoning concerning marital privacy, medical privacy, bodily autonomy, psychological liberty, and gender equality are all connected to myriad other cases concerning the rights of parents to rear their children, the right to marry, the right to use contraception, the right to have children, and the right to refuse unwanted medical treatment. Overturning *Roe* would unravel far more than the right to terminate a pregnancy, and many Americans who have never felt they had a personal stake in the abortion debate would suddenly find their own interests threatened, whether it was the elderly seeking to control their medical treatment, the infertile seeking to use IVF [in vitro fertilization] to have a child, the woman seeking to make a decision about genetic testing, the couple heeding public health messages to use a condom to reduce the risk of contracting AIDS or other sexually transmitted diseases, or the unmarried man who, with his partner, is trying to avoid becoming a father before he is ready to support a family. As a legal matter, the right of the government to regulate, or even prohibit, reproductive choices depends both on whether they are considered an exercise of especially protected personal liberties and whether their absence has a sufficiently disparate impact on women's lives that it amounts to a denial of equal protection of the law.

Various aspects of reproductive privacy rights have been articulated in a number of landmark cases in the U.S. Supreme Court. The earliest case limited the right of the government to order involuntary sterilization. In the 1960s and 1970s, the Court issued other landmark rulings that protected access to contraceptives and abortion services, declaring that the "decision whether or not to beget or bear a child is at the very heart of this cluster of constitutionally protected choices" and that "if the right of privacy means anything, it is the right of the individual...to be free of unwarranted governmental intrusion into matters so fundamentally affecting a person as the decision to bear or beget a child."

The earliest cases, such as those concerning forced sterilization, were grounded in a traditional, common-law concern about bodily integrity, but the later cases incorporated concerns about marital privacy and psychological autonomy. For example, a right to contraception for men—for whom conception is a psychological and potentially economic burden, but not a physical one—implicitly endorsed a theory of reproductive liberty that went beyond mere bodily integrity and included a more general right to set the course of one's future. This is a notion of reproductive liberty that embraces a variety of activities that have no physical implications but are at the core of the right to self-determination, for example the right to marry, the right to rear one's children in the manner of one's choosing, or the right to use medical services to predict one's risk of having offspring with devastating diseases.

Subsequent abortion decisions have recognized the scope and implications of this expansive notion of personal liberty. Where psychological autonomy was raised, as in Justice Sandra Day O'Connor's statement that "at the heart of liberty is the right to define one's own concept of existence, of meaning, of the universe, and of the mystery of human life," it was ravaged by some of her colleagues, as when Justice [Antonin] Scalia wrote that this "collection of adjectives...can be applied to many forms of conduct that this Court has held are not entitled to constitutional protection...(for example) homosexual sodomy, polygamy, adult incest and suicide, all of which are equally 'intimate' and 'deeply personal' decisions involving 'personal autonomy and bodily integrity,' and all of which can constitutionally be proscribed because it is our unquestionable constitutional tradition that they are proscribable." Left unsaid in Justice Scalia's dissent, however, is an equally strong historical tradition of banning contraception and interracial marriage, which would once again be an option for individual states should personal and psychological liberty no longer be constitutionally protected.

These comments by Scalia did presage a series of doctrinal struggles within the Supreme Court, and subsequent abortion cases have emphasized instead gender equality or bodily autonomy. Similarly, cases concerning control over the manner of one's death backed away from expanding upon *Roe v. Wade*'s vision of personal liberty. But by the same token, the Court has steadfastly upheld the right to refuse unwanted medical treatment as consistent with the right to privacy and bodily autonomy enunciated in *Roe*. Overturn *Roe* and one risks losing the constitutional grounds with which to challenge a state law that forces hospitals to inflict painful and even futile medical interventions on competent, protesting patients.

Thus, the implications of overturning *Roe v. Wade* are difficult to predict but certainly go beyond the narrow question of abortion. Much depends upon how the court would choose to identify the key justifications for the right to privacy deployed in *Roe* and which they would now propose to overturn.

If the court reverses *Roe v. Wade* and limits the right to privacy to intimate marital relations, then technologies such as artificial insemination and in vitro fertilization that often use a third party may not be protected, because they represent a departure from the purest form of marital privacy. Perhaps even more alarmingly, the longstanding right of unmarried persons to obtain contraceptives would be undermined, as would the right of unmarried persons to be free of coercive state efforts to prevent them from bearing children, for example, through forced sterilization or exorbitant tax penalties for having children outside marriage.

If it reverses *Roe v. Wade* and limits the right to privacy to preventing the government from casually interfering with the physical bodies and reproductive capabilities of its citizens, although there might still be protection from involuntary sterilization, there would be only a far weaker claim of any right to access medical services such as IVF that depend on extra-uterine maintenance or diagnosis of embryos. And again, perhaps more alarmingly, an interpretation narrowly focused on bodily autonomy would no longer support the more expansive notions of privacy and liberty that support parental discretion to choose the language of instruction for their children or to make other fundamental decisions about how to rear their children.

But however it chooses to reverse *Roe v. Wade*, it would be necessary to reject existing case law, which singles out human reproduction for the profound way in which it reflects individual choices, aspirations and self-identity. This is because neither marital intimacy nor bodily autonomy rights could explain the right of men to use a simple condom to avoid unintended pregnancy or the right of parents to freely choose whether or not to use genetic testing, that is, to freely choose whether to avoid or embrace the possibility of having a child with genetic disabilities. Rejecting the notion that our liberty rights encompass a right to control the path our lives would clear the way for a broad range of government intrusions into both reproductive decisions and other matters of personal life.

Of course, it is possible that the Court might overturn *Roe v. Wade* not by backing away from its principle of a fundamental right to privacy but rather by a claim that the fertilized egg and developing embryo have competing rights that outweigh even a fundamental right to privacy. One hears this point of view in the claim that the founding fathers listed "life, liberty, and the pursuit of happiness" in that order. But to accept this argument, however, the court would be forced to redefine the egg or embryo as a "person" for the purposes of the 14th Amendment; without that status, the interests imputed to the embryo could not outweigh the undisputed interests of an adult woman.

If the courts conclude that embryos are protected as persons by the 14th Amendment, it is not only the abortions that follow unprotected sex that could be outlawed. It is not only the abortions following failed contraceptive efforts that could be outlawed. It is also abortions following cases of rape and incest that could be outlawed, because the effect of ruling that embryos have the same rights as children is to rule that nothing short of a threat to a woman's life could justify their destruction.

And re-defining the egg or embryo as a 14th Amendment person, entitled to equal protection under the law, has implications that go far beyond the legality of abortion. Now viewed as legally equivalent to a live-born child, a parent would be required to provide nurture, to avoid undue risk, and to effect a rescue when the conceptus was in danger, just as a parent must do for a child. In practical terms, providing nurture and avoiding undue risk might well mean that women would lose the right to choose midwives over physicians, or to use herbal remedies and nutritional supplements rather than prescribed drugs during pregnancy. Indeed, they might even lose the right to treat their own illnesses, such as epilepsy or slow-growing cancer, if such treatments might destroy the embryo but foregoing the treatments would merely interfere with the health, but not the life, of the woman herself.

Even contraceptive techniques such as breast feeding and the rhythm method might be banned, as they not only reduce the odds of fertilization, but when fertilization nonetheless occurs, they reduce the chances that the fertilized egg will successfully implant in the uterine wall. This is precisely the reasoning by which many abortion opponents advocate a ban on birth control pills, IUDs and all other forms of hormonal contraception. Indeed, given that in most months a sexually active woman will lose a fertilized egg during her menstrual cycle, abandoning *Roe v. Wade* would mean, at least theoretically, that the government could prescribe the precise time of the month when sexual activity is permitted, in order to reduce the chances that a fertilized egg will fail to implant in the uterine wall. More realistically, a duty to rescue an embryo in danger could mean that women would be forced to have every IVF embryo they create put back in their bodies, even if additional embryos posed a threat to fetal and maternal health, and even if pregnancy attempts were likely futile.

Practical consequences such as these demonstrate not only the moral, ethical, and logistical challenges that await us if *Roe v. Wade* is overturned, but also the tremendous implications this would have for women's equality interests. A blanket principle that accords equal rights as between embryos and adults functions, in fact, to place virtually all responsibility and burden upon women. It is women who will be vulnerable to state mandated medical interventions. It is women whose educations will be interrupted, with potentially lifelong consequences. It is women whose jobs and careers will be at risk, with all the economic losses that entails.

That men and women are biologically different is a physiological fact. For some, this suggests that it is women's lot to bear the cost of intimate relations. For others, however, and for the Supreme Court in many of its decisions that go far beyond *Roe v. Wade*, it means that it is the duty of the government to avoid adopting policies or announcing principles that forever place women at the service of the state rather than as the mistresses of their own lives.

Overall, *Roe v. Wade* represents the culmination of decades of constitutional law on the need to restrain over-zealous governmental intrusions on personal decisions concerning our families, our bodies, and our lives. In turn, it has formed the basis for yet more decades of constitutional law on the importance of maintaining a zone of personal liberty and privacy, in which individuals may flourish. In a century that will bring ever greater temptations and technological capabilities for governmental surveillance and control of its citizens, maintaining the integrity of this zone of personal liberty and privacy is more important than ever.

Evaluating the "Right to an Abortion" Decision in *Roe v. Wade*: Negative Impact

TERESA COLLETT

Contrary to the intention of [its] authors and proponents, *Roe v. Wade* [has] significantly undermined the well being of women and children in the United States, as well as seriously damaged the political fabric of American civil society. Due to the time constraints of the committee, my testimony today will just address the first issue. Throughout this country's history women have struggled to gain political, social, and economic equality. By 1972 however, the year before *Roe* [was] decided, women were making considerable strides towards achieving these goals. According to a 1972 report by the United States Census Bureau, "Women who had completed 4 years or more of college were as likely as men with the same education to be professional, technical, administrative, or managerial workers." In 1964 [Senator] Margaret Chase Smith [R-ME] became the first woman in our nation's history to be nominated for the presidency of the United States by a national political party. In 1967 Muriel Seibert became the first woman to own a seat on the New York Stock Exchange, and five short years later Juanita Kreps became the first woman director of that eminent institution. Women were making great progress in our society, and it is not by means of denying their capacity to conceive and bear children. Rather than furthering these achievements while accommodating the unique maternal capacity of women, *Roe* adopted the sterile "male model" of society effectively forcing women to conform to ideal of childlessness in order to gain equality.

It was no accident that the early feminists, such as Elizabeth Cady Stanton and Susan B. Anthony, opposed abortion. They saw it as a tool of oppression, manifesting men's domination and mistreatment. Elizabeth Cady Stanton wrote, "When we consider that women are treated as property, it is degrading to women that we should treat our children as property to be disposed of as we see fit." Susan B. Anthony was of the same opinion:

> "Guilty? Yes. No matter what the motive, love of ease, or a desire to save from suffering the unborn innocent, the woman is awfully guilty who commits the deed. It will burden her conscience in life, it will burden her soul in death; But oh, thrice guilty is he who drove her to the desperation which impelled her to the crime!"

In their newspaper devoted to women's equality, *The Revolution*, Matilda Joslyn Gage wrote "[This] subject lies deeper down in woman's wrongs than any other...I hesitate not to assert that most of [the responsibility for] this crime lies at the door of the male sex." So strongly did these women reject abortion that they put the solvency of their publication, *The Revolution*, at risk rather than accept advertisements from abortionists.

By their rejection of abortion, these women demanded something more meaningful (and more radical) than what the majority [of the justices in] the *Roe* [case]...ordered—they demanded equality as full women, not as chemically or surgically altered surrogates of men. The early feminists understood that abortion on demand, not motherhood, posed the real threat to women's rights. The early feminists recognized that abortion was the product, not of choice, but of pressure, particularly from the men in women's lives. The current regime of abortion which *Roe* instigated has not changed this sad fact. A 1998 study published by the Guttmacher Institute, a research affiliate of Planned Parenthood, indicates that relationship problems contributed to the decision to seek abortions by 51% of American women.

Underlying this general reason are such specific ones as that the partner threatened to abandon the woman if she gives birth, that the partner or the woman herself refuses to marry to legitimate the birth, that a break-up is imminent for reasons other than the pregnancy, that the pregnancy resulted from an extramarital relationship, that the husband or partner mistreated the woman because of her pregnancy, or that the husband or partner simply does not want the child. Sometimes women combined these reasons with not being able to afford a baby, suggesting the importance of having a partner who can offer both emotional and financial support. The simple fact is that today, as in the 19th century, for many women abortion is the man's solution for what he views as the "woman's problem." *Roe's* harmful effects on women have not been confined to the social realm. Medical science has shown that abortion damages women's physical and mental health as well. By aborting their pregnancies, women lose the health benefits that childbirth and its accompanying lactation bring, including reduced risk of breast, ovarian, and endometrial cancer.

One-third of all women in the U.S. will suffer from cancer in their lifetime. Cancer is the second leading cause of death in the United States.

Breast cancer is the most common cancer diagnosed in women, and the second leading cause of cancer death in women. It is estimated that about 211,240 women in the United States will be diagnosed with invasive breast cancer in 2005, and about 40,410 women will die from the disease. One of the recognized risk factors for breast cancer is having no children or delaying childbearing until after the age of thirty.

In 1970 the World Health Organization published the results of an international study of breast cancer and reproductive experience involving 250,000 women from seven areas. The study established that women having their first child under age 18 have only about one-third the breast cancer risk of those whose first birth is delayed until age 35 or older. The researchers also noted that "data suggests an increased risk [of breast cancer] associated with abortion contrary to the reduction in risk associated with full-term births."

Childbirth also has a protective effect against ovarian cancer. Ovarian cancer is the seventh most common cancer, but ranks fourth as the cause of cancer death in women. It causes more deaths than any other cancer of the female reproductive system. The American Cancer Society estimates that there will be about 22,220 new cases of ovarian cancer in this country in 2005. About 16,210 women will die of the disease. While less common than breast cancer, it is more likely to be fatal. Childbirth reduces this risk.

Endometrial cancer is a cancer that develops from the inner lining of the uterus. In 2005, 40,880 new cases of endometrial cancer are expected to be diagnosed, and 7,310 women are expected to die from this cancer. Researchers have found that the process of childbirth results in the shedding of malignant or pre-malignant cells which lead to endometrial cancer. This protective effect increases with each birth.

In contrast, abortions render women thirty percent more likely to develop breast cancer and also increase the likelihood of developing cervical and ovarian cancer.

Abortion also creates numerous health hazards for subsequent pregnancies, including increasing the likelihood of death during childbirth. Furthermore, women who have had abortions experience varying degrees of emotional distress and are more likely to exhibit self-destructive behaviors, including suicide.

While it is often said that abortion is significantly safer than completing the pregnancy, the fact is we simply don't have the statistical information to know. Abortion providers have concede this fact in the published literature. Yet any attempts to remedy this critical lack of public health information are furiously fought by abortion-rights advocates.

Yet women are not the only ones harmed by the mentality reflected in the *Roe* [decision]. It is often said that the Court did not understand the physical development of the unborn at the case [was] heard. Yet I recently had occasion to go back and read the [legal] briefs presented to the *Roe* Court and was amazed by the amount of detail concerning the development of the unborn child, even in 1973. While there were no pictures as compelling as tiny Samuel Armas's hand apparently grasping the finger of the perinatal surgeon who was repairing his spine while Samuel was still in his mother's womb or those currently available from a 4-D ultrasound system, our common humanity was made clear by the Attorney General of Texas from the medical materials available, even at that time. The failure of the Court to engage this material in its opinion deeply troubles me.

Courts have traditionally recognized some rights in unborn children, and medical science continues to demonstrate with increasing veracity that even at the earliest stages of development, an unborn child is a human being. Even *Roe* recognized that the States have a compelling interest in protecting this human life. Nevertheless, this decision authorized expectant mothers to choose abortion over life, and since 1973, over thirty-nine million legal abortions have been performed in the United States. In this country alone, roughly 700 pregnancies per year continue after an initial abortion attempt, and children born after these failed attempts are likely to suffer from developmental abnormalities. Also, as previously noted, children conceived after an abortion and carried to term run a higher risk of prenatal complications.

Perhaps even more troubling is the mounting evidence that abortion has contributed to the reemergence of the idea of children as possessions. In 1972, one year before the *Roe v. Wade* decision, there were 2.05 reported abuse cases per 1,000 children, according to the U.S. Bureau of the Census. In April 2004 the U.S. Department of Health and Human Services reported 12.3 out of every 1,000 children were victims of abuse or neglect. In the six short years from 1986 to 1993 the total number of children endangered quadrupled. While many factors may have contributed to this increase, the attitude that we are free to dispose of human life that is "unwanted" certainly must be among them.

With the advent of in vitro fertilization, technology that only became available five years after *Roe v. Wade*, some would-be parents now dream of "custom-order" children resulting in today's debate regarding the morality of selecting the sex and other characteristics of a child. The parameters of this debate have expanded so far as to include those who defend the right of two deaf lesbians to intentionally create a deaf child.

All of these facts lead me to agree with a recent opinion of Judge Edith Jones of the United States Court of Appeals for the Fifth Circuit: Hard [science] and social science will of course progress even though the Supreme Court averts its eyes. It takes no expert prognosticator to know that research on women's mental and physical health following abortion will yield an eventual medical consensus, and neonatal science will push the frontiers of fetal "viability" ever closer to the date of conception. One may fervently hope that the Court will someday acknowledge such developments and re-evaluate *Roe* accordingly. Some of us think that day needs to be now.

THE CONTINUING DEBATE: Evaluating the "Right to an Abortion" Decision in *Roe v. Wade*

What Is New

In 2003 Congress banned D&X abortions, but the Second, Eighth, and Ninth Circuits of the U.S. Court of Appeals all ruled the act unconstitutional. The Supreme Court then agreed to hear the case during its 2006–2007 term. Anti-abortion forces are hopeful that Court will side with them because of the seating of two new and generally conservative members, Chief Justice John Roberts in 2005 and Justice Samuel Alito in 2006. Beyond this limited challenge to abortion, other efforts to radically restrict abortions continued. Most significantly, South Dakota squarely challenged *Roe v. Wade* by enacting in 2006 a law the makes it a felony to perform an abortion for any reason other than to save a woman's life. The law is already being challenged in U.S. District Court and could ultimately be heard by the Supreme Court.

As for public opinion, polls showed very mixed opinions. Some 60% said they thought the *Roe v. Wade* decision was a "good thing," but, as noted in the introduction, there was a nearly even split between those describing themselves as pro-choice and pro-life. Moreover 70% said abortion was "morally wrong" either always or sometimes. When asked about trimesters, 60% thought abortion should be legal in the first trimester, but only 26% supported in the second trimester, and a mere 12% favored it in the third trimester.

Where to Find More

The abortion debate in the United States dates back even beyond Connecticut's enactment of the first anti-abortion law in 1821. For a review of that debate, see Rosemary Nossiff, *Before Roe: Abortion Policy in the States* (Temple University Press, 2002). A study comparing abortion laws in 64 countries is Albin Eser and H. G. Koch, *Abortion and the Law: From International Comparison to Legal Policy* (Cambridge University Press, 2005).

Current information on the abortion debate and its politics can be found on the Web sites of those representing both points of view. That of the Center for Reproductive Rights, author of the first reading is at: www.crlp.org/. Representing the pro-life point of view is the National Right to Life Committee at www.nrlc.org/. A site that claims to be balanced and seems to strive for that can be found at: www.religioustolerance.org/abortion1.htm.

What More to Do

The greatest challenge is to try to reach an agreement on this emotionally charged issue. Certainly it will not be possible to reconcile everyone. There are ardent voices that see no middle ground between the right to choose and the right to life. But polls show that most Americans are less doctrinaire. A 2006 poll recorded 19% of its respondents thinking abortion should be legal in all cases, 32% saying legal in most cases, 27% arguing it should be illegal in most cases, 16% wanting abortion to be illegal in all cases, and 3% unsure. Somewhere in that majority of 62% Americans who are in the "most cases" or "uncertain" middle there may be a place that takes into account fetal/infant viability, maternal health, and other factors and creates a policy that most Americans can accept. Can your class craft a statement of standards that would receive a majority vote in the class?

CIVIL LIBERTIES

THE PHRASE "UNDER GOD" IN THE PLEDGE OF ALLEGIANCE: Violation of the First Amendment *or* Acceptable Traditional Expression?

VIOLATION OF THE FIRST AMENDMENT

ADVOCATE: Douglas Laycock, Professor, School of Law, University of Texas; and Counsel of Record for 32 Christian and Jewish clergy filing an amicus curiae brief with the Supreme Court in *Elk Grove School District v. Newdow*

SOURCE: A discussion of the topic "Under God? Pledge of Allegiance Constitutionality," sponsored by the Pew Forum on Religion and Public Life and held before the National Press Club, Washington, D.C., March 19, 2004

ACCEPTABLE TRADITIONAL EXPRESSION

ADVOCATE: Jay Alan Sekulow, Chief Counsel, American Center for Law and Justice; and Counsel of Record for 76 members of Congress and the Committee to Protect the Pledge filing an amicus curiae brief with the Supreme Court in *Elk Grove School District v. Newdow*

SOURCE: A discussion of the topic "Under God? Pledge of Allegiance Constitutionality," sponsored by the Pew Forum on Religion and Public Life and held before the National Press Club, Washington, D.C., March 19, 2004

This debate focuses on the establishment clause of the Constitution's First Amendment, which requires that "Congress shall make no law respecting an establishment of religion." It is clear that the authors of the First Amendment were reacting against the British practice of establishing and supporting an "official" church, in that case the Church of England. Also certain is that Congress meant the amendment to prohibit any attempt to bar any religion or religious belief. There the certainties end. For example, freedom of religion does not mean that the government cannot proscribe certain religious practices. Polygamy, animal sacrifice, and taking illegal drugs are just a few of the practices exercised in the name religion that have been legally with subsequent court approval.

Nevertheless, religion has always had a presence in government in the Untied States. The Great Seal of the United States, adopted in 1782 (and found on the back left of one dollar bills) contains an "all seeing eye of Providence," which probably means God, especially given that it is framed in a triangle, thought to represent the Christian trinity. The Great Seal also contains the Latin phrase "annuit coeptis," which translates as "It/He (Providence/God) has favored our undertakings." Also, first adopted in 1964 and currently on all U.S. paper currency is the motto "In God We Trust." That phrase is also found in the fourth stanza of the Star Spangled Banner (written 1813; officially adopted 1931), which concludes, "And this be our motto: "In God is our trust." Finally, in 1957 Congress added "under God" after one nation" to the Pledge of Allegiance. This last reference to God is the specific issue in this debate.

Government also has and continues to support religion and to choose among religions in other ways. For example, the military employs chaplains for all the major religious faiths, but does not employ atheist counselors. There is also a level of choosing among religions in having chaplains for the major religions, but not for the minor ones. Each year the president lights an immense Christmas tree, although these days in a bow to restrictions on religious displays on public property the giant fir is call the "national tree" and is lighted as part of the "Pageant of Peace," which, of course, corresponds with the Christmas season. Historically, it has been common to find the Ten Commandments carved in the walls of public buildings or otherwise displayed in them.

Traditionally, displays of the Ten Commandments or similar religious symbols on public property, prayers in public schools, references to God on the country's currency, or affirmations of patriotism were not high profile issues. This began to change because of the increasing stress on civil rights and liberties and because in *Everson v. Board of Education* (1947) the Supreme Court ruled that the due process cause of the Fourteenth Amendment made the establishment clause of the First Amendment applicable to the states, as well as federal government. During the ensuring years, a significant number of cases involving practices at the state and local levels were brought before the Supreme Court. With regard to the establishment clause, the Court struck down prayers and religious invocations in public schools, most religious displays on public property, and other explicit and implicit supports of religion by public officials. However, the Supreme Court has also allowed religious groups to meet in public buildings as long as there is no discrimination, has supported prayers opening legislative sessions, and having student groups fees go to student religious groups.

In this setting, Michael Newdow filed suit arguing that a California rule requiring students to recite the Pledge of Allegiance with its affirmative reference to God violated the establishment clause of the First Amendment. A U.S. District Court ruled for the school district, but the "Ninth Circuit of the U.S. Court of Appeals found for Newdow, and the Elk Grove school district appealed to the U.S. Supreme Court. Shortly before the High Court heard oral arguments, two opposing attorneys who had filed amicus curiae ("friend of the court") briefs with the Court debated the issue and responded to questions from the audience in the readings that follow.

POINTS TO PONDER

- Expressing an absolutist position when writing the majority opinion in the *Everson* case, Justice Hugo Black argued that the wall between church and state "must be kept high and impregnable. We [should] not approve any breach." What would be the implications of adopting that no-compromise standard?
- Compare the argument of Douglas Laycock that the Pledge, as government sanctioned religious expression, is "coercive" and Jay Sekulow's contention that the phrase "under God" is merely a "historical statement" reflecting the belief in God by most Americans throughout history.
- Does it make any difference that students are not required to say the pledge, only that schools must lead its recitation?

The Phrase "Under God" in the Pledge of Allegiance: Violation of the First Amendment

DOUGLAS LAYCOCK

Jay [Sekulow, the author of the second article in this debate] and I were on the same side in a case [*Locke v. Davey*, 2004] that the [Supreme] Court decided earlier this year, involving the student from Washington [State] who wanted to take his state scholarship to go to seminary with it. With this case, we're on opposite sides. How does that happen? What's up with me? Explaining that is relevant to what I think about the Pledge of Allegiance.

I come to these cases with a fairly simple theory, which is that people of every religion, including the majority and the minority, and people of no religion at all, are entitled to believe their own beliefs, speak their own beliefs, and act on their own beliefs as long as they're not hurting anybody else, and to be left alone by government and have government not take sides. And a corollary of that is that none of these groups can use the government to try to force the other side to join in or participate in their own religious observances. So when government tries to stop a student prayer club from meeting on its own after school, I think government is wrong. And when that student prayer club—or the supporters of that student prayer club—moves into the classroom and tries to induce everyone else who didn't want to come to participate anyway, I think they're wrong. And I think the Pledge of Allegiance falls on that side of the line.

The country has been fighting about this issue in various forms since the 1820s, when Catholics objected to Protestant religious observances in public schools. We've gotten better about it. In the 1840s and '50s, we had mobs in the street; we had people dead. We don't do that to each other any more, and that's progress. And "one nation under God" may seem like a pretty minimal violation of whatever principle is at stake here. The Supreme Court for 40 years has said consistently, without an exception, that government may not sponsor religious observances in the public schools, and they've said it with respect to things that were pretty short. The first school prayer case, *Engel v. Vitale* in 1962, was a pretty generic, monotheistic prayer composed not by clergymen but by the New York Board of Regents, and it was 22 words long, and the Court said you can't ask children to recite that prayer.

Now we're down to only two words, and it's not a prayer, and it's mixed up in the Pledge of Allegiance, and the question is, Does that change the answer? And the Supreme Court has repeatedly suggested, never in a holding, but over and over in what lawyers call dictums—side comments explaining what this opinion doesn't decide—there is some kind of threshold. It's got to be big enough to matter before it's an Establishment Clause violation [of the First Amendment to the Constitution]. There are little, ceremonial, rote, repetition things that the Court is not going to get involved in striking down. "In God We Trust" on the coins is a classic example; various state mottos around the country; certainly religious references in historical documents and in politicians' speeches, the Supreme Court is not going to strike down. And they have said—without a holding—two or three times that the Pledge of Allegiance is like "In God We Trust" on the coins. It's very short, and it's repeated by rote, and nobody really thinks about it much. Well, most people don't really think about it much.

The Court may say the Pledge of Allegiance—the religious part of the Pledge of Allegiance—is just too short to worry about. It's what lawyers call *de minimis*. That may happen.

I think the Pledge of Allegiance is different from all these other examples of things that might be de minimis. It's different from "In God We Trust" on the coins. It's different from politicians making speeches and so forth. The reason it's different is really unique in the culture. Government doesn't do this to adults; it doesn't do this to children in any other context. In the Pledge of Allegiance, we ask every child in the public schools in America every morning for a personal profession of faith. You don't have to take out your coin and read and meditate on "In God We Trust." You don't have to pay any attention when the politician is talking, and lots of us don't.

But this asks for a personal affirmation: I pledge allegiance to one nation under God. Now if God does not exist, or if I believe that God does not exist, then that isn't one nation under God. We can't have a nation under God unless there is a God. It doesn't say one nation under our god, or some gods, or one of the gods. It pretty clearly implies there is only one God, and if there is only one God, then the God of the Pledge is the one true God, and other alleged gods around the world are false gods.

It says one other thing about this God—it doesn't say much, can't say much in two words—but the nation is "under God." God is of such a nature that God exercises some sort of broad superintending authority so that it is possible for a whole nation to be under Him. Now that doesn't exclude many folks, but it excludes some, right? This is not God as First Cause who set the universe in motion and doesn't intervene any more; this is not God as a metaphor for all the goodness imminent in the universe or imminent in the population. This is God exercising some kind of authority over at least this nation; maybe over all nations.

It's a pretty generic concept of God, and it's comfortable for a lot of people. But we may overestimate how many people. The largest private opinion polls have about 15 percent of the population not subscribing to any monotheistic conception of God. Who is in that 15 percent? Buddhist and other non-theists, Hindus and other polytheists, those with no religion, atheist, agnostic, humanist, ethical culturalists. That's 15 percent of the population, with 7.2 million children in public schools who are being asked to personally affirm every morning a religious belief that is different from the religious belief that is taught or held in their home and by their parents. And it is the personal affirmation request in the Pledge, it seems to me, that makes the Pledge unique. It is different from all the other kinds of ceremonial deism that go on in the country.

In the attempt to defend the Pledge, government and the various friends of the Court supporting the Pledge have said a remarkable variety of things, but probably the most common thing they've said is variations on what appears in the brief of the United States. It is not religious. We don't mean for them to take it literally. We ask the children to say the nation is under God, but we don't expect them to really believe that the nation is under God. Here is a quote from the government's brief: "What it really means is, I pledge allegiance to one nation, founded by individuals whose belief in God gave rise to the governmental institutions and political order they adopted, indivisible, with liberty and justice for all."

Now if that were what it means, if anybody thought that was what it meant, we would not have had the great political outcry in response to the Ninth Circuit's decision. If people want to get mad about this because it had some recital about what the founders believed, or because of the other point the government makes—that it's in reference to historical and demographic facts that most Americans over time have believed in God—that would be one thing. But people don't get angry at a recital of historical and demographic facts. People get angry because they know what it means; it's plain English. They believe what it means, they want people to say what it means, they want their kids to say what it means. And I'll tell you a dirty little secret: They want to coerce other kids to say what it means and what they believe to be true. They know that "under God" means under God.

And if it doesn't mean under God, if we were to take the government seriously for asking children every morning to say the nation is under God but not to mean the nation is under God, well, Christians and Jews have a teaching about that, too. "Thou shalt not take the name of the Lord Thy God in vain." If we don't mean it, if it's a vain form of words that doesn't mean what it says, then it is indeed a taking of the name of the Lord in vain. That is why the [amicus curiae] brief that I filed [with the Supreme Court in the case of *Elk Grove School District v. Newdow*] is on behalf of 32 Christian and Jewish clergy who do care, not only about not coercing other people to practice their religion, but also care that if we are going to practice religion, we mean it seriously. We don't want a watered down religion that we don't really believe.

Jay Sekulow's version [in an opposing amicus curiae brief] is a little different. He says there's a category—and there's some of this in the government's brief as well—of patriotic observances with religious references. You can't do religion in the school, but you can do patriotism with a religious reference. The consequence of that would be, I suppose, that we could undo all the school prayer cases as long as we wrapped them in a coat of patriotism.

Mingling the patriotic and the religious seems to me to make it worse, not better. Think about what the Pledge does to a child who cannot in good faith affirm that the nation is under God and who actually thinks about it. And let me tell you, kids think about it. You don't think about it if you're comfortable with it, if it doesn't challenge anything you believe, you blur right over it. You can say it pretty fast, and most of us don't stop to reflect on the Pledge anymore. But for kids who don't believe it, and maybe most especially for kids who once went to a church and now don't believe it, whether or not to say "under God" becomes a big issue. I don't claim it becomes a big issue for all 7.2 million whose parents show up in opinion polls, but for a substantial minority of kids, to say "under God" or not becomes an issue.

Some kids drop it out. One of the saving graces here is that it's only two words, so you can get away with dropping it out, and your friends may not notice. But there are people who refuse to say those two words because they don't believe them, and there are a few who refuse to say those two words because it's religious in a governmental context, and it shouldn't be there. It belongs somewhere else.

And for the child who cannot say it, here's what we do by putting the religious reference in the middle of the Pledge of Allegiance to the nation: If you are doubtful about the existence of God, you are of doubtful loyalty to the nation. What kind of a citizen can you be? You can't even say the Pledge of Allegiance in the prescribed form that Congress has written. You can't pledge your loyalty to the nation without pledging your belief in the existence of God.

Now over and over and over the Supreme Court has said the reason it will not allow the government itself to take a position on a religious question, will not allow the government to endorse a religious viewpoint or an anti-religious viewpoint is because government should not make any citizen's political standing in the community depend upon his religious beliefs, not even implicitly, not even by implication. The Court says repeatedly that if the government says this is a Christian nation or this is a religious nation, then non-Christians and non-religious folks will think the government really views them as a second-class citizens. That's pretty indirect and implicit. This is very direct and explicit. Now, children, it is time to pledge your allegiance to the United States of America, and to do that, you have to pledge that the nation is under God. We have linked religion and politics, religion and patriotism, religious faith and patriotic standing inseparably right in the middle of one sentence. And the only way to avoid the religious part is literally to drop out mid-sentence and then come back in.

What would follow from a Supreme Court either striking down or upholding the Pledge? I think because of the fact that the Pledge is unique in asking for a personal affirmation, not much follows about other cases from a decision striking it down. Political volcano is going to follow, but not much is going to follow legally. "In God We Trust" doesn't come off the coins, the other religious references in the school curriculum don't come out. Of course the government can teach historical documents that have religious references in them because that is part of the history curriculum. I think they can teach music with religious references in it because that's music. It's important in the culture. I think schools should be more sensitive than they are about the problems faced by nonbelieving children when they're asked to sing that music. I think we can deal with those problems, but I don't think the Constitution requires that all—indeed, I think it forbids—certainly, it's sound educational policy—forbids stripping all religious references out of history. Religion is part of history.

None of those things ask the child to personally affirm his belief that the nation is under God, so in this sense, the Pledge case is unique. A decision taking "under God" out of the Pledge would not really portend much change on anything else.

A decision upholding the Pledge, well, you've got to see how they write it. If the Court wants to say the Pledge is special, we're going to let this go by, but it doesn't mean we're unraveling all the school prayer cases, it doesn't mean anything else much changes. They can write this very narrowly. There is a whole list of objective factors that are special about the Pledge that cut the other way. They could say it is only two words; it is recited by rote; it is not a prayer; it has been around in exactly the same form for 50 years before we got a hold of it; kids don't have to say it—we settled that in 1943 [in West Virginia v. Barnette]; they don't have to say it. For those reasons, in combination with all those reasons, we're going to uphold this. Nothing else will satisfy all those reasons. Nothing else is only two words, for starters, and that would be an opinion that doesn't change much.

If they write an opinion that's like the government's brief—we're going to declare that this really isn't religious—the problem with that is that it's completely standardless and therefore it's completely boundless. It's a fiat. The plain language is religious, but five of us on the Supreme Court—hey, with five votes, you can do anything—we're going to tell the country this is not religious. The Fifth Circuit recently held the Ten Commandments are not religious. A big monument across the top, giant letters, "I am the Lord, thy God. Thou shalt have no other gods before me." Not religious, the Fifth Circuit [of the U.S. Court of Appeals] says.

If the Supreme Court adopts that kind of approach—we'll just decree things not to be religious—then everything's up for grabs. If you're going to arbitrarily decree religious things to be secular, you can do it in any case, and district judges will be asked to do it in any case. So that would be a much scarier opinion, a much more potentially wide-ranging opinion, and then other possibilities sort of range in between. Any religion is okay if you're wrap it in patriotism. I think that's pretty wide open, too, because political officers can be pretty clever about wrapping things in patriotism.

So we may get an opinion either way—we may get a very narrow opinion either way or a very broad opinion, particularly if they uphold it. Watch not only for the result; watch for how they write it.

Question: Please comment on the "notion...of ceremonial deism," the idea that "references to God become meaningless if recited often enough in public places."

Mr. Laycock: I think you're right. I think the principal religious division in the country used to be Protestant-Catholic. It's not that anymore. It is a continuum from intense anti-religion to intensely religious. Intensely devout Protestants, Catholics, Muslims, Jews find themselves on the same side of a lot of issues, given that divide, and ceremonial deism is very comfortable for the vast range in the middle. The religious center in America is low-intensity theist.

I think these ceremonial references are very problematic for the anti-religious and for the seriously religious, and many of the seriously religious, in good faith, defend that kind of watered-down ceremonial deism in court on the theory that it's better than nothing; that's all they'll let us have, that's all we can get in a government-sponsored forum, and it's not for me to tell them they're making a mistake. But it seems to me it is a mistake, and a lot of folks who are intensely religious aren't comfortable with it, and to some extent, it is a position only for the Court. So the Justice Department, representing the United States, says, This is not religious at all. But the form letter from the White House that goes out to people who write in about this issue says it is profoundly religious. They're telling the Court one thing and the public something completely different. The ceremonial deism is a placeholder.

Question: Just to follow up,...comment on whether there is a path that we go down that essentially declares that the public realm—whatever is supported by government—must necessarily be godless, or is there an alternative to this? Does this case take you there or does it not necessarily take you there?

Mr. Laycock: There's no path that leads to the public sphere being godless. There is a path that leads to any activity sponsored by government being godless. The simple absolutist rule is that if the government's sponsoring it, there's no mention of God. In the public schools, the Court has never found a case where a government could mention God, but they've never said this is an absolutist rule with no exceptions either.

This case does not take us there. It does not present the question whether there can ever be any exceptions because this case has the unique feature of requesting a personal affirmation. So a decision in this case wouldn't say anything about whether the rule about what the teacher can do is absolute or the rule about what the president or the governor or the mayor at a public ceremony can do. That's never going to be absolute.

Question: I was wondering what implications this case would have for currency in the message "In God We Trust" on the U.S. dollar notes and coins?

Mr. Laycock: I'm sure there are people who fear it portends that any governmental reference to God goes, and so the currency all has to be changed. I don't think that follows at all because no one has to agree with the currency or pledge allegiance to the currency or even pay any attention to what it says on the currency, beyond the number.

Question: [You argue] "that the Pledge requires an affirmation of personal faith and consequently has got to go." Mr. Sekulow argues, "no, it doesn't—it's not an affirmation of personal faith, so it's okay. One point of view that's not represented here…is that yes, it requires an affirmation of personal faith and that's fine. And the Court should say that's fine. Is that a possible outcome? Can you play around with that a little bit?

Mr. Laycock: I think that's quite unlikely. It's not impossible, but let me just give you 30 seconds of the background. What the Court has said over the years on political issues the government can try to lead public opinion—which it does all the time, it tries to rally public support for its own agenda—but it cannot coerce people to agree with the government or to say that they agree with the government. And that's why in 1943, when the Pledge was entirely secular, it didn't have "under God" in it, and the Pledge case got to the Supreme Court, they said, You can't make students say it. Any student can opt out, but the teacher can lead it. On religious questions in the school prayer cases, they've said opt out isn't enough, because it's really outside the government's jurisdiction, the government isn't responsible for leading public opinion on religion, so the government can't do it at all. It can't ask the kids, even with an opt-out right, to say anything religious, and that's why I agree with Jay [Selulow].

It would be quite unlikely for them to say this really is religious, it really is an affirmation of faith and the government can ask you to say it as long as it gives you the right to opt out. That would be a striking departure from the structure of doctrine they've set up over the past 60 years.

Question: Much has been made of the fact that there are only two words here, but one of those words is a preposition, which, to at least some ears, implies a particular type of God, one that we are under, one that is transcendent. And I wonder if consideration of that aspect would move this particular phrase beyond ceremonial deism? I guess my concern is that if you reject the historical document argument, it does seem to imply that we're asking people to affirm a particular type of God, which in 2004, many, many people do not affirm.

Mr. Laycock: I think that if you want to talk about history, let's talk about history. "One nation under God" does not talk about history. It talks about theology and the relation of this nation today to God today and it does say we're under, that is a particular kind of God. I don't think that's going to trouble the Court much because it doesn't eliminate many conceptions of God, but it does eliminate some, as I said. But it's hard to talk about God without talking about some conception of God. It's impossible to be truly neutral in God-talk because humans have evolved too many radically diverse understandings of God.

Question: If our nation was not under Christianity at the birth of our Constitution, which I think scholars generally acknowledge Thomas Jefferson, whether he was a deist or a heretical Christian or a Unitarian, whatever he was, he was a religious man, obviously. But whether he was a Christian or not isn't relevant as far as the Constitution goes. But why did our Constitution refer to a Christian Sabbath, not a Jewish or a Muslim or an atheist Sabbath? And why was the document dated in the year of our

Lord? Would anyone dare to say that Lord is anyone other than Jesus Christ?

Mr. Laycock: I agree with most of what Jay just said. Let me elaborate a little bit further and add a piece that I think is very important here. The founding generation fought hard about religious liberty, but they fought about the issues that were controversial in their time. And the religious liberty issue that was controversial in their time was how do you fund the church? And it was controversial because Protestants disagreed about it, because Episcopalians and Congregationalists had had tax support and nobody else did, and fixing that, not surprisingly, produced a huge fight.

They did not fight about these sort of religious references in public documents and public events because there was broad diversity of opinion, but the country was overwhelmingly Protestant and there wasn't any disagreement there big enough to get a fight going. The disagreement became big enough to get a fight going in the 1820s, when they started creating public schools and conservative Protestants said you Unitarians—Horace Mann was a Unitarian, and he was the founder of the public school movement—you Unitarians are putting watered down Christianity. It's not much more than Unitarianism in the public schools. We want real religion in the public schools. And then the huge Catholic immigration began and you got much bigger fights between Protestants and Catholics about what to do with the schools. And really, today's battles over prayer in the public schools and funding for private religious schools both of those battles date to those early 19th century disputes and the Protestant-Catholic conflicts that comes all the way down.

Now if the Religion Clauses of First Amendment are a guarantee of principle that government will leave each of us alone, give us as much religious liberty as we can, that principle encountered a whole new set of applications when religious diversity became greater and when the public schools got going. And so to say that in the Declaration of Independence, which is our founding political theory but it's also a political document to rally opinion, that they invoked both the secular rationale, natural law, and the religious rationale, nature's God and our Creator, they did both, that's true. And that was shrewd, but I don't think that tells us anything about how the government should handle religion when it has other people's children in its custody.

The Phrase "Under God" in the Pledge of Allegiance: Acceptable Traditional Expression

ALAN SEKULOW

First, let me say that I probably agree with Doug [Laycock] on more cases than I disagree. In fact, the very first case I argued at the Supreme Court of the United States [*Airport Commissioners v. Jews for Jesus*]—which seems like a long time ago, because it was—Justice [Sandra Day] O'Connor wrote for the Court, and she relied primarily on an article that was written by Professor Laycock. So I've always appreciated that unanimous opinions are rare and getting rarer every day, especially in the Religion Clause cases.

Let me give you five reasons why the Pledge of Allegiance is constitutional and should be affirmed by the Court as not violating the Establishment Clause [of the First Amendment].

1. The Pledge of Allegiance is not in a form of prayer.
2. The Pledge of Allegiance does not refer to Christianity or any other particular religion.
3. The religious portion of the Pledge of Allegiance is only two words.
4. The Pledge of Allegiance was recited unchanged for 50 years before the Court considered the question.
5. And no one can be required to recite the Pledge of Allegiance.

That's the closing portion of the [amicus curiae] brief Professor Laycock filed [in *Elk Grove School District v. Newdow*], where he argued that if the Court was going to rule in favor the Pledge of Allegiance, here's five ways to do it. And it may well be what the Supreme Court does, because it does give a very specific approach, and I think a fairly persuasive one.

Doug [Laycock] talked about the 40 or 50 years of history when the Supreme Court has dealt with the school prayer issue and not allowing for school prayer in that context. There's another history that's over 200 years now, and it goes something like this: "God save the United States and this Honorable Court"—that's how this Supreme Court oral argument's going to start when Dr. [Michael] Newdow presents his arguments before the Supreme Court [in *Elk Grove School District v. Newdow*] next Wednesday.

So the fact of the matter is that the Supreme Court itself has had this cry as part of its opening ceremony described as an invocation. Students attend oral arguments frequently, including kids in high school and even elementary school. And when those justices stand up or walk in, the students stand up. And while they don't have to repeat it, students also don't have to repeat the Pledge of Allegiance, and correctly so, since the Supreme Court's decision in [West Virginia State Board of Education v. Barnette [(1943)], which is now dating back almost 60 years, said you can't be compelled to violate your conscience [by being required to recite the Pledge of Allegiance], and in that way, if you are objecting to the form of the Pledge of Allegiance.

I think that the words "God save the United States and this Honorable Court," like the words of the Pledge of Allegiance, echo what our founding fathers thought, and that was that our freedoms, rights and liberties are derived not from government but rather from God granting them to mankind. And in a sense, it's a very Lockean [English political philosopher John Locke, 1632–1704] concept. Thomas Jefferson talks about it. And even, of course, in the Declaration of Independence itself, how often have we learned or were required to learn and recite in school the words, the famous portion of the Declaration of Independence where it's written, "We hold these truths to be self-evident, that all men are created equal, endowed by their Creator with certain unalienable rights. Amongst them are life, liberty and the pursuit of happiness."

If the Pledge of Allegiance were to say something like that, I would suspect that there would be the same objection. Why? Because of its reliance on a Creator, and it is a concept where the Creator endows us with our rights. But in the context of the history of our country, that makes a lot of sense. Our country was founded on the concepts that the rights of man don't derive from a king and they can't be taken away from us by a king. The rights of mankind, the basic rights of mankind—liberty, freedom, the things that we cherish in this country—derive from a Creator. That's what our founding fathers mean.

It's often talked about, Thomas Jefferson's famous letter [in 1801] to the Danbury Baptist Connecticut Association, where he talked about what he called the "high and mighty duty in this wall of separation between church and state." There's something else that Jefferson wrote several years before he wrote that famous letter to the Danbury Baptists, and that was during the debates on the First Amendment and also in discussions with friends about the concept of liberty. He wrote, "Can the liberties of a nation be thought secure when we have removed their only firm basis, a conviction in the minds of the people that the liberties are a gift of God and that they are not violated but with His wrath?"

Now, Thomas Jefferson, in the classic understanding of his religious belief, would not fall within what most people would consider an orthodox Christian position. In my view of history anyway, I would not consider him to be—and I'm not speaking as a theologian—He had various views on religion and faith. I don't think faith was insignificant in his life, I don't mean to suggest that at all, but it wouldn't be what we would typically talk about today as a Protestant form of Christianity or Catholic form of Christianity. He kind of had his view of faith, Christianity, and the deity of Jesus, and that's a whole different topic.

But he recognized something very fundamental in that our rights don't come from a king; they are endowed to us. So if the requirement of the school district in *Elk Grove* was that we begin each school day by reminding ourselves, as students, that we should remember the history of this great nation, that we are endowed by our Creator with these rights, they're inalienable, and that the Creator bestowed them upon us—life, liberty and the pursuit of happiness—I submit that many people, Dr. Newdow included, would object, saying again it's this compelled reliance.

Now, nobody can be compelled, nor should they be, as I said, to recite the Pledge. Let's talk about the more recent history, and that is, what happened in 1954? Now, of course, the issue upon which certiorari is granted—and I am frequently reminded of that both when I'm watching arguments and when I argue them myself—is not the congressional action here, which is interesting. The United States asked for review of the 1954 congressional act amending the Pledge of Allegiance. The Supreme Court denied review there. They granted the school district's policy for review, which is a policy that said the school day will start with a patriotic expression. The Pledge of Allegiance would meet that patriotic expression.

In 1954, though, when the Pledge was modified to include the phrase "under God," what was motivating Congress? There were a lot of things motivating Congress. We were in the midst of the Cold War. There was this desire to treat and to establish the difference between how we viewed our rights and liberties, and how communism viewed these things, which is any rights that you have, whatever they might be, are derived from the state; the state is supreme. Congress, reflecting, again, on what the founding fathers thought, said, No, it doesn't work that way. We believe the foundation of our country is different, and this shows the difference. We believe that our rights come from God to mankind.

And I don't know if this is a true fact or not, but it's in one of the briefs, that Dr. Newdow is actually an ordained minister with the Universal Life Church, and I'm not sure if that's correct. What the Universal Life Church has as one of their—and I know they have a pretty broad view of what constitutes God—mission statements, it says that—and they use the phrase "gods" in terms of recognizing that individuals, us, are given what he calls "God-given rights"—freedoms, liberties. Again, this is part of the American experience.

Now, no one's required to believe that, and I don't think that that's the intent of saying the Pledge. Students who don't want to participate don't have to participate, and I think acknowledging the historical significance of how our rights are derived in the foundation of America is correct. The idea that you would be able to tell a student, You cannot be compelled to memorize the Declaration of Independence—which many of us remember having to do—and recite it because of its reference to a Creator, I would think would be wrong. Now, could you argue that there should be a religious exemption? Probably you could argue that under the Free Exercise Clause. These days, though, I don't know if any of us would be too persuasive on how that would go. But I will tell you this much: that is the historical fact. Our founding fathers did recognize—This was part of the Lockean concept of the rights of mankind, and you don't have to be a historian to check this out....

But I don't think it's correct contextually, with due respect, and that is "one nation"—the Pledge of Allegiance, "I pledge allegiance..." one nation under God," and of course ellipses in between. But that's not what the Pledge of Allegiance says. It doesn't say "one nation under God," and context matters in Establishment Clause cases. And I think the context of the Pledge and the history of how this country came into existence is going to point to what I would expect to be a Supreme Court decision affirming the constitutionality of the Pledge.

Let me close with this, and then I know there's going to be some questions. I think it would be revisionist history if we're going to start saying that students cannot say the Pledge of Allegiance, and revisionist in this context: the history, granted, of the Pledge itself is only 50 years old—it's not that old. But I'll tell you something: the religious heritage of the country goes back to its founding, and whether you take the very strict view of church-state separation or a more accommodationist view, or somewhere in between, denying the history is denying the fact. And I think that mandating a change in the Pledge or finding that those statements, those two words, as Professor Laycock pointed out so well in his brief, those two words create a constitutional crisis, I would hope the Court does not go there.

Question: [Pease comment on the] notion...of ceremonial deism...the idea that "references to God become meaningless if recited often enough in public places."

Mr. Sekulow: I'll go quickly, because I addressed the issue and covered it, but I'll give you two quick thoughts.

I don't for those who are anti-religious—and I know there are people who are anti-religious—I mean, the fact of the matter is you could be anti-something or pro-something; it's a free country, and neither the anti-religious nor the majority religion have a veto right over everybody else. And I think that's one thing.

Number two, a lot of people on my side of these issues normally, Doug [Laycock], get nervous about the phrase ceremonial deism. I've never had a problem with it. I think what Justice O'Connor said is right. It's one of these phrases that does tend to solemnize an occasion. It expresses hope for the future and reflects our past, but again, you're not compelling anybody to say this. You're not compelling anybody to believe this, but I suspect there'll be a lot of questions—I mean, I'm guessing again—on the issue of ceremonial deism. I've had that happen on a couple of the cases that I argued on those issues where prayer came up, and even in some of the earlier cases, in the early '90s. That's an issue that's going to come up. The ceremonial deism question is going to, I think, play in this probably significantly.

Question: Just to follow up,...comment on whether there is a path that we go down that essentially declares that the public realm—whatever is supported by government—must necessarily be godless, or is there an alternative to this? Does this case take you there or does it not necessarily take you there?

Mr. Sekulow: I think this case says you don't have to be godless. You can accurately reflect the historical precedent of the country's founding. That's how I would pitch this case. If I were arguing this case to the Court, I would be talking about the historic fact of patriotic expression. Sure, it's got religious overtones, but so does the "Star Spangled Banner" and a host of other religious music and songs and documents of our country. It's part of who we are.

So, yes, I think it can reflect—If you don't want to be in a situation where the next thing—and maybe some do—that we're fighting over is whether you really can have those students memorize the Declaration of Independence and be required to recite it as my teacher required me to recite it flawlessly, and if you didn't do it flawlessly you did it again, and it could go on, for many of us, for weeks.

Question: "I was wondering what implications this case would have for currency in the message "In God We Trust" on the U.S. dollar notes and coins?

Mr. Sekulow: I do think the lawsuit will follow, though. If the Pledge of Allegiance is declared unconstitutional—There have already been a series of cases on the national motto. Most recently, I handled one in Kansas. The district court ruled in our favor, and there was no appeal taken in that case. But I would expect that whether it applies or not, you will see those kind of lawsuits being filed if they declare the Pledge unconstitutional.

Whether they'll succeed or not, that's going to depend on how this opinion's written and what the Court says. But to say that it's not going to have far reaching consequences if the Pledge is struck down as unconstitutional—even if it is a four-four decision, which, as Professor Laycock said, is just an affirmance of the judgment—I will tell you that there will be school districts all over the United States that are going to say, Well, look, we're going to not read the tea leaves here. We don't want to get sued and lose again, so we're just going to stop saying the Pledge. I think that will be a ripple effect of this, too.

Question: Mr. Laycock argues "that the Pledge requires an affirmation of personal faith and consequently has got to go." Mr. Sekulow argues, "no, it doesn't—it's not an affirmation of personal faith, so it's okay." One point of view that's not represented here...is that yes, it requires an affirmation of personal faith and that's fine. And the Court should say that's fine. Is that a possible outcome? Can you play around with that a little bit?

Mr. Sekulow: I can't imagine the Court saying that—if they hold the Pledge constitutional, I think—actually, if they hold the Pledge constitutional, I think, it's going to be for the five reasons that Professor Laycock laid out in his brief. I think that is a pretty straightforward way for the Court to go if they decide it's constitutional. I can't imagine them saying the Pledge is constitutional, and you must believe it when you say it.

Question: "Much has been made of the fact that there are only two words here, but one of those words is a preposition, which, to at least some ears, implies a particular type of God, one that we are under, one that is transcendent. And I wonder if consideration of that aspect would move this particular phrase beyond ceremonial deism? I guess my concern is that if you reject the historical document argument, it does seem to imply that we're asking people to affirm a particular type of God, which in 2004, many, many people do not affirm.

Mr. Sekulow: But it's an historical fact that the phrase under God—Most people think it originated in the Gettysburg Address, when President Lincoln said "This nation under God shall have a new birth of freedom." But actually it predates that by almost a hundred years, because General Washington—I think he was Colonel Washington then actually—in his order to the Continental Army said, "Millions of lives are in jeopardy, both born and unborn"—talking about posterity—"and this army under God"—now, does that mean that this army's under God? That's how they viewed the interplay of Divine Providence. That's what they meant by that.

And, again, the Pledge is an historic statement. You can't change the history; you can debate what the history means, but the words they used are—Fortunately for all of us, we have them, and that's what they meant and that's what they said....

Let's say you don't agree with the historical document, say the Declaration of Independence. Again, Mrs. Sopher requiring us to memorize it when I was in junior high. There's no dispute that that's what the document says. It says we're endowed by our Creator with these rights. It was a Lockean concept that rights derived not from the King of England, because then the king could take them away, but derived from God to mankind. That's what they thought, whether they were deists or whatever their views were theologically, that is what their overall and overarching propositions were, and that's their thought process. So you could say you don't agree with the historical documents or you don't assume they're historic, you could argue anything, but I think they're pretty clear.

Question: If our nation was not under Christianity at the birth of our Constitution, which I think scholars generally acknowledge Thomas Jefferson, whether he was a deist or a heretical Christian or a Unitarian, whatever he was, he was a religious man, obviously. But whether he was a Christian or not isn't relevant as far as the Constitution goes. But why did our Constitution refer to a Christian Sabbath, not a Jewish or a Muslim or an atheist Sabbath? And why was the document dated in the year of our Lord? Would anyone dare to say that that Lord is anyone other than Jesus Christ?

Mr. Sekulow: I've just completed a dissertation on a lot of the historical backgrounds, mostly focusing on the Supreme Court justices, not on the founding fathers.

But what becomes very clear is that a lot of terminology was used by the founding fathers and by Supreme Court justices that we take in one context and, culturally, at the time, meant something very different. It's not to say that they were not people of faith, but there is no doubt about it, I mean, if you study history in America, it was a pretty broad—even within the founding fathers, a pretty broad swath of faith.

And statements like "In the year of our Lord" were the customary ways in which these documents were signed. It does not mean that they were anti-religious. Obviously they included them in there. The Declaration of Independence, I think, as a foundational document established how Americans viewed the relationship between rights, liberty, mankind and God, and I think they did it in one document and actually in one portion of that document.

A lot of the justices, for instance, had said this is a Christian nation, in 1892, 1864. We're Unitarians. Now, I'm not saying that they weren't Unitarians, weren't Christians, it's just that it wasn't what you would typically think of as Protestantism as we know it. So you've got to look at the cultural context to understand.

Now, having said all of that, to remove that history, I think, would be very dangerous. The fact that there was this general belief in the way rights derived to mankind, to remove that, I think, would be wrong....

THE CONTINUING DEBATE: The Phrase "Under God" in the Pledge of Allegiance

What Is New

The Supreme Court in essence ducked when it ruled in *Elk Grove Unified School District v. Newdow*. Instead of deciding the question, the Court dismissed the case on the grounds that since Michael Newdow's ex-wife had custody of their daughter, he did not have "standing" (enough legal interest) to sue on the girl's behalf. That almost certainly served only put off the day when the Court will have to rule. New law suits have been filed, and in 2005 a U.S. District Court judge found the Pledge unconstitutional. Taking an opposite view, North Carolina and other states have added a requirement that teachers in some school levels lead the pledge, and the U.S. House of Representatives passed a bill denying to the federal courts the authority to rule against the Pledge. How the Supreme Court might rule is unclear because it continues to demonstrate a careful, some might say inconsistent, view about the establishment clause. In *Van Orden v. Perry* (2005), the Court allowed a monument to the Ten Commandments to remain on the grounds of Texas' capitol building. The Court found the monument to be a historical reflection of the country's traditional recognition of the importance of the Ten Commandments and argued, "Simply having religious content or promoting a message consistent with a religious doctrine does not run afoul of the establishment clause." On the very same day, however, the Court also ruled in *McCreary County v. ACLU* (2005) that displays of the Ten Commandments in Kentucky state court houses, violated the establishment clause because, "When the government acts with the ostensible and predominant purpose of advancing religion, it violates...[the] central establishment clause."

Where to Find More

One site of a group that believes in a wall between church and state is the "nontheist" Freedom From Religion Foundation at www.ffrf.org/. Taking the opposite view is the Rutherford Institute at www.rutherford.org/issues/religiousfreedom.asp. A comprehensive view of the Supreme Courts role in the church-state issue is James Hitchcock, *The Supreme Court and Religion in American Life, Vol. 1: The Odyssey of the Religion Clauses* (Princeton University Press, 2004). Looking at the current strains over what the establishment clause means is Noah Feldman, *Divided by God: America's Church-State Problem—and What We Should Do About It* (Farrar, Straus and Giroux, 2005). The history of and controversies about the Pledge itself can be found in Richard J. Ellis, *To the Flag: The Unlikely History of the Pledge of Allegiance* (University of Kansas Press, 2005).

What to More to Do

One way to try to approach this debate and the difference between what is not permissible and what merely reflects tradition and is permissible is to ponder the seemingly contradictory decisions of the Supreme Court in *Van Orden v. Perry* (2005) and *McCreary County v. ACLU*. You can read opinions of the justices in these cases and also find supporting material at the site of the First Amendment Center at www.firstamendmentcenter.org/. Enter the name of the case in the search window. Once your views are clear, try jotting down some notes for a hypothetical essay, "How High Should the Wall Between Church and State Be?"

DEBATE

5

AMERICAN PEOPLE/ POLITICAL CULTURE

EVENTUAL CITIZENSHIP FOR UNAUTHORIZED IMMIGRANTS:
Rewarding Illegal Behavior *or* Rewarding Contributions to America?

REWARDING ILLEGAL BEHAVIOR

ADVOCATE: James R. Edwards, Jr., Adjunct Fellow, Hudson Institute

SOURCE: Testimony during hearings on "Should We Embrace the Senate's Grant of Amnesty to Millions of Illegal Aliens and Repeat the Mistakes of the Immigration Reform and Control Act of 1986?" U.S. House of Representatives, Committee on the Judiciary, Subcommittee on Immigration, Border Security, and Claims, July 18, 2006.

REWARDING CONTRIBUTIONS TO AMERICA

ADVOCATE: Tom Harkin, U.S. Senator (D-IA)

SOURCE: *Congressional Record,* March 29, 2006

The face of America is changing. A nation that was once overwhelmingly composed of European heritage whites is becoming more diverse ethnically and racially. In 1960 the U.S. population was approximately 82% white, 11% black, and 6% Hispanic, 0.5% Asian American, and 0.5% Native American. By 2000 the U.S. population had become 69% white, 12% African American, 13% Latino, 4% Asian American, and 1% Native American. This diversification is expected to continue, with the U.S. Census Bureau estimating that in 2050, the U.S. population will be 52% white, 24% Latino, 15% African American, 9% Asian American, and 1% Native American. One reason for the change is vary fertility rates, which is the average number of children a woman in her child-bearing years will have. In 2000 the fertility rate was 2.0 for whites, 2.1 for African Americans, 2.3 for Asian Americans, 2.5 for Native Americans, and 2.9 for Hispanics.

Immigration changes are a second factor accounting for growing diversity. Immigration has increased dramatically, nearly tripling for an annual average of 330,000 in the 1960s to an annual average of more than 900,000 since 1990. Moreover, the flow of immigration now brings in a much greater percentage of people from Asia, Latin American, and Africa. As late as the 1950s, more than 70% of immigrants were coming from Europe or from Canada and other European-heritage countries. Then Congress amended the immigration laws in 1965 to eliminate the quota system that favored immigration from Europe and replaced it with a qualifications system based on job skills and other criteria. Now, only about 16% of newcomers are from Europe, compared to 48% from Latin America and the Caribbean, 32% from Asia, and 4% from Africa. Adding to this influx are those who come to the United States without going through established immigration procedures. There are an estimate 10 million such immigrants in the United States, and between 400,000 and 500,00 new ones were arriving each year. About 80% of these illegal immigrants are from Central America, especially Mexico.

There are numerous issues related to unauthorized immigrants. These include such matters as whether or not they should be able to get drivers licenses and their access to social services. Another issue is whether to attempt to round up and expel as many unauthorized immigrants as possible or to give them temporary guest worker or even permanent residency status. Generally, there has been little official interest in a mass expulsion program. One reason is the sheer scope of trying to locate, detain, and repatriate unauthorized immigrants. A second reason is the economic importance of undocumented workers to many powerful interest groups (especially fruit and vegetable growers, meatpackers, and other "agribusiness" groups). The status of many of these immigrants changed in 1986 when Congress enacted the Immigration Control and Reform Act) extending amnesty to many undocumented residents by granting permanent residency to an estimated 3.9 million of them who had been living continuously in the United States since January 1, 1982. This status led those formerly illegal immigrants to seek citizenship. The ICRA also included heavier fines for employers hiring unauthorized workers and others provisions meant to stem illegal immigration. But they have been spottily enforced, and the flow of unauthorized immigrants continues.

During the past five years or so, the status of unauthorized workers and their families once again has once again become a major political issue. One reason is the post-9/11 fear that some of those slipping into the United States might be terrorists. A second factor has been the cumulative increase in foreign-born residents, both legal and illegal, as discussed above. Politics is a third factor. Democrats and Republicans are aware of the importance of the Latino vote, one the one hand, and, on the other hand strong concern about illegal immigration among most Americans. Attesting to that, a 2006 poll recorded 61% of respondents saying that illegal immigration was an "extremely" or "serious" problems, and another "30%" saying it was a "somewhat serious" problem. Only 8% had little or no concerns, with 1% unsure.

Congress and the George W. Bush administration have responded to these cross-pressures with a wide range of proposals. The administration favors a guest-worker program that could eventually lead to citizenship, a range of penalties on new illegal immigrants and their employers, and various measures, such as deploying National Guard troops along the border to deter and intercept unauthorized immigration. Some strong conservatives, like James Edwards in the first reading favor a more draconian approach, including such measures as making illegal entry a felony, setting up internment camps to hold illegal immigrants until they can be expelled, and making it impossible for illegal immigrants to ever get American citizenship. By contrast, Tom Harkins in the second reading and other liberals favor deemphasizing penalties and making it even easier than would Bush to obtain U.S. residency and eventual citizenship.

POINTS TO PONDER

- ➢Think about the security, budgetary, cultural, and other problems illegal immigrants allegedly cause and about why, if at all, such problems relate to illegal but not legal immigrants.
- ➢Do you think that the concern about undocumented immigrants would be as high if the vast majority were from Ireland, Canada, Germany, and Great Britain?
- ➢Consider whether it is reasonable for Tom Harkins to partly base is preferences on policy toward today's legal immigrants on the contribution's of yesterday's legal immigrants?

Eventual Citizenship for Unauthorized Immigrants: Rewarding Illegal Behavior

JAMES R. EDWARDS, JR.

Comparing the experience of 1986's [Immigration Reform and Control Act, IRCA] supposed "one-time only" legalization with the Senate-passed amnesty and its likely consequences should lead dispassionate observers to conclude that S. 2611 [which would allow eventual citizenship to illegal immigrants] would repeat past errors—only now, we should have learned better. The Senate amnesty would condemn the United States to the same harmful consequences that IRCA caused. Only now, its effects would be far, far worse.

Because spokesmen from the current administration and other advocates of out-of-control immigration perform all kinds of linguistic gymnastics and semantic magic tricks to deny that amnesty proposals such as the Reid-Kennedy-McCain-Hagel [Senators Harry Reid (D-NV; Edward Kennedy (D-MA), John McCain (R-AZ); and Charles Hagel 9R-NE)] amnesty are amnesties, allow me to offer a common-sense, conventional definition of "amnesty." Amnesty is the government forgiving all people or certain classes of people for certain unlawful acts they are guilty of. *Black's Law Dictionary* explicitly cites the 1986 IRCA as an example of amnesty. And by a normal person's reasonable judgment, the legalization provisions in S. 2611 and similar arrangements in other legislation can only be described as amnesty. That is so even with various conditions placed on the illegal aliens who would benefit, because most amnesties apply certain conditions for amnesty.

As a rule, amnesties should be employed sparingly and carefully. They indeed do affront the rule of law because amnesty is an act whereby the civil government overlooks lawbreaking. Amnesty in effect rewards lawbreakers for their lawbreaking. Amnesty lets off certain lawbreakers.

While individuals should forgive others their debts on the personal level, the principle doesn't carry over well to the government level. The job of the government is to uphold the law. That is how order is maintained in civil society. If amnesty is liberally or frequently or imprudently applied, then it undermines the principles of ordered liberty the Founders sought to embed in our system of government. In the immigration context, granting illegal aliens amnesty diminishes the honorable conduct of the many legal immigrants who abided by the law and persisted through the daunting process; amnesty of illegal aliens rewards their dishonorable, disorderly, lawless conduct in a highly public manner that effectively insults legal immigrants.

Today, I will focus my remarks on two areas: the 1986 IRCA amnesty and its similarities in S. 2611, and the connections between legal and illegal immigration.

IRCA, ITS MANY FLAWS, AND THE THREAT OF A REPEAT

In 1986, Congress struck a "grand bargain" on immigration—the Immigration Reform and Control Act, or IRCA. The keys to locking the "back door" to illegal immigration were supposed to be securing the border and demagnetizing the "jobs magnet:" employer sanctions.

The elements of IRCA are resurrected in the Senate bill. IRCA included:

◆ Border enforcement: IRCA authorized more Border Patrol and deportations (but ended warrantless INS [U.S. Immigration and Naturalization Service] farm sweeps).

◆ Employer sanctions: IRCA made it unlawful to "knowingly" hire illegal aliens; it established the visual-check, ID-based I-9 system (and also set up a regime to dissuade conscientious employers).

◆ Mass legalization: Three classes of illegal aliens were dealt with according to length of unlawful U.S. residency. Those here by 1972 got immediate amnesty of Lawful Permanent Residence. Those here since 1982 had to pay a nominal fee for a temporary visa, then could get a Green Card after a year and a half if they had minimal knowledge of English and U.S. civics. Special agricultural workers, or SAWs, claimed at least 90 days' farm work in 1986 or the previous three years to get amnesty; they became LPRs [lawful permanent residents] if they paid the nominal fee, the timing depending on their claimed farm work.

We observed in *The Congressional Politics of Immigration Reform* [a 1998 book written by Edwards and James G. Gimpel] and about IRCA's eventual consequences:

> At the time, few...accurately forecast the enormous demand that would be stimulated by the legalization program...Amnesty ultimately drove annual legal immigration levels to their peak in the 1980s, dramatically distorted historical immigration patterns, and contributed to the groundswell of opposition to legal and illegal immigration in the 1990s.

The contours of the Senate amnesty bill resemble IRCA's [amnesty provisions]. S. 2611, which would supposedly boost border enforcement and employer sanctions, mixes this sugar with the amnesty poison (though Reid-Kennedy includes many poison pills in the "enforcement" and "sanctions" sections that will guarantee the failure of those provisions, such as tying local law enforcement's hands and requiring federal, state, and local governments effectively to get Mexico's permission before taking any enforcement measures).

S. 2611, like IRCA, is long on promises, chock full of policy booby traps to ensure failure, and will be short on results other than a flood of foreign-born. S. 2611 is even worse than IRCA in that it includes mega-increases in legal immigration levels that will overwhelm America, break the treasury, flood the immigration bureaucracy, and ensure "chain migration" that doubles or triples immigration levels for the next two decades. Its "guest worker" program is nothing more than a means to launder the status of millions of foreign lawbreakers. There is nothing temporary about their "guest" status; they are assuredly here to stay, because "guest workers" may bring their families with them for the duration of their H-2C visas and status adjustment (many having been present already).

NumbersUSA's Rosemary Jenks has calculated that S. 2611 contains at least five amnesties. One, illegal aliens in the U.S. for at least five years get an instant Green Card. Two, illegal aliens present for two to five years get amnesty on the installment plan—three steps (plus a two-year tax amnesty). Three, there is an AGJOBS-type [agricultural jobs], two-step amnesty for those who purport to be part-time farm workers (alleging 21.6 weeks of work over two years). Four, a DREAM Act-type amnesty legalizes those claiming to have been here five years and to have entered illegally while under age

16. Five, those claiming to be a persecuted religious minority with an asylum claim pending on May 1, 2003, get immediate amnesty. And then there is mass amnesty for the illegitimate employers who hired these illegal aliens, privatized the benefits, and socialized their costs.

The employer sanctions and border enforcement legs of IRCA "failed"—which is to say, they were poorly or inadequately designed, not at all or poorly implemented, and were undermined by political pressure from the beginning. Only the amnesty "worked." That is, a lot of foreign lawbreakers got full amnesty. And IRCA spurred massive illegal immigration and "chain migration."

In 1980, there were an estimated 3 million illegal aliens in the United States. By IRCA, after six years of dangling the amnesty carrot as Congress debated, we had 5 million illegal aliens. IRCA legalized 3 million: 65,000 had been here since 1972; 1.6 million had been here since 1982; 1.1 million were SAWs. Some 2 million were Mexicans. IRCA imposed the equivalent of processing five years' worth of immigrants in just a couple of years (legal immigration in the 1980s ran about 700,000 a year).

IRCA, especially the SAW amnesty, was fraud-ridden. The INS estimated that there were 400,000 SAWs nationwide; 1.1 million were legalized. California was said to have fewer than 100,000 illegal SAWs, but 700,000 applied from that state alone. Most SAW applications were approved, despite suspicion of widespread fraud.

Rubber-stamping became the rule. Scrutiny and due diligence were out the door, as "INS essentially threw up its hands and decided not to spend the time and energy needed to sort out the fraudulent SAW applications," former Labor Department official David North said. INS approved 94.4 percent of regular amnesty applications and 93.5 percent of SAW applications.

IRCA fraud and amnesty benefited the Islamofascist cause. Mahmud Abouhalima, an Egyptian illegal alien, obtained amnesty as a SAW. This New York cab driver, who never worked on a farm, used his legalization to travel to Afghanistan for terrorist training. He was part of the first World Trade Center bombing plot. Given the internal corruption, mismanagement, and abuse within the Bureau of Citizenship and Immigration Services that has recently come to light by patriotic whistleblowers, the prospects of criminals and terrorists getting legalized is even more likely today.

Amnesty, premised on and promised as a once-only thing, encouraged and facilitated more illegal immigration. The 2 million residual illegal alien population of 1988 grew to 3.5 million in 1990—4 million in 1992—5 million in 1996 (i.e., replenished in a decade)—7 million in 2000—about 10 million in 2005.

Amnesty begat amnesty. IRCA was the first immigration amnesty in this nation, and now we have had seven since 1986. These include the "rolling amnesty" of Section 245(i) [of IRCA, as amended] in 1994, 1997, and 2000 (responsible for legalizing at least 1.5 million illegal aliens), the 1997 Central American-specific amnesty (NACARA, legalizing about one million), the 1998 Haitian-specific amnesty (of 125,000 illegal aliens), and the 2000 amnesty of illegal aliens claiming they deserved legalization under IRCA (benefiting about 400,000 illegal aliens).

THE UGLY TRUTH OF THE LEGAL-ILLEGAL CONNECTION

An underlying premise of the Hesburgh Commission's [The Select Commission on Immigration and Refugee Policy (1978–1981) headed by Theodore Hesburgh, president of Notre Dame University] recommendations, of IRCA, and of many Senators today is if you increase legal immigration, you'll reduce illegal immigration. But, in fact, legal and illegal immigration are two sides of the same coin. If legal immigration rose as S. 2611 proposes, illegal immigration would spike, too.

As legal immigration has risen markedly since 1965, illegal immigration has risen with it. Illegal aliens comprised 21 percent of the foreign-born population in 1980. Today, they're 28 percent. The top source countries of legal immigrants tend to be the top source countries of illegal aliens—Mexico, El Salvador, China, Dominican Republic, the Philippines. This is no coincidence.

Mexico is the largest source of both legal and illegal aliens. In 2000, Mexicans were 30 percent of the foreign-born. Over half of Mexicans in the U.S. were illegal aliens. Mexicans make up three times the proportion of the next three source countries combined: China, the Philippines, India.

Because of "chain migration"—the ability of an initial immigrant to sponsor distant family members for immigrant visas (e.g., adult siblings, adult married children), "new" immigrants aren't always new. The New Immigrant Survey unveiled that a third of LPRs had lived here illegally—for 5 to 8 years—before their Green Card came through. Two-thirds of Mexicans had first lived here unlawfully. This survey also found that the tourist visa is the most abused temporary visa by one-time-illegal, now-legal immigrants.

The existence of "chain migration" visa categories far beyond the reunification of spouses and of parents with their minor children, as well as full eligibility, to date, of amnestied aliens to naturalize and to sponsor additional immigrants, has swelled the numbers of immigrants (legal and illegal). Amnesties have exacerbated this exorbitant wave. These same phenomena have given would-be immigrants unrealistic expectations and an "entitlement mentality" toward immigration. Yet the reality, depending on country of origin and visa sought, is backlogs and waiting lists. These necessary delays, plus opportunities to plant roots via "anchor babies," INA and process loopholes, and visa abuse, increase the ties of this integral connection where high legal immigration fosters high illegal immigration.

In conclusion, what are the lessons we should draw from IRCA and from a realistic view of immigration?

We need to pursue enforcement first. Our strategy should be attrition through systematic, faithful, routinized enforcement. We need a border fence, vastly expanded expedited removal, meaningful, rigorous employer sanctions starting with the worst offenders, mandatory electronic employment verification of all workers, and empowering state and local law enforcement with the federal cooperation they need. We must cut legal immigration to more manageable levels. We should eliminate the "chain migration" categories of extended family and the visa lottery. Family or employer sponsors should bear greater responsibility for the immigrants they bring in—health insurance, life and disability insurance, for instance.

Given the IRCA disaster, the Reid-Kennedy amnesty is out of touch with reality and lacks common sense.

Eventual Citizenship for Unauthorized Immigrants: Rewarding Contributions to America

TOM HARKINS

For me, the current debate on immigration strikes very close to home. Those words at the base of the Statue of Liberty, "Give me your tired, your poor, your huddled masses, yearning to breathe free," have a profound personal meaning to me.

On my wall in my office, I have a picture of the house in which my mother was born and raised until she was 20 years of age in the small town of Suha, Slovenia. It is a small house with a dirt floor. Yes, my mother was born and raised in a house with a dirt floor until she was aged 20. Then she got steerage on the SS Argentina and came to America. She was going to land at Ellis Island, but landed in Boston because of bad weather. I have a copy of the documentation from when my mother landed here in America, it had her name and where she was from, and what she owned. She had one suitcase, a train ticket to Des Moines, IA, and $7. That is how my mother came to America. When she came, though, she was welcomed into the American community. She got married, obviously raised a family. She has since obviously passed away, but she became a productive citizen, a loyal American who gave a lot back to her adopted homeland.

I know the current debate has stirred up a lot of passions, but this is nothing new. Across the centuries, successive waves of immigrants—Germans, Irish, and again on my father's side my great-grandfather, who was an immigrant from the northern part of Ireland; Chinese, Italians, Greeks, others—every time they have come here they have aroused strong emotions. But in every case, Americans eventually rose above their economic fears and ethnic prejudices. We were true to those Statue of Liberty words and, as a result, America has become stronger and richer and fairer. We are indeed the envy of the world.

Today, once again, we are in the midst of a difficult and often emotional national debate about immigration. I am optimistic that we can arrive at a bill that addresses legitimate national security and law enforcement concerns, while also being faithful to our tradition and history as a nation of immigrants. I commend the senior Senator from Pennsylvania, Senator [Arlen] Specter [R], for his skill and leadership in reporting a bipartisan bill from the Judiciary Committee that takes us in the right direction. I want to commend his ranking member, Senator [Patrick] Leahy [D-VT], and Senator [Edward] Kennedy [D-MA] for his strong work on getting this bill through and making it a decent, fair, but yet strong bill to protect our national security and to protect our law enforcement in this country.

My State of Iowa, I am proud to say, has a long history of welcoming new immigrants. We have a growing immigrant Muslim population from Asia and the Middle East. In fact, Cedar Rapids, IA, is home to the oldest mosque in America, and we are proud of that. A quarter of a century ago, responding to the plight of Vietnamese and Laotian boat people, former Governor Robert Ray introduced programs to bring more than 30,000 of these refugees to our State. Because of his courageous humanitarian leadership, thousands of Iowans opened their homes and their hearts to these new immigrants.

More recently, tens of thousands of immigrants have come to Iowa from Latin America and elsewhere. They have come here in search of two things: work and freedom. Work, in order to feed and clothe their families; and freedom, to learn and to develop their talents, and to grow. In most cases, they have found work. The Iowa economy is hungry for immigrants who are willing to do jobs that basically are physically demanding, oftentimes dangerous, one example, of course, being the meat packing industry.

But not all of these new immigrants have found freedom—the freedom to learn and to grow and to develop their talents. Earlier this month, at United Trinity Methodist Church in Des Moines, I met with a group of new immigrants, an undocumented family. They told me about the hardships they face. They live in constant fear. They live in the shadows. What do they want? They want to become loyal, contributing Americans, to pursue the American dream, to contribute as my mother did, as my great-grandfather and his descendants did, to building this country we call America. But, instead, they are living an American nightmare of anxiety, exclusion, and exploitation.

So it is time for us to find a constructive and positive way to bring these people out of the shadows and into the sunlight. One thing we all agree on is that the current immigration system is broken and needs reform. It is totally out of sync with today's social and economic realities. It is time to come up with a just and fair immigration system, one true to our values and our tradition. I know we can come up with a bill that is a win-win for all of us.

To that end, we need at least three things: One, we need tough, consistent, effective enforcement of reformed immigration laws. Two, we need to enforce sanctions against employers who hire immigrants unauthorized to work. Three, we need a temporary worker program with documentation that gives immigrants a reasonable path to earning full American citizenship. As Senator *Kennedy* said earlier, we are not talking about amnesty. That would be wrong. We are talking about a process of earned legalization, giving people who are here a practical way to earn citizenship by working, paying taxes, paying a fine, learning English.

We need to deal with the reality before us. We have 11 million to 12 million undocumented people in this country, many of whom—as we listened to Senator [Richard] Durbin [D-IL] talk about—have lived here for many years, and many who came here as young children, as babies. Many of them who are here have children. They have other family members who are U.S. citizens. They are contributing to our prosperity. They are making a big contribution to our society. They may be undocumented; they may be living in the shadows; but make no mistake: They are de facto members of our American community. They are integrated into the fabric of our national life. They are filling jobs that, in most cases, go unfilled, and they are not going away. Frankly, we would face huge problems if they did. As the U.S. Chamber of Commerce said recently: "If you kick out 11 and-a-half to 12 million people, it will bring our economy to a screeching halt."

So let us acknowledge the reality. Let's establish a legal framework within which these immigrants can work and learn English and pass security background checks, pay a fine, the penalties that are necessary, and then earn the right to eventually become a U.S. citizen. At the same time, let's not delude ourselves with so-called simple solutions that are unworkable, unaffordable, or just plain mean-spirited. For example, the House has passed a bill that calls for criminalizing undocumented immigrants, rounding them up and deporting them, and charging with crimes anyone who might help, including clergy and church members.

Does anyone seriously believe we can round up 11 million to 12 million undocumented immigrants? Who is going to do it? Are we going to spend the $140 billion it would take to hire a vast army of agents to do this? And even if it were physically possible to round up 12 million people, how do you do it humanely? For example, would we be willing to break up families? Would we deport mothers and fathers but allow their U.S. citizen children to remain here? Would we deport an undocumented immigrant who is here, married, has children? Would she or he take the children with them, or leave them here? What is going to happen to all these people? How do you deal with this humanely?

Others advocate we spend tens of millions of dollars to build a 700-mile wall, a fence, across our southern border. That is nonsense. Did the Great Wall of China work? Maybe for a month or two. Think of the Berlin Wall. Just remember the Berlin Wall. And think about a wall between the United States and Mexico. Now we are going to build a wall across the Canadian border, too? Let's get serious. This is nonsense, absolutely nonsense.

And does anyone want to talk about those who come to the U.S. and overstay their visas? There are an estimated 4 million people in the United States who have overstayed their visas. They get visas, they are here, they are working. They overstay their visa and do not go back to their home countries; they decide to stay here illegally.

It is time to acknowledge why immigrants continue to come across our border, making enormous sacrifices, risking their lives. They are coming for economic opportunity to better themselves and to reunite, a lot of times, with their families.

In other words, they are coming for exactly the same reasons that my mother came to America—to get reunited with family members who were here, to work, to raise a family, to better her life and to better the lives of her children. The difference is they are coming now as undocumented because we failed to create a documented, legal avenue for our economy to get the workers we need. It is not their fault; it is our fault—because we have not designed a good immigration system.

We have heard it said that undocumented immigrants drive down wages for American citizens at the low end of the economic scale. According to this argument, undocumented immigrants are so desperate to work for the minimum wage or less, they will tolerate harsh, unsafe working conditions. Unfortunately, there is a lot of truth to that argument. So what is the answer, kick them out? No. The answer is to bring them out of the shadows. If they are given documentation and legal status, then employers will have to pay them a decent wage and treat them fairly. This will raise the floor. It will raise wages at the bottom rungs of the ladder, and this will benefit all American workers.

There is another huge cost and danger to allowing the status quo to continue. The current system has driven undocumented workers deep underground. We are not able to document, track, or control who is within our borders. This is the ideal environment for al-Qaida and others who aim to penetrate our society. Because of our preoccupation with chasing down undocumented immigrants, we are diverting scarce resources from addressing the real threats to our national security, and this needs to change. Instead, we are tracking down gardeners and dishwashers, let's focus on those who really want to do us harm.

Throughout America's history, the subject of immigration has lent itself to fear-mongering, demagoguery, and simplistic so-called solutions. But to our credit—and to America's great social and economic benefit—we have listened to the better angels of our nature. We have refused to slam the door. We have been true to our tradition as a nation of immigrants.

Today, once again, we are challenged to rise above fear and prejudice and to do the right thing. Legally or illegally, immigrants will continue to come to America as they have for four centuries. We need smart immigration reform, reform that will protect our borders, crack down on employers who hire those who are unauthorized to work, while creating a guest worker program that gives immigrants the opportunity to earn legalization and to have family reunification.

In closing, I commend the Judiciary Committee for sending to the floor a bipartisan bill that would accomplish these important things. It would bring undocumented immigrants out of the shadows so we know who they are, where they live, where they are from, and so we can identify any who could be a threat to our homeland security. It would allow earned legalization for those who pass security background checks.

It is going to take more than 10 years for an undocumented immigrant to demonstrate that he or she is a person of good moral standing, is paying taxes, learning English, and has paid the necessary fines. These people will not jump ahead of anyone who is already in line for citizenship. I want to stress that point. There is a thought: Oh, they will get in front of everybody. That is not true, not under the bill from the Judiciary Committee. They would work 6 years before they could apply for legal permanent residency or green card status, and after that they would work for another 5 years before they could apply for citizenship. During this process, they would have to pay a fine, and with those fines would help pay for this system.

Last, we don't need a wall around our borders. We can use unmanned aerial vehicles, sensors, guard posts. We can do this without building a wall, and we can protect our borders much better than we are doing now. That is what is in the Judiciary bill. It is an excellent starting point.

THE CONTINUING DEBATE: Eventual Citizenship for Unauthorized Immigrants

What Is New

There was a considerable political activity around the illegal immigration during 2006, but nothing was resolved. In April 2006, hundreds of thousands, perhaps a million, Hispanics and others supporting guest-worker status and possible citizenship for illegal aliens demonstrated in cities around the country. During a televised address in May, President Bush called for support for his guest worker program and also for tougher enforcement, including the dispatch 6,000 National Guard troops to help secure the border. Liberals criticized him for militarizing the border, while conservatives carped that he was making only a token gesture. Dozens of bills related to unauthorized immigration were introduced in Congress, and several committees held hearings. Then in August, a report from the Congressional Budget Office estimated that over ten years, a more lenient guest-worker and security bill would cost $126 billion, while a tougher, security-only bill would $78 billion. In the end, Congress was unable to muster a majority behind any proposal and failed to act. That spilled the issue into the electoral area, but its importance there was uncertain. Two-thirds of all Americans in one poll said that how they would vote for Congress in November would be strongly influenced by candidates' immigration policy positions. But when asked by another poll to rank the importance of immigration among nine issues, it finished only eighth, with just 8% identifying as the most important issue facing the country. Almost all Americans wanted greater border security, but 40% favored that alone, while 56% favored coupling heightened border security with also creating a way for some illegal immigrants already here to become citizens."

Where to Find More

A recent review of immigration policy is the Congressional Budget Office's *Immigration Policy of the United States*, a report to Congress (February 2006), available at the agency's Web site, www.cbo.gov/. An even more in-depth analysis is Daniel J. Tichenor, *Dividing Lines: The Politics of Immigration Control in America* (Princeton University Press, 2002). For a group favoring tough immigration laws, visit the site of NumbersUSA, an organization mentioned by James Edwards, at www.numbersusa.com/. An opposing viewpoint is held by the National Immigration Forum at www.immigrationforum.org/.

What More to Do

Congress and the president cannot agree what to do; maybe your class can. Write legislation that includes some or all of proposals to tighten borders (fences, troops, more border patrol agents), to deter unauthorized immigration (criminalization, imprisonment, no social or educational services, no drivers licenses, no hope for citizenship ever), to encourage immigrants to stay home (increased foreign aid to build up poor countries' economies), to impose heavy penalties on employers, to permit guest-worker status, to treat illegal immigrants humanely (services, education), and to permit some undocumented immigrants to eventually become citizens. Debate the issues until a majority can be formed in you class supporting a comprehensive bill.

DEBATE

6 PUBLIC OPINION/PARTICIPATION

VOLUNTEER BORDER PATROL GROUPS:
Laudable Patriots *or* Dangerous Vigilantes?

LAUDABLE PATRIOTS

ADVOCATE: Chris Simcox, President of Minuteman Civil Defense Corps

SOURCE: Testimony during hearings on "Securing Our Borders: What We Have Learned From Government Initiatives and Citizen Patrols," U.S. House of Representatives Committee on Government Reform, May 12, 2005

DANGEROUS VIGILANTES

ADVOCATE: Asheesh Siddique, Editor, *The Princeton Progressive Review*, Princeton University

SOURCE: "The New Nativism," *Campus Progress News*, Spring 2005

Americans are in strong disagreement about how to treat the illegal immigrants who are already in the United States, as Debate 5 discusses. Some Americans think that such immigrants who have established a good record or working and leading law-abiding lives should be legitimized by getting guest-worker status and being permitted to move toward eventual citizenship. Other Americans believe that you cannot build on a criminal act, entering the country illegally, toward citizenship. People with this perspective would increase detain and deport all unauthorized immigrants with no hope of legal return, much less citizenship.

What Americans do agree on, however, is that the flood of illegal immigrants entering the country, most via the 2,0000 mile long, porous U.S.-Mexico border has to be stemmed. One 2006 survey record 81% of Americans characterizing illegal immigration into the country as "out of control." Another poll asked respondents to grade the federal government's effort to address illegal immigration. The average grade given was a D+.

Such a woeful grade reflects the inability of U.S. Border Patrol forces, despite increased personnel and equipment since 2001, to substantially stem the tide of unauthorized immigrants entering the United States. Certainly, the Border Patrol has tried. During 2004, it intercepted and more than 1.1 million illegal immigrants trying to cross the southwest border alone. But many others gain entry and of those who are caught, many keep trying until they succeed. The president of the American Federation of Government Employees' National Border Patrol Council, estimates that the Border Patrol catches only between 25% and 33% of those trying to cross the border illegally. "We're just overwhelmed," he says. "We don't have enough people to keep up with the volume of traffic."

Adding to people's frustration was the sense that a solution was beyond the capabilities of the politicians in Washington, D.C. A poll that asked people if they approved of the way that President George Bush was handling the problem found that only 25% of the respondents did. But when asked if they thought that a Democratic president would do better, only 35% of those responding to the poll thought a change of political control of the White House would improve the situation. Showing perhaps an even deeper sense of public discouragement was a survey that asked people, "Which comes closer to your view—if the U.S. government took the right steps, it could prevent almost all illegal immigration to the U.S., or no matter what the U.S. government does, a sizeable number of illegal immigrants will still be able to get into the U.S? Only 36% of Americans thought that their country, the most powerful in the world, could prevent almost all illegal immigration compared to 61% who believed that a sizeable number of unauthorized immigrants would still make it over the border, with 3% unsure.

More than anywhere else, the sense of frustration with the federal response was felt in the states and communities nearest the Mexican border, the main point of entry for undocumented immigrants. Testifying before a congressional committee El Paso County, Texas, Sheriff Leo Samaniego conceded that "the majority of illegal aliens sneaking across our border are honest, hard working individuals looking for a better life and an opportunity to better their economic situation," but added, "There are [also] a great number of criminals, gang members and yes, potential terrorist, also entering among them." Sheriff Samaniego then charged:

> The federal government has failed to provide a measured response to the threat along the border. The silent majority, the law abiding tax paying rural residents in my county demand equal law enforcement protection from those who have no regard for human life or human dignity. They insist on an immediate response to the escalating threats by terrorist cells and drug and human trafficking organizations. They pay taxes to live free of intimidation. I will not fail them...the question is will you continue to fail them?

One response to the continuing flood tide of people entering the United States without permission has the formation of volunteer groups to patrol the border, particularly the frontier with Mexico, in support of the Border Patrol's mission or detaining and returning illegal immigrants. One such group was founded by Chris Simcox, owner and editor of the newspaper *Tombstone Tumbleweed.* He argues in the first reading that he and fellow volunteers are public-spirited citizens acting out of frustration after many years of seeing the federal government fail in its responsibility to secure U.S. borders. Taking a very different view in the second reading, Asheesh Siddique, a student at Princeton University, labels Simcox and his compatriots "right-wing activists allied with white supremacists" and accuses them of waging "a vigilante campaign of aggression against illegal Mexican migrants along the border."

POINTS TO PONDER

- What is the difference between patriotic groups laudably taking direct action and unsavory vigilante groups taking the law into their own hands? Were the 150 members of the American "Sons of Liberty" who, protesting what they saw as onerous British taxes on tea, bordered three ships in Boston in 1773 and dumped their cargo of tea into the harbor in the famous Boston Tea Party, patriots or vigilantes?
- Other than that they have entered the country without permission, what, if anything, about undocumented immigrants is worrisome.
- Does the fact that most illegal immigrants are from Latin American necessarily mean that those who want to halt the influx of undocumented people are racists?

Volunteer Border Patrol Groups: Laudable Patriots

CHRIS SIMCOX

Almost four years after the terrible terrorist attacks upon our country on September 11, 2001, citizens of the United States remain concerned about our national security, specifically our outrageously porous international border with Mexico. Those who live along the border-state region with Mexico have great concern for their personal safety as well as concern over the lack of border security.

Despite repeated warnings from citizens, local law enforcement and various public officials, our border remains intolerably porous and presents not only a threat to public safety but also a clear and present danger to the security of our nation. Millions of dollars have been thrown at the problem and new technology has been promised—some delivered, some conspicuously absent. Citizens who live with daily incursions of illegal aliens through our property and into the sparsely populated back country along the border realize one thing: the Department of Homeland security cannot effectively stop migrant workers, mothers carrying small children, vicious drug smugglers, known criminals and human smugglers from breaching our border security—we do not feel confident that our government is able to stop terrorist elements from entering our country with the intent of inflicting harm upon our citizens.

After years of writing letters, sending faxes, sending e-mails and making countless phone calls to elected officials pleading, begging and demanding redress of our grievances, frustration led us to but one conclusion—we must act and address the problem with a citizen movement. In November of 2002, I began assembling a group of citizens to undertake the responsibility in assisting what we realized was a Border Patrol woefully undermanned and, as it stood, unable to provide for the safety of the citizens of our local community, Cochise County, Arizona.

We began with a small group of about 40 concerned citizens who knew the only way to bring attention to the problem was with bold statement combined with effective active participation, and so a neighborhood border watch movement was born. Working with retired and active law enforcement and military personnel, we formed Civil Homeland Defense—a group of citizens who worked within the law to assist law enforcement with battling an overwhelming flood of incursions by foreign nationals from around the world who daily breached our border security. Since the formation of the CHD, over 400 citizens from Arizona and other states have participated in spotting, locating and reporting people who entered our country illegally. Our citizen effort has led to the capture, by the proper authorities, of 4,609 individuals from 26 different countries including China, Brazil, Colombia, Haiti, Poland and, yes, even people from Russia. During the same period, volunteers of our modest citizen patrol group have provided life saving water and medical attention to save the lives of 158 men, women and children. From the beginning, our volunteers have worked seamlessly with field agents of the U.S. Border Patrol; agents in the field have always acted with courtesy and have shown appreciation for our assistance with a problem they are not able to control, given the support they receive from the Congress.

Supervisors and sector chiefs of the U.S. Border Patrol have been a different story. Despite a public service campaign asking for the help of citizens, they contradict themselves when it comes to the point of actually going beyond picking up a phone to report groups of people who have obviously entered our country illegally.

Video provided by Civil Homeland Defense and the Minuteman Project illustrates just how porous our border is. Each of the nearly 5,000 identified illegal entrants is presented in videotape evidence supplied to this committee. Not only have local citizens documented persons from other countries entering Cochise County, but we also present evidence of incursions by Mexican military personnel—sometimes found up to a mile inside the borders of the United States. During the month of April 2005, 876 citizens volunteered at least one 8-hour shift manning static observation posts along a 26-mile sector of Cochise County. The areas were chosen because of their repeated use by human smugglers to bring thousands of foreign nationals into our country illegally. We identified the most heavily traveled routes used by smugglers and we formed static observation posts spaced approximately one-quarter of a mile apart, to create an obvious presence that resulted in deterring anyone from entering the country in those areas. Sixty-three volunteers spent the entire 30-day period working multiple shifts to maintain a presence. On our "Naco line," an area east of Bisbee, Arizona, stretching towards Douglas, Arizona, an area notorious for up to 500 illegal crossings a day, we saw a drop to nearly zero during the 30-day mission.

On our "Huachuca line," an area 5-miles from the Mexican border at the base of the Huachuca Mountains, we witnessed a dramatic decrease in groups of illegal aliens descending through canyons leading through neighborhoods south of Sierra Vista and the unincorporated area known as Hereford, Arizona.

During the month-long mission, volunteers of the Minuteman Project assisted Border Patrol with locating and apprehending 349 people entering the United States illegally. Also during the month of April, calls to Border Patrol from local residents led to more than 1,500 apprehensions that would not have been made had citizens not taken the initiative to report suspicious illegal activity in their neighborhoods. Border Patrol officials reported that apprehensions of illegal aliens in the Naco sector dropped 65% from the previous year during the same time period. During the month-long project, volunteer encounters with Border patrol field agents were nothing less than amicable and friendly. Agents were overtly appreciative and supportive of the assistance provided by citizens. Agents thanked the volunteers for bringing national attention to their plight and their frustration with being ignored by supervisors as well as the lack of support both in equipment and personnel by Congress, and expressed anger at comments made by the President of the United States, George W. Bush.

When volunteers of the Minuteman Project made calls for assistance to the Border Patrol they responded quickly and shared words of appreciation for the efforts of the volunteers. At no time did any field agent state concerns about citizens impeding their duties or getting in the way. At no time did field agents express frustration regarding the setting off of sensors.

The Minuteman Project was a phenomenal success due to the law abiding and conscientious efforts of many retired law enforcement and military veterans who gave their time and offered expertise in organizing, supervising and ensuring volunteers remained explicitly aware of the tactics outlined in our carefully written Standard Operating Procedures (S.O.Ps.). That S.O.P. format is included in the packet of information offered as testimony to this committee. The S.O.Ps. provided a framework that assured citizens' exemplary behavior and code of conduct during the month-long protest.

Our message is clear: Congress must move immediately to assign military reserves to the border to assist with controlling our border, or we the people will continue to organize, train and act to assist doing the job—right alongside our courageous Border Patrol agents. Our effort now continues in Cochise County, and will expand towards a much larger citizen volunteer group preparing for a month-long effort in all four southern border states in October 2005.

Each of our volunteers must submit to a criminal background check; they must be interviewed by recruitment personnel and must understand their participation hinges on their strict adherence to a policy of law-abiding engagement with those who willfully break the laws of our nation by entering our country illegally. We intend to share all intelligence information with the proper authorities and will work in ways that do not impede their operations.

We know our border is rife with hardened criminals who have no respect for human life. Volunteers are prepared for the consequences of violent encounters with criminals; we are prepared to defend our lives and our country with reasonable counter-force if necessary. Volunteers will abide strictly by the laws of the states in which they operate such patrols. Volunteers fully understand the weight of responsibility heaped upon their shoulders by the lack of attention to this problem by Congress and the President of the United States. It is your duty to immediately respond to our grievances and quickly act to supply professional personnel who would bring an end to the necessity for ordinary citizens to band together to provide the services that are clearly delegated by the Constitution to the Federal Government.

Our plan is continue recruiting retired law enforcement personnel and we are actively recruiting military veterans, from WWII vets to veterans returning from the most recent war in Iraq—they are ready and willing to serve their country again by assisting with border security.

The success has led to an outpouring of support and volunteerism, skyrocketing to the point where organizers have been contacted by over 15,000 people wishing to volunteer for future operations.

We consider this a mandate from the citizens of the United States who are no longer demanding better border security—they are now willing to participate in securing the borders themselves. Our intentions are to follow the will of the people. The Minuteman Civil Defense Corps. is now undertaking the task of recruiting, training and deploying thousands of U.S. citizens to the four southern border states with Mexico. This effort will also continue to expand to northern border states with Canada.

We now consider the movement to be a revival of the Civil Defense movement of the World War II era. While our troops are fighting on foreign soil, while our Department of Homeland Security applies its resources and efforts to provide for our national security in other areas, we the people will take up the slack by developing civil defense volunteers to support the U.S. Border Patrol.

We consider this a no-compromise situation. Until the time that Congress appropriates sufficient funding and develops personnel levels to the numbers needed to effectively secure our borders, we the people will roll up our sleeves in the time-honored tradition and creed of a "cando" society, and we will assist until honorably relieved from duty by the government of the United States.

Only one scenario is possible in convincing citizens to return to our normal everyday lives: deployment of U.S. military reserves and/or assigning National Guard personnel, to augment a woefully understaffed Border patrol; only this will convince ordinary citizens to retire from this endeavor.

The tactics and logistics now seem obvious. Static observation posts are the only effective method of deterrence short of building a wall along the almost 2,000 mile border with Mexico. Elevated observation outposts spaced approximately one-half-mile apart and staffed with teams of two to four Border Patrol or military personnel are needed to deter drug and human smugglers from entering the country. It is all about creating an obvious presence that deters individuals from entering our country illegally.

We know that posse comitatus [an 1878 law prohibiting the use of the military for civilian law enforcement] cannot be used as an excuse for preventing the deployment of military reserves to assist with border security. President Theodore Roosevelt set aside the 60 foot right of way known as the international border road in 1907 explicitly for the purpose of using the military to protect the United States. We of course are not concerned about the military being used against citizens of the United States; we are asking for the military to augment Border Patrol to improve national security and to prevent people and illicit goods from entering the U.S. illegally.

U.S. military reserves and National Guard personnel could use the border for training exercises, creating a presence to deter illegal activity. Border Patrol could work as a secondary layer of protection and would pursue and apprehend people who breach the first line of defense. For the citizens who have worked the border, we know first hand this tactic works. While we watched the border during April, every illegal alien who chanced crossing the border in our area of operations was quickly apprehended by the proper authorities. Using advanced technology, ground sensors, cameras and UAVs [Unmanned Aerial Vehicles] are important in providing security; however, nothing is as effective as a physical presence of personnel on the border.

Volunteer Border Patrol Groups: Dangerous Vigilantes

ASHEESH SIDDIQUE

The Arizona-Mexico border is one of the most arid parts of America, but also holds some of this country's most beautiful national landmarks. Deep canyons, along with ancient pueblos built as early as 700 AD, dot the land, making the region a prime tourist destination. Tall mountain ranges, swift rivers, jackrabbits, and coyotes create a natural environment like no other in the world.

But there's trouble in paradise.

Right-wing activists allied with white supremacists this past month to wage a vigilante campaign of aggression against illegal Mexican migrants along the border. Throughout April [2005], a coalition of anti-immigration activists calling themselves the Minuteman Project engaged in an effort to "peacefully observe" the border for signs of illegal immigration. The organizers of the effort, which came to a temporary end this past Sunday, claimed that their intentions are legal, benign, and free of racist motivations. "Our objective will be to spot these intruders and inform the U.S. Border Patrol of their location so that border patrol agents can intercept and detain them," read the project's web site. "We will NOT be confronting the illegal aliens or making citizens' arrests."

But the Project was not as innocent as it claimed to be. Many members of the National Alliance, the largest Neo-Nazi group in America, attended meetings of the vigilante group, and even distributed flyers to local residents on behalf of the Minutemen stating that "Non-Whites are turning America into a Third World slum." And even as the Minutemen claimed to be acting to protect America, their actions directly violated basic human rights protections guaranteed to migrant workers under international treaties—irrespective of their status under U.S. immigration law (Part III, Article 10. Note: no distinction made in terms of legal status).

The rhetoric of the participating organizations' leadership also belied their true motivations. Glenn Spencer, one of America's leading anti-immigration activists and the founder of American Border Patrol, has argued that "Mexican culture is based on deceit" and "Chicanos and Mexicanos lie as a means of survival." Civil Homeland Defense's founder, Chris Simcox, has argued that Mexican immigrants "have no problem slitting your throat and taking your money or selling drugs to your kids or raping your daughters and they are evil people." Most of the funding for these groups has come from organizations with extremist connections, such as the Federation for American Immigration Reform—an organization that has ties to the racist Council of Conservative Citizens. And while the Minuteman Project has denied being a racist organization, James Gilchrist, its founder, recently defended white supremacists on Fox News' Hannity & Colmes.

Southeast Arizona has a long history of racially motivated violence against immigrants, but things had been fairly calm during the 1980s and 1990s. Tensions between the white population and Mexican migrants, however, flared up beginning in 1999 as groups like American Border Patrol, Ranch Rescue, the Minuteman Project, and Civil Homeland Defense began to organize campaigns of harassment and intimidation against these laborers.

These new efforts among conservatives have surged in the wake of 9/11, seeking to capitalize on the new climate of fear to push an anti-immigrant, jingoistic agenda that seeks to curtail due-process rights to non-citizens and impose federal restrictions on the types of documentation government officials can accept as valid types of identification.

Legal observers from the American Civil Liberties Union and other organizations spent the month monitoring the activities of the Minutemen and their allies. They reported several disturbing civil liberties violations by the vigilantes, including one incident where volunteers allegedly held a migrant against his will and photographed him wearing clothing with the slogan "Bryan Barton caught an illegal alien and all I got was this t-shirt," and even occasions where the Minutemen took migrants hostage and tried to attack them with dogs.

Furthermore, the Minuteman Project's activities disrupted the work of the legal immigration authorities. Volunteers unfamiliar with the provisions the Border Patrol already has in place tripped sensors, caused false alarms that taxed the efforts of law enforcement agents. One agent noted the toll of these mistakes: "Every sensor has to be addressed. It has taken away from our normal operations."

In spite of the group's radical views and racist ties, the Minutemen received resounding endorsement from prominent political figures, including at least ten members of Congress, including [U.S. Representative] Tom Tancredo [R-CO], chairman of the House Immigration Reform Caucus, and California Governor Arnold Schwarzenegger, who has been criticized by immigration rights groups for making comments "nothing short of base racism" in support of the Project. In addition, prominent conservative pundits and journalists, including Michelle Malkin, Cal Thomas, and George Metcalf, strongly defended the Minutemen—suggesting that the extremism of Spencer, Simcox, and Gilchrist is very much within the mainstream of conservative political discourse on immigration.

The conclusion of the Minutemen's month of vigilantism came as Congress continues to debate how to address the genuine problem of illegal immigration. In March, the Pew Hispanic Center estimated that there are about 10.3 million undocumented residents in the United States, with 57% coming from Mexico. Arizona has experienced one of the most rapid growths in its undocumented migrant population. One proposal being floated in Washington is the REAL ID Act, which passed the House in February [2005] and is currently pending in the Senate. Written by Representative James Sensenbrenner [R-WI], the legislation attempts to make it easier to send asylum-seekers back to the country they are fleeing, and makes it more difficult for the courts to review unlawful actions made by the government in deportation cases. [Democratic National Committee] Chairman Howard Dean has explicitly highlighted the similarities between the REAL ID Act and the Minuteman Project, saying that both create "an atmosphere of hostility." Dean also noted that the Act would provide incentives for vigilantes to corral immigrants without ensuring their identity, creating the potential for more Minutemen-style civil liberties violations. [The proposed Real ID Act (H.R. 418) was included as a provision of a supplemental appropriation bill (H.R. 1286), which was enacted by Congress, signed by the president, and became law (P.L. 109–13) in May 2005.

Progressives continue to wrestle with this issue. Some who advocate for change argue that we need to have a skills-based approach to immigration, encouraging the immigration of highly skilled workers from abroad who will be able to contribute significantly to American economic growth, while at the same time gradually reducing the number of unskilled workers. This is, of course, quite different from the more aggressive approach favored by conservatives and the Minutemen.

If there's anything to be learned from the sorry saga of the Minuteman Project, it's that efforts to make America a land of exclusion, not freedom, are pervasive even in the age of globalization. Declaring "victory" in their efforts on April 30, the Minutemen have now announced plans to expand their efforts northward to the U.S.-Canada border, and into other Southwestern states. Progressives must be just as vigilant in ensuring that this nation remains a genuine land of opportunity for millions of immigrants from around the world. In her famous 1883 poem "The New Colossus," Emma Lazarus offered a vision of an America open to receiving the "huddled masses yearning to breathe free," a "city on a hill" where people could come and create a better life free of poverty, sickness, and persecution. We must remain true to Lazarus' dream of opportunity—a dream that both defines us and unites us as Americans.

THE CONTINUING DEBATE: Volunteer Border Patrol Groups

What Is New

The Minutemen's plan to patrol the U.S.–Mexico border in 2005 set off alarm and criticism. Mexican President Vicente Fox of Mexico denounced such groups "immigrant hunters," and President Bush declared, "I'm against vigilantes." However, what unfolded once the Minutemen had been patrolling for a while led the *Wall Street Journal* to comment, "Those on both sides of the issue [agree that] the Minuteman…initiative in Arizona came off largely without incident." The Minutemen did not try to detain suspected illegal immigrants. Instead they reported them and followed them until the Border Patrol arrived. According to that agency, over 1,000 such citizen reports led to over 2,000 intercepts during April 2005 in the 20-mile zone the Minutemen were patrolling. Skeptics noted that 900 Minutemen had patrolled a small area, and, by the same coverage of the entire 2,000 U.S.–Mexico border would take 60,000 people.

The relatively few volunteers have kept patrols severely limited in terms of both time and geography. The Minuteman movement has also suffered due to internal feuding between Chris Simcox and his Minuteman Civil Defense Corps and his former collaborator, Jim Gilchrist and his Minuteman Project. However, the border efforts by the volunteer continue and to a degree have been augmented. In 2006, for example, a high-tech firm donated $7 million worth of fiber-optic security fencing to Simcox's group. Thus the controversy continues, epitomized by an August 2006 story in the *Fort Worth Start Telegram* entitled, Patriots or Vigilante Nuts?"

Where to Find More

The Web site of the Minuteman Civil Defense Corps is www.minutemanhq.com/hq/ and that of the Minuteman Project is www.minutemanproject.com/. A sympathetic book on the movement is Jim Gilchrist, Jerome R. Corsi, and (U.S. Representative) Tom Tancredo (R-CO), *Minutemen: The Battle to Secure America's Borders* (World Ahead Publishing, 2006). There are no specific anti-Minuteman groups, but one critical organization and its commentary are the People for the American Way at www.rightwingwatch.org/2006/07/border_vigilant.html.

What More to Do

The core debate for the future is whether to (1) spend the financial resources necessary to seal the border against future illegal immigration and also locate, detain, and repatriate the millions of undocumented immigrants already in the United States, (2) increase both the level of enforcement against and penalties on the many Americans and U.S. businesses that employ undocumented workers, (3) adopt one of the various proposals to "legalize" these immigrants by either granting them temporary workers/family status or even permanent residency/citizenship, (4) give enough aid to the countries the immigrants come from so that they can find economic opportunity at home, and/or (5) do no more or even less along the border and devote financial resources to other issues facing the country. How would you prioritize these five options?

DEBATE 7

MEDIA

SHIELDING JOURNALISTS' SOURCES FROM SUBPOENA: Protecting Democracy *or* Impeding Justice?

PROTECTING DEMOCRACY

ADVOCATE: Norman Pearlstine, Editor-in-Chief, Time Inc.

SOURCE: Testimony during hearings on "Reporters' Shield Legislation: Issues and Implications," U.S. Senate Committee on the Judiciary, July 20, 2005

IMPEDING JUSTICE

ADVOCATE: James B. Comey, Deputy Attorney General, U.S. Department of Justice

SOURCE: Testimony during hearings on "Reporters' Shield Legislation: Issues and Implications," U.S. Senate Committee on the Judiciary, July 20, 2005

Journalists have long used "anonymous" or "confidential" sources to obtain information. They argue that unless they can assure their sources of anonymity, the flow of news will decrease because their sources will fear retaliation. Sometimes, such anonymous sources have been instrumental in major stories. Most famously, "Deep Throat" was an anonymous source for the press during the Watergate scandal that led President Richard M. Nixon to resign in 1974. The press did not identify that source (Mark Felt, former deputy director of the FBI) until he gave his permission in 2005. Historically, there has been little effort to, and no court support of, efforts to force journalists to reveal their sources in such cases.

The ability of journalists to shield sources in criminal matters is another issue. The matter first became a legal issue in the 1890s when a reporter for the Baltimore *Sun* was jailed for contempt of court after he refused to disclose his sources related to a voting bribery scandal and ensuing criminal investigation. Responding to his incarceration, Maryland in 1896 enacted the country's first "shield law" giving journalists the legal right to maintain confidential news sources, even during criminal investigation. Since then, almost all states have passed shield laws to protect reporters, although the extent of protection varies widely among the states.

On the federal level, the key Supreme Court ruling came in the *Branzburg v. Hayes* (1972), a case involving the refusal of a reporter for the Louisville *Courier-Journal* to reveal sources related to drug dealing. In a 5 to 4 decision, the court held that the First Amendment did not exempt journalists from having "to respond to grand jury subpoena and answer relevant questions." However, the court kept its focus on criminal investigating by adding, "Official harassment of the press undertaken not for purposes of law enforcement but to disrupt a reporter's relationship with his news sources would have no justification."

There the matter rested until the recent events that prompted this debate. They began in 2003 amid the controversy over whether or not the administration of President George W. Bush had reason to believe that Iraq had a nuclear weapons program. On July 6, 2003, the *New York Times* published an op-ed piece by former Ambassador Joseph Wilson claiming that the CIA had sent him to Niger in early 2002 to look into whether the Iraqis had tried to buy uranium from that country and that he had found no evidence of any attempted purchase. Soon thereafter, syndicated columnist Robert Novak reported that two high-level Bush officials had told him that the CIA had sent Wilson on the recommendation of his wife, Valerie Plame. Novak described her as a spy, "an agency operative on weapons of mass destruction." Soon thereafter, *Time* published articles based on the investigative reporting of Matthew Cooper, Judith Miller, and others indicating that government officials had also revealed to *Time* that Plame was a CIA operative. One story-line suggested that officials leaked Plame's status in order to ruin her career by blowing her cover in retaliation for the op-ed piece written by her husband.

Knowingly disclosing the identity of U.S. spies violates the Intelligence Identities Protection Act, and federal investigators subpoenaed Cooper, Miller, and *Time*, demanding that they submit all documents related to the stories and reveal their sources. Such subpoenas are not common. According to Department of Justice data, federal officials and courts issued only 17 subpoenas between 1991 and 2001 asking for journalist's sources.

In the cases at hand, the reporters and *Time* declined to comply. In subsequent court actions, they all were held in contempt of court by a U.S. district judge, the U.S. Court of Appeals upheld that action, and the Supreme Court refused to take the case. *Time* gave way and submitted the documents it possessed. Cooper also complied with the court order after receiving a waiver of confidentiality from his source, White House senior political adviser Karl Rove. But Miller remained in contempt and was sent to jail and was still incarcerated when the testimony that makes the up following articles was given.

One response to the Plame affair was the introduction of the Free Flow of Information Act of 2005 in Congress. The legislation is designed to further limit the ability of the government to force journalists to reveal their sources. In the first of the following articles, *Time's* editor-in-chief Norman Pearlstine tells the Senate that using confidential sources is necessary to enabling reporters to protect an essential element of democracy: providing vital information to the public so that people can make informed decisions about the government and thereby fully participate in democracy. Deputy U.S. Attorney General James Comey counters that he recognizes the importance of the press in a free society, but argues that sufficient protection for the press already exists and that new legislation to shield journalists' sources would upset the proper balance between the need for free dissemination of ideas and information in a democracy and the equally important need for effective law enforcement and the fair administration of justice.

POINTS TO PONDER

- Note the difference between the reporters right to shield sources about non-criminal matters and those under investigation as violations of the law.
- Think about whether by refusing to reveal sources, the media is not withholding important information that would help citizens evaluate the stories based on anonymous sources.
- Pay attention to the detailed commentary on the pending bill in James Comey's commentary. As the line goes, "the devil is in the detail," and you can favor some aspects of the bill and not others.

Shielding Journalists' Sources from Subpoena: Protecting Democracy

NORMAN PEARLSTINE

I...support...the proposed federal legislation that would protect journalists from being compelled to testify about confidential sources and other unpublished information obtained during newsgathering. This type of protection, which has been adopted in one form or another by 49 states and the District of Columbia, is commonly called a "reporter's privilege," but this is something of a misnomer. The laws are really intended to protect the public, not reporters, by ensuring the free flow of information about governmental activities and other matters of public concern and interest. I believe there is an urgent need for such protection at the federal level.

Until today, I had never testified in a Senate hearing or, for that matter, in any other legislative proceeding. As a journalist, I am far more comfortable reporting, writing, or editing news about the government than urging the government to adopt new laws. But the absence of federal legislation protecting sources has created extraordinary chaos, limiting the public's access to important information that is so necessary in a democratic society. The Supreme Court's sharply divided decision 33 years ago in *Branzburg v. Hayes* (1972) has mystified courts, lawyers and journalists alike. As a result, the federal courts are in a state of utter disarray about whether a reporter's privilege protecting confidential sources exists. The conflicting legal standards throughout the federal courts defeat the nearly unanimous policies of the states in this area. This uncertainty chills essential newsgathering and reporting. It also leads to confusion by sources and reporters, and the threat of jail and other harsh penalties for reporters who do not know what promises they can make to their sources. I recently witnessed the problems firsthand. As the Committee is no doubt aware, for almost two years, Time Inc. and its reporter Matthew Cooper fought against compelled disclosure of confidential sources in response to grand jury subpoenas in Special Counsel Patrick Fitzgerald's investigation of the Valerie Plame affair. The federal district judge presiding over the matter called this battle a "perfect storm" in which important First Amendment rights clashed with the important interest in law enforcement. We fought all the way to the Supreme Court and lost.

My decision to turn over confidential documents to the Special Counsel after we had pursued every possible legal remedy was the toughest decision of my career—and one I should never have had to make. The experience has only deepened my commitment to ensure protection for confidential sources and made clear to me the urgent need for federal legislation....[In the following commentary] I shall...discuss why the careful use of confidential sources is indispensable to ensuring that the press can fulfill its constitutionally established duty of providing vital information to the public so that people can make informed decisions about the government and thereby fully participate in democracy. I shall [also] explain why I so strongly believe that federal legislation is necessary—and long overdue.

THE IMPORTANCE OF PROTECTING CONFIDENTIAL SOURCES

It is Time Inc.'s editorial policy that articles in our publications should identify sources by name whenever possible. But sometimes we can obtain information only by promising confidentiality to a source, because many persons with important information won't speak to the press unless they are assured anonymity. Information given in confidence is especially valuable when it contradicts or undermines public positions asserted by governments or powerful individuals or corporations. Without confidential sourcing, the public would never have learned the details of many situations vital to its interests, from Watergate to the controversies that led to the impeachment (and then acquittal) of President [Bill] Clinton to the Enron and Abu Ghraib scandals.

Time Inc. has a long history of fighting to preserve press freedoms because we believe it is in the public interest to do so. It is no coincidence that the Supreme Court held in a case involving our company that freedom of the press was created "not for the benefit of the press so much as for the benefit of all of us." *Time Inc. v. Hill* (1967). We know that when gathering and reporting news, journalists act as surrogates for the public. Protecting confidential sources is thus intended not to protect the rights of news organizations, individual reporters or sources, but to safeguard the public's rights. [As argued by constitutional expert] Ronald Dworkin..., "The special position of the press is justified, not because reporters have special rights but because it is thought that the community as a whole will benefit from their special treatment, just as wheat farmers might be given a subsidy, not because they are entitled to it, but because the community will benefit from that." Our "Constitution specifically selected the press" to fulfill an "important role" in our democracy ...[according to the Supreme Court in] *Mills v. Alabama* (1966). [In that case, the court also said that] the press "serves and was designed to serve as a powerful antidote to any abuses of power by governmental officials as a constitutionally chosen means for keeping officials elected by the people responsible to all the people whom they were elected to serve." [In another case, *Estes v. Texas* (1965), the court commented that] the press "has been a mighty catalyst in awakening public interest in governmental affairs, exposing corruption among public officers and employees and generally informing the citizenry of public events and occurrences." [In a 1981 ruling], the Second Circuit Court of the Court of Appeals wrote, "[N]ews gathering is essential to a free press" and "[t]he press was protected so that it could bare the secrets of government and inform the people." Without an unfettered press, citizens would be far less able to make informed political, social, and economic choices. But the press's function as a vital source of information is weakened whenever the ability of journalists to gather news is impaired.

Some reliance on confidential sources is necessary to protect the press's ability to fulfill its constitutionally ordained role. Over the years *Time* and our other magazines have published many stories regarding issues of significant public interest that could not have been published unless we could rely on confidential sources. To cite a few examples from the weeks prior to the Supreme Court's denial of our petition for certiorari, I worked with colleagues at *Time* on important stories about a suicide bomber in Iraq, the treatment and interrogation of a detainee at Guantanamo [Bay, U.S. Naval Base], and the vulnerability of our nation's commercial nuclear facilities should they be subjected to terrorist attack. None of these stories could have been published without the use of information from confidential sources. As one court explained it:

> The interrelationship between newsgathering, news dissemination and the need for a journalist to protect his or her source is too apparent to require belaboring. A journalist's inability to protect the confidentiality of sources s/he must use will jeopardize the journalist's ability to obtain information on a confidential basis. This in turn will seriously erode the essential role played by the press in the dissemination of information and matters of interest and concern to the public.

Following my decision to obey the courts by providing the Special Counsel with the subpoenaed documents, I met last week with *Time's* Washington bureau, and later that day with many of its New York writers and editors. Many of them showed me e-mails and letters from valuable sources who insisted that they no longer trusted the magazine and that they would no longer cooperate on stories.

The chilling effect is obvious. Without confidentiality—that express promise or implied understanding that a source's identity won't be revealed—it will often be impossible for our reporters to sustain relationships with sources and to obtain sensitive information from them. As Professor Alexander Bickel observed in a celebrated essay:

> Indispensable information comes in confidence from officeholders fearful of superiors, from businessmen fearful of competitors, from informers operating at the edge of the law who are in danger of reprisal from criminal associates, from people afraid of the law and of government—sometimes rightly afraid, but as often from an excess of caution—and from men in all fields anxious not to incur censure for unorthodox or unpopular views. ...Forcing reporters to divulge such confidences would dam the flow to the press, and through it to the people, of the most valuable sort of information: not the press release, not the handout, but the firsthand story based on the candid talk of a primary news source.

THE URGENT NEED FOR A FEDERAL SHIELD LAW

The need for a federal shield law has never been clearer. Judith Miller is in jail and Matthew Cooper would have been had his source not released him at the last minute from his bond of confidentiality. As we argued in our certiorari petition [to the Supreme Court], the law is a mess—so much so that the three judges on the D.C. Circuit panel each took a very different view of whether the federal common law recognizes a reporter's privilege. Some judges...believe that *Branzburg* bars not only First Amendment protection, but any form of judicially recognized privilege, and the Supreme Court has refused to revisit that decision, leaving federal legislation as the sole realistic possibility for a uniform federal rule. As the Supreme Court in *Branzburg* recognized, "[a]t the federal level, Congress has freedom to determine whether a statutory newsman's privilege is necessary and desirable and to fashion standards and rules as narrow or broad as deemed necessary to deal with the evil discerned and, equally important, to refashion those rules as experience from time to time may dictate."

Federal law recognizes many other evidentiary privileges, including privileges protecting spousal communications, and communications between social workers and those seeking counseling from them, doctors and patients, attorneys and clients, and clergy and penitents. These privileges may lead to the loss of evidence in some instances, but they are viewed as necessary to protect and foster communications deemed valuable to society as a whole. The same is true for communications between reporters and confidential sources.

When courts compel disclosure of confidential sources, it endangers our ability to do our jobs, and this practice inevitably stems the flow of information on public events vital to an informed citizenry and a healthy democracy. In this case, for instance, Cooper's story *A War on Wilson?* raised the important question whether government officials improperly retaliated against a critic of the Administration's decision to go to war.

The Plame case is part of a disturbing trend. In the last two years, dozens of reporters have been subpoenaed to reveal their confidential sources, many of whom face the prospect of imminent imprisonment. The use of such subpoenas in the Plame case represents a profound departure from the practice of federal prosecutors when this case is compared to other landmark cases involving confidentiality over the past 30 years. Neither Archibald Cox, the Watergate Special Prosecutor, nor Judge John Sirica sought to force *The Washington Post* or its reporters to reveal the identity of "Deep Throat," the prized confidential source. We are deeply concerned that the rulings in the Plame case will exacerbate the danger of prosecutorial excesses when it comes to issuing subpoenas in all types of cases. To be sure, the Department of Justice guidelines limit subpoenas to the press and require the Attorney General's approval of such subpoenas. But the courts in the Plame case held that these regulations are not judicially enforceable. And where a special (or "independent") counsel is leading the investigation, the Attorney General's approval is no longer required, posing special dangers to the press. As Judge Tatel noted in the Plame case, "[I]ndependent prosecutors...may skew their assessments of the public interests implicated when a reporter is subpoenaed. After all, special prosecutors, immune to political control and lacking a docket of other cases, face pressure to justify their appointments by bagging their prey.

To make matters worse, reporters and their sources are subject to a tangle of contradictory privilege rules that vary widely depending on the jurisdiction in which they are subpoenaed. These differing rules lead to arbitrary, unpredictable and conflicting outcomes. This uncertainty has a chilling effect on speech, and ultimately results in less information reaching the public, as many individuals will hesitate to communicate with a reporter if a promise of confidentiality is good in some jurisdictions but not in others. In particular, a state-law reporter's privilege is of little value if it offers no reliable protection from forced disclosure in federal court.

The 34 states and the District of Columbia said it best in their amicus curiae brief urging the Supreme Court to grant review in the Plame case. All of these states and the District have adopted some form of reporter's shield law and these laws, "like those of the other fifteen jurisdictions that have them, share a common purpose: to assure that the public enjoys a free flow of information and that journalists who gather and report the news to the public can do so in a free and unfettered atmosphere. The shield laws also rest on the uniform determination by the states that, in most cases, compelling newsgatherers to disclose confidential information is contrary to the public interest. That the chief law enforcement officers for these 35 jurisdictions weighed in to endorse their reporter's shield laws is powerful evidence that these laws do not interfere with the government's ability to prosecute crimes.

At the same time, the states also declared in their brief that a "federal policy that allows journalists to be imprisoned for engaging in the same conduct that these State privileges encourage and protect 'buck[s] that clear policy of virtually all states,' and undermines both the purpose of the shield laws, and the policy determinations of the State courts and legislatures that adopted them." And they emphasized that the states "have a vital interest in this issue independent of protecting the integrity of their shield laws. Uncertainty and confusion...have marked this area of the law in the three decades that have passed since...*Branzburg*....This increasing conflict has undercut the state shield laws just as much as the absence of a federal privilege."

CONCLUSION

I strongly believe in the need for confidential sources and that we must protect our sources when we grant them confidentiality. This is an obligation I take with the utmost seriousness. I also believe we must resist government coercion. But defying court orders, accepting imprisonment and fines, shouldn't be our only way of protecting sources or resisting coercion. Put simply, the issues at stake are crucial to our ability to report the news to the public. Without some federal protection for confidential sources, all of this is in jeopardy. The time has come for enactment of a shield law that will bring federal law into line with the laws of the states and ensure the free and open flow of information to the public on the issues of the day.

Shielding Journalists' Sources from Subpoena: Impeding Justice

JAMES B. COMEY

INTRODUCTION

This statement will focus on S. 340, the "Free Flow of Information Act of 2005." An identical bill has been introduced in the House of Representatives as H.R. 581. S. 340 would establish a federal shield law that would preclude the federal government from issuing compulsory process to obtain information about sources from members of the news media. It would shift from the Department of Justice to the courts the authority to evaluate requests for subpoenas to members of the media and make final decisions during criminal investigations and prosecutions as to whether subpoenas should be issued. It would create a bar against any subpoena issued to certain third parties that reasonably could be expected to lead to the discovery of the identity of a source. It would apply to all forms of federal compulsory process, including court orders and national security letters used in terrorism and espionage investigations, to selected categories of news and informational outlets. The bill would create serious impediments to the department's ability to effectively enforce the law and fight terrorism.

[The proposed legislation] would significantly impair the flexibility of the Executive branch in enforcing federal law, both by imposing inflexible, mandatory standards in lieu of existing voluntary ones and by applying its restrictions on the use of compulsory process more broadly than existing regulations. The bill is bad public policy primarily because it would bar the government from obtaining information about media sources—even in the most urgent of circumstances affecting the public's health or safety or national security—and would place an unreasonable burden upon the government to justify to the court, in a public evidentiary proceeding, that it requires non-source information from the media in connection with sensitive grand jury investigations.

The Department of Justice recognizes that the media plays a critical role in our society. The freedom of the press is a hallowed American right, and in a time when news can be sent around the world almost instantaneously, it is as important as ever that the American people be kept informed of what is happening overseas, in Washington, and in their hometowns. For this reason, the department's disciplined approach to subpoenas directed towards members of the news media carefully balances the public's interest in the free dissemination of ideas and information with the public's interest in effective law enforcement and the fair administration of justice.

For the last 33 years, the Department of Justice has authorized subpoenas to the news media only in the most serious cases. The guidelines [that the Department of Justice follows] require the Attorney General personally to approve all contested subpoenas directed to journalists, following a rigorous multi-layered internal review process involving various components of the department. [The proposed legislation] would disrupt the department's ability to balance the competing interests involved in a decision to subpoena a member of the media and would strip the department of its ability to obtain crucial evidence in criminal investigations and prosecutions. It would also effectively overrule the Supreme Court's decision in *Branzburg v. Hayes* (1972), which held that reporters have no privilege, qualified or otherwise, to withhold information from a grand jury. *Branzburg* has been followed consistently by the federal courts of appeals, and was recently reaffirmed by the United States Court of Appeals for the District of Columbia in *In re Grand Jury Subpoena, Judith Miller* (2005). Indeed, the bill would give more protection to the reporter's "privilege"—which has not been recognized by the Supreme Court—than exists for other forms of privilege that are recognized, *e.g.*, the attorney-client privilege or the spousal privilege.

These results are completely unjustified and would pose a great threat to public safety. In the absence of a credible demonstration that the subpoena power is being abused by the department in this area, such that sources have dried up, with the result that journalists are unable to do effective investigative reporting, there is no need for a legislative fix that substantially skews the carefully maintained balance against legitimate law enforcement interests. The next part of this statement will address the specific provisions of the bill.

SECTION 2

Section 2 of the bill is intended to...prevent the department from issuing subpoenas to members of the news media unless a court determines by clear and convincing evidence: (i) that there are reasonable grounds to believe, based upon non-media evidence, that a crime has occurred; (ii) that the testimony or document sought is essential to the investigation or prosecution; and (iii) that the department has unsuccessfully attempted to obtain the evidence from non-media sources. While, to some degree, subsection 2(a) is similar to the guidelines the department follows in its governing regulation, the bill departs dramatically from the regulation's requirements, first, by requiring the department to make its case before a court, after providing the news media an opportunity to be heard, and, second, by imposing a new "clear and convincing standard" to meet the section's requirements. In effect, this provision would require public mini-trials whenever the department seeks relevant information in a criminal grand jury investigation or to justify a trial subpoena.

The bill would seriously jeopardize traditional notions of grand jury secrecy and unnecessarily delay the completion of criminal investigations. To meet the bill's "clear and convincing" standard, the department frequently will have to present other evidence obtained before the grand jury. It is unclear how the department can present such justifying evidence consistent with its secrecy obligations under Rule 6(e) of the Federal Rules of Criminal Procedure. Further, the provision would require that in order to issue to the media a trial subpoena for non-source information, such as a reporter's eyewitness testimony or video outtakes, the department must showcase its evidence prematurely. These new burdens could significantly cripple effective law enforcement and thereby wreak havoc on the public's interest in the fair administration of justice. We note that media outlets often are happy to provide certain types of non-sensitive information to the federal government, but are more comfortable doing so in response to a subpoena. By making it quite difficult to issue almost any type of subpoena, the bill would make it more difficult for media outlets to cooperate with the federal government. Subsection 2(b) is directed toward...limiting compelled evidence from a member of the media to: (i) verifying published information; or (ii) describing surrounding circumstances relevant to the accuracy of published information. But the regulatory provision [the department follows] has been interpreted consistently to permit compulsion of additional types of evidence if it is apparent that there are no other sources to obtain the information and that the information is otherwise essential to the case. While subsection 2(b) includes language that the limitation is applicable "to the extent possible," it is manifestly unclear under what circumstances the court would allow other types of evidence to be subpoenaed. The provision certainly would substitute the judgment of the court for that of the prosecutor in determining what evidence was necessary in a criminal investigation or prosecution.

SECTION 4

Section 4 would ban compelling members of the news media to identify their sources of information. It would preclude the department from compelling a journalist to identify a confidential source of information from whom the journalist obtained information. More importantly, it also would prevent the compulsion of any information that reasonably could lead to the discovery of the identity of the source. These limitations are not in the department's governing regulation and represent a significant departure from the state of federal law.

The effect of this provision cannot be overstated. A provision that bars process that might obtain "any information that could reasonably be expected to lead to the discovery of the identity of...a source" might effectively end an investigation, particularly one that involved release of national security information. Moreover, even if the intent of the investigation were not to identify a source, the investigation might be barred because it may compel information that a court may find could reasonably lead to the discovery of a source's identity. This provision would create a perverse incentive for persons committing serious crimes involving public safety and national security to employ the media in the process.

Historically, in applying its governing regulation to requests involving source information, the department has carefully balanced the public's interest in the free dissemination of ideas with the public's interest in effective law enforcement. The department's regulation has served to limit the number of subpoenas authorized for source information to little more than a handful over its 33-year history. The authorizations granted for source information have been linked closely to significant criminal matters that directly affect the public's safety and welfare. Section 4 of the bill would preclude the department from obtaining crucial evidence in vital cases, and would overrule settled Supreme Court precedent that protects the grand jury's ability to hear every person's evidence in pursuit of the truth.

The harm that this provision might cause is demonstrably greater than the purported benefit it may serve. It is essential to the public interest that the department maintain the ability, in certain vitally important circumstances, to obtain information identifying a source when a paramount interest is at stake. For example, obtaining source information may be the only available means of abating a terrorist threat or locating a kidnapped child. Certainly, in the face of a paramount public safety or health concern or a national security imperative, the balance should favor disclosure of source information in the possession of the news media. For example, on September 11, 2001, the U.S. Attorney's Office for the Northern District of California requested authorization to subpoena facsimiles that were sent to a San Francisco, California television station from individuals who had predicted eight weeks earlier that September 11th would be "Armageddon." Under the bill, the government would have been unable to obtain that information.

This provision would go far beyond any common law privilege. As the United States Court of Appeals for the District of Columbia Circuit recently held in *Miller*, there is no First Amendment privilege for journalists' confidential sources, and if a common law privilege exists, it is not absolute and must yield to the legitimate imperatives of law enforcement. Further, comparing the bill to existing state shield laws is inapt. None of the states deals with classified information in the way that the federal government does, and no state is tasked with defending the nation as a whole or conducting international diplomacy. The bill makes no recognition of these critical federal responsibilities, and would allow no exceptions for situations that endanger the national security or the public's health and safety.

Finally, section 4's definition of a confidential source is overly broad. Under subparagraph 4(1)(B), any individual whom the journalist subjectively claims to be a confidential source automatically would be afforded that status. This is the case although the source may have not sought confidential status with the journalist or even cared whether his or her identity was disclosed.

SECTION 5

Section 5 appears to be an attempt to codify the regulation governing requests to subpoena the telephone toll records of a member of the news media. It would add other business transaction records between a reporter and a third party, such as a telecommunications service provider, Internet service provider, or operator of an interactive computer service for a business purpose.

Taken together with section 4's prohibition against obtaining information that reasonably could lead to the identification of a source, this section largely ends the ability of law enforcement authorities to conduct *any* investigation involving third parties. For example, a ransom demand made to a kidnap victim's family home telephone could be investigated by compulsory process; a ransom demand made by an anonymous person to a media outlet could not be investigated by such compulsory process. This provision is inconsistent with common law and goes far beyond any statute in any State.

Like section 2, section 5 would require a public mini-trial every time the department sought telephone or other communications service provider records in a grand jury investigation or criminal trial. For the reasons articulated above, section 5 is also bad public policy. While section 5 would establish an exception to the notice requirement if the court determines by clear and convincing evidence that notice "would pose a substantial threat to the integrity of a criminal investigation," there are no built-in mechanisms to protect from public disclosure the very information that the department would be seeking to protect by resisting notice.

SECTION 6

Even if the information sought has already been published or disseminated, section 6 of the bill would continue the ban on compelling source material and would continue to require court approval for other media evidence. The purpose of this provision is unclear. Moreover, reporters could use the provision to provide selective testimony; they could choose what facts to disclose in testimony, while every court would be barred from ordering the reporter to provide any information that the reporter chose not to share. It is possible that the provision is intended to protect a reporter from disclosing source information that already has been publicly disclosed (inadvertently or otherwise) by someone else. Other well-established privileges are waived under certain circumstances when the information sought to be protected has been disclosed. We believe that the issue of waiver should be determined on a case-by-case basis.

SECTION 7

The definition of a "covered person" contained in the bill raises several distinct concerns. Most significantly, it would extend the bill's protections well beyond its presumably intended objective, that is, providing special statutory protections for the kind of news- and information-gathering activities that are essential to freedom of the press under the First Amendment. For example, "covered persons" protected by the bill include non-media corporate affiliates, subsidiaries, or parents of any cable system or programming service, whether or not located in the United States. It would also include any supermarket, department store, or other business that periodically publishes a products catalog, sales pamphlet, or even a listing of registered customers.

Far more dangerously, it would cover criminal or terrorist organizations that also have media operations, including many foreign terrorist organizations, such as al Qaida (which, from its founding, maintained a media office that published a newsletter). Indeed, the inherent difficulty of appropriately defining a "covered person" in a world in which the very definition of "media" is constantly evolving, suggests yet another fundamental weakness in the bill. What could be shielded here is not so much the traditional media—which already is protected adequately by existing Justice Department guidelines—as criminal activity deliberately or fortuitously using means or facilities in the course of the offenses that would cause the perpetrators to fall within the definition of the media under the bill.

In addition, the provisions of the bill reach well beyond the department of Justice. The bill applies broadly to any "federal entity," defined under the bill to include "an entity or employee of the judicial, legislative, or executive branch of the federal government with the power to issue a subpoena or provide other compulsory process." The bill also would reach beyond the guidelines in imposing its restrictions upon any requirement for a covered person to testify or produce documents "in any proceeding or *in connection with any issue arising under federal law.*" Section 2(a). For example, although section 3 of the bill attempts to exclude from coverage "requests for...commercial or financial information unrelated to news gathering or news and information dissemination," the meaning of this section is unclear and may not be sufficient to prevent the bill from empowering news companies to block legitimate antitrust investigations into their potentially anticompetitive mergers and business practices.

CONCLUSION

Recent events no doubt have raised the public's awareness of the issue of compelling evidence from journalists. There are legitimate competing interests involved in the ongoing dialogue on this issue. However, history has shown that the protections already in place, including the department's rigorous internal review of media subpoena requests coupled with the media's ability to challenge compulsory process in the federal courts, are sufficient and strike the proper balance between the public's interest in the free dissemination of ideas and information and the public's interest in effective law enforcement and the fair administration of justice.

THE CONTINUING DEBATE: Shielding Journalists' Sources from Subpoena

What Is New

After 85 days imprisonment, Judith Miller was released in October 2005 after testifying before the grand jury and identifying her source as I. Lewis "Scooter" Libby, chief of staff for Vice President Dick Cheney. Miller indicated that Libby had given her permission to reveal his identify. Later that month, a grand jury indicted Libby for perjury and other crimes related to the investigation. The Free Flow of Information Act of 2005 remained in committee in both the House and Senate, and died when the 109th Congress passed into history after the 2006 election.

It is unclear how Americans feel about shielding journalists' sources in criminal investigation. A May 2005 poll found that 55% of those asked approved "of the use of anonymous sources in news stories," compared to 43% who disapproved and 4% who were unsure. But that did not address the nuanced issues of shielding a source during a criminal investigation. It is probable that public support of the press would be much lower. One reason is that Americans are skeptical of press motives, with another 2005 poll showing that 75% of Americans think the press is primarily motivated by attracting bigger audiences, with only 19% thinking that journalists mostly act to keep the public informed, and 6% unsure.

Where to Find More

A journalists' group at the center of the fight for shield law is the Reporters Committee for Freedom of the Press at www.rcfp.org. For printed commentary from the media's point of view of the impact of the Plame affair on reporter-source relations and on news gathering, read Rachel Smolkin, "Uncharted Terrain," *American Journalism Review* (October 2005). The opposite stand is taken by Dan Ackman, "Expose the Press Players," *Forbes* (February 2005). To explore Americans' attitudes about the news media and issues surrounding freedom of the press, read David A. Yalof and Kenneth Dautrich, *The First Amendment and the Media in the Court of Public Opinion* (Cambridge University Press, 2002).

What More to Do

Debate shield laws in the abstract, but also get into the details of specific legislation. Go to Thomas (thomas.loc.gov/), the basic Web site for Congress, and enter "Free Flow of Information Act" in the search window labeled "Search Bill Text 109th Congress (2005–2006)." Pick one of the related House or Senate bills, such as S. 1419 or H.R. 3323, then click "Text of Legislation" to access the bill. Debate it in class provision by provision. If you support the basic thrust of the legislation, try to build a majority coalition of your class members. Anyone can offer amendments to your bill.

DEBATE 8

INTEREST GROUPS

THE PRO-ISRAEL LOBBY IN THE UNITED STATES: Goliath *or* David?

GOLIATH

ADVOCATES: John Mearsheimer, R. Wendell Harrison Distinguished Service Professor of Political Science and co-director of the Program on International Security Policy, University of Chicago; and Stephen Walt, Robert and Rene Belfer Professor of International Affairs, John F. Kennedy School of Government, Harvard University

SOURCE: "The Israel Lobby," *London Review of Books*, March 23, 2006

DAVID

ADVOCATE: Alan Dershowitz, Professor, School of Law, Harvard University

SOURCE: "Debunking the Newest—and Oldest—Jewish Conspiracy: A Reply to the Mearsheimer-Walt 'Working Paper,'" Faculty Research Working Papers, Kennedy School of Government, Harvard University

Being an American is an idea. It is the notion of belonging to people, a nation, that cultural, historical, and political ties that bind it. A primary political tie is that Americans identify first and foremost as a citizen of the United States and put the interests of their country and its people above all others. This does not mean that Americans do not or should not also feel links to the outside world. Indeed, many Americans think of themselves as, African Americans, Jewish Americans, and many other kinds of Americans. The hyphen to denote these groups (as in Irish-American) has gone out of style, but its earlier use has left the term "hyphenated American" to designate such groups.

Identification with a specific country is the most common link, and many Americans think of themselves as, say, Italian Americans or Mexican Americans. Religion is another possible tie. For example, many Jewish Americans have a strong sense of community with Israel. Other groups have a regional connection. Because slavery wiped out the ability of most blacks to trace their heritage to a specific location, that group's sense of heritage is linked more to sub-Saharan Africa than to a single country.

Throughout American history, hyphenated American groups have often acted as interest groups trying to influence U.S. foreign policy to be favorable to their homeland and ancestral culture. For one, Jewish Americans who support Israel are represented by such organizations as the American-Israel Public Affairs Committee (AIPAC), which declares itself, "America's Pro-Israel Lobby" and features on its home page a quote by the New York Times heralding AIPAC as "The most important organization affecting America's relationship with Israel." Among the groups trying to counterbalance the efforts of AIPAC is the Arab American Institute. It lists one of its missions as representing "Arab Americans throughout the United States...[on] a variety of public policy issues that concern...U.S.—Arab relations." To this list of ethnic lobbies could be added the Cuban American National Foundation, American Latvian Association, the TransAfrica Forum, the Armenian National Committee of America, the American Hellenic Institute (Greek Americans), the Irish National Caucus, the Polish American Congress, and myriad others.

The language of the First Amendment guaranteeing the right "to petition the government for a redress of grievances," clearly gives such hyphenate-American interest groups, like all other interest groups, the right to lobby the U.S. government. Equally certain is that lobbying by groups of every policy persuasion is an accepted and perhaps necessary element of the American democratic tradition and process. Some people, however, believe that lobbying for foreign policy that benefits another country, region, or people falls outside the boundaries of what is or should be acceptable. They charge that such pressures distort U.S. foreign policy in ways that can actually contravene U.S. national interests.

The readings in this debate address the power of what John Mearsheimer and Stephen Walt call the "Israel lobby." They argue that the group has a powerful influence on U.S. foreign policy toward the Middle East and that the lobby has pushed American policy in a direction that is not in the U.S. national interest. Alan Dershowitz responds that the supposed Israel lobby is not the Goliath that Mearsheimer and Walt portray it to be nor is the lobby a corrosive influence on U.S. policy.

Be aware that this is a very emotionally charged debate. The complexity of the argument, the emotions it evokes, and the questioning even the motives of Mearsheimer and Walt are the reason that these readings are longer than typical for this volume. Some charge that criticizing Israel and/or the supposed Israel lobby in the United States is rooted in anti-Semitism. Surely, it is important to be aware that anti-Semitism, just like racism and other forms of prejudice, can lead to negativity about Israel and its American supporters. But Israel is country that, like any other country, is capable of laudable and deplorable actions. Moreover, the Israel lobby, to the degree it exists, is an interest group like any other. As such it is not above criticism. Still, its existence is part of the American democratic political process and not an un-American activity any more than are the American Latvian Association or the TransAfrica Forum.

POINTS TO PONDER

➢ Carefully consider whether you agree with Dershowitz's charge that Mearsheimer and Walt misuse evidence to make their point.

➢ Think about whether it is possible to simultaneously be a loyal American concerned foremost with the interest of the United States and its people and also to have a strong attachment to a foreign country or cause. What if what is good for one is not good for the other?

➢ Arguing that ethnic lobby groups sometimes advocate policies contrary to the national interest assumes that an objective national interest exists. Is that so, or is the national interest only a matter of opinion?

➢ There are foreign policy lobby groups based on economic interests, ideological views, gender, and many other bases, as well as ethnicity. Are your views on the legitimacy of foreign policy lobbying the same for all these groups? If you differentiate, why?

The Pro-Israel Lobby in the United States: Goliath

JOHN MEARSHEIMER AND STEPHEN WALT

For the past several decades, and especially since the Six-Day War [between Israel and several neighboring Arab countries] in 1967, the centerpiece of U.S. Middle Eastern policy has been its relationship with Israel. The combination of unwavering support for Israel and the related effort to spread "democracy" throughout the region has inflamed Arab and Islamic opinion and jeopardized not only U.S. security but that of much of the rest of the world. This situation has no equal in American political history. Why has the U.S. been willing to set aside its own security and that of many of its allies in order to advance the interests of another state? One might assume that the bond between the two countries was based on shared strategic interests or compelling moral imperatives, but neither explanation can account for the remarkable level of material and diplomatic support that the U.S. provides.

Instead, the thrust of U.S. policy in the region derives almost entirely from domestic politics, and especially the activities of the "Israel Lobby." Other special-interest groups have managed to skew foreign policy, but no lobby has managed to divert it as far from what the national interest would suggest, while simultaneously convincing Americans that U.S. interests and those of the other country—in this case, Israel—are essentially identical.

Since the October War in 1973 [Egypt and Syria vs. Israel], Washington has provided Israel with a level of support dwarfing that given to any other state. It has been the largest annual recipient of direct economic and military assistance since 1976, and is the largest recipient in total since World War Two, to the tune of well over $140 billion (in 2004 dollars). Israel receives about $3 billion in direct assistance each year, roughly one-fifth of the foreign aid budget, and worth about $500 a year for every Israeli. This largesse is especially striking since Israel is now a wealthy industrial state with a per capita income roughly equal to that of South Korea or Spain.

Other recipients get their money in quarterly installments, but Israel receives its entire appropriation at the beginning of each fiscal year and can thus earn interest on it. Most recipients of aid given for military purposes are required to spend all of it in the U.S., but Israel is allowed to use roughly 25 per cent of its allocation to subsidize its own defense industry. It is the only recipient that does not have to account for how the aid is spent, which makes it virtually impossible to prevent the money from being used for purposes the U.S. opposes, such as building settlements on the West Bank. Moreover, the U.S. has provided Israel with nearly $3 billion to develop weapons systems, and given it access to such top-drawer weaponry as Blackhawk helicopters and F-16 jets. Finally, the U.S. gives Israel access to intelligence it denies to its NATO allies and has turned a blind eye to Israel's acquisition of nuclear weapons.

Washington also provides Israel with consistent diplomatic support. Since 1982, the U.S. has vetoed 32 Security Council resolutions critical of Israel, more than the total number of vetoes cast by all the other Security Council members. It blocks the

Mearsheimer, John. "The Israel Lobby," *London Review of Books*, March 23, 2006. www.lrb.co.uk. Reprinted by permission.

efforts of Arab states to put Israel's nuclear arsenal on the IAEA's [International Atomic Energy Agency] agenda. The U.S. comes to the rescue in wartime and takes Israel's side when negotiating peace. The Nixon administration protected it from the threat of Soviet intervention and resupplied it during the October War. Washington was deeply involved in the negotiations that ended that war, as well as in the lengthy "step-by-step" process that followed, just as it played a key role in the negotiations that preceded and followed the 1993 Oslo Accords. In each case there was occasional friction between U.S. and Israeli officials, but the U.S. consistently supported the Israeli position. One American participant at Camp David in 2000 later said,. "Far too often, we functioned...as Israel's lawyer." Finally, the Bush administration's ambition to transform the Middle East is at least partly aimed at improving Israel's strategic situation.

This extraordinary generosity might be understandable if Israel were a vital strategic asset or if there were a compelling moral case for U.S. backing. But neither explanation is convincing. One might argue that Israel was an asset during the Cold War. By serving as America's proxy after 1967, it helped contain Soviet expansion in the region and inflicted humiliating defeats on Soviet clients like Egypt and Syria. It occasionally helped protect other U.S. allies (like King Hussein of Jordan) and its military prowess forced Moscow to spend more on backing its own client states. It also provided useful intelligence about Soviet capabilities.

Backing Israel was not cheap, however, and it complicated America's relations with the Arab world. For example, the decision to give $2.2 billion in emergency military aid during the October War triggered an OPEC [Organization of Petroleum Exporting Countries] oil embargo that inflicted considerable damage on Western economies. For all that, Israel's armed forces were not in a position to protect U.S. interests in the region. The U.S. could not, for example, rely on Israel when the Iranian Revolution in 1979 raised concerns about the security of oil supplies, and had to create its own Rapid Deployment Force instead.

The first Gulf War [1991] revealed the extent to which Israel was becoming a strategic burden. The U.S. could not use Israeli bases without rupturing the anti-Iraq coalition, and had to divert resources (e.g. Patriot [anti-missile] missile batteries) to prevent Tel Aviv doing anything that might harm the alliance against Saddam Hussein. History repeated itself in 2003: although Israel was eager for the U.S. to attack Iraq, Bush could not ask it to help without triggering Arab opposition. So Israel stayed on the sidelines once again.

Beginning in the 1990s, and even more after 9/11, U.S. support has been justified by the claim that both states are threatened by terrorist groups originating in the Arab and Muslim world, and by "rogue states" that back these groups and seek weapons of mass destruction. This is taken to mean not only that Washington should give Israel a free hand in dealing with the Palestinians and not press it to make concessions until all Palestinian terrorists are imprisoned or dead, but that the U.S. should go after countries like Iran and Syria. Israel is thus seen as a crucial ally in the war on terror, because its enemies are America's enemies. In fact, Israel is a liability in the war on terror and the broader effort to deal with rogue states.

"Terrorism" is not a single adversary, but a tactic employed by a wide array of political groups. The terrorist organizations that threaten Israel do not threaten the United States, except when it intervenes against them (as in Lebanon in 1982). Moreover, Palestinian terrorism is not random violence directed against Israel or "the West"; it is largely a response to Israel's prolonged campaign to colonize the West Bank and Gaza Strip.

More important, saying that Israel and the U.S. are united by a shared terrorist threat has the causal relationship backwards: the U.S. has a terrorism problem in good part because it is so closely allied with Israel, not the other way around. Support for Israel is not the only source of anti-American terrorism, but it is an important one, and it makes winning the war on terror more difficult. There is no question that many al-Qaida leaders, including Osama bin Laden, are motivated by Israel's presence in Jerusalem and the plight of the Palestinians. Unconditional support for Israel makes it easier for extremists to rally popular support and to attract recruits.

As for so-called rogue states in the Middle East, they are not a dire threat to vital U.S. interests, except inasmuch as they are a threat to Israel. Even if these states acquire nuclear weapons—which is obviously undesirable—neither America nor Israel could be blackmailed, because the blackmailer could not carry out the threat without suffering overwhelming retaliation. The danger of a nuclear handover to terrorists is equally remote, because a rogue state could not be sure the transfer would go undetected or that it would not be blamed and punished afterwards. The relationship with Israel actually makes it harder for the U.S. to deal with these states. Israel's nuclear arsenal is one reason some of its neighbors want nuclear weapons, and threatening them with regime change merely increases that desire.

A final reason to question Israel's strategic value is that it does not behave like a loyal ally. Israeli officials frequently ignore U.S. requests and renege on promises (including pledges to stop building settlements and to refrain from "targeted assassinations" of Palestinian leaders). Israel has provided sensitive military technology to potential rivals like China, in what the State Department inspector-general called "a systematic and growing pattern of unauthorized transfers." According to the General Accounting Office, Israel also "conducts the most aggressive espionage operations against the U.S. of any ally." In addition to the case of Jonathan Pollard, an American naval intelligence analyst] who gave Israel large quantities of classified material in the early 1980s (which it reportedly passed on to the Soviet Union in return for more exit visas for Soviet Jews), a new controversy erupted in 2004 when it was revealed that a key Pentagon official called Larry Franklin had passed classified information to an Israeli diplomat. Israel is hardly the only country that spies on the U.S., but its willingness to spy on its principal patron casts further doubt on its strategic value.

Israel's strategic value isn't the only issue. Its backers also argue that it deserves unqualified support because it is weak and surrounded by enemies; it is a democracy; the Jewish people have suffered from past crimes and therefore deserve special treatment; and Israel's conduct has been morally superior to that of its adversaries. On close inspection, none of these arguments is persuasive. There is a strong moral case for supporting Israel's existence, but that is not in jeopardy. Viewed objectively, its past and present conduct offers no moral basis for privileging it over the Palestinians.

Israel is often portrayed as David confronted by Goliath, but the converse is closer to the truth. Contrary to popular belief, the Zionists had larger, better equipped and better led forces during the 1947–49 War of Independence, and the Israel Defense Forces [IDF] won quick and easy victories against Egypt in 1956 and against Egypt, Jordan and Syria in

1967—all of this before large-scale U.S. aid began flowing. Today, Israel is the strongest military power in the Middle East. Its conventional forces are far superior to those of its neighbors and it is the only state in the region with nuclear weapons. Egypt and Jordan have signed peace treaties with it, and Saudi Arabia has offered to do so. Syria has lost its Soviet patron, Iraq has been devastated by three disastrous wars and Iran is hundreds of miles away. The Palestinians barely have an effective police force, let alone an army that could pose a threat to Israel. According to a 2005 assessment by Tel Aviv University's Jaffee Centre for Strategic Studies, "the strategic balance decidedly favors Israel, which has continued to widen the qualitative gap between its own military capability and deterrence powers and those of its neighbors." If backing the underdog were a compelling motive, the United States would be supporting Israel's opponents.

That Israel is a fellow democracy surrounded by hostile dictatorships cannot account for the current level of aid: there are many democracies around the world, but none receives the same lavish support. The U.S. has overthrown democratic governments in the past and supported dictators when this was thought to advance its interests—it has good relations with a number of dictatorships today.

Some aspects of Israeli democracy are at odds with core American values. Unlike the U.S., where people are supposed to enjoy equal rights irrespective of race, religion or ethnicity, Israel was explicitly founded as a Jewish state and citizenship is based on the principle of blood kinship. Given this, it is not surprising that its 1.3 million Arabs are treated as second-class citizens, or that a recent Israeli government commission found that Israel behaves in a "neglectful and discriminatory" manner towards them. Its democratic status is also undermined by its refusal to grant the Palestinians a viable state of their own or full political rights.

A third justification is the history of Jewish suffering in the Christian West, especially during the Holocaust. Because Jews were persecuted for centuries and could feel safe only in a Jewish homeland, many people now believe that Israel deserves special treatment from the United States. The country's creation was undoubtedly an appropriate response to the long record of crimes against Jews, but it also brought about fresh crimes against a largely innocent third party, the Palestinians.

This was well understood by Israel's early leaders. David Ben-Gurion [Israel's first prime minister] told Nahum Goldmann, the president of the World Jewish Congress:

> If I were an Arab leader I would never make terms with Israel. That is natural: we have taken their country...We come from Israel, but two thousand years ago, and what is that to them? There has been anti-Semitism, the Nazis, Hitler, Auschwitz, but was that their fault? They only see one thing: we have come here and stolen their country. Why should they accept that?

Since then, Israeli leaders have repeatedly sought to deny the Palestinians' national ambitions. When she was prime minister [1969–1974], Golda Meir famously remarked that "there is no such thing as a Palestinian." Pressure from extremist violence and Palestinian population growth has forced subsequent Israeli leaders to disengage from the Gaza Strip and consider other territorial compromises, but not even [Prime Minister] Yitzhak Rabin [1974–1977, 1992–1995] was willing to offer the Palestinians a viable state.

[Prime Minister] Ehud Barak's [1999–2001] purportedly generous offer at Camp David would have given them only a disarmed set of Bantustans [a reference to one of the segregated, theoretically autonomous, areas that white South Africans once forced many of the country's blacks (who speak Bantu and other languages) blacks to live in] ethnic enclaves controlled by a country surrounding them] under de facto Israeli control. The tragic history of the Jewish people does not obligate the U.S. to help Israel today no matter what it does.

Israel's backers also portray it as a country that has sought peace at every turn and shown great restraint even when provoked. The Arabs, by contrast, are said to have acted with great wickedness. Yet on the ground, Israel's record is not distinguishable from that of its opponents. Ben-Gurion acknowledged that the early Zionists were far from benevolent towards the Palestinian Arabs, who resisted their encroachments—which is hardly surprising, given that the Zionists were trying to create their own state on Arab land. In the same way, the creation of Israel in 1947–48 involved acts of ethnic cleansing, including executions, massacres and rapes by Jews, and Israel's subsequent conduct has often been brutal, belying any claim to moral superiority. Between 1949 and 1956, for example, Israeli security forces killed between 2700 and 5000 Arab infiltrators, the overwhelming majority of them unarmed. The IDF murdered hundreds of Egyptian prisoners of war in both the 1956 and 1967 wars, while in 1967, it expelled between 100,000 and 260,000 Palestinians from the newly conquered West Bank, and drove 80,000 Syrians from the Golan Heights.

During the first intifada [a Palestinian uprising beginning in 1987], the IDF distributed truncheons to its troops and encouraged them to break the bones of Palestinian protesters. The Swedish branch of Save the Children estimated that "23,600 to 29,900 children required medical treatment for their beating injuries in the first two years of the intifada." Nearly a third of them were aged ten or under. The response to the second intifada has been even more violent, leading *Ha'aretz* to declare that "the IDF…is turning into a killing machine whose efficiency is awe-inspiring, yet shocking." The IDF fired one million bullets in the first days of the uprising. Since then, for every Israeli lost, Israel has killed 3.4 Palestinians, the majority of whom have been innocent bystanders; the ratio of Palestinian to Israeli children killed is even higher (5.7:1). It is also worth bearing in mind that the Zionists relied on terrorist bombs to drive the British from Palestine, and that Yitzhak Shamir, once a terrorist and later prime minister, declared that "neither Jewish ethics nor Jewish tradition can disqualify terrorism as a means of combat."

The Palestinian resort to terrorism is wrong but it isn't surprising. The Palestinians believe they have no other way to force Israeli concessions. As Ehud Barak once admitted, had he been born a Palestinian, he "would have joined a terrorist organization."

So if neither strategic nor moral arguments can account for America's support for Israel, how are we to explain it?

The explanation is the unmatched power of the Israel Lobby. We use "the Lobby" as shorthand for the loose coalition of individuals and organizations who actively work to steer U.S. foreign policy in a pro-Israel direction. This is not meant to suggest that "the Lobby" is a unified movement with a central leadership, or that individuals within it do not disagree on certain issues. Not all Jewish Americans are part of the Lobby, because Israel is not a salient issue for many of them. In a 2004 survey, for example, roughly 36 per cent of American Jews said they were either "not very" or "not at all" emotionally attached to Israel.

Jewish Americans also differ on specific Israeli policies. Many of the key organizations in the Lobby, such as the American-Israel Public Affairs Committee (AIPAC) and the Conference of Presidents of Major Jewish Organizations, are run by hardliners who generally support the [conservative] Likud Party's expansionist policies, including its hostility to the Oslo peace process. The bulk of U.S. Jewry, meanwhile, is more inclined to make concessions to the Palestinians, and a few groups—such as Jewish Voice for Peace—strongly advocate such steps. Despite these differences, moderates and hardliners both favor giving steadfast support to Israel.

Not surprisingly, American Jewish leaders often consult Israeli officials, to make sure that their actions advance Israeli goals. As one activist from a major Jewish organization wrote, "it is routine for us to say, "This is our policy on a certain issue, but we must check what the Israelis think. We as a community do it all the time." There is a strong prejudice against criticizing Israeli policy, and putting pressure on Israel is considered out of order. Edgar Bronfman Sr, the president of the World Jewish Congress, was accused of "perfidy" when he wrote a letter to President Bush in mid-2003 urging him to persuade Israel to curb construction of its controversial "security fence" [between Israel and the West Bank]. His critics said that "it would be obscene at any time for the president of the World Jewish Congress to lobby the president of the United States to resist policies being promoted by the government of Israel."

Similarly, when the president of the Israel Policy Forum, Seymour Reich, advised [U.S. Secretary of State] Condoleezza Rice in November 2005 to ask Israel to reopen a critical border crossing in the Gaza Strip, his action was denounced as "irresponsible." "There is," his critics said, "absolutely no room in the Jewish mainstream for actively canvassing against the security-related policies…of Israel." Recoiling from these attacks, Reich announced that the word "pressure" is not in my vocabulary when it comes to Israel."

Jewish Americans have set up an impressive array of organizations to influence American foreign policy, of which AIPAC is the most powerful and best known. In 1997, *Fortune* magazine asked members of Congress and their staffs to list the most powerful lobbies in Washington. AIPAC was ranked second behind the American Association of Retired People, but ahead of the AFL-CIO and the National Rifle Association. A *National Journal* study in March 2005 reached a similar conclusion, placing AIPAC in second place (tied with AARP) in the Washington "muscle rankings."

The Lobby also includes prominent Christian evangelicals like Gary Bauer, Jerry Falwell, Ralph Reed and Pat Robertson, as well as Dick Armey [R-TX] and Tom DeLay [R-TX], former majority leaders in the House of Representatives, all of whom believe Israel's rebirth is the fulfillment of biblical prophecy and support its expansionist agenda; to do otherwise, they believe, would be contrary to God's will. Neo-conservative gentiles such as John Bolton; Robert Bartley, the former *Wall Street Journal* editor; William Bennett, the former secretary of education; Jeane Kirkpatrick, the former UN ambassador; and the influential columnist George Will are also steadfast supporters.

The U.S. form of government offers activists many ways of influencing the policy process. Interest groups can lobby elected representatives and members of the executive branch, make campaign contributions, vote in elections, try to mould public opinion etc. They enjoy a disproportionate amount of influence when they are committed to an issue to which the bulk of the population is indifferent. Policymakers will tend to accommodate those who care about the issue, even if their numbers are small, confident that the rest of the population will not penalize them for doing so.

In its basic operations, the Israel Lobby is no different from the farm lobby, steel or textile workers' unions, or other ethnic lobbies. There is nothing improper about American Jews and their Christian allies attempting to sway U.S. policy: the Lobby's activities are not a conspiracy of the sort depicted in tracts like the *Protocols of the Elders of Zion*. For the most part, the individuals and groups that comprise it are only doing what other special interest groups do, but doing it very much better. By contrast, pro-Arab interest groups, in so far as they exist at all, are weak, which makes the Israel Lobby's task even easier.

The Lobby pursues two broad strategies. First, it wields its significant influence in Washington, pressuring both Congress and the executive branch. Whatever an individual lawmaker or policymaker's own views may be, the Lobby tries to make supporting Israel the "smart" choice. Second, it strives to ensure that public discourse portrays Israel in a positive light, by repeating myths about its founding and by promoting its point of view in policy debates. The goal is to prevent critical comments from getting a fair hearing in the political arena. Controlling the debate is essential to guaranteeing U.S. support, because a candid discussion of U.S.-Israeli relations might lead Americans to favor a different policy.

A key pillar of the Lobby's effectiveness is its influence in Congress, where Israel is virtually immune from criticism. This in itself is remarkable, because Congress rarely shies away from contentious issues. Where Israel is concerned, however, potential critics fall silent. One reason is that some key members are Christian Zionists like Dick Armey, who said in September 2002, "

My No. 1 priority in foreign policy is to protect Israel." One might think that the No. 1 priority for any congressman would be to protect America. There are also Jewish senators and congressmen who work to ensure that U.S. foreign policy supports Israel's interests.

Another source of the Lobby's power is its use of pro-Israel congressional staffers. As Morris Amitay, a former head of AIPAC, once admitted, "there are a lot of guys at the working level up here"—on Capitol Hill—"who happen to be Jewish, who are willing...to look at certain issues in terms of their Jewishness...These are all guys who are in a position to make the decision in these areas for those senators...You can get an awful lot done just at the staff level."

AIPAC itself, however, forms the core of the Lobby's influence in Congress. Its success is due to its ability to reward legislators and congressional candidates who support its agenda, and to punish those who challenge it. Money is critical to U.S. elections (as the scandal over the lobbyist Jack Abramoff's shady dealings reminds us), and AIPAC makes sure that its friends get strong financial support from the many pro-Israel political action committees. Anyone who is seen as hostile to Israel can be sure that AIPAC will direct campaign contributions to his or her political opponents. AIPAC also organizes letter-writing campaigns and encourages newspaper editors to endorse pro-Israel candidates.

There is no doubt about the efficacy of these tactics. Here is one example: in the

1984 elections, AIPAC helped defeat Senator Charles Percy from Illinois, who, according to a prominent Lobby figure, had "displayed insensitivity and even hostility to our concerns." Thomas Dine, the head of AIPAC at the time, explained what happened: "All the Jews in America, from coast to coast, gathered to oust Percy. And the American politicians—those who hold public positions now, and those who aspire—got the message."

AIPAC's influence on Capitol Hill goes even further. According to Douglas Bloomfield, a former AIPAC staff member, "it is common for members of Congress and their staffs to turn to AIPAC first when they need information, before calling the Library of Congress, the Congressional Research Service, committee staff or administration experts." More important, he notes that AIPAC is "often called on to draft speeches, work on legislation, advise on tactics, perform research, collect co-sponsors and marshal votes."

The bottom line is that AIPAC, a de facto agent for a foreign government, has a stranglehold on Congress, with the result that U.S. policy towards Israel is not debated there, even though that policy has important consequences for the entire world. In other words, one of the three main branches of the government is firmly committed to supporting Israel. As one former Democratic senator, Ernest Hollings, noted on leaving office, "you can't have an Israeli policy other than what AIPAC gives you around here." Or as [Israeli Prime Minister] Ariel Sharon [2001–2006] once told an American audience, "when people ask me how they can help Israel, I tell them: "Help AIPAC."

Thanks in part to the influence Jewish voters have on presidential elections, the Lobby also has significant leverage over the executive branch. Although they make up fewer than 3 per cent of the population, they make large campaign donations to candidates from both parties. The *Washington Post* once estimated that Democratic presidential candidates "depend on Jewish supporters to supply as much as 60 per cent of the money." And because Jewish voters have high turn-out rates and are concentrated in key states like California, Florida, Illinois, New York and Pennsylvania, presidential candidates go to great lengths not to antagonize them.

Key organizations in the Lobby make it their business to ensure that critics of Israel do not get important foreign policy jobs. Jimmy Carter wanted to make George Ball his first secretary of state, but knew that Ball was seen as critical of Israel and that the Lobby would oppose the appointment. In this way any aspiring policymaker is encouraged to become an overt supporter of Israel, which is why public critics of Israeli policy have become an endangered species in the foreign policy establishment.

When Howard Dean [former governor of Vermont who sought the Democratic presidential nomination in 2004] called for the United States to take a more "even-handed role" in the Arab-Israeli conflict, Senator Joseph Lieberman [D-CT] accused him of selling Israel down the river and said his statement was "irresponsible." Virtually all the top Democrats in the House signed a letter criticizing Dean's remarks, and the *Chicago Jewish Star* reported that "anonymous attackers…are clogging the email inboxes of Jewish leaders around the country, warning—without much evidence—that Dean would somehow be bad for Israel."

This worry was absurd; Dean is in fact quite hawkish on Israel: his campaign co-chair was a former AIPAC president, and Dean said his own views on the Middle East more closely reflected those of AIPAC than those of the more moderate

Americans for Peace Now. He had merely suggested that to "bring the sides together," Washington should act as an honest broker. This is hardly a radical idea, but the Lobby doesn't tolerate even-handedness.

During the Clinton administration, Middle Eastern policy was largely shaped by officials with close ties to Israel or to prominent pro-Israel organizations; among them, Martin Indyk, the former deputy director of research at AIPAC and co-founder of the pro-Israel Washington Institute for Near East Policy (WINEP); Dennis Ross, who joined WINEP after leaving government in 2001; and Aaron Miller, who has lived in Israel and often visits the country. These men were among Clinton's closest advisers at the Camp David summit in July 2000. Although all three supported the Oslo peace process and favored the creation of a Palestinian state, they did so only within the limits of what would be acceptable to Israel. The American delegation took its cues from Ehud Barak, coordinated its negotiating positions with Israel in advance, and did not offer independent proposals. Not surprisingly, Palestinian negotiators complained that they were "negotiating with two Israeli teams—one displaying an Israeli flag, and one an American flag."

The situation is even more pronounced in the Bush administration, whose ranks have included such fervent advocates of the Israeli cause as Elliot Abrams, John Bolton, Douglas Feith, I. Lewis ("Scooter") Libby, Richard Perle, Paul Wolfowitz and David Wurmser. As we shall see, these officials have consistently pushed for policies favoured by Israel and backed by organizations in the Lobby.

The Lobby doesn't want an open debate, of course, because that might lead Americans to question the level of support they provide. Accordingly, pro-Israel organizations work hard to influence the institutions that do most to shape popular opinion.

The Lobby's perspective prevails in the mainstream media: the debate among Middle East pundits, the journalist Eric Alterman writes, is "dominated by people who cannot imagine criticising Israel." He lists 61 "columnists and commentators who can be counted on to support Israel reflexively and without qualification." Conversely, he found just five pundits who consistently criticize Israeli actions or endorse Arab positions. Newspapers occasionally publish guest op-eds challenging Israeli policy, but the balance of opinion clearly favors the other side. It is hard to imagine any mainstream media outlet in the United States publishing a piece like this one.

"Shamir, Sharon, Bibi [Israeli Prime Minister Benjamin Netanyahu, 1996–1999),—whatever those guys want is pretty much fine by me," Robert Bartley once remarked. Not surprisingly, his newspaper, the *Wall Street Journal*, along with other prominent papers like the *Chicago Sun-Times* and the *Washington Times*, regularly runs editorials that strongly support Israel. Magazines like *Commentary*, the *New Republic* and the *Weekly Standard* defend Israel at every turn.

Editorial bias is also found in papers like the *New York Times*, which occasionally criticizes Israeli policies and sometimes concedes that the Palestinians have legitimate grievances, but is not even-handed. In his memoirs the paper's former executive editor Max Frankel acknowledges the impact his own attitude had on his editorial decisions: "I was much more deeply devoted to Israel than I dared to assert…Fortified by my knowledge of Israel and my friendships there, I myself wrote most of our Middle East commentaries. As more Arab than Jewish readers recognized, I wrote them from a pro-Israel perspective."

News reports are more even-handed, in part because reporters strive to be objective, but also because it is difficult to cover events in the Occupied Territories without acknowledging Israel's actions on the ground. To discourage unfavorable reporting, the Lobby organizes letter-writing campaigns, demonstrations and boycotts of news outlets whose content it considers anti-Israel. One CNN executive has said that he sometimes gets 6000 email messages in a single day complaining about a story. In May 2003, the pro-Israel Committee for Accurate Middle East Reporting in America (CAMERA) organized demonstrations outside National Public Radio stations in 33 cities; it also tried to persuade contributors to withhold support from NPR until its Middle East coverage becomes more sympathetic to Israel. Boston's NPR station, WBUR, reportedly lost more than $1 million in contributions as a result of these efforts. Further pressure on NPR has come from Israel's friends in Congress, who have asked for an internal audit of its Middle East coverage as well as more oversight.

The Israeli side also dominates the think tanks which play an important role in shaping public debate as well as actual policy. The Lobby created its own think tank in 1985, when Martin Indyk helped to found WINEP. Although WINEP plays down its links to Israel, claiming instead to provide a "balanced and realistic" perspective on Middle East issues, it is funded and run by individuals deeply committed to advancing Israel's agenda.

The Lobby's influence extends well beyond WINEP, however. Over the past 25 years, pro-Israel forces have established a commanding presence at the American Enterprise Institute, the Brookings Institution, the Center for Security Policy, the Foreign Policy Research Institute, the Heritage Foundation, the Hudson Institute, the Institute for Foreign Policy Analysis and the Jewish Institute for National Security Affairs (JINSA). These think tanks employ few, if any, critics of U.S. support for Israel.

Take the Brookings Institution. For many years, its senior expert on the Middle East was William Quandt, a former NSC official with a well-deserved reputation for even-handedness. Today, Brookings's coverage is conducted through the Saban Center for Middle East Studies, which is financed by Haim Saban, an Israeli-American businessman and ardent Zionist. The center's director is the ubiquitous Martin Indyk. What was once a non-partisan policy institute is now part of the pro-Israel chorus.

Where the Lobby has had the most difficulty is in stifling debate on university campuses. In the 1990s, when the Oslo peace process was underway, there was only mild criticism of Israel, but it grew stronger with Oslo's collapse and Sharon's access to power, becoming quite vociferous when the IDF reoccupied the West Bank in spring 2002 and employed massive force to subdue the second intifada.

The Lobby moved immediately to "take back the campuses." New groups sprang up, like the Caravan for Democracy, which brought Israeli speakers to U.S. colleges. Established groups like the Jewish Council for Public Affairs and Hillel joined in, and a new group, the Israel on Campus Coalition, was formed to co-ordinate the many bodies that now sought to put Israel's case. Finally, AIPAC more than tripled its spending on programs to monitor university activities and to train young advocates, in order to "vastly expand the number of students involved on campus...in the national pro-Israel effort."

The Lobby also monitors what professors write and teach. In September 2002, Martin Kramer and Daniel Pipes, two passionately pro-Israel neo-conservatives, established a website (Campus Watch) that posted dossiers on suspect academics and encouraged students to report remarks or behavior that might be considered hostile to Israel. This transparent attempt to blacklist and intimidate scholars provoked a harsh reaction and Pipes and Kramer later removed the dossiers, but the website still invites students to report "anti-Israel" activity.

Groups within the Lobby put pressure on particular academics and universities. Columbia has been a frequent target, no doubt because of the presence of the late Edward Said on its faculty. "One can be sure that any public statement in support of the Palestinian people by the pre-eminent literary critic Edward Said will elicit hundreds of emails, letters and journalistic accounts that call on us to denounce Said and to either sanction or fire him," Jonathan Cole, its former provost, reported. When Columbia recruited the historian Rashid Khalidi from Chicago, the same thing happened. It was a problem Princeton also faced a few years later when it considered wooing Khalidi away from Columbia.

A classic illustration of the effort to police academia occurred towards the end of 2004, when the David Project produced a film alleging that faculty members of Columbia's Middle East Studies program were anti-Semitic and were intimidating Jewish students who stood up for Israel. Columbia was hauled over the coals, but a faculty committee which was assigned to investigate the charges found no evidence of anti-Semitism and the only incident possibly worth noting was that one professor had "responded heatedly" to a student's question. The committee also discovered that the academics in question had themselves been the target of an overt campaign of intimidation.

Perhaps the most disturbing aspect of all this is the efforts Jewish groups have made to push Congress into establishing mechanisms to monitor what professors say. If they manage to get this passed, universities judged to have an anti-Israel bias would be denied federal funding. Their efforts have not yet succeeded, but they are an indication of the importance placed on controlling debate.

A number of Jewish philanthropists have recently established Israel Studies programs (in addition to the roughly 130 Jewish Studies programs already in existence) so as to increase the number of Israel-friendly scholars on campus. In May 2003, NYU announced the establishment of the Taub Center for Israel Studies; similar programs have been set up at Berkeley, Brandeis and Emory. Academic administrators emphasize their pedagogical value, but the truth is that they are intended in large part to promote Israel's image. Fred Laffer, the head of the Taub Foundation, makes it clear that his foundation funded the NYU centre to help counter the "Arabic [*sic*] point of view" that he thinks is prevalent in NYU's Middle East programs.

No discussion of the Lobby would be complete without an examination of one of its most powerful weapons: the charge of anti-Semitism. Anyone who criticizes Israel's actions or argues that pro-Israel groups have significant influence over U.S. Middle Eastern policy—an influence AIPAC celebrates—stands a good chance of being labeled an anti-Semite. Indeed, anyone who merely claims that there *is* an Israel Lobby runs the risk of being charged with anti-Semitism, even though the Israeli media refer to America's "Jewish Lobby." In other words, the Lobby first boasts of its influence and then attacks anyone who calls attention to it. It's a very effective tactic: anti-Semitism is something no one wants to be accused of.

Europeans have been more willing than Americans to criticize Israeli policy, which some people attribute to a resurgence of anti-Semitism in Europe. We are "getting to a point," the U.S. ambassador to the EU said in early 2004, "where it is as bad as it was in the 1930s." Measuring anti-Semitism is a complicated matter, but the weight of evidence points in the opposite direction. In the spring of 2004, when accusations of European anti-Semitism filled the air in America, separate surveys of European public opinion conducted by the U.S.-based Anti-Defamation League and the Pew Research Center for the People and the Press found that it was in fact declining. In the 1930s, by contrast, anti-Semitism was not only widespread among Europeans of all classes but considered quite acceptable.

The Lobby and its friends often portray France as the most anti-Semitic country in Europe. But in 2003, the head of the French Jewish community said that "France is not more anti-Semitic than America." According to a recent article in *Ha'aretz*, the French police have reported that anti-Semitic incidents declined by almost 50 per cent in 2005; and this even though France has the largest Muslim population of any European country. Finally, when a French Jew was murdered in Paris last month by a Muslim gang, tens of thousands of demonstrators poured into the streets to condemn anti-Semitism. [President] Jacques Chirac and [Premier] Dominique de Villepin both attended the victim's memorial service to show their solidarity.

No one would deny that there is anti-Semitism among European Muslims, some of it provoked by Israel's conduct towards the Palestinians and some of it straightforwardly racist. But this is a separate matter with little bearing on whether or not Europe today is like Europe in the 1930s. Nor would anyone deny that there are still some virulent autochthonous anti-Semites in Europe (as there are in the United States) but their numbers are small and their views are rejected by the vast majority of Europeans.

Israel's advocates, when pressed to go beyond mere assertion, claim that there is a "new anti-Semitism," which they equate with criticism of Israel. In other words, criticize Israeli policy and you are by definition an anti-Semite. When the synod of the Church of England recently voted to divest from Caterpillar Inc on the grounds that it manufactures the bulldozers used by the Israelis to demolish Palestinian homes, the Chief Rabbi complained that this would "have the most adverse repercussions on...Jewish-Christian relations in Britain," while Rabbi Tony Bayfield, the head of the Reform movement, said, "There is a clear problem of anti-Zionist—verging on anti-Semitic—attitudes emerging in the grass-roots, and even in the middle ranks of the Church." But the Church was guilty merely of protesting against Israeli government policy.

Critics are also accused of holding Israel to an unfair standard or questioning its right to exist. But these are bogus charges too. Western critics of Israel hardly ever question its right to exist: they question its behavior towards the Palestinians, as do Israelis themselves. Nor is Israel being judged unfairly. Israeli treatment of the Palestinians elicits criticism because it is contrary to widely accepted notions of human rights, to international law and to the principle of national self-determination. And it is hardly the only state that has faced sharp criticism on these grounds.

In the autumn of 2001, and especially in the spring of 2002, the Bush administration tried to reduce anti-American sentiment in the Arab world and undermine support for terrorist groups like al-Qaida by halting Israel's expansionist policies in the Occupied Territories and advocating the creation of a Palestinian state. Bush had very significant means of persuasion at his disposal. He could have threatened to reduce economic and diplomatic support for Israel, and the American people would almost certainly have supported him. A May 2003 poll reported that more than 60 per cent of Americans were willing to withhold aid if Israel resisted U.S. pressure to settle the conflict, and that number rose to 70 per cent among the "politically active." Indeed, 73 per cent said that the United States should not favor either side.

Yet the administration failed to change Israeli policy, and Washington ended up backing it. Over time, the administration also adopted Israel's own justifications of its position, so that U.S. rhetoric began to mimic Israeli rhetoric. By February 2003, a *Washington Post* headline summarized the situation: "Bush and Sharon Nearly Identical on Mideast Policy." The main reason for this switch was the Lobby.

The story begins in late September 2001, when Bush began urging Sharon to show restraint in the Occupied Territories. He also pressed him to allow Israel's foreign minister, Shimon Peres, to meet with Yasser Arafat, even though he (Bush) was highly critical of Arafat's leadership. Bush even said publicly that he supported the creation of a Palestinian state. Alarmed, Sharon accused him of trying "to appease the Arabs at our expense," warning that Israel "will not be Czechoslovakia."

Bush was reportedly furious at being compared to Chamberlain, and the White House press secretary called Sharon's remarks "unacceptable." Sharon offered a pro forma apology, but quickly joined forces with the Lobby to persuade the administration and the American people that the United States and Israel faced a common threat from terrorism. Israeli officials and Lobby representatives insisted that there was no real difference between Arafat and Osama bin Laden: the United States and Israel, they said, should isolate the Palestinians' elected leader and have nothing to do with him.

The Lobby also went to work in Congress. On 16 November, 89 senators sent Bush a letter praising him for refusing to meet with Arafat, but also demanding that the U.S. not restrain Israel from retaliating against the Palestinians; the administration, they wrote, must state publicly that it stood behind Israel. According to the *New York Times*, the letter "stemmed" from a meeting two weeks before between "leaders of the American Jewish community and key senators," adding that AIPAC was "particularly active in providing advice on the letter."

By late November, relations between Tel Aviv and Washington had improved considerably. This was thanks in part to the Lobby's efforts, but also to America's initial victory in Afghanistan, which reduced the perceived need for Arab support in dealing with al-Qaida. Sharon visited the White House in early December and had a friendly meeting with Bush.

In April 2002 trouble erupted again, after the IDF launched Operation Defensive Shield and resumed control of virtually all the major Palestinian areas on the West Bank. Bush knew that Israel's actions would damage America's image in the Islamic world and undermine the war on terrorism, so he demanded that Sharon "halt the incursions and begin withdrawal." He underscored this message two days later, saying he wanted Israel to "withdraw without delay." On 7 April, Condoleezza Rice, then Bush's national security adviser, told reporters, "Without delay means without delay. It means now." That same day Colin Powell set out for the Middle East to persuade all sides to stop fighting and start negotiating.

Israel and the Lobby swung into action. Pro-Israel officials in the vice-president's office and the Pentagon, as well as neo-conservative pundits like Robert Kagan and William Kristol, put the heat on Powell. They even accused him of having "virtually obliterated the distinction between terrorists and those fighting terrorists." Bush himself was being pressed by Jewish leaders and Christian evangelicals. Tom DeLay and Dick Armey were especially outspoken about the need to support Israel, and DeLay and the Senate minority leader, Trent Lott, visited the White House and warned Bush to back off.

The first sign that Bush was caving in came on 11 April—a week after he told Sharon to withdraw his forces—when the White House press secretary said that the president believed Sharon was "a man of peace." Bush repeated this statement publicly on Powell's return from his abortive mission, and told reporters that Sharon had responded satisfactorily to his call for a full and immediate withdrawal. Sharon had done no such thing, but Bush was no longer willing to make an issue of it.

Meanwhile, Congress was also moving to back Sharon. On 2 May, it overrode the administration's objections and passed two resolutions reaffirming support for Israel. (The Senate vote was 94 to 2; the House of Representatives version passed 352 to 21.) Both resolutions held that the United States "stands in solidarity with Israel" and that the two countries were, to quote the House resolution, "now engaged in a common struggle against terrorism." The House version also condemned "the ongoing support and co-ordination of terror by Yasser Arafat," who was portrayed as a central part of the terrorism problem. Both resolutions were drawn up with the help of the Lobby. A few days later, a bipartisan congressional delegation on a fact-finding mission to Israel stated that Sharon should resist U.S. pressure to negotiate with Arafat. On 9 May, a House appropriations subcommittee met to consider giving Israel an extra $200 million to fight terrorism. Powell opposed the package, but the Lobby backed it and Powell lost.

In short, Sharon and the Lobby took on the president of the United States and triumphed. Hemi Shalev, a journalist on the Israeli newspaper *Ma'ariv*, reported that Sharon's aides "could not hide their satisfaction in view of Powell's failure. Sharon saw the whites of President Bush's eyes, they bragged, and the president blinked first." But it was Israel's champions in the United States, not Sharon or Israel, that played the key role in defeating Bush.

The situation has changed little since then. The Bush administration refused ever again to have dealings with Arafat. After his death, it embraced the new Palestinian leader, Mahmoud Abbas, but has done little to help him. Sharon continued to develop his plan to impose a unilateral settlement on the Palestinians, based on "disengagement" from Gaza coupled with continued expansion on the West Bank. By refusing to negotiate with Abbas and making it impossible for him to deliver tangible benefits to the Palestinian people, Sharon's strategy contributed directly to Hamas's electoral victory. With Hamas in power, however, Israel has another excuse not to negotiate. The U.S. administration has supported Sharon's actions (and those of his successor, Ehud Olmert). Bush has even endorsed unilateral Israeli annexations in the Occupied Territories, reversing the stated policy of every president since Lyndon Johnson.

U.S. officials have offered mild criticisms of a few Israeli actions, but have done little to help create a viable Palestinian state. Sharon has Bush "wrapped around his little finger," the former national security adviser Brent

Scowcroft said in October 2004. If Bush tries to distance the U.S. from Israel, or even criticizes Israeli actions in the Occupied Territories, he is certain to face the wrath of the Lobby and its supporters in Congress. Democratic presidential candidates understand that these are facts of life, which is the reason John Kerry went to great lengths to display unalloyed support for Israel in 2004, and why Hillary Clinton is doing the same thing today.

Maintaining U.S. support for Israel's policies against the Palestinians is essential as far as the Lobby is concerned, but its ambitions do not stop there. It also wants America to help Israel remain the dominant regional power. The Israeli government and pro-Israel groups in the United States have worked together to shape the administration's policy towards Iraq, Syria and Iran, as well as its grand scheme for reordering the Middle East.

Pressure from Israel and the Lobby was not the only factor behind the decision to attack Iraq in March 2003, but it was critical. Some Americans believe that this was a war for oil, but there is hardly any direct evidence to support this claim. Instead, the war was motivated in good part by a desire to make Israel more secure. According to Philip Zelikow, a former member of the president's Foreign Intelligence Advisory Board, the executive director of the 9/11 Commission, and now a counselor to Condoleezza Rice, the "real threat" from Iraq was not a threat to the United States. The "unstated threat" was the "threat against Israel," Zelikow told an audience at the University of Virginia in September 2002. "The American government," he added, "doesn't want to lean too hard on it rhetorically, because it is not a popular sell."

On 16 August 2002, 11 days before Dick Cheney kicked off the campaign for war with a hardline speech to the Veterans of Foreign Wars, the *Washington Post* reported that "Israel is urging U.S. officials not to delay a military strike against Iraq's Saddam Hussein." By this point, according to Sharon, strategic co-ordination between Israel and the U.S. had reached "unprecedented dimensions," and Israeli intelligence officials had given Washington a variety of alarming reports about Iraq's WMD programs. As one retired Israeli general later put it, "Israeli intelligence was a full partner to the picture presented by American and British intelligence regarding Iraq's non-conventional capabilities."

Israeli leaders were deeply distressed when Bush decided to seek Security Council authorisation for war, and even more worried when Saddam agreed to let UN inspectors back in. "The campaign against Saddam Hussein is a must," Shimon Peres told reporters in September 2002. "Inspections and inspectors are good for decent people, but dishonest people can overcome easily inspections and inspectors."

At the same time, Ehud Barak wrote a *New York Times* op-ed warning that "the greatest risk now lies in inaction." His predecessor as prime minister, Benjamin Netanyahu, published a similar piece in the *Wall Street Journal*, entitled, "The Case for Toppling Saddam." "Today nothing less than dismantling his regime will do," he declared. "I believe I speak for the overwhelming majority of Israelis in supporting a pre-emptive strike against Saddam's regime." Or as *Ha'aretz* reported in February 2003, "the military and political leadership yearns for war in Iraq."

As Netanyahu suggested, however, the desire for war was not confined to Israel's leaders. Apart from Kuwait, which Saddam invaded in 1990, Israel was the only country in the world where both politicians and public favored war. As the journalist Gideon Levy observed at the time, "Israel is the only country in the West whose leaders support the war unreservedly and where no alternative opinion is voiced." In fact, Israelis were so gung-ho that their allies in America told them to damp down their rhetoric, or it would look as if the war would be fought on Israel's behalf.

Within the U.S., the main driving force behind the war was a small band of neo-conservatives, many with ties to Likud. But leaders of the Lobby's major organizations lent their voices to the campaign. "As President Bush attempted to sell the...war in Iraq," the *Forward* reported, "America's most important Jewish organizations rallied as one to his defense. In statement after statement community leaders stressed the need to rid the world of Saddam Hussein and his weapons of mass destruction." The editorial goes on to say that "concern for Israel's safety rightfully factored into the deliberations of the main Jewish groups."

Although neo-conservatives and other Lobby leaders were eager to invade Iraq, the broader American Jewish community was not. Just after the war started, Samuel Freedman reported that "a compilation of nationwide opinion polls by the Pew Research Center shows that Jews are less supportive of the Iraq war than the population at large, 52 per cent to 62 per cent." Clearly, it would be wrong to blame the war in Iraq on "Jewish influence." Rather, it was due in large part to the Lobby's influence, especially that of the neo-conservatives within it.

The neo-conservatives had been determined to topple Saddam even before Bush became president. They caused a stir early in 1998 by publishing two open letters to Clinton, calling for Saddam's removal from power. The signatories, many of whom had close ties to pro-Israel groups like JINSA or WINEP, and who included Elliot Abrams, John Bolton, Douglas Feith, William Kristol, Bernard Lewis, Donald Rumsfeld, Richard Perle and Paul Wolfowitz, had little trouble persuading the Clinton administration to adopt the general goal of ousting Saddam. But they were unable to sell a war to achieve that objective. They were no more able to generate enthusiasm for invading Iraq in the early months of the Bush administration. They needed help to achieve their aim. That help arrived with 9/11. Specifically, the events of that day led Bush and Cheney to reverse course and become strong proponents of a preventive war.

At a key meeting with Bush at Camp David on 15 September, Wolfowitz advocated attacking Iraq before Afghanistan, even though there was no evidence that Saddam was involved in the attacks on the U.S. and bin Laden was known to be in Afghanistan. Bush rejected his advice and chose to go after Afghanistan instead, but war with Iraq was now regarded as a serious possibility and on 21 November the president charged military planners with developing concrete plans for an invasion.

Other neo-conservatives were meanwhile at work in the corridors of power. We don't have the full story yet, but scholars like Bernard Lewis of Princeton and Fouad Ajami of Johns Hopkins reportedly played important roles in persuading Cheney that war was the best option, though neo-conservatives on his staff—Eric Edelman, John Hannah and Scooter Libby, Cheney's chief of staff and one of the most powerful individuals in the administration—also played their part. By early 2002 Cheney had persuaded Bush; and with Bush and Cheney on board, war was inevitable.

Outside the administration, neo-conservative pundits lost no time in making the case that invading Iraq was essential to winning the war on terrorism. Their efforts were designed partly to keep up the pressure on Bush, and partly to overcome opposition to the war inside and outside the government. On 20 September, a group of prominent neo-conservatives and their allies published another open letter: "Even if evidence does not link Iraq directly to the attack," it read, "any strategy aiming at the eradication of terrorism and its sponsors must include a determined effort to remove Saddam Hussein from power in Iraq." The letter also reminded Bush that "Israel has been and remains America's staunchest ally against international terrorism." In the 1 October issue of the *Weekly Standard*, Robert Kagan and William Kristol called for regime change in Iraq as soon as the Taliban was defeated. That same day, Charles Krauthammer argued in the *Washington Post* that after the U.S. was done with Afghanistan, Syria should be next, followed by Iran and Iraq: "The war on terrorism will conclude in Baghdad," when we finish off "the most dangerous terrorist regime in the world."

This was the beginning of an unrelenting public relations campaign to win support for an invasion of Iraq, a crucial part of which was the manipulation of intelligence in such a way as to make it seem as if Saddam posed an imminent threat. For example, Libby pressured CIA analysts to find evidence supporting the case for war and helped prepare Colin Powell's now discredited briefing to the UN Security Council. Within the Pentagon, the Policy Counterterrorism Evaluation Group was charged with finding links between al-Qaida and Iraq that the intelligence community had supposedly missed. Its two key members were David Wurmser, a hard-core neo-conservative, and Michael Maloof, a Lebanese-American with close ties to Perle. Another Pentagon group, the so-called Office of Special Plans, was given the task of uncovering evidence that could be used to sell the war. It was headed by Abram Shulsky, a neo-conservative with long-standing ties to Wolfowitz, and its ranks included recruits from pro-Israel think tanks. Both these organizations were created after 9/11 and reported directly to Douglas Feith.

Like virtually all the neo-conservatives, Feith is deeply committed to Israel; he also has long-term ties to Likud. He wrote articles in the 1990s supporting the settlements and arguing that Israel should retain the Occupied Territories. More important, along with Perle and Wurmser, he wrote the famous "Clean Break" report in June 1996 for Netanyahu, who had just become prime minister. Among other things, it recommended that Netanyahu "focus on removing Saddam Hussein from power in Iraq—an important Israeli strategic objective in its own right." It also called for Israel to take steps to reorder the entire Middle East. Netanyahu did not follow their advice, but Feith, Perle and Wurmser were soon urging the Bush administration to pursue those same goals. The *Ha'aretz* columnist Akiva Eldar warned that Feith and Perle "are walking a fine line between their loyalty to American governments...and Israeli interests."

Wolfowitz is equally committed to Israel. The *Forward* once described him as "the most hawkishly pro-Israel voice in the administration," and selected him in 2002 as first among 50 notables who "have consciously pursued Jewish activism." At about the same time, JINSA gave Wolfowitz its Henry M. Jackson Distinguished Service Award for promoting a strong partnership between Israel and the United States; and the *Jerusalem Post*, describing him as "devoutly pro-Israel," named him "Man of the Year" in 2003.

Finally, a brief word is in order about the neo-conservative'" prewar support of

Ahmed Chalabi, the unscrupulous Iraqi exile who headed the Iraqi National Congress. They backed Chalabi because he had established close ties with Jewish-American groups and had pledged to foster good relations with Israel once he gained power. This was precisely what pro-Israel proponents of regime change wanted to hear. Matthew Berger laid out the essence of the bargain in the *Jewish Journal*: "The INC saw improved relations as a way to tap Jewish influence in Washington and Jerusalem and to drum up increased support for its cause. For their part, the Jewish groups saw an opportunity to pave the way for better relations between Israel and Iraq, if and when the INC is involved in replacing Saddam Hussein's regime."

Given the neo-conservatives' devotion to Israel, their obsession with Iraq, and their influence in the Bush administration, it isn't surprising that many Americans suspected that the war was designed to further Israeli interests. Last March, Barry Jacobs of the American Jewish Committee acknowledged that the belief that Israel and the neo-conservatives had conspired to get the U.S. into a war in Iraq was "pervasive" in the intelligence community. Yet few people would say so publicly, and most of those who did—including Senator Ernest Hollings and Representative James Moran—were condemned for raising the issue. Michael Kinsley wrote in late 2002 that "the lack of public discussion about the role of Israel…is the proverbial elephant in the room." The reason for the reluctance to talk about it, he observed, was fear of being labeled an anti-Semite. There is little doubt that Israel and the Lobby were key factors in the decision to go to war. It's a decision the U.S. would have been far less likely to take without their efforts. And the war itself was intended to be only the first step. A front-page headline in the *Wall Street Journal* shortly after the war began says it all: "President's Dream: Changing Not Just Regime but a Region: A Pro-U.S., Democratic Area Is a Goal that Has Israeli and Neo-Conservative Roots."

Pro-Israel forces have long been interested in getting the U.S. military more directly involved in the Middle East. But they had limited success during the Cold War, because America acted as an "off-shore balancer" in the region. Most forces designated for the Middle East, like the Rapid Deployment Force, were kept "over the horizon" and out of harm's way. The idea was to play local powers off against each other—which is why the Reagan administration supported Saddam against revolutionary Iran during the Iran-Iraq War—in order to maintain a balance favorable to the U.S..

This policy changed after the first Gulf War, when the Clinton administration adopted a strategy of "dual containment." Substantial U.S. forces would be stationed in the region in order to contain both Iran and Iraq, instead of one being used to check the other. The father of dual containment was none other than Martin Indyk, who first outlined the strategy in May 1993 at WINEP and then implemented it as director for Near East and South Asian Affairs at the National Security Council.

By the mid-1990s there was considerable dissatisfaction with dual containment, because it made the United States the mortal enemy of two countries that hated each other, and forced Washington to bear the burden of containing both. But it was a strategy the Lobby favored and worked actively in Congress to preserve. Pressed by AIPAC and other pro-Israel forces, Clinton toughened up the policy in the spring of 1995 by imposing an economic embargo on Iran. But AIPAC and the others wanted more. The result was the 1996 Iran and Libya Sanctions Act, which imposed sanctions on any foreign companies investing more than $40 million to develop petroleum resources in Iran or Libya. As Ze'ev Schiff, the military correspondent of *Ha'aretz*, noted at the time, "Israel is but a tiny element in the big scheme, but one should not conclude that it cannot influence those within the Beltway."

By the late 1990s, however, the neo-conservatives were arguing that dual containment was not enough and that regime change in Iraq was essential. By toppling Saddam and turning Iraq into a vibrant democracy, they argued, the U.S. would trigger a far-reaching process of change throughout the Middle East. The same line of thinking was evident in the "Clean Break" study the neo-conservatives wrote for Netanyahu. By 2002, when an invasion of Iraq was on the front-burner, regional transformation was an article of faith in neo-conservative circles.

Charles Krauthammer describes this grand scheme as the brainchild of Natan Sharansky, but Israelis across the political spectrum believed that toppling Saddam would alter the Middle East to Israel's advantage. Aluf Benn reported in *Ha'aretz* (17 February 2003):

> Senior IDF officers and those close to Prime Minister Ariel Sharon, such as National Security Adviser Ephraim Halevy, paint a rosy picture of the wonderful future Israel can expect after the war. They envision a domino effect, with the fall of Saddam Hussein followed by that of Israel's other enemies ...Along with these leaders will disappear terror and weapons of mass destruction.

Once Baghdad fell in mid-April 2003, Sharon and his lieutenants began urging Washington to target Damascus. On 16 April, Sharon, interviewed in *Yedioth Ahronoth*, called for the United States to put "very heavy" pressure on Syria, while Shaul Mofaz, his defense minister, interviewed in *Ma'ariv*, said, "We have a long list of issues that we are thinking of demanding of the Syrians and it is appropriate that it should be done through the Americans." Ephraim Halevy told a WINEP audience that it was now important for the U.S. to get rough with Syria, and the *Washington Post* reported that Israel was "fuelling the campaign" against Syria by feeding the U.S. intelligence reports about the actions of Bashar Assad, the Syrian president.

Prominent members of the Lobby made the same arguments. Wolfowitz declared that "there has got to be regime change in Syria," and Richard Perle told a journalist that "a short message, a two-worded message" could be delivered to other hostile regimes in the Middle East, "You're next." In early April, WINEP released a bipartisan report stating that Syria "should not miss the message that countries that pursue Saddam's reckless, irresponsible and defiant behavior could end up sharing his fate." On 15 April, Yossi Klein Halevi wrote a piece in the *Los Angeles Times* entitled "Next, Turn the Screws on Syria," while the following day Zev Chafets wrote an article for the *New York Daily News* entitled "Terror-Friendly Syria Needs a Change, Too." Not to be outdone, Lawrence Kaplan wrote in the *New Republic* on 21 April that Assad was a serious threat to America.

Back on Capitol Hill, Congressman Eliot Engel had reintroduced the Syria Accountability and Lebanese Sovereignty Restoration Act. It threatened sanctions against Syria if it did not withdraw from Lebanon, give up its WMD and stop supporting terrorism, and it also called for

Syria and Lebanon to take concrete steps to make peace with Israel. This legislation was strongly endorsed by the Lobby—by AIPAC especially—and "framed," according to the *Jewish Telegraph Agency*, "by some of Israel's best friends in Congress." The Bush administration had little enthusiasm for it, but the anti-Syrian act passed overwhelmingly (398 to 4 in the House; 89 to 4 in the Senate), and Bush signed it into law on 12 December 2003.

The administration itself was still divided about the wisdom of targeting Syria. Although the neo-conservatives were eager to pick a fight with Damascus, the CIA and the State Department were opposed to the idea. And even after Bush signed the new law, he emphasized that he would go slowly in implementing it. His ambivalence is understandable. First, the Syrian government had not only been providing important intelligence about al-Qaida since 9/11. It had also warned Washington about a planned terrorist attack in the Gulf and given CIA interrogators access to Mohammed Zammar, the alleged recruiter of some of the 9/11 hijackers. Targeting the Assad regime would jeopardize these valuable connections, and thereby undermine the larger war on terrorism.

Second, Syria had not been on bad terms with Washington before the Iraq war (it had even voted for UN Resolution 1441), and was itself no threat to the United States. Playing hardball with it would make the U.S. look like a bully with an insatiable appetite for beating up Arab states. Third, putting Syria on the hit list would give Damascus a powerful incentive to cause trouble in Iraq. Even if one wanted to bring pressure to bear, it made good sense to finish the job in Iraq first. Yet Congress insisted on putting the screws on Damascus, largely in response to pressure from Israeli officials and groups like AIPAC. If there were no Lobby, there would have been no Syria Accountability Act, and U.S. policy towards Damascus would have been more in line with the national interest.

Israelis tend to describe every threat in the starkest terms, but Iran is widely seen as their most dangerous enemy because it is the most likely to acquire nuclear weapons. Virtually all Israelis regard an Islamic country in the Middle East with nuclear weapons as a threat to their existence. "Iraq is a problem...But you should understand, if you ask me, today Iran is more dangerous than Iraq," the defense minister, Binyamin Ben-Eliezer, remarked a month before the Iraq war.

Sharon began pushing the U.S. to confront Iran in November 2002, in an interview in the *Times*. Describing Iran as the "center of world terror," and bent on acquiring nuclear weapons, he declared that the Bush administration should put the strong arm on Iran "the day after" it conquered Iraq. In late April 2003, *Ha'aretz* reported that the Israeli ambassador in Washington was calling for regime change in Iran. The overthrow of Saddam, he noted, was "not enough." In his words, America "has to follow through. We still have great threats of that magnitude coming from Syria, coming from Iran."

The neo-conservatives, too, lost no time in making the case for regime change in Tehran. On 6 May, the AEI co-sponsored an all-day conference on Iran with the Foundation for the Defense of Democracies and the Hudson Institute, both champions of Israel. The speakers were all strongly pro-Israel, and many called for the U.S. to replace the Iranian regime with a democracy. As usual, a bevy of articles by prominent neo-conservatives made the case for going after Iran. "The liberation of Iraq was the first great battle for the future of the Middle East...But the next great battle—not, we hope, a military battle—will be for Iran," William Kristol wrote in the *Weekly Standard* on 12 May.

The administration has responded to the Lobby's pressure by working overtime to shut down Iran's nuclear program. But Washington has had little success, and Iran seems determined to create a nuclear arsenal. As a result, the Lobby has intensified its pressure. Op-eds and other articles now warn of imminent dangers from a nuclear Iran, caution against any appeasement of a "terrorist" regime, and hint darkly of preventive action should diplomacy fail. The Lobby is pushing Congress to approve the Iran Freedom Support Act, which would expand existing sanctions. Israeli officials also warn they may take pre-emptive action should Iran continue down the nuclear road, threats partly intended to keep Washington's attention on the issue.

One might argue that Israel and the Lobby have not had much influence on policy towards Iran, because the U.S. has its own reasons for keeping Iran from going nuclear. There is some truth in this, but Iran's nuclear ambitions do not pose a direct threat to the U.S. If Washington could live with a nuclear Soviet Union, a nuclear China or even a nuclear North Korea, it can live with a nuclear Iran. And that is why the Lobby must keep up constant pressure on politicians to confront Tehran. Iran and the U.S. would hardly be allies if the Lobby did not exist, but U.S. policy would be more temperate and preventive war would not be a serious option.

It is not surprising that Israel and its American supporters want the U.S. to deal with any and all threats to Israel's security. If their efforts to shape U.S. policy succeed, Israel's enemies will be weakened or overthrown, Israel will get a free hand with the Palestinians, and the U.S. will do most of the fighting, dying, rebuilding and paying. But even if the U.S. fails to transform the Middle East and finds itself in conflict with an increasingly radicalized Arab and Islamic world, Israel will end up protected by the world's only superpower. This is not a perfect outcome from the Lobby's point of view, but it is obviously preferable to Washington distancing itself, or using its leverage to force Israel to make peace with the Palestinians.

Can the Lobby's power be curtailed? One would like to think so, given the Iraq debacle, the obvious need to rebuild America's image in the Arab and Islamic world, and the recent revelations about AIPAC officials passing U.S. government secrets to Israel. One might also think that Arafat's death and the election of the more moderate Mahmoud Abbas would cause Washington to press vigorously and evenhandedly for a peace agreement. In short, there are ample grounds for leaders to distance themselves from the Lobby and adopt a Middle East policy more consistent with broader U.S. interests. In particular, using American power to achieve a just peace between Israel and the Palestinians would help advance the cause of democracy in the region.

But that is not going to happen—not soon anyway. AIPAC and its allies (including Christian Zionists) have no serious opponents in the lobbying world. They know it has become more difficult to make Israel's case today, and they are responding by taking on staff and expanding their activities. Besides, American politicians remain acutely sensitive to campaign contributions and other forms of political pressure, and major media outlets are likely to remain sympathetic to Israel no matter what it does.

The Lobby's influence causes trouble on several fronts. It increases the terrorist danger that all states face—including America's European allies. It has made it impossible to end the Israeli-Palestinian conflict, a situation that gives extremists a powerful recruiting tool, increases the pool of potential terrorists and sympathizers, and contributes to Islamic radicalism in Europe and Asia.

Equally worrying, the Lobby's campaign for regime change in Iran and Syria could lead the U.S. to attack those countries, with potentially disastrous effects. We don't need another Iraq. At a minimum, the Lobby's hostility towards Syria and Iran makes it almost impossible for Washington to enlist them in the struggle against al-Qaida and the Iraqi insurgency, where their help is badly needed.

There is a moral dimension here as well. Thanks to the Lobby, the United States has become the de facto enabler of Israeli expansion in the Occupied Territories, making it complicit in the crimes perpetrated against the Palestinians. This situation undercuts Washington's efforts to promote democracy abroad and makes it look hypocritical when it presses other states to respect human rights. U.S. efforts to limit nuclear proliferation appear equally hypocritical given its willingness to accept Israel's nuclear arsenal, which only encourages Iran and others to seek a similar capability.

Besides, the Lobby's campaign to quash debate about Israel is unhealthy for democracy. Silencing skeptics by organizing blacklists and boycotts—or by suggesting that critics are anti-Semites—violates the principle of open debate on which democracy depends. The inability of Congress to conduct a genuine debate on these important issues paralyses the entire process of democratic deliberation. Israel's backers should be free to make their case and to challenge those who disagree with them, but efforts to stifle debate by intimidation must be roundly condemned.

Finally, the Lobby's influence has been bad for Israel. Its ability to persuade Washington to support an expansionist agenda has discouraged Israel from seizing opportunities—including a peace treaty with Syria and a prompt and full implementation of the Oslo Accords—that would have saved Israeli lives and shrunk the ranks of Palestinian extremists. Denying the Palestinians their legitimate political rights certainly has not made Israel more secure, and the long campaign to kill or marginalize a generation of Palestinian leaders has empowered extremist groups like Hamas, and reduced the number of Palestinian leaders who would be willing to accept a fair settlement and be able to make it work. Israel itself would probably be better off if the Lobby were less powerful and U.S. policy more even-handed.

There is a ray of hope, however. Although the Lobby remains a powerful force, the adverse effects of its influence are increasingly difficult to hide. Powerful states can maintain flawed policies for quite some time, but reality cannot be ignored for ever. What is needed is a candid discussion of the Lobby's influence and a more open debate about U.S. interests in this vital region. Israel's well-being is one of those interests, but its continued occupation of the West Bank and its broader regional agenda are not. Open debate will expose the limits of the strategic and moral case for one-sided U.S. support and could move the U.S. to a position more consistent with its own national interest, with the interests of the other states in the region, and with Israel's long-term interests as well.

The Pro-Israel Lobby in the United States: David

ALAN DERSHOWITZ

INTRODUCTION

The publication, on the Harvard Kennedy School web site, of a "working paper," written by a professor at the Kennedy School and a prominent professor at the University of Chicago, has ignited a hailstorm of controversy and raised troubling questions. The paper was written by two self-described foreign-policy "realists," Professor Stephen Walt and Professor John Mearsheimer. It asserts that the Israel "Lobby"—a cabal whose "core" is "American Jews"—has a "stranglehold" on mainstream American media, think tanks, academia, and the government. The Lobby is led by the American-Israel Public Affairs Committee ("AIPAC"), which the authors characterize as a "de facto agent of a foreign government" that places the interests of that government ahead of the interests of the United States. Jewish political contributors use Jewish "money" to blackmail government officials, while "Jewish philanthropists" influence and "police" academic programs and shape public opinion. Jewish "congressional staffers" exploit their roles and betray the trust of their bosses by "look[ing] at certain issues in terms of their Jewishness," rather than in terms of their Americanism. [Note: The article by Mearsheimer and Walt that is used here did not differ any important respect from the working paper referred to by Dershowitz.]

The authors claim that the Lobby works against the interests of the United States because Israel's interests are not only different from ours, but antagonistic to them for several reasons, including that:

> America's "terrorism problem" is directly attributable to its "alli[ance] with Israel"; Israel has gotten us to fight wars, such as those against Iraq, which are not in our general interest; and Israel spied on the United States during the Cold War and provided information to our enemy, the Soviet Union.

The authors also assert that Israel lacks any moral claim to American support, because the "creation of Israel entailed a moral crime against the Palestinian people"; Israel has continued to commit crimes including "massacres…and rapes by Jews"; Israel is not a true democracy, because "citizenship is based on the principle of blood kinship"; Israel is a "colonizing" regime, on the road to achieving "pariah status" reserved for "apartheid states like South Africa"; Israel has always refused to grant the "largely innocent" Palestinians "a viable state of their own"; and "Israel's conduct is not morally distinguishable from the actions of its opponents."

This particular lobby—which the authors ominously capitalize and reference with the definite article ("the Lobby")—uses the undue influence of Jews in America to get the United States to do the "fighting, dying…and paying" for wars that are not in its own interest, causing American soldiers to die for Israeli interests. It was "the Lobby" that, according to Walt and Mearsheimer, drove the United States into the war against Iraq, and threatens to drive us into a war against Iran. In other words, real Americans are being killed because other Americans, whose primary loyalty is to the Jewish nation, are manipulating America's political, media, academic and cultural leaders, as well as ordinary American citizens. American Jews who support Israel—even in a critical way—are thus being disloyal to the United States by placing the interests of a foreign state above the interests of their own country.

If these charges sound familiar, it is because, as I will show, they can be found on the websites of extremists of the hard right, like David Duke, and the hard left, like Alexander Cockburn. They appear daily in the Arab and Muslim press. They are contemporary variations on old themes such as those promulgated in the notorious czarist forgery, *The Protocols of the Elders of Zion*, in the Nazi and America First literature of the 1930s and early '40s, and in the propaganda pamphlets of the Soviet Union.

In essence, the working paper is little more than a compilation of old, false, and authoritatively discredited charges dressed up in academic garb. The only thing new about it is the imprimatur these recycled assertions have now been given by the prominence of its authors and their institutional affiliations. As David Duke observed: "The Harvard report contains little new information. I and a few other American commentators have for years been making the same assertions as this new paper." It "validates every major point I [Duke] have been making." It should have been easily predictable—especially to "realists"—that their "Harvard report" would be featured, as it has been, on neo-Nazi and extremist websites, and even by terrorist organizations, and that it would be used by overt anti-Semites to "validate" their paranoid claims of a worldwide Jewish conspiracy.

One of the authors of this paper has acknowledged that "none of the evidence [in their paper] represents original documentation or is derived from independent interviews"—a surprising admission, considering that professors at great universities are judged by the originality of their research. Moreover, the paper is filled with errors and distortions that should be obvious to any critical reader, all of which are directed against Israel and the Jewish Lobby. As I will show, there are at least three major types of errors: First, quotations are wrenched out of context (for example, the authors distort a Ben-Gurion [Israel's first prime minister] quote to make him appear to favor evacuation of Arabs by "brutal compulsion," when he actually said that, because an evacuation would require "brutal compulsion," it should not become "part of our program"). Second, facts are misstated (for example, that Israeli citizenship is based on "blood kinship," thus confusing Israel's law of citizenship with its Law of Return; fully a quarter of Israel's citizens are not Jewish). And third, embarrassingly poor logic is employed (for example, whenever America and Israel act on a common interest, it must be the result of pressure from "the Lobby," and that "the mere existence of the Lobby" is proof that "support for Israel is not in the American national interest"). [Emphasis here and elsewhere in the Dershowitz original.]

In light of its many errors and the admission that their paper contains nothing original, it is fair to ask why these distinguished professors would have chosen to publish a paper that does not meet their usual scholarly standards, especially given the obvious risk that recycling these old but explosive charges under the imprimatur of prominent authors and their universities would be seized on by bigots to promote their anti-Semitic agendas.

As an advocate of free speech and an opponent of censorship based on political correctness, I welcome a serious, balanced, objective study of the influences of lobbies—including Israeli lobbies—on American foreign policy. I also welcome reasoned, contextual and comparative criticism of Israeli policies and actions. Let the marketplace of ideas remain open to all. But, as I will show, this study is so filled with distortions, so empty of originality or new evidence, so tendentious in its tone, so lacking in nuance and balance, so unscholarly in its approach, so riddled with obvious factual errors that could easily have been checked (but obviously were not), and so dependent on biased, extremist and anti-American sources, as to raise the question of motive: what would motivate two well recognized academics to depart so grossly from their usual standards of academic writing and research in order to produce a "study paper" that contributes so little to the existing scholarship while being so susceptible to misuse?

Academics do not generally respond to the kinds of assertions and accusations made on hate sites. But because of the academic setting in which the Walt-Mearsheimer paper appears, I feel compelled to respond in detail and to these recycled charges and to demonstrate how the paper fails the most basic tests of scholarship and accuracy.

In this paper, I expressly raise questions about motive. As I have argued elsewhere, the issue of motive is a legitimate concern of scholarship, especially to "realists" who often look behind rationales for the actual reasons that underlie actions. This is especially so when the Walt-Mearsheimer paper itself questions the motives and loyalties of others, and when so many critics of the paper have raised the question of motive.

I have requested the Kennedy School to distribute this counter working paper on its website and to give it the same circulation and prominence as the original paper. Dean David Ellwood has graciously acceded to this request. I am confident that we share a commitment to the open marketplace of ideas as a vehicle to establish the validity or falsehood of ideas.

I have had only a few days to write this preliminary response to a paper that took much more time to produce, and so my response is truly a "working paper"—a work in progress. But because of the attention the original paper has received, it is essential to publish and circulate this response as soon as possible. I hope that readers will be stimulated by my work to do research of their own to test my points as well as those of Mearsheimer and Walt. My reply is not meant to be exhaustive; I address only the central points, beginning with the charge that "the Lobby" exists to undercut the interests of the United States on behalf of an antagonistic foreign power.

THE LOBBY

Who belongs to "the Lobby"? Walt and Mearsheimer acknowledge that the lobby is not monolithic in its composition. They point to extremists on the religious and political right as included in this Lobby, though they consciously omit non-Jewish liberal supporters of Israel, ranging from Senators Edward Kennedy [D-MA] and Evan Bayh [D-IN] to former President Bill Clinton and Vice President Al Gore to Father Robert Drinan [professor of law, Georgetown University] and [Harvard] Professor Henry Louis Gates, Jr. Yet they claim that the Lobby is single-minded in its pursuit of Israel's interests over that of the United States.

Walt and Mearsheimer include in their catalogue of "Lobby"-ists: journalists Robert Kagan, William Kristol, and Charles Krauthammer; Princeton professor Bernard Lewis; Clinton administration diplomats Dennis Ross and Martin Indyk; Bush staffers [I. Lewis] Scooter Libby and

Paul Wolfowitz; Democratic Senator Joseph Lieberman (CT) and Congressman Eliot Engel [D-NY]; former Republic Congressman Dick Armey [R-TX]; the Brookings Institute and just about every other major think tank. The *New York Times* and the *Wall Street Journal* are willing members of the conspiracy, whereas CNN and NPR are being dragged into it by pressure from Jewish donors and letter writers. This explains why, according to Mearsheimer and Walt, "the American media contains few criticisms of Israeli policies." This statement will sound especially bizarre to anyone who regularly reads *The New York Times*, which is frequently critical of Israel, and whose editorial board seems particularly antagonistic toward the Likud Party, which dominated Israeli politics during the period under discussion by the authors. Indeed, some members of the so-called Lobby organized a boycott of *The New York Times* for its perceived bias against Israel. A careful review of other media outlets that are allegedly part of the Lobby will also show repeated criticism of specific Israeli policies. Mearsheimer and Walt are demonstrably wrong when the assert that "the American media contains few criticisms of Israeli policies."

They are also wrong when the say that the Lobby conspires to manipulate the U.S. government into making war on Arab and Muslim nations. Never mind that the chief figures in the Bush Administration responsible for the Iraq war, including the President, the Vice President, both Secretaries of State, and the Secretary of Defense, are all non-Jewish. A pesky detail like that can be explained away by the claim that America's top politicians are all heavily "influenced by the neoconservatives" (read: Jews), and pressured by Jewish congressional staffers into doing Israel's bidding, even though it is against the interests of the United States. As the conclusion warns, "American leaders" must "distance themselves from the Lobby" in order to act in a manner "more consistent with broader U.S. interests."

The reality, of course, is that the so-called members of "the Lobby" have little in common with each other, except for a preference for democracy over tyranny, belief in Israel's strategic importance to the United States, support for an endangered American ally, commitment to the survival of a small democracy in which Jewish culture can thrive, and the recognition of the need for one nation that will always be open to Jews threatened with discrimination and persecution in a world with continuing if not increasing anti-Semitism. As Brett Stephens explained why the *Wall Street Journal*'s Robert Bartley—a moderate Christian—supported Israel:

> He supported Israel for much the same reason he supported Great Britain, Poland and Taiwan—because they were friends of the United States, because they were democracies, because they were places where his core beliefs in free men and free markets held sway. In this respect, and like so many of us who are friends of the Jewish state, he was not privy to an Israeli conspiracy but part of an American consensus.

Some supporters of Israel are of the left and support extensive territorial compromise and a two state solution. Others are of the right and favor more limited steps. Some are secular, others religious. Some are Democrats, others Republican. Some supported the war in Iraq, while others—a majority of Jews—opposed it. They have no more in common with each other than do "members" of the anti-Israel lobby, which includes David Duke, Pat Buchanan, Noam Chomsky, Alexander

Cockburn, numerous Arab and Muslim organizations, some church groups and now the authors of this working paper.

Indeed, there are many lobbies that support diverse approaches to the Arab-Israeli conflict, just as there are many lobbies with differing perspectives on Cuba, China, North Korea, and Russia. Among the powerful lobbies related to the Middle East are the American oil lobby, the Saudi lobby, the lobbies for the Emirates, and various church groups that urge divestiture against Israel. AIPAC—to its credit—has been an influential lobby. So have others. When Saudi lobbyists have clashed with the Israel lobby, the Saudi lobby has often won. For example, the Israel lobby was no match against the Saudi lobby in securing the $8.5 billion sale of American Airborne Warning and Control System (AWACS) jets to Saudi Arabia [in the 1980s], over strong Israeli objection. The chief lobbyist for the Saudis, until recently, was Prince Bandar bin Sultan, who was described as "so close to the President's father, George H. W. Bush, that he was considered almost a member of the family," and was nicknamed "Bandar Bush" by the President's family. And yet Walt and Mearsheimer omit any reference to competing lobbies.

The [Mearsheimer and Walt] paper is filled with thinly veiled charges of Jewish control of American thought. The authors refer to Jewish "manipulation" and "influence" over American media and government thirty-four times. They identify an American-Jewish lobbying group as a "*de facto* agent for a foreign government," of having a "stranglehold" over American policy, and of "controlling the debate." These charges are indistinguishable from Pat Buchanan's invocation of the U.S. government as Israel's "amen corner" and his reference to Congress as "Israeli Occupied Territory," allegations, among others, that led William F. Buckley to characterize Buchanan's views as "amount[ing] to anti-Semitism."

Mearsheimer and Walt go out of their way to deny that their paper's dominant thesis is similar to the notorious anti-Semitic forgery, *The Protocols of the Elders of Zion*. They bring up the *Protocols* to distance themselves from it—while generally adhering to a variation on its conspiratorial theme. Again, listen to Bret Stephens in the *Wall Street Journal*:

> [T]he gist of the Mearsheimer-Walt hypothesis should be clear. So should its pedigree. The authors are at pains to note that the Israel Lobby is by no means exclusively Jewish, and that not every American Jew is a part of it. Fair enough. But has there ever been an anti-Semitic conspiracy theory that does not share its basic features? Dual loyalty, disloyalty, manipulation of the media, financial manipulation of the political system, duping the *goyim* (gentiles) and getting them to fight their wars, sponsoring and covering up acts of gratuitous cruelty against an innocent people—every canard ever alleged of the Jews is here made about the Israel Lobby and its cause.

As an added precaution, the authors preemptively accuse the Lobby of indiscriminately crying anti-Semitism: "Anyone who criticizes Israeli actions or says that pro-Israel groups have significant influence over U.S. Middle East policy...stands a good chance of getting labeled an anti-Semite." "In other words criticize Israeli policy and you are by definition an anti-Semite." This is demonstrably false, though it is a charge made frequently in the hate literature. Several years ago, I challenged those who made similar accusations to identify a single Jewish leader who equated mere criticism of Israeli policy with anti-

Semitism. No one accepted my challenge, because no Jewish leader has made such an absurd claim. Among the harshest critics of Israeli policy are Jews and Israelis. Just read the mainstream Israel and Jewish-American press—a research task that Mearsheimer and Walt should have but did not undertake before they falsely generalized about its content. Mearsheimer and Walt's strawman argument—which, if true, would make me and other critical supporters of Israel anti-Semites—simply does not stand up to scrutiny.

Nor are Mearsheimer and Walt merely criticizing Israeli policies, or even Israel itself. They are very explicitly targeting American *Jews*: "The core of the Lobby is comprised of American Jews who make a significant effort in their daily lives to bend U.S. foreign policy so that it advances Israel's interests" over those of the United States. In one of the paper's more peculiar passages, the authors try to refute the allegation that anti-Semitism is on the rise in France by pointing out that "85 percent of practicing French Catholics reject the charge that Jews have too much influence in business and finance." By citing this strange statistic—very few French people are, in fact, practicing Catholics—they seem to be acknowledging that those who do argue that Jews have too much influence may well be making a bigoted argument.

The fact is that anti-Semitism is on the rise in France, as evidenced by a recent poll showing that sixty-four percent of French citizens themselves (not limited to, but including, "practicing French Catholics") "think anti-Semitism is on the rise in France." The *New York Times* recently reported on "an undeniable problem: anti-Semitism among France's second generation immigrant youth...." It headlined its story "Jews in France feel sting as anti-Semitism surges among children of immigrants," and it documented "the deteriorating climate" that "has led thousands of French Jews to move to Israel in the past five years...." Yet Mearsheimer and Walt insist on denying the "undeniable," because a rise in anti-Semitism would undercut their thesis of an all-powerful Jewish cabal.

Regardless, the real trouble with the paper is that it presents a conspiratorial view of history. This type of paranoid worldview, in which Jews manipulate and control the media and government, is not the sort of argument one would expect from prominent academics. It more closely resembles what Professor Richard Hofstadter described in "The Paranoid Style of American Politics," in which extremists on both the far right and the far left harbor exaggerated fantasies about an individual demographic group's influence. Prominent among the hard-right Jewish conspiracy theorists are David Duke and Pat Buchanan, and on the hard left are Noam Chomsky, Norman Finkelstein, and Alexander Cockburn. Their hateful views are consistent with other types of conspiracy theories spouted by those who, for instance, blame all of their own and America's economic troubles on immigrants, or those who blame all crime on African-Americans, those who blame a perceived cultural decline on gays, or moral decline on secular humanists. The sort of people who articulate such views might defend themselves against charges of prejudice by insisting that they do not believe that *all* immigrants are harmful to America, or that *all* blacks violate the law. But just because a person believes there are some exceptions to his pejorative generalizations does not erase the underlying prejudice.

There are three areas of the Mearsheimer-Walt paper that I will address in more detail: their method of scholarship, their marshalling of facts, and their logical analysis.

SCHOLARSHIP

Mearsheimer and Walt rely heavily on discredited allegations and out of context quotations found on extremist, disreputable sources, including well-known hate websites. It is ironic that in support of the proposition that American Jews are disloyal *to America*, Mearsheimer and Walt cite America *haters* who classify our country as the leader of the real axis of evil, who call America a worse terrorist organization than al Qaeda, and who claim that we deserved what happened to us on September 11.

Consider some of the sources. Mearsheimer and Walt favorably cite Cockburn's *CounterPunch.org* on four different occasions. Cockburn is best known for his anti-American charges (he referred to "the shared enthusiasm of the Fuehrer [Adolf Hitler] and all U.S. Presidents (with the possible exception of Warren Harding) for mass murder as an appropriate expression of national policy") and for airing accusations that Israel may have been complicit in September 11, ultimately concluding that he is not sure "whether [the charges] are true or not." They cite [professors] Noam Chomsky [Massachusetts Institute of Technology] and Norman Finkelstein [DePaul University] three times apiece. Chomsky has repeatedly expressed hatred for the United States, making such claims as: "[i]f the Nuremberg laws were applied today, then every Post-War American president would have to be hanged." Finkelstein's anti-Americanism has led him to support Hezbollah and to blame the United States for September 11: "[W]e [the U.S.] deserve the problem on our hands because some things Bin Laden says are true." On the question of Palestinian refugees, Mearsheimer and Walt cite Finkelstein's for the absurd proposition that Israel essentially started the War of Independence in order to ethnically cleanse its land of Palestinians. Why would serious academics choose to cite as an authority on the contentious refugee issue a man who is not an expert on Israel and who wrote a book that the *New York Times Book Review* called "irrational and insidious" and a "conspiracy theory"? This is a man whom the *Washington Post* has described as "a writer celebrated by neo-Nazi groups for his Holocaust revisionism and comparisons of Israel to Nazi Germany." University of Chicago historian Peter Novick had it exactly right when he said Finkelstein's so-called scholarship—which he says includes made up quotes and sources—is a "twenty-first century updating of the 'Protocols of the Elders of Zion." Novick continued:

> As concerns particular assertions made by Finkelstein...the appropriate response is not (exhilarating) debate but (tedious) examination of his footnotes. Such an examination reveals that many of those assertions are pure invention....No facts alleged by Finkelstein should be assumed to be really facts, no quotation in his book should be assumed to be accurate, without taking the time to carefully compare his claims with the sources he cites.

If there were other, more reputable sources, they would not have had to dig through recycled trash to support their untenable assertions.

Mearsheimer and Walt do not make up quotes, but they wrench them out of context. They twice quote [Israel's first prime minister] David Ben-Gurion so out of context that they make him appear to be saying the exact opposite of what he actually did say. First, the authors have Ben-Gurion saying, "After the formation of a large army in the wake of the establishment of the state, we shall abolish partition and expand to the whole of Palestine." The clear implication is that this would be done by force. Yet, in a follow-up question to that statement, Ben-Gurion was asked whether he meant to achieve this "By force as well?" He responded in the negative. "Through mutual understanding and Jewish-Arab agreement." Yet, Mearsheimer and Walt omit this important qualifying answer. Ben-Gurion is then quoted by Mearsheimer and Walt as saying that "it is impossible to imagine general evacuation [of the Arab population] without compulsion, and brutal compulsion," making it seem as if Ben-Gurion was advocating a "brutal compulsion." But they omit what Ben-Gurion said after that: "but we should in no way make it part of our program." By omitting Ben-Gurion's critical conclusions, they falsely suggest that Ben-Gurion was proposing the opposite of what he said. There are only two possible explanations for these pregnant omissions: either they were unaware of the context of the quotes because they read only the misleading excerpts ripped out of context by the biased sources in which they found them but did not cite; or they themselves made the decision to misuse the quotes so as to mislead the reader. The burden is on them to tell us which it is.

These particular quotations from Ben Gurion appears on several hard-left or hate sites, where they are always wrenched out of context to make it appear that he said the opposite of what he actually said. The same is true of other quotations, also taken out of context. For example, the Max Frankel quotations are trumpeted on holywar.org, a website which claims that "Israel is a Satanic state." Mearsheimer and Walt quote [Israeli Prime Minister] Ehud Barak as saying that "had he been born a Palestinian, he 'would have joined a terrorist organization.'" This quote, too, appears on many hard-left websites, and omits his condemnation of terrorism. The same goes for the Ben-Gurion quote, "If I were an Arab leader I would never make terms with Israel." And the quotation of Morris Amitay, about how Jewish Congressional staffers will "look at certain issues in terms of their Jewishness," was included in an article 22 years ago that sounded many of the same themes as Mearsheimer and Walt. On NukeIsrael.com and other hate sites, one can also find many of the same points: "A group of powerful U.S. Jews have grotesquely distorted U.S. foreign policy in blind fanatic support of Israel." And the following, which is somewhat more nuanced than the Mearsheimer-Walt formulation, appears in a neo-Nazi on-line publication: "Although criticism of specific Israeli policies is permissible in the United States, it is more or less forbidden to express fundamental criticism of the Zionist state, of America's basic policy of support for Israel, or of the Jewish-Zionist grip on the U.S. media or America's political and academic life."

In addition to relying on quotes wrenched out of context by dubious sources, Mearsheimer and Walt also recite historic facts out of context. They willfully omit the most important contextual history. The authors mention the wars of 1948, 1967, and 1973 to cite evidence of Israeli military superiority, but they never mention *why* the wars were fought in the first place. In other words, there is absolutely no indication that on all three occasions, Arab countries attacked Israel in order, according to their own well-known formulation, to "drive the Jews into the Sea."

Mearsheimer and Walt say that Israel won "quick and easy victories" in these wars, without mentioning casualty rates that claimed the lives of a full one percent of Israel's population (many of them Holocaust survivors) during the 1948 war, or the high casualty rates and near-disaster Israel suffered by the Egyptian surprise attack on Yom Kippur of 1973. Nor is there any mention of Palestinian terrorism, except to blithely dismiss it as a minor nuisance and to justify it as an understandable reaction to occupation. Needless to say, the authors' rationalization does not explain the prevalence of Palestinian terror campaigns beginning in 1929, nor does it address terrorist organizations that consider all of Israel to be "occupied territory" (including Hamas, which now controls the Palestinian Authority). After all, al-Fatah ("The Conquest," the main branch of the PLO) was founded as an organization committed to Israel's destruction by terrorism *before* the 1967 war and subsequent occupation.

The authors' discussion of American involvement in Israel's affairs is similarly skewed. They mention that "Washington was deeply involved in the negotiations that ended [the 1973] war" without saying that Washington's intervention was to Israel's *disadvantage*. They say that Israel was a potential liability in the first Gulf War coalition without mentioning that Israel refrained from entering the conflict, at the United States' request, despite the Iraqi Scuds that rained down on Tel Aviv. Walt and Mearsheimer also fail to mention that it would have been considerably more difficult, if not impossible, for the United States to confront Iraq in the first Gulf War if Israel had not destroyed the Osirak nuclear reactor [in Iraq] ten years earlier [in 1981]. Then-Secretary of Defense Dick Cheney acknowledged Israel's crucial role in facilitating America's victory when, in December 1991, he presented the Israeli general who had organized the attack on Osirak a satellite photograph of the destroyed reactor with the following inscription: "With thanks and appreciation for the outstanding job...on the Iraqi nuclear program in 1981, which made our job much easier in Desert Storm."

[Mearsheimer and Walt] The authors write, "Even when Israel was founded, Jews were only about 35 percent of Palestine's population and owned 7 percent of the land," without citing the more important demographic statistic, namely, that Jews were a clear majority in the areas assigned to Israel under partition, thus making their reference to South Africa's Apartheid inapt.

[Mearsheimer and Walt's] The authors' bias is most clearly demonstrated when they write that "the creation of Israel entailed a moral crime" without adequately explaining the history behind Israel's birth and the near-unanimous Arab refusal to accept a Jewish state in the Middle East. There is no recognition that during and after the Holocaust, no nation would accept more than a handful of Jews in need of refuge. There is no word of the several partition plans—Balfour (1917), Peel (1937), and the UN (1947)—that the Arabs rejected but that the Jewish leadership accepted so that it might establish peaceful sovereignty alongside its of a great crime, rather than the to one. Neighbors, no matter how small, disconnected, and indefensible were the borders of the proposed Jewish state. There is no word about the great statesmen of the time, from Woodrow Wilson through Harry Truman and Winston Churchill, who wholeheartedly supported Jewish self-determination through the establishment of Israel. The authors invert cause and effect by presenting Israel's founding, without any historical context, as the cause reaction.

These are only a few examples. Nearly every paragraph of the paper is riddled with similar errors, omits crucial details, and misleads the reader. As an editorial in the *Forward* put it:

> Countless facts are simply wrong. Long stretches of argument are implausible, at times almost comically so. Much of their research is oddly amateurish, drawn not from credible [sources]....Some are wildly misquoted. An undergraduate submitting work like this would be laughed out of class.

But this is no laughing matter since the authors of this "junk" social science study—one of Mearsheimer's colleagues called it "piss-poor, monocausal social science"—hold prominent positions in major universities. Accordingly, the alleged "facts" on which their study is based must be tested against the reality.

II. FACTS

It would take a much longer article to debunk all the factual errors in the paper, which truly is a collage of misinformation. I will point out only a very few of the most obvious misstatements Mearsheimer and Walt have borrowed from Israel bashers.

1. "By contrast, Israel was explicitly founded as a Jewish state and citizenship is based on the principle of blood kinship."

This mendacious emphasis on Jewish "blood" is a favorite of neo-Nazi propaganda. It is totally false. In reality, a person of any ethnicity or religion can become an Israeli citizen. In fact, approximately a quarter of Israel's citizens are not Jewish, a higher percentage of minority citizenry than in nearly any other country. Mearsheimer and Walt admit that Israel has 1.3 million Arab citizens—about 20 percent of Israel's population. Yet they repeat the blood accusation. The paper's authors confuse Israel's law of return—which was designed to grant asylum to those who were victims of anti-Semitism, including non-Jewish relatives of Jews—with its law of citizenship. All Israeli citizens, whether Jews or non-Jews, enjoy the same legal rights and liberties, as evidenced by the many thriving Arab political parties represented in the Israeli Knesset and Muslim judges in the Israeli judiciary. (Where is there a single Jewish legislator or judge in any Muslim-majority nation?) As evidence of the "undemocratic" nature of Israel in relation to its Arab citizens, Walt and Mearsheimer cite "The Official Summation of the Or Commission Report." They fail to mention, however, that the report explicitly noted that "Israel's Arab citizens have the right to equality because of the essence of the State of Israel as a democracy, and because it is a basic right of every citizen." The report goes on to state that existing inequalities between the Jewish and Arab citizens are due in part to efforts by some Arab leaders to delegitimize the government:

> The committee determined that, while most of Israel's Arab citizens are loyal to the state, the messages transmitted during the October disturbances blurred and sometimes erased the distinction between the state's Arab citizens and their legitimate struggle for rights, and the armed struggle against the state being conducted by organizations and individuals in the West Bank and Gaza. More than once, the two struggles are presented by leaders of the Arab community as one struggle against one adversary, often an enemy. The committee emphasized that the concept of citizenship is incompatible with the presentation of the state as the enemy...

Conveniently, Mearsheimer and Walt ignore the nuances and qualifications of the report.

If Mearsheimer and Walt were truly concerned about racist citizenship statutes, they could have looked right next door, to Jordan, which openly and explicitly refuses to grant citizenship to Jews. (This, from everyone's favorite "moderate" Arab nation!) When asked about Arab citizenship laws, Walt responded, "We were not writing on Saudi Arabia and Jordan." First of all, that is not true. Mearsheimer and Walt compare Israel to its Arab neighbors on several occasions, finding—incredibly—that "[i]n terms of actual behavior, Israel's conduct is not morally distinguishable from the actions of its opponents." Second, Walt's evasive answer reminds me of an argument attributed to another Harvard administrator—President A. Lawrence Lowell—who fought fiercely to keep Jews out of Harvard. His reasoning was that "Jews cheat." When a distinguished alumnus pointed out that some non-Jews cheat, too, Lowell allegedly responded, "You're changing the subject. I'm talking about Jews." Mearsheimer and Walt are using the same tactic: singling out Jews and Israel without any historical or contemporary comparative data. When someone identifies their bias, they accuse the objector of changing the subject.

2. "[T]he United States has a terrorism problem in good part because it is so closely allied with Israel, not the other way around.... There is no question, for example, that many al Qaeda leaders, including bin Laden, are motivated by Israel's presence in Jerusalem and the plight of the Palestinians."

In fact, bin Laden was primarily motivated by the presence of American troops in Saudi Arabia. Saudi Arabia, recall, had asked the United States to defend the Arabian Peninsula against Iraqi aggression prior to the first Gulf War. So it was America's ties to and defense of an *Arab* state—from which fifteen of the nineteen 9/11 hijackers originated—and not the *Jewish* state, that most clearly precipitated September 11. Prior to September 11, Israel was barely on bin Laden's radar screen.

Nor does Israel's supposed domination of American public life explain terrorist massacres in Bali, Madrid, London, and elsewhere. Europe, after all, is praised for being more immune to the Lobby's manipulation tactics.

3. "Contrary to popular belief, the Zionists had larger, better-equipped, and better-led forces during the 1947–49 War of Independence...."

Here, the authors are trying to persuade the readers that, despite the Arab world's several attempts to eliminate the Jewish State and exterminate its inhabitants, Israel has never been in serious danger. To the contrary, the invading Arab armies—trained professional militaries—possessed armor and a steep manpower advantage, whereas Israel "had few heavy weapons and no artillery, armored vehicles, or planes."

There are enormously varying accounts of the number of soldiers and armament in the 1948 War. One estimate shows the Arab armies with ten times more aircrafts, thirty times more artillery, and ninety times more tanks than the Israelis, not to mention thousands more combat soldiers available to the Arabs because of their enormous population advantage. Other accounts suggest that the Arab advantage was less lopsided. Some numbers are indisputable. It is easy, for example, to count the hundreds of aircrafts under the control of Arab armies, versus the nominal number of planes that the young Jewish state was able to secure for its defense. Manpower is more difficult to evaluate, because the numbers depend on whether one counts front-line soldiers in Israel at any given time, or the full standing armies of the several allied Arab nations. Typical of Walt and Mearsheimer's style, the authors select the most extreme interpretation, omitting all nuance and conflicting accounts, and present it as if it were non-controversial.

4. "Israeli officials have long claimed that the Arabs fled because their leaders told them to, but careful scholarship (much of it by Israeli historians like Morris) have demolished this myth."

No such academic consensus exists. On the contrary, nearly all scholars acknowledge that the issue is complex and that some Arab leaders did urge Palestinians to flee their homes in Israel. Nor does the Israeli historian Benny Morris say anything resembling what Mearsheimer and Walt cite him as saying. Here is what he wrote:

> In some areas Arab commanders ordered the villagers to evacuate to clear the ground for military purposes or to prevent surrender. More than half a dozen villages—just north of Jerusalem and in the Lower Galilee—were abandoned during these months as a result of such orders.

Morris insists that "there was no Zionist policy to expel the Arabs or intimidate them into flight...." Certainly, many innocent Palestinians fled because they feared the approaching Jewish army. Such flight from the scenes of battle occurs in most wars, if the winning side allows it, rather than seeking to kill those running away, as the Arabs proposed doing. As Abdel al-Rahman Azzam Pasha, the secretary general of the Arab League, predicted immediately prior to the Arab invasion of Israel: "This will be a war of extermination and a momentous massacre, which will be spoken of like the Mongolian massacres and the Crusades." And, indeed, the Palestinians murdered many unarmed Israelis as well as soldiers who had surrendered.

Keep in mind, too, that it was the Palestinians and surrounding Arab armies that initiated the war. There would be no refugees if, as Israel did, the Arabs had been willing to accept Partition, leading to a full Palestinian state alongside a Jewish homeland.

This particular falsehood also illustrates Mearsheimer and Walt's co-opting of Noam Chomsky's favored method of argumentation: they simply claim that their most preposterous assertions are universally accepted as true. They call their evidence entirely "not controversial," just as Chomsky says "the most significant facts"—that is, the facts that he invents and relies upon—"are not controversial."

5. "But the creation of Israel involved additional crimes against a largely innocent third party: the Palestinians."

Considering Palestinian collaboration and support for Nazism during World War II, and its participation in an offensive war of extermination in 1948–49, the Palestinian people can hardly be called "a largely innocent third party." The recognized leader of the Palestinian people, Grand Mufti of Jerusalem Haj Amin al-Husseini, supported Hitler wholeheartedly. He asked the Axis powers for help in solving the Jewish problem in Palestine based on the "racial interests of the Arabs and along lines similar to those used to solve the Jewish question in Germany...." He even asked if he could send Jews to "Poland, in order thereby to protect oneself from their menace."

Following the war, when the UN partitioned the British Mandate between Jews and Palestinians, the Jews agreed to a peaceable division, while the Palestinians sided with the invading Arab armies in a war whose object was to rid the former

Mandate of its Jews. Mearsheimer and Walt never mention the Peel Commission (1937) or the UN Partition Plan (1947) and Israel's acceptance of tiny, non-contiguous cantons, because it would undermine their false argument that Israel has never agreed to a full and contiguous Palestinian state.

6. "The mainstream Zionist leadership was not interested in establishing a binational state or accepting a permanent partition of Palestine."

Israel has accepted every partition plan proposed, from the 1917 Balfour Declaration, to the 1937 Peel Commission plan, to the 1947 UN Partition, to the 2000 Camp David proposals, and finally, to the December 23 Clinton Parameter plans. The Palestinian leadership has rejected all of these international partition proposals. But you wouldn't know that from reading this one-sided account.

7. "Pressure from extremist violence and the growing Palestinian population has forced subsequent Israeli leaders to disengage from some of the occupied territories and to explore territorial compromise, but no Israeli government has been willing to offer the Palestinians a viable state of their own. Even Prime Minister Ehud Barak's purportedly generous offer at Camp David in July 2000 would only have given the Palestinians a disarmed and dismembered set of 'Bantustans' under de facto Israeli control."

The Bantustan accusation is Mearsheimer and Walt's boldest misstatement. They cite Ehud Barak for this proposition, though what he actually said was that the Bantustan accusation was "one of the most embarrassing lies" Arafat told about Camp David. They do *not* cite to the map Dennis Ross published in his book, *The Missing Peace*, which contrasts the "Palestinian Characterization of the Final Proposal at Camp David" with the "Map Reflecting Actual Proposal at Camp David." The second map—which reflected President Clinton's proposals and which Arafat rejected—shows a contiguous Palestinian state in the West Bank. Saudi Prince Bandar was so astounded by the generosity of Israel's offer at Camp David that he told Arafat in no uncertain terms, "If we lose this opportunity, it is not going to be a tragedy. This is going to be a crime." Mearsheimer and Walt choose to repeat Arafat's lie over the word of virtually everyone else at Camp David and the published maps proving exactly what it was that Arafat turned down. Yet they insist on characterizing their demonstrably false description as "uncontroversial." On Planet Chomsky perhaps, but not in the real world!

8. "Neither America nor Israel could be blackmailed by a nuclear-armed rogue [Iran], because the blackmailer could not carry out the threat without receiving overwhelming retaliation. The danger of a 'nuclear handoff' to terrorists is equally remote, because a rogue state could not be sure the transfer would be undetected or that it would not be blamed and punished afterwards."

Mearsheimer and Walt minimize the dangers posed by Iran both to the United States and to Israel. They assume that Iran would be as subject to a deterrent threat of massive retaliation as was the Soviet Union during the Cold War or North Korea today. This argument ignores the fact that the leaders of Iran have quite clearly asserted that they do not fear nuclear retaliation. Hashemi Rafsanjani, the former president of Iran, has threatened Israel with nuclear destruction, boasting that an Iranian attack would kill as many as five million Jews. Rafsanjani estimated that even if Israel retaliated by dropping its own nuclear bombs, Iran would probably lose only fifteen million people, which he said would be a small "sacrifice" from among the billion Muslims in the world. And he told a crowd in Tehran:

> "If a day comes when the world of Islam is duly equipped with the arms Israel has in its possession, the strategy of colonialism would face a stalemate because application of an atomic bomb would not leave any thing in Israel but the same thing would just produce damages in the Muslim world."

At a conference entitled "The World Without Zionism" in October 2005, Rafsanjani's successor, Mahmoud Ahmadinejad, declared that Israel "must be wiped off the map." Accordingly, neither the United States nor Israel could be confident that a "handoff" of nuclear weapons to terrorists would necessarily be deterred by the threat of retaliation. That is why both nations, as well as European countries, have mutual interests in preventing Iran from developing nuclear weapons.

9. "There is also a strong norm against criticizing Israeli policy, and Jewish-American leaders rarely support putting pressure on Israel."

If the [Mearsheimer and Walt] believe that American Jews are reluctant to criticize Israel or to try to pressure Israeli public officials, they are not familiar with the American Jewish community, which thrives on controversy.

10. The Lobby is engaged in a "campaign to eliminate criticism of Israel from college campuses."

If this absurd assertion were true, it would prove that "the Lobby" is a lot less powerful than the authors would have us believe, considering the fact that anti-Israel sentiment is nearly ubiquitous on college campuses. Mearsheimer and Walt try to have it both ways. On the one hand, the Lobby is an all-powerful force for manipulating American thought, conversation, and policy. On the other, the Lobby is ineffectual in its desperate attempt to stifle debate about Israel on university campuses.

In fact, the Mearsheimer-Walt *paper* may be one of the strongest pieces of evidence of the powerful culture of anti-Israeli animus on college campuses. As Caroline Glick [deputy managing editor of the *Jerusalem Post*] pointed out:

> Walt and Mearsheimer—who are both rational men—undoubtedly considered the likely consequences of publishing their views and concluded that the anti-Israel nature of their article would shield them from criticisms of its substandard academic quality. That is, they believe that hostility towards Israel is so acceptable in the U.S. that authors of shoddy research whose publication would normally destroy their professional reputations can get away with substandard work if it that work relates to Israel.

III. LOGIC

Even if the scholarship were sound and the facts accurate—neither come close—the paper's thesis would still be unsound. Mearsheimer and Walt's "reasoning" is simply illogical.

The very first argument they offer exemplifies their illogical and conspiratorial approach. They contend that the very existence of an Israeli lobby proves that support for Israel is essentially un-American. Here is what they say:

> Indeed, the mere existence of the Lobby suggests that unconditional

support for Israel is not in the American national interest. If it was [*sic.*], one would not need an organized special interest group to bring it about.

In other words, any group that *needs* a lobby must be working against "American national interest." The absurdity of this argument is demonstrated by the fact that the most powerful lobby is the AARP. According to Mearsheimer and Walt's "logic," that would mean that the rights of retired people are inconsistent with American national interests, as is equality for African-Americans (NAACP), choice for women (reproductive rights lobbies), clean air for environmentalists (Environmental Defense Fund), and the thousands of other groups that maintain powerful lobbies in Washington. By their reasoning, the very existence of the ACLU proves that civil liberties are not in America's national interest! The reality, of course, is that virtually all interest groups and many foreign countries employ lobbying, but only the "Israel lobby" is accused of being contrary to American national interest.

One of the authors' most common arguments is to suggest that if a Jew admits something negative about other Jews, then it must necessarily be true. Gideon Levy wrote a column saying that no one in Israel opposed the Iraq war—a ridiculous and easily falsifiable claim—but Mearsheimer and Walt quote it as Gospel. Akiva Eldar accused Douglas Feith and Richard Perle of "walking a fine line between their loyalty to American governments...and Israeli interests." The authors copy the quotation and present it as credible evidence. The authors quote Morris Amitay, another Jew, to suggest that Jewish staffers view their primary professional allegiance to their "Jewishness" rather than to their nation. It is a serious accusation, substantiated by only a single quotation from a person who, like many in Washington, had a professional stake in exaggerating his access to decision-makers. But he's a Jew, so it must be true!

These are example*s* of the *ad hominem* fallacy, in which the authors rest the soundness of their arguments on the identity of the speaker, rather than on the truth of the ideas. As I wrote about this style of argumentation in *The Case For Israel*:

> It is a fundamental fallacy to conclude that one side of a dispute must be right if some people who are ethnically identified with that side support the other side. For example, the fact that there is a handful of Jewish Holocaust deniers—as well as some prominent Jews, like Noam Chomsky, who are prepared to endorse the "extensive research" done by a Holocaust denier—does not mean that the Holocaust did not occur. Nor does the fact that some Italian Jews supported Mussolini in the early 1930s prove that fascism was right. Yet a staple of pro-Palestinian propaganda is the argument that is structured as follows: "See, even a Jew like [fill in the name] believes that Israel is wrong and the Palestinians are right about [fill in the issue]." This "argument by ethnic admission" is both logically and empirically fallacious.

The paper's thesis is equally nonsensical. Mearsheimer and Walt attribute anything that Israel and America do or aspire to achieve in common to Israeli manipulation. The professors make the most basic of all logical fallacies—they confuse correlation with causation. Listen to the following passage:

> By February 2003, a *Washington Post* headline summarized the situation: "Bush and Sharon Nearly

Identical on Mideast Policy." The main reason for this switch is the Lobby.

The upshot of their naked conclusory assertion is that Ariel Sharon *duped* President Bush into overthrowing Saddam Hussein. Mearsheimer and Walt never consider the more likely explanation: that Bush and Sharon shared the same worldview and vision for the Middle East. This is not academic writing. There is no weighing of evidence. Mearsheimer and Walt simply chose the most insidious explanation—which also happened to be the *least plausible* explanation—and dismissed all other possibilities without even an acknowledgement that other interpretations are *possible.* No wonder Mearsheimer's colleague critiqued the research as poor "monocausal social science."

Walt's colleague David Gergen—who has far more experience in the actual decision-making process in the White House—finds the paper's thesis "wildly at variance" with what he witnessed. Yet Walt and Mearsheimer apparently never interviewed Gergan. Had they done so, they would have learned the following:

> Over the course of four tours in the White House, I never once saw a decision in the Oval Office to tilt U.S. foreign policy in favor of Israel at the expense of America's interest. Other than Richard Nixon—who occasionally said terrible things about Jews, despite the number on his team—I can't remember any president even talking about an Israeli lobby. Perhaps I have forgotten, but I can remember plenty of conversations about the power of the American gun lobby, environmentalists, evangelicals, small-business owners, and teachers unions.

Gergen added the following:

> Not only are these charges wildly at variance with what I have personally witnessed in the Oval Office over the years, but they also impugn the loyalty and the unstinting service to America's national security by public figures like Dennis Ross, Martin Indyk, and many others. As a Christian, let me add that it is also wrong and unfair to call into question the loyalty of millions of American Jews who have faithfully supported Israel while also working tirelessly and generously to advance America's cause, both at home and abroad. They are among our finest citizens and should be praised, not pilloried.

Just because Israel and the United States often have similar interests does not mean that America is pursuing its policies on Israel's behalf. By that reasoning, anyone who agrees with Mearsheimer and Walt's paper must in fact be manipulating the authors into holding their particular beliefs. The most vocal proponent of their paper so far has been David Duke, but that does not mean that Mearsheimer and Walt are beholden to the Klan Lobby. The better explanation is simply that Walt, Mearsheimer, and Duke happen to have reached the same conclusions, and share the same interest in vilifying Jewish leaders and spouting conspiracy theories about Zionist plots against American interests.

What is most astounding about Mearsheimer and Walt's conspiratorial worldview is that they think that a population of five million Jews—which is less than 2% (not 3%, as Mearsheimer and Walt assert) of the U.S. population—is somehow able to bully and confuse two hundred ninety-five million non-Jews into consistently acting against their own true interests. They are parroting the Marxist principle of "false consciousness," that is, the idea that "the masses" do not truly recognize what is in their own self-interest. Professor Ruth Wisse [Harvard University], with whom I have often respectfully disagreed on matters of Israel and the Jewish community, gets is right this time when she writes:

> Yet it would be a mistake to treat this article on the "Israel Lobby" as an attack on Israel alone, or on its Jewish defenders, or on the organizations and individuals it singles out for condemnation. Its true target is the American public, which now supports Israel with higher levels of confidence than ever before. When the authors imply that the bipartisan support of Israel in Congress is a result of Jewish influence, they function as classic conspiracy theorists who attribute decisions to nefarious alliances rather than to the choices of a democratic electorate. Their contempt for fellow citizens dictates their claims of a gullible and stupid America. Their insistence that American support for Israel is bought and paid for by the Lobby heaps scorn on American judgment and values.

Again, the more likely explanation is that the majority of Americans—Jew and non-Jew alike—often perceive their interests to be parallel to Israel's interests. Both are democratic nations born out of Western traditions with rich Western cultures. Is it any wonder that Americans would more closely identify with a secular democratic nation than with the totalitarian theocracies or oppressive dictatorships that surround Israel—or with a nation that is fervently pro-American, rather than with countries with considerable anti-American sentiment.

The implication of Mearsheimer and Walt's paper, that American Jews put the interests of Israel before those of America, raises the ugly specter of "dual loyalty," a canard that has haunted Diaspora Jews from time immemorial. Today in America, it is rightfully considered vile to suggest that American Catholic politicians such as John F. Kennedy and John Kerry owe their primary allegiance to the Vatican over the United States. But Mearsheimer and Walt have no qualms about making the analogous accusation against Jewish politicians and their staffers. "There are also Jewish senators and congressmen who work to make U.S. foreign policy support Israel's interests." When America acts in concert with Britain, Italy, Germany, India, or China, no one questions the loyalty and patriotism of the descendants from those nationalities. Mearsheimer and Walt target only Jews for their accusations of disloyalty and subversion of American interests.

CONCLUSION

It is not only the words—false and unbalanced as they are—that invoke old stereotypes and canards. It is the "music" as well—the tone, pitch, and feel of the article—that has caused such outrage from academics and concerned citizens from all across the political and religious spectrum (with the exception of the hard right and hard left). What would motivate two recognized academics to issue a compilation of previously made assertions that they must know will be used by overt anti-Semites to argue that Jews have too much influence, that will give an academic imprimatur to crass bigotry, and that will place all Jews in government and the media under suspicion of disloyalty to America? Imagine if two professors compiled as many negative statements, based on shoddy research and questionable sources, about African-Americans causing all the problems in America, and presented that compilation as evidence that

African-Americans behave in a manner contrary to the best interest of the United States. No matter how many footnotes there were, who would fail to recognize such a project as destructive?

I wonder what the authors believed they would accomplish by recycling such misinformation about Jewish "blood kinship," by raising discredited and false connections between Jonathan Pollard and the Soviet Union, by saying that the "Zionist" army was larger and better equipped than the Arab armies that tried to destroy it in 1948, and by repeating so many other easily refutable distortions? Why pay so much attention to Jewish congressional staffers? Is it so that Congresspeople will stop hiring Jews or demand loyalty tests of them? I simply do not understand, *what is the motive*?

And so I repeat my challenges to Stephen Walt and John Mearsheimer. I challenge them to tell us which arguments are new and have not previously been made on hate sites and in anti-Israel screeds. What new evidence has been gathered? Why are there so many factual errors, all cutting against Israel? Why didn't they present important counterfacts or address any counterarguments?

Walt and Mearsheimer repeatedly claim that they have written their paper, at least in part, in order to stimulate dialogue concerning the influence of the Lobby. They claim that it is the pro-Israel side that seeks to suppress public discussion: "[The Lobby] does not want Americans to question the level of support they currently provide." Yet the pro-Israel side has risen to the Walt-Mearsheimer challenge and has participated in the marketplace of ideas, only to be greeted by silence from the authors, who have generally refused to defend their views. I have personally offered Walt and Mearsheimer an opportunity to debate the issues raised in their paper, but to date they have not done so. My invitation to debate remains open. I challenge Mearsheimer and Walt to look me in the eye and tell me that because I am a proud Jew and a critical supporter of Israel, I am disloyal to my country.

THE CONTINUING DEBATE: The Pro-Israel Lobby in the United States

What Is New

The appearance of the John Mearsheimer and Stephen Walt paper, set off a storm of controversy. As one commentary noted, seldom "has an academic essay detonated with such force." Some critics hurled charges of anti-Semitism. Professor Eliot A. Cohen of John Hopkins University charged that Mearsheimer and Walt's article was "not scholarship or policy advocacy. It is merely, and unforgivably, bigotry." Others were more general, with, for instance, U.S Representative Jerrold Nadler calling the article "dishonest piece of crap." However, other commentators either gave some or full support to Mearsheimer and Walt or faulted some critics for overreacting. Syndicated columnist Richard Cohen wrote that associating Mearsheimer and Walt with such avowed racists as David Duke was unfair "guilt by association," and columnist Tony Lundt regretted that fears of being labeled anti-Semitic were causing a "failure to consider a major issue in public policy."

Soon the outbreak of violence between Israel and Hezbollah in Lebanon put U.S. policy to the test. The Bush administration stood solidly behind Israel, but American public opinion was not overwhelmingly supportive. More Americans (62%) are sympathetic toward Israel than not, and during the conflict almost none favored U.S. support of Hezbollah. But only 31% wanted the U.S. government to take Israel's side, while 65% favored not taking either side, with 4% were unsure.

Where to Find More

A review of the reactions to the Mearsheimer and Walt article is Michael Massing's "The Storm Over Israel," *New York Review of Books* (June 8, 2006). For an argument that the United States is too pro-Israel, but discounts the influence of AIPAC, see Stephen Zunes, "The Israel Lobby: How Powerful is it Really?" *Mother Jones* (May 16, 2006). The reactions of Mearsheimer and Walt to the criticism is in an interview, "Grabbing the Third Rail," *Mother Jones* (June 18, 2006). The website of the American-Israel Public Affairs Committee is www.aipac.org/, that of the Arab American Institute is www.aaiusa.org/.

What More to Do

Although those in the United States who favor Israel and lobby the U.S. government to support it are the focus of this article, remember that they are but an example of the larger question that this debate addresses. That is whether and/or there is conflict of interest when Americans promote the interests of another country or foreign group. If such lobbying is not acceptable, how would you regulate it?

DEBATE 9

POLITICAL PARTIES

HILLARY CLINTON AND THE 2008 PRESIDENTIAL ELECTION: The Democrats' Best Bet *or* a Problematic Candidate?

THE DEMOCRATS' BEST BET

ADVOCATE: Carl Cannon, White House correspondent for the *National Journal*

SOURCE: "She Can Win the White House," *Washington Monthly*, July/August 2005

A PROBLEMATIC CANDIDATE

ADVOCATE: Amy Sullivan, editor, *Washington Monthly*

SOURCE: "Not So Fast," *Washington Monthly*, July/August 2005

Kermit the Frog has often sung a plaintiff tune that begins, "It's not easy being green." Members of the currently out-of-power political party in the United States can identity with Kermit's struggle because for them, "It's not easy being a Democrat." Once that was easier. Indeed the Democrats had a great run beginning with Franklin D. Roosevelt's entry into the White House in 1933. From then until 1969, a Democrat sat in the Oval Office for all but eight years (1953–1961, Dwight D. Eisenhower). Making life even happier for the Democrats, they also controlled both houses of Congress except for four years (1947–1949 and 1953–1955).

Then the political fortune of the Democrats began to decline. Republican Richard M. Nixon became president in 1969, and since then a Republican has been president two-thirds of the time (exceptions: Jimmy Carter, 1977–1981; Bill Clinton, 1993–2001). The power of the Democrats also declined in Congress, although they held on longer there. The Republicans took control of the Senate in 1981 and held it for six years. They then lost the majority to the Democrats for eights years but regained control in 1997 and have held it ever since. Democrats ceded power in the House even more slowly, but they lost it in 1997 and remain the minority party. Republicans also dominate marginally at the state level. In 2005, Republican state governors outnumber their Democratic counterparts 28 to 22. Of the various state legislative chambers, Republicans control 50, the Democrats 47; one is tied.

This tale of nearly 40 disappointing years for the Democrats brings us to the 2008 presidential election and the potential of New York Senator Hillary R. Clinton as the Democratic nominee. Prior to that, of course, there is the 2006 congressional elections. With public discontent over the war in Iraq and other matters hurting the popularity of President Bush and, by extension, other Republicans, the Democrats have the best chance in a decade to regain a majority in one or both houses of Congress. However, the Republicans have enough of a majority in both houses and the chances of defeating incumbents are so slim, that Democratic control of the Senate would be a major upset and there is only a fifty-fifty chance the Democrats will control the House. Thus 2008 is a key year for the Democrats. With President

Bush ineligible to run again, the Democratic incumbent will not have to run against an incumbent president. Moreover of the 33 Senate seats up for election in 2008, Republicans are vulnerable because they hold 19 of them. Additionally, a winning Democratic presidential "coat tails," even if limited, could provide the margin of victory to gain a majority in the House.

Is Senator Clinton the candidate most likely to lead Democrats to control of the White House and both houses of Congress in 2009? That is the issue which divides Carl Cannon, who believes she is, and Amy Sullivan, who contends that she is not.

Clinton was born on October 26, 1947, as Hillary Diane Rodham and grew up in Park Ridge, Illinois. She began her active political career while at Wellesley College, where she served as president of the Wellesley College Chapter of the College Republicans. During her junior year, however, Rodham became a Democrat. She first gained a glimmer of national note when her valedictory graduation speech at Wellesley was considered so outstanding that she was featured in a *Life* magazine article. After that, she attended Yale Law School, where she met future husband Bill Clinton, and from where she graduated in 1972. After marrying Clinton in 1975, she moved to Arkansas, where she practiced law.

Hillary Clinton became first lady in 1993, and was soon appointed by her husband to head the Task Force on National Health Care Reform. Its eventual recommendations were much too far reaching to be accepted by Congress and were soon abandoned. This ended any overt political role for Ms. Clinton until the very end of her husband's tenure in the White House. It was not, however, the last of her trouble during those years. There were charges of unethical, even illegal activities in the huge gain she had made in 1979, turning an investment of $1,000 into $100,000, trading cattle futures on the Chicago Mercantile Exchange. Later, in the so-called Whitewater scandal, Ms. Clinton was summoned to testify before a grand jury regarding any part she might have played in a real estate fraud involving a venture in which she and her husband were among the partners. Several of the partners went to jail, but the Clintons were not charged. Ms. Clinton's time in the White House was also troubled by her spouse's alleged and acknowledged extra-marital affairs, most notably with White House intern Monica Lewinsky. With her husband's years as president ending, Ms. Clinton sought and won the Democratic nomination for the U.S. Senate in New York, then handily beat her Republican opponent with 55% of the vote. It was widely thought then, as it is now, that she would try to use the New York Senate seat as a platform to launch a bid for the presidency.

POINTS TO PONDER

- For this early in a campaign, Senator Clinton has an unusually high percentage of "positive" and "negatives," people who like and dislike her. The authors disagree about what this means. Who is right?
- What, if anything, would it mean to have former president Bill Clinton in the White House as the "first gentleman"?
- To what degree if any is gender a reasonable standard to any voter to make a decision for or against supporting Clinton?

Hillary Clinton and the 2008 Presidential Election: The Democrats' Best Bet

CARL CANNON

In 1978, while covering California politics, I found myself on election night at the Century Plaza Hotel in Los Angeles, which was serving as a kind of election central. Waiting for the returns to come in, I was sitting in the lobby having a drink with my father—who, then as now, was the leading expert on Ronald Reagan. As iron cue, the former actor and ex-California governor came striding into the hotel. Even then Reagan looked the part: wide-shouldered, flanked by a security detail, sporting his trademark blue serge suit, every black hair in place.

The only thing missing, I thought, was the Marine Corps Band.

No one back east took Reagan nearly as seriously as he seemed to be taking himself. Despite a devoted following among what were then known as Goldwater Republicans, the Washington cognoscenti casually dismissed Reagan as too conservative, too old, a B-movie actor who once played second fiddle to a chimpanzee—"Who does he think he is?" I asked my dad. "The president of the United States?"

"No," came the reply. "He thinks he's the next president of the United States." After a pause, he added, "And he might be."

I remember that vignette every time a political sage says authoritatively that [Senator] Hillary Rodham Clinton [D-NY] will "never" be president.

This is a particularly entrenched bit of conventional wisdom, which seems to have metastasized into a kind of secret handshake. If you "know" Clinton can't be president, you're a member of the Washington in-crowd. If you don't, you're an outsider, some boob from the sticks of, I don't know, Sacramento or somewhere. Suburban Chicago, maybe. You know the rap: She's too liberal, too polarizing, a feminist too threatening to male voters. Too much baggage. Too... *Clinton.*

And these are Democrats talking. Bizarrely, the party's insiders are going out of their way to tear down the credentials and prospects of one of their rare superstars. Conservative columnist Robert Novak ran into this phenomenon recently while speaking to eight local Democratic politicians in Los Angeles. Novak told them matter-of-factly that Hillary was the odds-on favorite to be their party's 2008 nominee—and that no one was in second place. Novak was surprised by their reaction: Not one was for Mrs. Clinton. Why? "They think she is a loser," said one of the Democrats.

With some exceptions, the journalistic pack seems nearly as negative about Hillary Clinton's chances. I'm a charter member of an informal lunch group of writers who runs the gamut from conservative to liberal, and each month when we meet, Hillary's name arises. Around the table it goes: She can't be elected in a general election; men aren't willing to vote for a woman like Hillary; women don't think much of her marriage—or her, for staying in it; which red state could she possibly carry? What swing voter would she convince? Each month, I marshaled my arguments in favor of Hillary's candidacy until finally I began sparing my friends the whole rap by just noting—for the minutes of the meeting, as it were—that I disagree with them.

Perhaps my lunch mates, those worried activist Democrats, and the majority of Washington pundits are correct. But I don't think so.

They certainly weren't right about Reagan.

Conservatives (and liberals) would consider it heresy to compare Ronald Reagan and Hillary Clinton. And Reagan is certainly a hard act to follow. He combined Main Street sensibilities and a soothing Middle America persona with an uplifting vision of America's place in the world that earned him a stunningly decisive victory in 1980—and 60 percent of the vote when he ran for reelection four years later. Senator Clinton is a more polarizing figure, in more polarized times. Yet Clinton, like Reagan, can lay claim to the passions of diehard grassroots members of her party. With the exception of incumbents and vice presidents, no candidate since Reagan has had a hammerlock on his or her party's nomination this long before the election. And like Reagan, the charisma gap between her and any would-be challengers in her own party is palpable.

Of course, the question is not whether she can win in the primary. Most Democrats concede the primary is probably hers for the taking. "I don't know how you beat her for the Democratic nomination," former Senator Bob Kerrey [D-NE] told *New York* magazine. She's a rock star. But that, as the cognoscenti see it, is the problem. She can't lose the primary, and she can't win the general election. And so they look vainly for an alternative—Warner? Biden? Bayh? Oh my!—always circling back to the same despairing fear of another four years in the political wilderness. Democrats have raised this kind of defeatism to a high art. But it's time for Democrats to snap out of it and take a fresh look at the hand they've been dealt. Hillary Rodham Clinton can win the general election no matter who the Republicans throw at her. The Democrats just might be holding aces.

POLL POSITIONED

The available data do not suggest she is unelectable—they suggest just the opposite. A Gallup poll done a week before Memorial Day showed Senator Clinton with a favorable rate of 55 percent. True, her unfavorable number is 39 percent, which is high enough for concern—but one that is nearly identical to Bush's on the eve of his reelection. And the unfavorable rating registered by Republican contender [Senator] Bill Frist [R-TN] was nearly as high as his favorable numbers, with 32 percent saying they'd never heard of him.

"Then there was this eye-opening question:

If Hillary Rodham Clinton were to run for president in 2008, how likely would you be to vote for her—very likely, somewhat likely, not very likely, or not at all likely?

Very likely	29%
Somewhat likely	24
Not very likely	7
Not at all likely	40
No opinion	1

At the risk of laboring the point, 29 percent plus 24 percent adds up to a majority. I can hear my pals answering this as they read these numbers: "Yes, but that's before the conservative attack machine gets a hold of her..."

Well, no, it isn't. They've been going at her with verbal tire irons, machetes, and sawed-off shotguns for 12 years now. Senator Clinton's negatives are already figured into her ratings. What could she be accused of that she hasn't already confronted since she entered the public eye 14 years ago? Clinton today is in a position similar to Bush's at the beginning of 2004. Democrats hoped that more information about the president's youth would "knock him down." But voters had already taken the president's past into account when they voted for him in 2000. More information just wasn't going to make a dent. In fact, as the spring of 2005 turned to summer there were yet another book and a matched spate of tabloid broadsides. In the face of it all, Hillary appears, if anything, to be getting stronger. Indeed, the more the right throws at her, the easier it is for her to lump any criticism in with the darkest visions of the professional Clinton bashers.

Let's also look deeper into that Gallup survey because the closer you look at it, the more formidable Senator Clinton seems. Thirty percent of the poll's respondents consider Hillary a "moderate," while 9 percent described her a "conservative." Now, I'm not sure which newspapers that 9 percent have been reading (the *Daily Worker*?), but the fact that nearly 40 percent of the electorate does not identify her as liberal mitigates the perception that she's considered too far to the left to be a viable national candidate.

Such perceptions are hardly set in stone, however, and senators' voting records can come back to haunt them in the heat of a campaign as [Senator] John Kerry [D-MA] learned in 2004 and countless others have learned before him. It's no accident that the last sitting U.S. senator elected president was John F. Kennedy. Thus, Clinton's Senate voting record, and where it puts her on the ideological scale, is worth some additional scrutiny.

The most comprehensive annual analysis of voting records is undertaken by my magazine, *National Journal*, which for 2004 used 24 votes on economic issues, 19 votes on social issues, and 17 foreign policy-related roll calls to rate all 100 U.S. senators. Its resulting ranking of John Kerry as the Senate's most liberal member (at least during 2003) was a gift from on high for the Bush campaign, and the Massachusetts senator spent the better part of his campaign trying to explain away this vote or that. But Senator Clinton is harder to pigeon-hole. For 2004, Clinton's composite liberal score was 71 percent—putting her roughly in the middle of the Democratic caucus. While adhering to her party's liberal dogma on issues such as race, gun control, and judicial appointees, Hillary lists slightly toward the center on economic issues, and even more so on national security and foreign-policy issues. There's no telling at this point how the war in Iraq will play in 2008, but one thing is certain: Senator Clinton won't struggle the way Kerry did to reconcile a vote authorizing the war with one not authorizing the $87 billion to pay for it. For better or worse, she voted "aye" both times.

Yet another piece of received Washington wisdom holds that the party could never nominate someone in 2008 who has supported the Iraq war. Perhaps. But history suggests that if Bush's mission in Iraq flounders, a politician as nimble as Clinton will have plenty of time to get out in front of any anti-war movement. If it succeeds, Hillary would have demonstrated the kind of steadfastness demanded by the soccer moms turned security moms with whom Bush did so well in 2004.

On domestic issues, Senator Clinton has also shown a willingness to step out of the safety zone. She is bolstering her bipartisan credentials by teaming up with Republicans from the other side of the aisle, such as [Senator] Lindsey Graham [R-SC] and Frist himself, making her more difficult to portray as some kind of radical. And while her liberal voting record on social issues remains intact, she has taken rhetorical steps toward the middle. The most notable example occurred during a January speech in Albany, in which she advised abortion-rights activists to seek "common ground ...with people on the other side." While pledging to defend *Roe v. Wade*, Mrs. Clinton relented to abortion as a "sad, even tragic, act" and called on Democrats to embrace a moral language for discussing the issue. Some conservatives even seemed receptive. In some quarters, Hillary's centrist posture was portrayed as new; but it actually isn't: She butted heads with the Arkansas teachers' union in the mid-1980s over a proposal she led to improve teacher quality.

The abortion speech was reminiscent of her husband's 1992 campaign-trail criticism of Sister Souljah for advocating violence against white people. Her remarks simultaneously showed she was willing to talk common sense to a key Democratic interest group while putting herself in sync with the ambivalent sensibilities most Americans have toward abortion. And because of the high standing she enjoys among Democratic women, she was able to do it without any fear of liberal backlash. Let's face it: When a feminist with Hillary's credentials discusses abortion in the way she has, it causes people to sit up and take notice.

Which brings us to the ultimate question: Hillary's gender. Will Americans vote for a woman?

They certainly say they will: 74 percent told Gallup that they'd be either "somewhat" or "very" likely to vote for a woman in 2008. This number is actually on the low side compared to polls from the pre-Hillary era, for the obvious reason that Clinton casts a shadow over 2008, and many of the respondents are Republicans who plan to vote against her. Again, I can hear some of my friends murmuring that these voters aren't telling the truth. But that's precisely the kind of snobbish thinking that never gets Democrats anywhere, that is usually wrong, and that infuriates swing voters. My advice to my Democratic friends is to ignore your inner elitist, and trust the American people to tell the truth, and, moreover, to do the right thing.

In fact, there is no reason to doubt them, as they've been proving their willingness to pull the lever for female candidates for a long time. In 1999, when Hillary first entered the national scene, 56 women sat in the House of Representatives, and nine in the Senate. Only three women were governors, but many women were in the pipeline in state government: Nearly 28 percent of statewide elective offices in the country were occupied by women. In one state, Arizona, women held the top five statewide offices. And that pipeline produced. Six years later, there are 14 women in the Senate, and 66 in the House (along with another three non-voting delegates). There are eight, not three, women governors. "The day will come when men will recognize woman as his peer, not only at the fireside, but in councils of the nation," [Women's suffrage leader] Susan B. Anthony [1820–1906] once predicted. That day is fast approaching whether or not conservatives are ready for it, and whether or not liberals are willing to acknowledge it.

Nonetheless, anyone who maintains that the American electorate is ready for a female president (and this particular female candidate) must at some point confront the Electoral College map. This, my skeptical friends claim, is where Hillary's hopes run aground. Putting it plainly, they challenge anyone to come up with a red state that Hillary can carry—someplace, anyplace, where Senator Clinton could run stronger than the Kerry/Edwards ticket.

It is, of course, absurd to look at electoral politics at such an atomic level this far out. In due time, pollsters and the press will christen 2008's must-have swing voters and must-win swing states. But calibrating a candidacy to the last election is a fool's errand. The near-frozen electoral map of the last five years has been an historical anomaly, not the rule. So there's no reason to believe that a 2004 electoral map would be terribly useful three years hence.

But if we must, let's play along. What red state could Clinton snatch away from the GOP column? How about Florida? The Gold Coast considers itself part of New York anyway, and Clinton's moderate overtures might draw swing voters from upstate. Cuban Americans are no longer the sole Latino voting bloc in Florida—and even Cubans are no longer monolithic. If not Florida, how about Iowa and New Mexico? They are centrist, bellwether states—and states Hillary's husband carried both times he ran. Meanwhile, the Republican Party hardly has a lock on Ohio, which went for Clinton twice, and which was close in 2000 and 2004.

The fact is, there are a thousand movable parts in a presidential campaign, but the two most indispensable are (1) a candidate with charisma, money, and a broad following in his or her party; and (2) a ticket that espouses values and policies that Middle Americans agree with. A candidate, the polls now suggest, like Hillary Clinton.

Or [Senator] John McCain [R-AZ].

THE BUBBA FACTOR

After dissecting an upcoming race, any good horse player will look at the *Racing Form* again and figure out if he (or she) missed anything: Who could beat the obvious horse? For the 2008 presidential run, there is an answer that jumps off the page: If the Republican faithful are smart enough to nominate him, John Sydney McCain III would probably be their most formidable candidate—if he gets the GOP nomination, a big "if."

It's fanciful to suggest that anyone is unbeatable this far out, even McCain. While he makes the media swoon, the Arizona senator would have to thread a pretty tight needle to get to the White House. A Quinnipiac Poll taken in March showed a McCain-Clinton election virtually tied, 43–41. These are good numbers, but they're hardly in the Colin Powell range. The Republican conservative base remains leery of him. That this antipathy is self-defeating (or even inexplicable) makes it no less real. In addition, the easiest circumstances to envision that would benefit McCain would be if there were widespread disillusion with Bush. But the issue most likely to bring that about—a dire result to the occupation in Iraq—probably doesn't help McCain anyway: If anything, he's been more hawkish on foreign policy than the president. Even if other factors—a rotten economy or a scandal—led to a McCain general election candidacy, a GOP meltdown might carry McCain to the nomination, but it wouldn't help him against Hillary Clinton. First, if conservatives could muster only halfhearted passion for the man (not unlike the less-than-enthusiastic support John Kerry received from many Democrats), well, we've seen that movie. No candidate is without vulnerabilities, and certainly Hillary has hers. (I'll leave their enumeration to my counterpart, Amy Sullivan.) The difference between a winning and losing campaign, though, is whether you have the strategy to weather the inevitable rough waters.

On the USS *George W. Bush*, Karl Rove is considered the indispensable navigator. But when one looks on the Democratic side, who is a match for the man Bush called "The Architect" of his triumph? What recent Democrat has shown such an ability to see the political chessboard 20 moves ahead and plot a winning game plan? Only one, and to find him, Senator ***Clinton*** need only look to the other side of the breakfast table.

President Clinton doesn't come without strings attached. While it is an article of faith among the Clintonistas that Al Gore hurt his own campaign in 2000 by not using Bill Clinton more on the stump, there was plenty of polling to back up Gore's gambit. While Clinton could stir up the party faithful, his presence wasn't always a net plus. Hillary faces a similar dilemma when it comes to her husband—and a lot closer to home. But in addition to being able to draw upon Clinton's strategic gifts, Senator Clinton would almost certainly not make the more serious mistake Gore made: not being able to successfully make use of the Clinton administration's record of 22 million new jobs; steady income growth for workers of every level; precipitous declines in the welfare rolls; and an expanded NATO [North Atlantic Treaty Organization] alliance that ushered in the post–Cold War geopolitical map.

Will Americans remember the optimism and idealism espoused in 1992 by The Man From Hope [a reference to Hope, Arkansas, the childhood home of Bill Clinton], and the way Clinton would parry policy questions with long, coherent, informative answers? Or will they remember their disgust at the revelations about the infamous blue dress, and how Clinton often shaded the truth?

No repentance, however sincere, could spare Bill Clinton from his eternity as fodder for the tabloids and late-night monologues. But he seems to be growing increasingly sure-footed and confident in his role as elder statesman. He has formed a friendship with the man he defeated for the office, and a productive working relationship with the current president. If he is to help his wife, all Clinton needs to do is remind us of his better angels, as he did during his tour of tsunami-devastated South Asia.

This brings us back to Hillary herself. Even if Bill Clinton rises to the occasion, voters are going to remember the yin and the yang of our 42nd president, and they are going to chew on the fact that the woman who wants to be our 44th is married to him. She will be asked about the marriage. How she answers will go a long way toward determining the viability of her candidacy. In his astute book [*The Survivor*: Random House, 1992] on the Clinton presidency, John F. Harris recounts how aides broached the subject of her marriage as Hillary prepared to run for the Senate. How would she answer this basic question: Why had she stayed with him?

"Yes, I've been wondering that myself," Hillary says playfully.

Then Bill interjects: "Because you're a sticker! That's what people need to know—you're a sticker. You stick at the things you care about."

Clintonites love this story, but there are a couple of things wrong with it. First, Bill Clinton is providing the answer, but it's not his answer to give. Second, it's a talking point. The Clintons are good at slogans, but this is a question women will have for Hillary Clinton, women looking to identify with her. A sound bite answer just might confirm voters' fears that her marriage is a sham, and that she's an opportunist. On the other hand, if the answer emerges that she loves Bill Clinton, despite his flaws, and that she's in an imperfect marriage—well, most marriages are imperfect. Moreover, if she suggests that the deciding factor was her concern for their daughter, well, that's the kind of pro-family cred that really matters. Cute answers won't cut it. Authenticity will. And there's every reason to believe both Clintons could summon it when talking about the daughter to whom they are so obviously devoted.

Finally, there is one perceived pitfall—and that's Hillary's penchant for the jugular. Party activists admire her for this, but successful general election candidates learn to temper the instincts that result in outbursts like the "vast, right-wing conspiracy."

In upstate New York, Senator Clinton has charmed independent Yankee farmers and small-town Republican businessmen from Buffalo with an inclusive, upbeat style of campaigning and governing. This is the dress rehearsal for running nationwide, yet when she gets going on the red meat circuit Senator Clinton retains a fondness for ad hominem attacks and paranoid world views.

"There has never been an administration, I don't believe in our history, more intent upon consolidating and abusing power to further their own agenda," Clinton said at a recent Democratic fundraiser. "Why can't the Democrats do more to stop them? I can tell you this: It's very hard to stop people who have no shame about what they're doing....It is very hard to stop people who have never been acquainted with the truth." The crowd loved it, but this rant manages to ignore Nixon, while simultaneously sounding Nixonian. Hillary can definitely have a tin ear.

Hillary Clinton, whether she realizes it or not, is relieved of the obligation to pander in this way. She has paid her dues to the Democratic Party, and she doesn't have to prove her bona tides to anyone. From now on, she only need emulate Reagan, a fellow Illinois native, who campaigned with positive rhetoric and a smile on his face, trusting that the work he'd done cultivating his base would pay off, and that he needed mainly to reassure independent-minded voters. When we in the press corps tried to bait Reagan into going negative by asking why he'd abandoned the party of his youth, he invariably smiled, cocked his head, and gave the same line. "I didn't leave the Democratic Party," Reagan would say. "The Democratic Party left me."

As a girl, Hillary Rodham was a Goldwater Republican. She could use the same line in reverse. It might remind swing voters why they are looking, once again, at casting their lot with a candidate named Clinton. She can do this because Democrats are poised to back her already, and because much of the rest of America is watching, open-minded, half-hoping that she gives them a reason to support her, too.

Hillary Clinton and the 2008 Presidential Election: A Problematic Candidate

AMY SULLIVAN

For a first-time candidate and controversial first lady, Hillary Clinton's bid for the open New York Senate seat in 2000 was going surprisingly well. From the beginning, she had staked out a seemingly impossible strategy; given who she was: ignore the press, go straight to the voters, and focus exclusively on issues, never on herself. "You make a mistake if you let any campaign become about you," she told Michael Tomasky, one of the reporters who followed her that year. Given that even campaigns not involving Hillary Clinton sometimes manage to become about Hillary Clinton, it was difficult to imagine how she could pull off this feat. Still, she stuck doggedly to policy talk, boring the press corps but impressing New York voters. Two weeks before Election Day, she enjoyed a comfortable lead, polling eight points ahead of opponent [Republican candidate, Representative] Rick Lazio.

And that's when Lazio decided to take matters into his hands and make the race about Clinton whether she liked it or not. His campaign put together a commercial intended to target her biggest vulnerability: white suburban women. All throughout the campaign, this demographic had been the most skeptical; in focus groups, even women who liked Clinton said she reminded them of an unpleasant woman in their lives—a mother-in-law or a stern Catholic nun or a judgmental neighbor. The ad sought to remind them that, deep down, they didn't really like Hillary Clinton, that they thought she was too ambitious. On the screen, a woman making dinner in a kitchen talked on a phone, her tone angry: "We started out at the bottom and worked our tushes off to get somewhere. No, but Hillary, she wants to start at the top, you know, the senator from New York?"

The ad was the most personal of the race, and it worked. Within days, Clinton's lead had shrunk to three points, within the margin of error. Although she recovered to win the Senate seat with 55 percent of the vote, Clinton's advantage among women was only half that of Al Gore's, who won New York's female vote by a margin of 65 to 31.

Five years later, Senator Clinton is a major player on the political scene. Her name is first on the lips of anyone who talks about the 2008 race for the White House. Potential rival John McCain says she would make a fine president. Conservatives such as [former Speaker of the U.S. House of Representatives] Newt Gingrich and Bill Kristol [editor of *The Weekly Standard*] are talking up Clinton, warning their partisan colleagues that she would be a formidable opponent. That's not surprising—after all, Republicans have long fantasized about the prospect of taking on Hillary Clinton again at a national level. But now, talk of her candidacy has gone from conservative wishful thinking to serious discussions within her own party, which is anxious to end its losing streak and is considering the advantages of closing ranks behind an early frontrunner. One glance at polls showing that 53 percent of Americans are willing to consider putting Clinton in the White House makes visions of sugar plums and oval offices dance in the heads of Democratic Party leaders. The high name recognition, impressive early poll numbers, and desperate party all carry the Senate whiff of inevitability that accompanied George W. Bush's campaign for the 2000 election.

In the face of this momentum, someone has to say it, so here goes: Please don't run, Senator.

Don't get me wrong. I'm a longtime Hillary Clinton fan. As in a back-when-she-was-still-wearing-headbands fan. I have found her warm and utterly charming in person; more than that, she understands the challenges facing Democrats in a way that few others in the party do, and her ability to absorb policy nuances rivals her husband's. This country is long past due for a female president, and I would love to see Hillary Clinton in that trailblazing role (and not just because it would make Ann Coulter break out in giant hives). But—at the risk of getting myself permanently blackballed by her loyal and protective staff while Clinton can win nearly any debate that is about issues, she cannot avoid becoming the issue in a national campaign. And when that happens, she will very likely lose.

NO SUCH THING AS UNDECIDED

It's not exactly news that Hillary Clinton is a polarizing figure. Ever since Newt Gingrich's mother whispered to Connie Chung on national television that she thought Mrs. Clinton was, well, a bitch, Americans have understood that the ex-first lady provokes intense emotions on all sides. Still, it's not hard to see why Hillary boosters are tempted to think that voters might be willing to take a new look at her and why politically astute people are turning cartwheels over the idea of her candidacy.

Over the last five years, Clinton has developed into perhaps the most interesting politician in America. She has a reputation for bipartisanship in the Senate, forming partnerships with some of her most conservative Republican colleagues, including Bill Frist (R-Tenn.), Rick Santorum (R-Pa.), and Sam Brownback (R-Kan.). She has quietly, but firmly, assumed a leadership role in her own caucus. And she has shown vision and backbone in a party that is accused of having none.

Years before most Washington Democrats started worrying about the party's reputation on "moral values," Clinton was bringing Jim Wallis and other progressive religious leaders to talk with her colleagues about reclaiming the concepts of faith and values. She voted for the Iraq war when that wasn't a popular position for a Democrat to take, and has been willing to speak uncomfortable truths in difficult venues. In January, she told a crowd of over 1,000 assembled pro-choice activists that the way they have been talking about abortion is wrong, that many Americans won't even listen to them until they admit that it would be better if most women didn't have to face the "sad, even tragic choice" of having one. More recently, she cosponsored the "Workplace Religious Freedom Act" after intense lobbying from women's groups that oppose the legislation.

There's no one tougher. No one understands better that Middle America cares about both economic issues and cultural concerns. At the same time, no one is better at firing up the liberal base. Add to all of that approval ratings in the high 50s, and it sounds like you have the makings of a surefire winner for the Democrats.

And if it were any other candidate, that might be true. But with Hillary Clinton, everything's more complicated.

Let's look at those poll numbers that have Democrats pasting "Hillary '08" bumper stickers onto their Subaru Outbacks and Republicans pulling their Whitewater files out of the basement. Right now, Clinton is leaving her fellow Democratic contenders—including Sens. John Kerry (D-Mass.), John Edwards (D-

N.C.), and Joseph Biden (D-Del.)—in the dust. In polls that ask voters to identify which potential Democratic nominee they would back in 2008, she regularly clocks in at around 40 percent while her closest competitor rarely breaks the 20 percent mark.

It's important to remember, however, that polls taken this early in the process tend simply to reflect how well known a candidate is. (Kerry is surely as well-known as Clinton, but may be suffering in the polls from Democratic loser fatigue.) In 1997, for instance, George W. Bush led most polls of Republican prospects, in large part because many respondents thought they were being asked about his father. Hillary Clinton occupies the spot held by Al Gore at this point in the 2004 election cycle. She may well be the candidate most Democrats want to see as their nominee; or she could just be the one they know best. Right now, it's too early to know for certain.

In addition, while her "favorables" are good—57 percent of Americans have a positive impression of her—her negatives are disturbingly high as well. This long before an election, most voters have yet to make up their mind about a candidate. Even as close to the primaries as December 2003, 66 percent of voters didn't know what they thought of John Kerry. That's not the case with Clinton. While at this point in George W. Bush's first presidential campaign, Bush also had favorable ratings around the mid-50s, an additional 30 percent of voters said they either hadn't made up their minds about him or they didn't know who he was. Compare that to Hillary: Only 7 percent of respondents aren't sure what they think of her, and—not surprisingly—no one says they haven't heard of her.

Never in American political history has a candidate faced such a decided electorate at this early a point in a presidential race. That's a disadvantage when you consider that one of the lessons of 2004 was that once voters develop a perception about a candidate, it's as immovable as superglue. No one who thought George W. Bush was a likable, friendly guy could be convinced that he was corrupt or misleading. And once John Kerry became identified in voters' minds as a "flip-flopper," no amount of arguing could change that image. It's a problem for any candidate. For Senator Clinton, it could be fatal. Americans know exactly what they think of her. And nearly 40 percent say they would never consider voting for her.

SHAKING HANDS, CHANGING MINDS

Of course, there is one proven way that Hillary Clinton has damaged voters' perceptions. In her first Senate race, the strategy was simple: Meet as many voters as possible, and ignore the scandal-focused press. It paid off—when Clinton hunched her campaign, only 41 percent of New Yorkers were prepared to vote for her; she won in November 2000 with 55 percent of the vote after having visited each of the state's 62 counties, many of them repeatedly.

Operation Smother the Voters worked in large part because the real Hillary Clinton is a far cry from the caricature of a manipulative, power-hungry, shrewish woman that has been propagated by the right. One of the unexpected benefits of being demonized and attacked by conservatives for more than a decade turns out to be that voters are surprised and relieved when she doesn't fly into town on a broomstick. Tomasky relates the response of voters when they actually met the woman they'd heard so much about for eight years in *Hillary's Turn*, his excellent book about Clinton's 2000 campaign. "People had expected Hillary to instruct and talk, and, let's face it, to come across as pushy and judgmental," he wrote. "So when she paid genuine attention to the things people were saying, she really threw them." Indeed, the first time I met the Clintons, the president distractedly shook some hands after a speech and then left fairly quickly while the first lady was the one who displayed the vaunted Clinton political skills—chatting easily about policy details, focusing intently on what my colleague and I had to say, and then throwing her arms around our shoulders for a photo that looks more like three college friends than two awed congressional staffers and a first lady.

The strategy also succeeded because many voters—weaned on a diet of conservative talking points during the 1990s—expected Clinton to be a liberal of the bluest sort, to the left of Ted Kennedy and unable to understand their concerns. What they found was that her positions on welfare, crime, and foreign policy, among other issues, were far more centrist than liberal. In addition, while most professional political observers dismissed her "Listening Tour" as a stunt, Clinton actually used it to query New Yorkers about their problems and obsessively study up on local issues.

All of this is impressive. But if the ability to work a rope line or a town hall meeting was the key ingredient to winning a national race, our political history would be quite different. In *What It Takes*, his chronicle of the 1988 presidential race, the journalist Richard Ben Cramer describes watching Dick Gephardt entrance voters with his earnest, determined approach and piercing blue eyes. "Sweet Jesus, he is terrific," Cramer writes. "There aren't ten voters in the country who would work against him, once he's had them face-to-face." Similarly, last winter, many political reporters chalked up John Kerry's surprising comeback in Iowa to the fact that he'd spent countless evenings in individual homes, talking to voters until he had convinced each person to support him. No candidate, however, meets every voter face-to-face en route to the White House.

Anyone running for office would prefer to meet as many voters as possible in person. The stakes are higher for Hillary Clinton: She has to meet personally with voters in order to have a chance of changing their minds about her. If she runs for the White House, the vast majority of Americans will learn what they know about her campaign through the media. And that's where the second half of Senator Clinton's New York strategy falls apart.

"NURSE RATCHED"

When a candidate's name recognition is at 100 percent in a statewide campaign, she can afford to turn a few campaign saws about the media upside-down. For the 2000 Clinton campaign, no press was good press; "the smaller the circus, the better," one of her staffers told Tomasky. They considered it a victory when the traveling press corps—bored by the lack of news made by Clinton's "Listening Tour" and its endless focus on the minutiae of dairy compacts and traffic conditions on the Canadian border—winnowed from 250 reporters to 70 to about a dozen permanent scribes. Although the *New York Post*, and columnist Dick Morris in particular, nipped at Clinton's heels for the length of the campaign, she was able to conduct her image transformation largely in a vacuum.

It's safe to say that wouldn't be the case in 2008. The only way to reach voters in a nationwide campaign is through the media, both through purchased airtime and what is referred to as "free" media—coverage of campaign events and interviews with print and television reporters. It's a two-sided coin for candidates. They need journalists in order to get their messages across to the majority of Americans who won't get a chance to hear them in person, but they have no control over what gets reported or how it's framed in the press. Any Democrat running in the general election would face that challenge, although they might not yet know precisely how the press would cover their candidacy. Senator Clinton, however, knows all too well what to expect. Her instincts were correct in 2000: When you're Hillary Clinton, "free" media always comes with a cost.

Journalists are often no different from voters in general—when they form an impression of a politician, many reporters filter coverage through what they think they know about the candidate. Reporters "knew" Al Gore was a serial exaggerator, that Kerry was an out-of-touch, aristocratic elitist, and that Bush was an amiable goof. They may not let ideological leanings color their coverage, but personal biases can affect what they choose to report and the narratives they choose to tell.

Jill Lawrence, one of *USA Today*'s campaign correspondents in 2004, has observed that very few political reporters wrote about the way Kerry used religious language—even though, she noted, it occurred every week on the campaign wail—because they assumed that Democratic candidates weren't deeply religious. "The stereotype of the Democratic Party is so deep that it never broke through," she said. That's already happening with Clinton, whose religious references and comments on abortion generated headlines early in 2005. Most news outlets characterized her remarks as a distinct break from the past—implying that she was transforming herself for a White House run—even though she is a former Sunday School teacher who has spoken publicly about religion for decades and her comments on abortion were consistent with her husband's mantra that abortion should be "safe, legal, and rare?"

Chemistry is also important for the press corps. Reporters are attracted to straight-talkers like [Senator] John McCain [R-AZ], Rudy Giuliani [former Republican mayor of New York City], and—in 2003, at least—Howard Dean [former Democratic governor of Vermont]. Inaccessibility is definitely a turn-off; in the early years of the Clinton administration, the First Lady famously fought with the *Washington Post* over the release of documents about Whitewater. Her chilly relationship with the press has warmed considerably during her first term in the Senate, but Hillary Clinton still has far more skeptics than fans have the press corps.

Sometimes they go far beyond reportorial cynicism. The *Washington Post's* reporter assigned to cover Clinton's first Senate race, [*Washington Post* reporter] Michael Grunwald, provides one illustration of how the press corps already feels about her. Describing the first lady as "bor[ing] New York into submission, droning on endlessly about focus-grouped Democratic issues," Grunwald accused her of "baldly deceptive and intentionally vacuous behavior" and "an intellectually and emotionally dishonest scheme to get a job without a résumé" and charged that "her only consistent ideology was a faith in political popularity." Ouch. More recently, on the Feb. 20, 2005, installment of "The Chris Matthews Show," a panel discussed Hillary's candidacy while calling her "Nurse Ratched" [an unflattering reference to a domineering, repressed character in the 1975 film *One Flew Over the Cuckoo's Nest*] and a "castrating female persona" things really got going when journalist Gloria Borger mimicked Clinton's laugh and mannerisms while her colleagues sniggered.

And that's coming from members of the mainstream media. The conservative press—never shy when it comes to Hillary Clinton—has spent the spring teeing up for another game of Hillaryball. The trial of David Rosen, the fundraiser for Clinton's 2000 campaign, who was accused of hiding about $800,000 of costs for a campaign event held in Los Angeles, came first. In the three months leading up to the verdict (Rosen was acquitted), the FOX News Channel ran more than a dozen segments on Rosen, including a "Hannity & Colmes" segment titled "Are Hillary's Presidential Chances Over?" Rosen's eventual acquittal merited barely a hiccup on FOX, which simply replaced Rosen coverage with segments on the next Clinton scandal story—yet another bestselling book taking on the Senator.

THE HILLARY EFFECT

Edward Klein's *The Truth About Hillary: What She Knew, and How Far She'll Go to Become President* [Sentinel, 2005] is, even by the low standards of the genre, vile. In seeking to portray Hillary Clinton as a cold, manipulative woman who will do anything for power, Klein relies on wholly unsubstantiated accusations of corruption, lesbianism, and marital rape. Most conservatives who gleefully anticipated the book's release are now distancing themselves from it. And liberals have derived some joy from scenes such as right-wing talk show host Scan Hannity sharply questioning Klein over his use of sources.

Klein apparently didn't get the memo about anti-Hillary strategy. Frontal assaults and reckless accusations are sooo 1990s, definitely déclassé. More to the point, they make conservatives sound scary and are counterproductive. But while Democrats are surely hoping that these attacks will spur a backlash and sympathy for Clinton, the more likely outcome is a draw. Americans may have lost their appetite for books like *Madame Hillary: The Dark Road to the White House* [by R. Emmett Tyrrell, Jr., and Mark W. Davis, 2004] and *Hillary's Scheme: Inside the Next Clinton's Ruthless Agenda to Take the White House* [by Carl Limbacher, 2004], but many of them share the underlying concern about Clinton's motives and character. Likewise, while a Republican nominee would benefit from anti-Hillary donations—in the last few months of the 2000 race, Lazio averaged $1 million each week in hard money contributions from Hillary-haters outside of New York—Senator Clinton's prodigious fundraising has the potential to neutralize that effort.

Conservatives won't trot out supposed lesbian lovers in 2008; they'll go after her more subtly. They know that 40 percent of the country can't stand Senator Clinton, another 40 percent adores her, and the remaining 20 percent (which, according to those recent polls, seem to feel generally positive about her) is made up of fairly soft support. The best way to turn that support into opposition is to voice those age-old questions about the Clintons: She's inappropriately power-hungry and ambitious—remember that Tammy Wynette crack? He lacks moral character—do you really want him roaming the White House again? And don't forget health care—who elected her to that post anyway?

Another golden oldie—the charge that the Clintons will say anything to get ahead—is already being revived elliptically by conservatives. The day after Senator Clinton's news-making abortion speech this past January, conservatives were all over the media, charging that she was undergoing a "makeover" of her political image. "I think what we're seeing is, at least rhetorically, the attempt of the ultimate makeover," Gary Bauer told the *Washington Times. Investors Business Daily* editorialized: "When husband Bill did it, it was called triangulation.... Now another Clinton running for president is telling different audiences what they want to hear." In the six months since, the "makeover" charge has been repeated more than 100 times in the press. Give them another six, and "makeover" will be the new "flip-flop."

The target audience for these whispers and insinuations—and, let's not be naive, occasional television commercials—is a familiar demographic: suburban women. Democrats lost ground in the 2004 elections among white, married, working women, and it's generally accepted that to win back the White House, the party needs a nominee who can appeal to these women. There's no reason to think that Republicans wouldn't revive the same kind of personal attacks that Lazio brought out in the last week of the 2000 campaign. In that race, the Hillary effect that resulted in the loss of suburban women was masked by gains among upstate men. She'll have a much harder time winning their counterparts in those essential swing states, which makes it even more important that she be able to count on the women's vote. If the Republican strategy in 2008 results in the same outcome as 2000—if, in other words, Clinton's advantage among women was half that of Gore's—the margin of victory in states like Iowa, Minnesota, New Mexico, and Wisconsin will disappear. Game, set, match.

No, Democrats, it's not fair. Hillary Clinton is smart, she's paving a promising new path for her party, she's a much better campaigner than anyone ever expected, and she's already survived more personal assaults than anyone should have to endure. But wishing the country would grow up and get over the 1990s already, that she could wage a campaign of issues and be evaluated on her political merit, won't make it so. What's more, those daydreams—pleasant as they are to contemplate on a sunny afternoon—cast a shadow over the Democratic field that makes it difficult for a potentially viable candidate to emerge.

It's too early for anyone to say with certainty that Hillary Clinton can't win the White House. But it's far too early—and dangerous—to conclude that she's the best chance that Democrats have.

THE CONTINUING DEBATE: Hillary Clinton and the 2008 Presidential Election

What Is New

It would be surprising if Hillary Clinton did not seek the presidency in 2008. First, however, Clinton has to be reelected to the Senate in 2006. Few analysts doubt she can win, but a victory with less than the 55% of the vote she amassed in 2000 will dull her luster somewhat. Several factors will influence her prospects in 2008. One is what the impact of her being a woman will be. A 2006 poll found 32% saying her sex was a reason to vote for Clinton, 17% seeing it as a reason to vote against her, and 51% saying it made no difference. A second factor is Clinton's image. She is very well known and opinions on her tend to be strong. In mid 2006, her "favorable" rating (51%) was high, but so was her "unfavorable" rating (44%), with only 5% of poll respondents without an opinion. Among other things, the electorate is moderate, and the Republicans will portray her as a liberal. This characterization is supported by Clinton's voting record, which the liberal group Americans for Democratic Action has given a "liberal quotient" of 96%, for her first five years (2001–2005) in the Senate. Also standing in Clinton's way is the 2004 vice presidential nominee John Edwards and the many other Democrats who would like their party's nomination in 2008. Finally, if nominated, she will have to defeat the Republican candidate, with Senator John McCain (Arizona) the early front-runner for the nomination. It is a long way from to November 2008 from June 2006, but at that point, one poll found 22% saying they would definitely vote for Clinton and 28% saying that they would consider doing so. But 47% were already committed to "definitely not" voting for her, with 3% venturing no opinion.

Where to Find More

Autobiographies are worth reading if not fully believing, and Hillary Clinton's is *Living History* (Simon & Schuster, 2003). In somewhat the same genre, visit her 2006 Senate reelection site at www.hillaryclinton.com/ and her Senate office site at http://clinton.senate.gov/. An official Hillary Clinton for president organization is Votehillary at www.votehillary.org/. Directly rebutting Clinton's autobiography is *Rewriting History* (Regan Books, 2004) by Dick Morris, a former top political adviser to President Clinton. A group that takes a dim view of the senator is STOP Hillary PAC at http://stophillarypac.com/.

What More to Do

Whether you support or oppose Senator Clinton, you have two fairly immediate chances to affect her political future and perhaps the country's too. One opportunity is to get involved in the 2006 New York Senate race, the other is to participate in the 2008 presidential campaign, including the nomination and election. If you are not sure, gather information about Clinton, form an opinion, then get active.

PROVIDING PROOF OF CITIZENSHIP WHEN REGISTERING TO VOTE:

Reasonable Requirement *or* Unnecessary Barrier to Participation?

REASONABLE REQUIREMENT

Advocate: Patrick J. Rogers, attorney and member of the Board of Directors of the American Center for Voting Rights Legislative Fund

Source: Testimony during hearings on "Non-citizen Voting," before the House of Representatives, Committee on House Administration, June 22, 2006

UNNECESSARY BARRIER TO PARTICIPATION

Advocate: Christine Chen, Executive Director of Asian and Pacific Islander American Vote

Source: Testimony during hearings on "Non-citizen Voting," before the House of Representatives, Committee on House Administration, June 22, 2006

A core requirement of democracy is that people must be able to vote without undue restrictions. No democracy allows everyone to vote. Children, for example, are universally excluded. However, democracy demands that the burden of proof for excluding anyone should rest on those who favor the exclusion rather than on those who favor inclusion.

Historically, voter eligibility has generally expanded. The Fifteenth (1870), Nineteenth (1920), and Twenty-sixth (1971) Amendments respectively barred denying the vote to anyone because, respectively, of race, sex, or age (once their were eighteen years old). Numerous other actions have attacked barriers designed to circumvent these amendments or to otherwise limit voting. For example, the Twenty-fourth Amendment to the Constitution forbids poll taxes in federal elections. Various federal laws sought to remove obstacles. Most importantly, the Voting Rights Act (1965) empowered the federal government to regulate election procedures in states with a record of discrimination and barred such voting hurdles as literacy tests. A 1975 amendment to the VRA required that states provide voting material in languages other than English where necessary, and the Americans with Disabilities Act of 1990 required states to ensure that disabled Americans could vote. The decisions of the U.S. Supreme Court in modern times have also almost always favored broadening the franchise. For example, the Court ruled in *Harper v. Virginia State Board of Elections* (1966) extended the ban on poll taxes to state and local elections under the Fourteenth Amendment (1868).

States also contributed to expanding the franchise. It was once common for only property owners to be eligible to vote for state and national offices; North Carolina became the last state to eliminate that requirement in 1856. Often barriers to women and others voting were eliminated in many states before federal action took place.

A related set of issues related to voting has been the requirements to register prior to voting. Traditionally set by state law, registration was rarely required until the 1870s. This changed because of voting fraud perpetrated by big city political machines and others, and by 1925 almost all states required voter registration prior to election day. Certainly many abuses were eliminated, but the requirements also caused some eligible voters to stay away from the polls. As a result, turnout dropped off. With turnout even for presidential elections at only about half of all eligible voters by the 1990s and with turnout for other election even lower, reforms moved in the other direction and attempted to make it easier for people to register. For instance, the National Voter Registration Act (NVRA) of 1993 (or "motor-voter" law) mandates that states requiring pre-election day voter registration must permit individuals to register by mail. Same-day (as the election) registration and wider eligibility to vote by mail are other examples of steps to make voting easier. How effective such measures to reduce technical registration and voting barriers have been is controversial, but research has generally found that the impact of voting registration and turnout has been very modest at best and that any increases have mostly involved young adults and poor and less educated individuals.

Even more recently, other concerns have created pressure to increase voting and registration requirements. The difficulties in the Florida presidential vote in 2000, allegations of fraudulent registration (especially by the increased number of legal and illegal immigrants in the United States, see Debate 5), and other worries led to calls for election reforms. As a result, the Commission on Federal Election Reform, co-chaired by former President Jimmy Carter and former Secretary of State James A. Baker III, was established. It found, "There is no evidence of extensive fraud in U.S. elections or of multiple voting," but went on to argue, "but both occur, and...could affect the outcome of a close election." It is unclear whether the report mean only that isolated instances of fraud and multiple voting both occur or extensive instances of fraud and multiple voting both occur. In any case, the Carter-Baker report called for "Real ID" cards be required to register and vote. This type of identification had emerged from post 9/11 concerns about terrorists using fake identity, with Congress enacting the Real ID Act of 2005. It requires that by 2008, states only issue driver's license and non-driver's ID cards after receiving documentary proof of the applicant's (1) full legal name and date of birth, (2) Social Security number or exemption from having one, (3) principal legal residence address, and (4) citizenship.

Where the debate here picks is with a bill in the U.S. House of Representatives, H.R. 4844, the Federal Election Integrity Act of 2006. It proposes to implement the Carter-Baker recommendation by requiring individuals registering to vote in a federal election to prove U.S. citizenship to election officials. Richard J. Rogers supports the bill in the first reading, arguing that it will help restore voter confidence in the electoral system. Christine Chen disagrees, and in the second reader contends that H.R. 4844 is a misguided approach that would disenfranchise large numbers of legal voters.

POINTS TO PONDER

- There is an inevitable trade off between preventing fraud and making voting more accessible. Which is more important: preventing fraud or making voting easy?
- Carefully weigh the evidence presented by Rogers that fraud is widespread enough to merit H.R. 4844 and Chen's evidence that H.R. 4844 will deter many eligible voters.
- Ponder whether the Real ID Act of 2005 and H.R. 4844 are part of a step-by-step move toward a national identification card and how you fell about that possibility.

Providing Proof of Citizenship When Registering to Vote: Reasonable Requirement

Patrick J. Rogers

I appreciate this opportunity to address the Committee about the important issues of voter identification and ensuring that only United States citizens can vote to elect our leaders in the elections of our country....I am a member of the Board of Directors of the American Center for Voting Rights Legislative Fund ("ACVR-LF"). ...ACVR-LF is a national, non-partisan, non-profit organization that was founded on the belief that public confidence in our electoral system is the cornerstone of our democracy. ACVR-LF supports election reform that protects the right of all citizens to participate in the election process free of intimidation, discrimination or harassment. ACVR-LF's aim is for election reform that will make it easy to vote but tough to cheat. ACVR-LF supports election reforms such as those proposed by the nonpartisan Carter-Baker Commission.

....I am concerned about fraud in the registration and voting process, and that legal voters have been disenfranchised by ballots illegally and fraudulently cast in our state and federal elections. I was involved in litigation over the conduct of the election in New Mexico in 2000 when [Vice President Al] Gore was credited with a 366 vote lead, when the county recounts, related suits, and investigations were halted. In 2004, I was involved in a host of lawsuits concerning the election process including voter identification requirements and ballot access issues. Presently, I am counsel to three individuals who seek to intervene in a federal suit in which the American Civil Liberties Union has challenged the constitutionality of the City of Albuquerque's photo identification requirements....

Fraudulent voting and problems with registration in 2004 brought new attention to these topics in [my home state of] New Mexico, but these problems are not new problems for New Mexico. In 1952, the Senate Subcommittee on Privileges and Elections of the Committee on Rules and Administration investigated the New Mexico Senate election of November 4, 1952. The Senate Committee Report suggests New Mexico has not made much progress in the ensuing fifty-four years:

> An election must authoritatively express the will of the people. This can be accomplished only by an electoral system which clearly identifies those who are qualified to vote, establishes conditions under which the voter can freely express his choice, and creates standards to accurately record the results of the election. Although the system is important, the exercise of the electoral franchise depends not alone upon procedures but equally upon its honest and efficient administration. *The investigation into the New Mexico senatorial election of 1952 revealed the deplorable spectacle of the exploitation and breakdown of an electoral system through irresponsible and ineffective administration.* [emphasis added by Rogers]

The report noted that illegal aliens had registered and voted. The subcommittee suggested:

> the registration system is so loose and ineffective that it is an invitation to fraud and dishonesty in elections. Since the registration laws must be strictly enforced to encourage full participation by the citizens and to readily determine the qualifications of those who present themselves to vote on election day.

Voting by non-citizens is not just a concern in New Mexico. In the wake of the 1996 election, as this committee is well aware, the contest of the Dornan-Sanchez election [in California for the U.S. House of Representatives, with Democrat Loretta Sanchez narrowly defeating Republican incumbent Robert K Dornan]; identified at least 784 illegally cast votes and this committee's report concluded that the exact number of illegal residents who were registered and cast ballots could not be conclusively determined.

I am not in a position today to quantify or even begin to quantify the magnitude of the problem. However, I am in a position to assure you in the strongest terms possible that fraudulent registration and fraudulent voting is a problem.…

PROOF OF CITIZENSHIP TO REGISTER TO VOTE

Voting by illegal immigrants is one of the toughest issues to study in the election and voting area. This is because there is no centralized or accessible list of illegal immigrants that can be compared to voter registration lists or lists of persons who actually cast ballots. The closest "list" I am aware of that could be used as a basis for systematic research is a list maintained by the Bureau of Immigration and Customs Enforcement ("ICE") at the Department of Homeland Security. This is a list of those illegal immigrants who have overstayed their Visas or are "deportable." But the list is not available to election officials to check or validate voter registration rolls.

New Mexico was truly plagued in 2004 by fraudulent voter registration by some employees of the Association of Community Organizations for Reform ("ACORN") and a few other 527 groups. The Bernalillo County Clerk reported more than three thousand fraudulent registrations after media reports highlighted the registration of a thirteen year old, by an ACORN employee. In the 2004 New Mexico voter identification cases, the ACORN director responsible for the oversight of the registration drive invoked his Fifth Amendment right at the trial. Another 527 witness invoked her Fifth Amendment right to remain silent about the details of the registration process. The Albuquerque Police Department Special Gang Unit arrested a Cuban national for possession of crack cocaine paraphernalia, and the investigation disclosed the fellow was supplementing his income by gathering fraudulent voter registration forms for ACORN. This type of voter registration fraud seriously undermines the public confidence in the election process.

In a pending federal suit in the Federal District Court of New Mexico, *ACLU v. Santillanes*, I represent Dwight Adkins who applied to intervene in the suit because in 2004 his vote was stolen. He was not allowed to vote when he appeared at his polling place because someone had voted fraudulently in his place. His "provisional ballot" was cast and denied on the basis, he was told, that he had already voted. Rosemary McGee of Albuquerque suffered the same fate.

While some advocates for illegal immigrants claim that illegals want nothing to do with the government and therefore won't register to vote or attempt to vote, there are other advocates for both legal and illegal immigrants who are actively pushing to legalize non-citizen voting.

Whole organizations exist to advocate for "rights" of immigrants to vote include, for example, the Immigrant Voting Project at the New School in New York City.

Last spring, Tufts University funded a study on the "feasibility" of non-citizen voting in Massachusetts. That study opened with this summary: "...There is growing support for non-citizen voting nationwide, and action taken by lobbyists, activists, non-citizens, and other key stakeholders can lay the foundation for a more favorable outcome in the future."

And this sort of advocacy is not confined to academics in Massachusetts. The UCLA Chicano Studies Research Center issued a report in December of 2003 entitled "Political Apartheid in California: Consequences of Excluding a Growing Noncitizen Population." The press release announcing the report said the author concluded that "a de facto political apartheid will exist in California if steps are not taken to include more than 4.6 million non-citizen adults in the voting process." Other legal journals are publishing similar articles, such as "Prospects for Democratic Change: Non-Citizen Suffrage in America" published in the *Hamline Journal of Public Law & Policy*, and "Noncitizen Voting Rights: The History, the Law and Current Prospects for Change" published in the *Law and Inequality Journal*.

Several of these articles gloss over the issue of who may be in the United States lawfully and who may be in the United States in violation of our laws. In advance of the 2004 elections, the affirmation of U.S citizenship required by the National Voter Registration Act ("Motor Voter") law was at issue in several states. Despite the clear mandate of the Motor Voter law that any potential voter must affirm citizenship on the voter registration application, South Dakota and Iowa issued directives to voter registration officials that voters should be added to the roles even if their application did not affirmatively indicate they are United States citizens. One case even went to litigation (*Diaz v. Hood*) in Florida because Florida maintained that this citizenship box affirming citizenship needs to be affirmatively "checked" in order for the person to register to vote. And, I should note, this case was essentially re-filed in the last few months in Florida.

In Maryland, the state elections director reportedly told the Associated Press in August of 2004 that he was "shocked" to learn that non-citizens were on the state's voter registration rolls. ICE reportedly did not cooperate with the state's attempt to identify and remove non-citizens from the state's voting rolls. Maryland has at least six municipalities that affirmatively allow non-citizens to vote in local elections.

In 2005, Utah's legislative audit bureau attempted to undertake a systematic study of illegal immigrants who had obtained state identification cards—either driver's license or state identification cards. Utah determined that some 383 possibly illegal immigrants were registered to vote. Utah asked ICE to review these registered voters to determine if, in fact, they were U.S. citizens. ICE examined a sample consisting of 135 of these individuals and determined that 5 were naturalized citizens, 20 were "deportable," one was a permanent legal resident and the other 109 had no record and were likely in the United States illegally. Fourteen of these 383 individuals voted in a recent election in Utah, but ICE did not provide enough information to the state to allow it to determine whether these 14 individuals were in fact citizens.

The State of Arizona is currently embroiled in litigation over Proposition 200. The citizens of Arizona passed by popular initiative a requirement that before someone can register to vote, they must be a citizen of the state and United States. This passed in a landslide and a CNN poll analyzing Proposition 200 found that nearly fifty percent of the Hispanic/Latino community supported Proposition 200. This is not a racial or ethnic issue.

The Federal Election Assistance Commission has issued an opinion claiming that states may not require more than is provided on the federal voter registration application while, at the same time, the Department of Defense is instructing its personnel to provide proof of citizenship as the state of Arizona requests when registering to vote in Arizona using the postcard application. The concept is simple. It is proper and appropriate for a state to request proof of citizenship before a person is added to the voter rolls. This is a simple commonsense measure to protect the right of all honest citizens of whatever partisan or ethnic background to participate in our elections without having their vote canceled by a ballot cast by someone who is not legally entitled to vote.

In the past few days, the federal court in the pending Arizona lawsuit has denied a request for a temporary restraining order and reaffirmed the critical nature of the right to vote and the need to assure eligibility to vote: "Determining whether an individual is a United States citizen is of paramount importance when determining his or her eligibility to vote. In fact, the NVRA repeatedly mentions that its purpose is to increase registration of 'eligible citizens.' Proving proof of citizenship undoubtedly assists Arizona is assessing the eligibility of applicants. Arizona's proof of citizenship requirement does not conflict with the plain language of the NVRA."

A large number of individual cases of illegal immigrants registering to vote or voting have been reported in the news media. Here are just a few examples:

- In Maryland, a 2006 email from a member of the Montgomery County Board of Elections in Montgomery County, Maryland was made public indicating he was going to register people to vote "regardless of status." I've attached a copy of that email to this testimony.
- Donna Hope, a non-citizen immigrant from Barbados who resides in Philadelphia, was told by a representative of the voter registration group "Voting is Power," the voter mobilization arm of the Muslim American Society, that she could register to vote if she has been in the United States at least 7 years. Ms. Hope completed the registration form and was added to the voting rolls. In November of 2004, Ms. Hope did not vote because she was not a citizen, but someone illegally cast a ballot in her name. *See* Attachments 2–7.
- The Wall Street Journal reported that "[t]he man who in 1994 assassinated Mexican presidential candidate Luis Donaldo Colosino in Tijuana had registered to vote at least twice in the U.S. although he was not a citizen."
- In 1998, California Secretary of State Bill Jones referred to the INS claims by nearly 450 people called for jury duty in Orange County, California who claimed they were exempt from jury duty because they were non-citizens. The jury duty lists are pulled from driver's license and registered voter files.

Let me close with this thought on the illegal immigration registration portion of H.R. 4844: A Congressional Research Service report from September of 2005 indicated that more than 25 states did not require proof of legal presence in the United States in order to apply for and obtain a driver's license. And, as a consequence of the Motor Voter law, every single person who applies for a driver's license is asked if they want to register to vote. Voter rolls in the United States, particularly in states that allow illegal immigrants to obtain driver's licenses, are inflated by non-citizens who are registered to vote. The only question is the number.

VOTER IDENTIFICATION REQUIREMENTS

The voter identification portion of H.R. 4844 [the Federal Election Integrity Act of 2006] appears to be a significant step forward to address the cynicism, skepticism and fraud that keep many American citizens on the sidelines and out of the voting booth. Requiring a person to identify themselves with photo identification before casting a ballot enjoys broad public support. The American Center for Voting Rights—Legislative Fund's polling in Pennsylvania and Missouri found that more than 80% of the population favors photo ID requirement in order to vote. Other state specific polls in Wisconsin and Washington have found similar levels of public support for voter identification requirements. Nationally, a *Wall Street Journal*/NBC poll conducted by on April 21–26, 2006 found that more than eighty percent of U.S. citizens support the requirement that a person show a photo ID before they are allowed to cast a ballot.

When the issue of voter photo ID is placed on the ballot, there is strong non-partisan support for the measure. Albuquerque voters, with the support of Hispanic Democrat Mayor Chavez, adopted a photo ID requirement for all Albuquerque elections. In Arizona, voters passed a popular state-wide initiative (Proposition 200) that, separate and apart from providing proof of citizenship to register, required voters to present identification before voting.

Voter photo identification requirements—including photo identification requirements—have emerged as a national consensus. More than twenty-four states currently require every voter to provide identification before casting a ballot and seven states currently require photo identification in order to vote.

Election reform legislation requiring photo identification before casting a ballot has been introduced this legislative session in at least four more states and a national photo ID requirement amendment introduced by Senator [Mitch] McConnell [R-KY] was part of the Senate debate on the immigration reform bill, although it was not included in the final version of the Senate bill.

New Mexico and Albuquerque voters support photo ID by a significant percentage. Prior to 2004, the polls indicated an overall margin of 77–17% support including significant bipartisan support with sixty-six percent of Democrats supporting photo ID. [According to the] *Albuquerque Journal* (8/24/05), polling showed photo ID with overwhelming support "among Republicans and Democrats, Anglos and Hispanics and across all income levels" in Albuquerque. The Albuquerque City photo identification requirements currently in affect are the subject of the federal suit. However, the press reported broad support for the measure and the implementation of the change. Albuquerque City Clerk Judy Chavez and other election officials said the rule change did not cause any problems. Shirley Bartel, an election clerk at Chelwood Elementary School, said many voters had their IDs out already when approaching the polls. "They said, 'It should have been done a long time ago. It makes for a more honest election,' Bartel said." "Herbert Gutierrez, a retiree who voted Tuesday, said producing an

ID was no problem. 'I wish they would make it mandatory for everything,' he said." (*Id.*)

In connection with the 2004 New Mexico Voter ID lawsuits, a poll that was conducted established that first time voters, those people who had registered, but not in person before a clerk, were more concerned about fraudulent voting and fraudulent registrations than people who have been voting for years. I submit to you that any steps Congress might take to ensure and assure voters and potential voters that only citizens and registered voters are allowed to vote is important, not just for the integrity of the vote itself, but for the increasing numbers of voters who are skeptical or cynical about the honesty and fairness of our elections.

CONCLUSION

As to need for effective identification requirements before voting, it is impossible to come to any conclusion other than the obvious. If the 2008 Presidential Election in New Mexico matters, if the count is close, I absolutely guarantee this Committee that without effective voter identification requirements, real limitations and real safeguards to prevent fraud and ineligible persons from voting, then any New Mexico result certainly will be subject to challenge for fraud and ineligible persons voting. My preliminary view of HR 4844 is that it is a significant and important step forward in the effort to restore and honor the right to vote. Increased confidence in the system that our elections are fair and honest will increase participation.

Providing Proof Of Citizenship When Registering To Vote: Unnecessary Barrier To Participation

CHRISTINE CHEN

[As] Executive Director of Asian and Pacific Islander American Vote (APIAVote), I appreciate the opportunity to present to you the views of APIAVote regarding identification requirements in U.S. elections. I am privileged to represent organizations, partners and volunteers from my community who continue to promote democracy by expanding access to the electoral process by submitting testimony before the Committee this morning.

APIAVote is a national nonpartisan, nonprofit organization that encourages and promotes civic participation of Asian Pacific Islander Americans in the electoral and public policy processes at the national, state and local levels. By working with national and local partners, APIAVote focuses on coordinating activities related to voter registration, education, outreach, mobilization and voting rights advocacy. APIAVote also prioritizes strengthening local capacity by serving as a clearinghouse for information and providing resources & trainings. Within the last ten years, this historic grassroots effort ultimately formed partnerships with more than 150 local organizations and over a dozen national organizations across the country. We have been able to build and establish relationships in communities where voter turnout has been traditionally low.

VOTER REGISTRATION

Participating in the electoral process is a relatively new concept for the Asian Pacific Islander community. It was only with the enactment of the 1952 McCarren-Walter Act (also known as the Immigration and Nationality Act) that racial and ethnic barriers to naturalization were lifted to allow Asian immigrants to be naturalized citizens for the first time in history. As a largely immigrant community, APIAs were deeply impacted by the anti-immigrant sentiment during the legislative wave of 1996. Awakened to the need to become a politically engaged force, electoral organizing in the APIA community hit groundbreaking levels. Between 1990 and 2000, Asian American voters grew from less than a million to 1.98 million, a 118% growth. In 2004 3.2 million APIAs registered to vote with an 85% turnout rate.

But the APIA community still faces many challenges in accessing and understanding the electoral system. In 2004, 6.3 million Asian Americans were eligible to vote, but only 3.2 million registered. The APIA community has not historically been reached by mainstream voter mobilization activities, and the capacity of many nonprofits and volunteers working with the APIA and largely immigrant community is very low. This is one of the main challenges that APIAVote faces as we focus on building the capacity to outreach to the community and help them access the ballot box.

H.R. 4844, the Federal Election Integrity Act of 2006, *may sound* like a good idea. But H.R. 4844 is a misguided approach that would disenfranchise large numbers of legal voters. Congress and the states are already successful in accomplishing the important task of preventing noncitizens from voting and ensuring voters are who they claim to be. Instead of safeguarding elections, H.R. 4844 would suppress access to the building blocks of our democracy, the right to vote for U.S. citizens.

BUREAUCRATIC BARRIER

According to APIAVote's national post-2004 election conference held last year, our partners across the country implemented a common practice and successful strategy to register potential voters by implementing voter registration drives at community events and festivals. Many of these first time registrants were people filling out their registration form onsite and were not likely to be carrying around passports, birth certificates, and naturalization papers. H.R. 4844 would have a chilling impact on similar outreach activities in the future and ultimately depress APIA voter registration. In addition, these voter registration efforts are implemented by members of the community, most of whom are volunteers. These nonprofit organizations do not have the equipment and resources to obtain a photo copier and an outdoor power source to make copies of these documents. In addition, these volunteers are not document experts, and they may not know what documents are required to comply with this proposed legislation.

Proof of citizenship places onerous requirements on voters as well as voter registration and voter engagement organizations. A citizenship requirement to register and a photo ID to vote are so unrealistic and administratively burdensome that civic engagement will be the only activity effectively discouraged. These requirements undermine the legislative intent behind both the NVRA and HAVA, which sought to minimize barriers to vote and facilitate access to the ballot. Further election reform should promote greater participation in and turnout for elections.

NATURAL AND/OR PERSONAL DISASTERS

Other barriers include individuals and families who were recently impacted by natural disasters such as Hurricane Katrina. In Biloxi, Mississippi where 5.11% of the community are Asian American and Pacific Islanders (AAPIs) and in New Orleans, Louisiana where over 462,269 AAPIs reside are citizens struggling to rebuild their lives. Many are in the process of trying to obtain copies of all their legal documents that were lost in the disaster. We must not penalize these communities by taking away their voice and power of their individual vote in their time of need.

LANGUAGE BARRIER

According to the National Korean American Service & Education Consortium (NAKASEC), Korean Americans now numbering over 1.3 million and representing the 7th largest group of immigrants at close to a million. An estimated 520,000 are naturalized citizens. The majority are immigrant and Limited English Proficient voters with language access needs.

If H.R. 4844 is enacted, it will be very difficult for LEP voters to understand new requirements. Even for those jurisdictions with Section 203 coverage, this new requirement will take time for AAPI LEP voters to understand and comply. And in addition, many counties will not have resources to explain and reach out to Limited English speaking voters of the new requirements. The result is that many voters will be disenfranchised for several elections. Further, many will feel fed up with the additional requirements and not bother to vote.

ECONOMIC BARRIER

Additionally, according to Southeast Asia Resource Action Center (SEARAC), over 85,000 Southeast Asians reside mostly in the Twin cities region of Minnesota. Voter participation has increased recently with the election of two Hmong former refugees into the Minnesota State Legislature and where voters in precincts with large APIA communities utilized the same-day voter registration option at higher rates than average. Between Hennepin and Ramsey Counties, 56,996 voters in precincts with large APIA communities registered on election day. That represents almost one-fifth of total voters in APIA precincts that were able to cast a ballot on election day.

At the same time, the Asian Americans and Pacific Islander population in this region have a per capita income of $15,536, far below that of the Twin Cities area income average of $26,219. For communities who are financially struggling, requiring a photo ID of voters is the equivalent of a poll tax. By mandating that voters provide photo identification, H.R. 4844 would require voters to pay for a photo ID or documentation such as a passport, if they don't already have it.

For example, a birth certificate usually costs $10 to $15. According to the Department of Bureau of Consular Affairs, only 25–27% of eligible Americans have passports, which now cost $97. Naturalization papers, if they are lost or damaged and need to be replaced, cost $210. Not all eligible voters in this country can afford to purchase such identification, and H.R. 4844 does not provide remedies to help them get one. This simply means that many people will no longer be able to "afford" to exercise their constitutional right to vote.

This bill simply creates additional barriers to voter participation.

MISTRUST IN GOVERNMENT

An APIAVote study released after the 2004 elections reveals a plurality of APIAs (27%) registered to vote through the mail. This contrasts with Non-Hispanic Whites and Blacks who favored going to government elections offices.

If H.R. 4844 was to be enacted, it will decrease the number of AAPI's registered through Vote by Mail. Many AAPI's will not send their identification in the mail for the fear of their identification will be misused and or stolen. The additional requirement for identification will increase voter's fear and their distrust in their government.

Asian and Pacific Islanders immigrated to the United States because we are a democratic nation. Many members of the Asian community traditionally come from countries that do not believe in the democratic process and did not integrate individuals into the electoral and decision making process. We are no longer a democracy when the majority of eligible voters are hindered and discouraged from participating due to policies that create barriers instead of breaking them down.

APIAVote is able to register eligible individuals to vote and complement voter outreach efforts by local and state election officials. We help facilitate and develop trust amongst those engaged in civic and voter participation. It is commonly understood that officials need more resources to administer elections, and as partners in the administration of elections, voter registration groups facilitate access to communities that have been historically less active in voting. Our efforts should be focused on promoting democracy and advancing the goal to increase civic engagement an voter turnout.

Instead of discussing ways to create barriers and discourage civic participation, perhaps we should be talking about ways to increase participation. For example, APIAs are more likely to use alternative methods of voting when available. In Clark County, Nevada, a majority of voters in

APIA precincts chose "early voting" or "vote-by-mail" methods to cast their ballots. For APIA precinct voters in Hennepin and Ramsey Counties, Minnesota, almost 20% registered and voted under the "same day registration" provisions.

VOTER IDENTIFICATION

APIAVote has serious concerns regarding how the voter identification law would be implemented. According to the Asian American Legal Defense and Education Fund who conducted the largest nonpartisan exit poll of Asian Americans, nearly 70% of Asian voters were asked for ID in states where no ID was required. In the 2004 elections, nearly 3,000 Asian American voters reported to AALDEF that they were improperly required to present identification to vote, sometimes in the form of naturalization certificates. AALDEF poll monitors also found that Asian American voters were racially profiled at the polls and that demands for a naturalization certificate were only made upon Asian American voters, and no other voters.

We believe that even if photo identification is available, many eligible voters will be turned away. A large number of poll workers are usually overworked, underpaid, and not properly trained. Deciding whether a voter matches or does not match the photo in an ID card is a very subjective process.

In addition, volunteer ballot observers from VNTeamwork in Houston, Texas noted that since many Vietnamese and Asian names seem similar for those not familiar with these surnames, they are often entered incorrectly into the system. Also, many Asian names place the last name before the first name which can be confusing and entered incorrectly as well. As a result, the record does not accurately match the name on the identification and documentation.

H.R. 4844 does not explain how disputes over the validity of an ID card would be handled, and because it would keep voters who don't have "valid" ID from obtaining provisional ballots, it could easily open the door to widespread racial and ethnic discrimination at polling places.

According to the Chinese Progressive Association in Boston, Massachusetts, first time voters with limited English proficiency were sometimes sent back 2–3 times to obtain improper ID. It was observed that poll workers didn't even bother trying to speak with voters directly to get their names to look them up in poll books but instead demanded identification. Some voters were turned away form voting. It is important to note that because of these problems the U.S. Department of Justice filed a lawsuit against the City of Boston in 2005 for anti-Asian voter discrimination which resulted in a settlement requiring fully translated Chinese and Vietnamese ballots.

An example of how improper handling of documents increases racial and ethnic discrimination is illustrated with the implementation of the Immigration Reform and Control Act of 1986 (IRCA). Under IRCA, employers may hire only persons who may legally work in the U.S. The employer must verify the identity and employment eligibility of anyone to be hired, which includes completing the Employment Eligibility Verification Form (I-9), but in many cases, employers asked for additional documentation than necessary from Latinos, Asians, and anyone that could be perceived as foreign. In a study conducted in March of 1990, GAO [the U.S. Government Accountability Office] found that IRCA had created a widespread pattern of discrimination throughout the country, and it was most prevalent in areas with the greatest numbers of Latinos and Asians. This study also showed that over

891,000 employers, who by their own admission, adopted discriminatory hiring practices as a result of employer sanctions.

Since 2004, APIAVote helped build a model of mentoring and organizing to get out the vote among APIA youth. For the first time in history, APIA sororities and fraternities joined a coordinated effort to mobilize 20,004 APIA youth to vote. By working closely with the Asian Pacific Islander student organizations and networks, such as the South Asian American Voting Youth, Asian Greek Alliance and the National Asian American Student Conference, APIAVote, participation increased. APIAVote is weary of how H.R. 4844 would be implemented seeing that legitimate voters with Photo ID could be turned away for benign reasons such as a driver's license not containing the voter's current address. Many college students change addresses multiple times within their college career. For example in Wisconsin, 97% of all students do not have their current address on their photo ID. H.R. 4844 could undermine the important safety net under the Help America Vote Act. If an eligible voter does not bring proper ID, H.R. 4844 would keep him or her from registering and voting.

CONCLUSION

APIAVote understands and advocates that we maintain the integrity of the United States electoral process, but we also believe that current laws are already extremely tough on individuals who try to vote illegally. It is already a federal offense for falsely claiming citizenship and for voting fraud. In addition, ever since U.S. immigration laws were reformed in 1996, noncitizens who try to vote are automatically given a one-way ticket out of the country, with no criminal conviction necessary. Proof of citizenship requirements will only penalize U.S. citizens who want to exercise their right to vote.

We believe that the type of fraud cited in support of photo ID requirements—individual voters who misrepresent their identity at the polls—is nothing but an anomaly. For example, despite the accusations of fraud as support for the new Georgia law, Secretary of State Cathy Cox stated that in her ten-year tenure, she could not recall one documented case of voter fraud involving the impersonation of a registered voter at the polls. ID requirements passed at the state level are already having a chilling effect on voter registration groups around the country.

Some states have enacted laws that create criminal penalties that may be applied to organizations conducting voter registration. As a result, these nonprofit organizations must decide whether or not the goal to promote democracy outweighs potential criminal penalties. Instead, civic organizations should be encouraged to support methods that strengthen democracy and ensure the voice of every American is heard.

APIAVote stands in strong opposition to H.R. 4844 and the barriers to voting this law will create for all Americans.

THE CONTINUING DEBATE: Providing Proof of Citizenship When Registering to Vote

What Is New

As of early September 2006, the Committee on Administration had made a decision on whether to send H.R. 4844 to the floor of the House of Representatives. Whether or not the bill makes it out of committee during the hectic and truncated session time during the fall 2006 election season and what its fate would be in the Senate and the House is unclear. However, whatever the specific fate of H.R. 4844 is, the issues surrounding it are likely to grow in intensity. These issues are tied up in the push for identification cards based on worries about terrorism and the general concern about the impact of immigrants, both legal and illegal, on the country. Moreover, whatever the overt arguments are for and against tightening voter registration, such proposals have partisan consequences. The reason is that restrictions are more likely to be a barrier to people who are apt to vote Democrat than those who are likely to vote Republican. That factor is usually not acknowledged, but it is the reason that all the members of Congress who spoke for H.R. 4844 during the hearings by the Committee on Administration were Republicans and all the members who opposed the bill were Democrats.

Where to Find More

A study reviewed a range of issues associated with this debate is Benjamin Highton, "Voter Registration and Turnout in the United States," *Perspectives on Politics* (2004). The 2005 report of the (Carter-Baker) Commission on Federal Election Reform is available at www.american.edu/ia/cfer/. After reading that, turn to Wendy R. Weiser, Justin Levitt, Catherine Weiss, and Spencer Overton, "Response to the Report of the 2005 Commission on Federal Election Reform," on the Website of the Brennan Center For Justice, New York University School of Law at www.brennancenter.org. Not surprisingly, the Brennan Center's site also has material in opposition to H.R. 4844. For more from proponents of the bill and similar proposals, go to the Website of Patrick Rogers' American Center for Voting Rights Legislative Fund at www.ac4vr.com.

What More to Do

At first glance, this debate seems simple. Since only citizens can vote, who could oppose demonstrating citizenship prior to voting. Yet it is more complex than that. Debate, in part, why a change is needed now if the country has gotten along for over two centuries without it. Also wrestle with the subtleties of this debate. Even if there is a problem, how big is it, what is the price of fixing it, and is the cure worth the cost?

CONGRESS

CONGRESSIONAL TERM LIMITS:
Promoting Choice *or* Restricting Choice?

PROMOTING CHOICE

ADVOCATE: Paul Jacob, Executive Director, U.S. Term Limits

SOURCE: Testimony during hearings on "Limiting Terms of Office for Members of the U.S. Senate and U.S. House of Representatives," U.S. House of Representatives, Committee on the Judiciary, Subcommittee on the Constitution, January 22, 1997

RESTRICTING CHOICE

ADVOCATE: John R. Hibbing, Professor of Political Science, University of Nebraska

SOURCE: Testimony during hearings on "Limiting Terms of Office for Members of the U.S. Senate and U.S. House of Representatives," U.S. House of Representatives, Committee on the Judiciary, Subcommittee on the Constitution, January 22, 1997

One way this debate could have been entitled was with a riddle: "When Does Restricting Voter Choice Improve Democracy?" An alternative riddle/title might have been, "When Does Unrestricted Voter Choice Diminish Democracy?" Those who advocate limiting the number of terms members of Congress may serve argue that incumbents have advantages that make it nearly impossible for challengers to unseat them, thereby limiting the "real" choice of voters. Opponents counter that, among other drawbacks, term limits abridge the voters' democratic right to choose whomever they wish to represent them for as long as they wish.

Statistically, once someone gets elected to Congress they have an extraordinarily good chance of being reelected again. For example, during elections between 1980 and 2002, about 90% of all incumbent members of Congress sought another term, and of those who did, voters returned 93% of the representatives and 89% of the senators. Moreover, incumbents in House races received an average of 71% of the vote in 2002. The senators in office in 2003 had amassed an average 62% of the vote in their previous election. Also indisputable is the fact that the average number of years a person spends in Congress has increased over time. During the 1800s only 3% of representatives and 11% of senators served more than 12 years. Those figures jumped to 27% and 32% during the 1900s, and since 1947 to 35% and 41% respectively.

There are numerous reasons why incumbents have an advantage, which, in sum, create a positive view by most people of their individual members of Congress. One survey found that 62% of respondents approved of the job their members of Congress were doing, only 17% disapproved, and 21% were not sure. This is remarkable given that only 43% of those respondents approved of the job Congress as an institution was doing, with 33% disapproving and 24% unsure.

Term limits have long applied to the tenure of many chief executives. The presidency had a two-term tradition until Franklin Roosevelt sought and won four terms. Soon thereafter, the Twenty-Second Amendment (1951) made the two-term limit mandatory. Additionally, 36 states have term limits for governor. Recently, the idea of also limiting the terms of state and national legislators began to become prominent. California and Oklahoma passed the first such legislation in 1990. It was an idea whose time had come, and soon 20 other states followed suit. Most of these restrictions were enacted by direct democracy techniques, including initiatives and referendums.

Opponents of term limits quickly challenged their constitutionality. In 1995 by a 6 to 3 vote in *U.S. Term Limits, Inc. v. Thornton*, the U.S. Supreme Court struck down the limits that Arkansas (and by implication all other states) had placed on terms in the U.S. Congress. Term limits on state legislatures, by contrast, are matters primarily of state constitutional law, and in this realm, the federal courts and most state courts have upheld term limits.

The Supreme Court decision means that it would be necessary to amend the Constitution in order to limit the number of terms that members of the U.S. Senate and House of Representatives can serve. Part of the "Contract with America" put forth by the successful Republican congressional campaign in 1994 was a pledge to work for such a constitutional amendment, with a limit of two terms (12 years) for senators and 6 terms (12 years) for members of the House. Numerous such proposals were introduced in Congress in 1995, and others have been submitted since then. But none have gathered sufficient support. The "hot topic" of the 1990s faded somewhat in face of the daunting prospect of getting two-thirds of each of the two houses to pass a constitutional amendment and thereby truncate their own political careers. This fate has, among other things, increased the calls to adopt national direct democracy procedures (see Debate 19) and to amend the Constitution so that states can initiate amendments to the U.S. Constitution (see Debate 20). What many see as the problem of entrenched legislators remains, however. The senior senator in the 108th Congress, Robert Byrd, has held his seat since 1959 when Dwight D. Eisenhower was president, and the dean of the House, John Dingle, began his tenure four years before that in 1955 when the current president, George W. Bush was nine years old. As a historical note, the record for the longest combined service in Congress (57 years) is held by Carl Hayden, who served in the House from the time of Arizona's admission to the union in 1912 to 1927, then was in the Senate until 1969. The oldest member ever of Congress was South Carolina Strom Thurmond, who retired at age 100 in 2003 after 48 years in the Senate.

POINTS TO PONDER

- Would term limits enhance or diminish Congress' power compared to the president?
- John Hibbing notes that senior members of Congress are often more effective in terms of getting legislation passed. Is this because they gain expertise or because they use the power structure to limit the role of junior members?
- What impact do you think term limits would have on the proportion of underrepresented groups (such as women and racial and ethnic minorities) in Congress?

Congressional Term Limits: Promoting Choice

PAUL JACOB

America has one clear and decisive advantage over the rest of the world: Our political system.

Our system is a unique democratic republic with constitutional limits on the federal government. It's a system designed to maximize individual freedom and citizen control of government at all levels. Our forebears not only set up this system of protected freedoms, but also recognized the need for change, for continual reform, and for constitutional amendment in order to preserve and enhance our freedom.

George Washington said in his farewell address, "The basis of our political systems is the right of the people to make and alter their constitutions of government." President [Abraham] Lincoln explained: "The country, with its institutions, belongs to the people who inhabit it. Whenever they shall grow weary of the existing government, they can exercise their Constitutional right of amending it." As Thomas Jefferson said to those who object to amending the Constitution, "We might as well require a man to wear still the coat which fitted him when a boy."

The vast majority of Americans today want to amend their Constitution. They want congressional term limits of three terms for House members and two terms for Senators.

EXPERIENCE WITH TERM LIMITS

Term limits is not a new idea. Democracy as far back as Aristotle has known term limits, or rotation in office. Certainly our Founders appreciated rotation in office. John Adams, Ben Franklin, Thomas Jefferson all spoke to the need for limited tenure in public office. Today, term limits are the law of the land for the President, 40 state governors, 20 state legislatures and thousands of local elected officials including many large cities most notably New York and Los Angeles. Americans support congressional term limits not only for what they hope it will do to the culture in Congress, but for what it has already done at other levels of government.

According to Jody Newman, former head of the National Women's Political Caucus, "Our political system is tremendously biased in favor of incumbents." While this has slowed the progress of women and minorities into elected office, term limits are helping to bring more women, minorities and people from all walks of life into politics. This has been the case in cities like New Orleans and Kansas City where record numbers of minorities now hold office as well as the legislature in California which, according to the *Los Angeles Times*, now includes "a former U.S. Air Force fighter pilot, a former sheriff-coroner, a paralegal, a retired teacher, a video store owner, a businesswoman-homemaker, a children's advocate, an interior designer...and a number of businessmen."

Term limits are bringing more competition, and arguably fairer competition. A recent study by Kermit Daniel of the University of Pennsylvania and Joan R. Lott of the University of Chicago concluded: "California's legislative term limits have dramatically reduced campaign expenditures, while at the same time that more candidates are running for office and races are becoming more competitive. The changes are so large that more incumbents are being defeated, races are closer, more candidates are running, and there are fewer single candidate races than at any other time in our sample."

In Ohio, state legislative term limits were credited with helping pass serious ethics reform. "Term limits established a kind of public-interest momentum" according to Ohio Common Cause executive director Janet Lewis, whose group had led the fight against term limits. Robert McCord, a columnist with the *Arkansas Times* declared "the Arkansas House of Representatives has been reborn" after the state's voters enacted a six-year House limit and representatives were quick to dismantle the seniority system.

Anecdotal and empirical evidence abounds that term limits have reduced partisanship, gridlock, and special interest influence. At the same time, more people are running for office, additional reforms are following in the term limits wake, and the disastrous predictions of opponents are being quietly forgotten.

Unfortunately, Congress continues to be locked in partisan warfare, ethics problems, and largely uncompetitive elections. Congress needs term limits.

CONGRESS HAS A CONFLICT OF INTEREST

When the amendment process of the Constitution was originally debated [in 1787], delegate George Byron of Pennsylvania had tremendous vision. He saw the potential of a congressional conflict of interest and warned, "We shall never find two-thirds of a Congress voting for anything which shall derogate from their own authority and importance."

Even with consistent and overwhelming public support, about three out of four Americans believe Congress will refuse to propose a constitutional amendment for term limits. Why? Because Congress has a clear conflict of interest. Term limits is about limiting your personal power and the power of any individual who takes your place in our system.

Most members of Congress do support the concept of term limits and have for some time. After all, Congress voted by two-thirds of both Houses to propose the Twenty-Second Amendment limiting the President to two terms, eight years, in office. More recently (in the 104th Congress) [1995–1996], 355 members of the House voted to limit committee chairs to three terms. Yet, while supporting and imposing the concept on others, many members do not want limits to apply to them personally.

The congressional conflict of interest results in many members of Congress favoring limits twice as generous as most voters, that is, if they favor any limits at all. Congress has also shown a tremendous ability for political maneuvering on the issue.

Last Congress, the House of Representatives failed to represent their constituents as term limits were defeated by outright opponents and "loved to death" by some questionable friends. The three-term House limit enacted by 15 states and supported by gigantic percentages of voters was opposed by a majority of Republicans, as well as Democrats. Only the freshman Republicans were in sync with the wishes of the American people 72 percent voting for a three-term limit, a constitutional majority itself demonstrating the benefit of regular rotation in office.

This conflict also can be found in some members' demand that Congress, rather than the voters, set the limits. As David Mason of the Heritage Foundation wrote, "At a February 28 [1995] House Judiciary Committee mark-up session on these proposals, a coalition of opponents and wavering supporters amended the McCollum bill, so that it...explicitly would preempt state term limit laws (the original bill was silent on state powers)." What Mr. Mason didn't report was Representative McCollum proposed this amendment to his own bill that would have specifically struck down the shorter term limit imposed on him by the voters of Florida. That the House GOP's point-man on the issue would seek to preempt his own state's term limit law passed by a 77 percent vote is a striking example of his conflict of interest.

The commitment of the House Republican Leadership, especially Speaker Newt Gingrich, has been the subject of much doubt. Television producer Brian Boyer, who spent a great deal of time with Gingrich while filming a 1995 documentary, said, "It was very surprising, and this was, remember, from very long conversations with Gingrich, to learn that he personally is not in favor of term limits." Gingrich's spokesperson Tony Blankley told the *American Spectator* in July of 1994 that term limits was "something conceptually [Newt] doesn't like." Columnist Robert Novak wrote in the *Washington Post*, "Republican leaders profess to want 12 years, but it is clear they prefer no limits at all."

A number of Republicans in the leadership voted against every term limit bill as did five committee chairs. Only one member of the leadership, Majority Leader Dick Armey, and only one committee chair voted for the three-term House limit passed by most states. Yet while Mr. Armey said he would have stripped a member of a committee chairmanship had they like Senator Mark Hatfield voted against the Balanced Budget Amendment, there was no such pressure brought to bear for term limits.

Freshman Michael Forbes of New York told the *New York Times* after the failed House vote, "Candidly, this leadership didn't want [term limits] anymore than the old leadership did." But the American people were not fooled—a *Washington Post*/ABC News poll found close to two-thirds believe neither Republicans nor Democrats in Congress really tried to pass term limits.

THREE TERMS VS. SIX TERMS

The question as to the proper length of the term limits is not merely: What should the limits be? Rather, the essential question is: Who should set the limits? U.S. Term Limits is dedicated to the proposition that the people, not Congress, should set the limits.

Some observers of the battle in Congress over whether House terms should be limited to three terms or six terms have posited that the term limits movement is split. This is simply not the case. The term limits movement is strongly united behind three terms. Only in Congress (and especially among longtime members whose support for any limit whatsoever is questionable) is there significant approval of six terms and fierce opposition to three terms.

Throughout the rest of America, support for three terms far surpasses support for six terms. The American people, prolimits scholars and virtually every state term limit group in the country supports a three-term limit in the House and a two-term limit in the Senate. Poll after poll demonstrates public support for three terms over six. A 1996 Fabrizio-McLaughlin poll of 1,000 adults nationally found supporters favored three terms 81 percent to 16 percent over six terms.

Not surprisingly, election results bear this out. In every head to head vote three terms has won over six terms. Colorado voters went to the polls in 1994 and voted to lower their limits from six terms to three terms. The arguments in favor of a six-term House limit are so barren, that one such Beltway advocate brazenly and erroneously claims this is "compelling" evidence of support for the longer limit.

ONLY IN WASHINGTON

South Dakota has voted on both a 12-year House limit and a 6-year House limit in separate elections where one would not replace the other. The 6-year limit received 68 percent of the vote to 63 percent for the 12-year limit. After the Wyoming legislature voted to double its state House limits from three terms to six, voters said keep the three-term limit 54 to 46 percent. This even after the sitting governor and three former governors came out in favor of the longer limits.

In fact, the latest trend for politicians opposed to term limits is to pretend to favor term limits, but only longer ones like 12 Years. In New York City, Peter Vallone, Council President and adamant term-limit opponent, was unsuccessful in his attempt to defeat term limits in 1993. Just this past election, he sought to extend the limits from eight years to twelve years. Even with a purposely slanted and misleading ballot title, the voters saw through the council's scheme and rejected this term extension. The same effort to claim support for the term limits concept in order to extend the limits has been and is being repeated in many cities and states with term limits. The voters continue to oppose these term extensions.

The intellectual support for a shorter House limit is also very substantial. A working group of 31 scholars formed by Empower America in December of 1994 studied the term limits issue and concluded, "We put term limits on our agenda, and would even go so far as to favor the specific proposal to limit terms to 6 years in the House and 12 in the Senate."

Mark Petracca, a professor at the University of California-Irvine and a leading scholar on limits, told Congress "my preference is strongly for a limit less expansive than 12 years or 6 terms in the House.... A six-term or 12-year limit in the House...won't do much to deprofessionalize the House. Neither may it do much to remedy the other exigencies driving the term limits movement."

David M. Mason of the Heritage Foundation points to "Senate-envy" as the number one reason House members favor the much longer six-term limit and reminds us, "The incumbents' plea for experience only echoes arguments of term limits opponents."

Senator Fred Thompson of Tennessee pointed out one of the reasons people oppose a six-term limit and support three terms. In his 1995 House and Senate testimony, he stated, "Limiting House Members to six terms, instead of the three terms as I have proposed, would leave the seniority system intact and do little to level a playing field that has huge advantages for incumbents." Missouri Senator John Ashcroft recognizes a three-term limit would reduce the incentive for gerrymandering congressional districts for the benefit of incumbents, stating, "it would be one of several benefits exclusive to the 3/2 term proposal..."

Of the major Republican candidates for president in 1996, Lamar Alexander, Pat Buchanan, Steve Forbes, Phil Gramm, and Alan Keyes all supported a limit of three House terms. As Pat Buchanan told the Senate, "Now, what about this 12-year proposal? Well, let me associate myself with what...Lamar Alexander...said. I am unalterably opposed to 12 years. I am for 6 years and out. I know that folks say let's treat both Houses the same way. But the Founding Fathers did not treat both Houses the same way."

There are a plethora of other important policy reasons for enacting a three-term limit as opposed to six terms. Three-term limits will mean greater turnover, more competitive elections, more and quicker campaign reform, and a larger dose of fiscal sanity.

The "Legislative Backgrounder" attached as an appendix to this testimony details further evidence of the public policy benefits associated with a three-term rather than six-term limit.

In reality, many in Congress supposedly favoring a six-term limit appear to not support term limits at all. Representative Bill Barrett of Nebraska has supported the six-term McCollum bill, but wrote in 1995, "I understand voters are frustrated and dissatisfied with the performance of Congress, but I doubt term limits are the answer." Another cosponsor of the McCollum bill is Representative David Camp of Michigan who like Barrett voted against the three-term limits passed in his state. Camp told the *Michigan Midland Daily News* [May 23, 1995], "Voters understand that if they want to limit a member of Congress' term, they can vote for the opponent." These are not the statements of term limit enthusiasts.

In the face of popular and intellectual reasons that three-term limits are superior, the main argument advanced by the longer limit advocates in Congress is that they will simply refuse to support any limits shorter than 6 terms regardless of any support or rationale evidenced against them. This is presented as realism and practicality, but at its core it's the intellectual integrity of a hijacker. Congress in such a case is saying, "The people may have right on their side, but we have the power to ignore them."

INFORMED VOTER LAWS

Nobel prize-winning economist Milton Friedman recognizes the congressional conflict, but also appreciates the ingenuity of the American people in declaring, "Congress is never, not in a million years, going to impose term limits on itself unless it has to."

After the vote in the House in 1995, the American people understood they would have to take matters into their own hands, and they did. The result? In 1996, nine states passed Informed Voter Laws sometimes called Term Limits Accountability Laws. These states are Alaska, Arkansas, Colorado, Idaho, Maine, Missouri, Nebraska, Nevada and South Dakota.

The laws are very simple. First, they instruct members of Congress to support a specific 3/2 term limits amendment written precisely in the initiative. With differing opinions among members of Congress in the past, and the built-in conflict of interest, the voters of these states seek to make the term limits amendment they want explicitly clear.

Secondly, these laws create a procedure for informing the voters if their instructions on term limits are simply disregarded. If members from these states fail to support the 3/2 amendment or attempt to enact watered-down limits longer than 3/2, the Secretary of State will inform the voters by printing "DISREGARDED VOTER INSTRUCTION ON TERM LIMITS" next to the incumbents' names on the ballot.

Candidates who are not incumbents are allowed to sign a pledge to abide by the voters' instructions when they file for the office. If they do not so pledge, the voters will again be informed by the Secretary of State printing "DECLINED TO PLEDGE TO SUPPORT TERM LIMITS" next to their name on the ballot.

Some will argue these laws are unconstitutional. The opponents of term limits have long used the lawsuit as their primary weapon. Already the voters are being sued by special interests and politicians in a number of states trying to overturn the people's vote. But let me suggest the courts will not save politician-kind this time.

Prior to the 1996 election, the Arkansas Supreme Court declared the state's Informed Voter Initiative unconstitutional and removed it from the ballot. The state court argued the measure would cause "potential political deaths" if elected officials did not heed the instructions of an informed public. To this end, I can only say I certainly hope so. But the U.S. Supreme Court did not allow the Arkansas court to deny the people a vote on this measure. In a highly unusual move, the High Court 7 to 2 issued an emergency stay of the state court decision and the voters got their opportunity to cast ballots for or against the Informed Voter Law.

On November 5, more than 60 percent of Arkansans voted to add the Term Limits Informed Voter amendment to their state constitution. Now the U.S. Supreme Court has been petitioned to take the case, and we believe the people of Arkansas will prevail on the merits.

The response to these Informed Voter Laws has been universal shock and horror from the political establishment. What is there to cause such objection? These laws offer congressmen non-binding instructions from the people they work for and are charged with representing. The republican right of instruction is nothing new and surely no elected official could object to his or her constituents making their desires known regarding their government and their very own representative.

The informational aspect of the initiative has been attacked as the Scarlet Letter. Yet term limit enemies do not argue the information is anything but accurate. Their claims that such an "instruct and inform" tactic is coercive are all predicated on their understanding that the public deeply favors term limits and will likely use the accurate information to oppose those not representing their position. Do incumbents have a right to block truthful information harmful to them from the voting public? If citizens are free to make their instructions known, are they to be denied any knowledge as to how their elected representatives have acted? There is no public good in promoting public ignorance on term limits.

Some have argued that the voters will demand similar information on a whole host of issues. They imagine ballot information such as "VOTED TO RAISE TAXES" or "SUPPORTED CONGRESSIONAL PAY RAISE" next to candidates' names. What if it were so? Isn't public education a good thing? If the voters want more information, then they should have it. Yet, similar voter instructions were given and ballot notations used 90 years ago by the Progressives in pursuit of the Seventeenth Amendment for popular election of U.S. Senators and not until now on term limits have citizens returned to this device. The reasons are obvious. Voters understand they must call the tune if they can hope to overcome the political self-interest of members on the issue.

Harry Truman was called "Give 'em Hell Harry." But Truman remarked, "I never did give anybody hell. I just told the truth and they thought it was hell." These Informed Voter Laws likewise only tell the truth, and while they have popular support, term limits opponents will think they're hell. With public knowledge, politicians lose their wiggle-room on an issue that truly matters to voters.

The American people want a constitutional amendment for a three-term limit in the House and a two-term limit in the Senate. The sooner this body proposes such an amendment, the sooner Congress can be reconnected to this great country. For as the great Englishman Edmund Burke said: "In all forms of Government the people [are] the true legislator."

I ask you to put aside all political games and offer a proposal the American people have endorsed. If this Congress chooses to vote it down, so be it. At least the people will have a clean vote on real term limits.

Congressional Term Limits: Restricting Choice

JOHN R. HIBBING

I urge you to do what you can to keep the terms of members of Congress from being limited to a set number. I will organize my case against term limits around three points: the value of congressional experience, the uncertain consequences of term limits for representation, and the inability of term limits to improve the public's opinion of Congress.

CONGRESSIONAL EXPERIENCE

The term limit movement believes it is important to have a constant infusion of "new blood" in Congress lest the body become stale and set in its ways. Opponents of term limits worry that too much new blood would lead to a decrease in both legislative quality and institutional memory as inexperienced members wrestle with devilishly complex issues. Which side is correct? What is the optimal level of membership turnover for an institution like Congress? Most of the debate on these questions has proceeded without any firm evidence for the value of congressional experience. I would like to interject some evidence now.

About 10 years ago, I attempted to determine the manner in which members of this house changed as their careers in Congress unfolded. I found that, with a few exceptions of course, most members did not change much ideologically. Liberals stayed liberal and conservatives stayed conservative. Early career roll call patterns were good predictors of late career roll call patterns. Surprisingly, perhaps, early career electoral results were also good predictors of late career electoral results. It is not the case that many members transform marginal seats into safe seats. The chances of losing office because of an election are nearly as great for senior members as they are for junior members. Attention to the district, as measured by the number of trips home, diminishes with increasing tenure but only by a little. Most senior members work quite hard at maintaining a presence in the district. Finally, the odds of a member being involved in some type of scandalous behavior do not increase with tenure. Junior members are just as likely as senior members to be scandal-ridden. The popular vision of an inert, uncaring, corrupt, and electorally unchallengeable senior member is simply inaccurate. On each of these counts, senior members are almost no different from junior members.

This statement does not apply, however, when attention shifts to legislative activity, that is, actually formulating and passing legislation. Here I found substantial differences between junior and senior members. Senior members, it turns out, are the heart and the soul of the legislative process. They are more active on legislation (giving speeches, offering amendments, and sponsoring bills), they are more specialized (a greater portion of their legislative attention goes to a focused substantive area), and they are more efficient (a greater percentage of their legislation becomes law). These patterns, I might add, persist even when senior members do not become leaders on committees or subcommittees, so it is not just that member activity reflects the positions of power that some senior members hold. The reasons for altered legislative contributions are broader than that and have to do, simply, with increased legislative experience.

Now, I will be the first to admit that many of these indicators of legislative involvement are badly flawed. It is impossible to measure quantitatively a representative's overall legislative contribution. As members know better than anyone, the legislative process is too rich and subtle to be captured by counting speeches or calculating legislative batting averages. But we must try to understand the relative contributions of senior members if we are to know the consequences of statutorily prohibiting the service of senior members, and here it can be said with some confidence that senior members have more active, focused, and successful legislative agendas. Junior members tend to introduce bills on topics about which they know very little. The subject matter of these bills is all over the map and the bills have precious little chance of making it out of committee let alone becoming law. These are empirical facts. We need more senior members; not fewer.

UNCERTAINTY ABOUT CONSEQUENCES

Many people support the term limit movement because they believe it would make members more responsive to the people. The argument is that Congress has grown out of touch and that if members served only short time periods, along the lines of the citizen legislatures of old, they would be more in touch with the needs and concerns of ordinary people. But there are others who support the term limit movement for exactly the opposite reason. [Columnist] George Will is probably the best-known proponent of the position that term limits should be enacted in order to make Congress less sensitive to the desires of ordinary people. Will and others believe that mandatory term limits would embolden representatives, giving them the nerve to go against public opinion. Only when members know their stint in Congress will soon end, the argument is, will members stop pandering to unrealistic public demands for both lower taxes and more government services. I do not know which side is correct about the consequences of term limits for the proximity of Congress to the people but I do know that the inability of those in the term limit movement to agree amongst themselves on whether Congress is too close or not close enough to the people together with their inability to know whether term limits would in actuality reduce or increase the distance between the people and their Congress should give us pause. Before we enshrine a reform in the Constitution of the United States, should we not at least expect the champions of that reform to know what they want to accomplish?

Public Opinion of Congress

My current research interests have to do with the reasons the public tends to be displeased with Congress. People believe Congress has been captured by special interests, extremist parties, and professionalized politicians and that ordinary folks have been lost in the shuffle. They want changes that would restore the public's role in the process. The only way we can restore public confidence in Congress, some reformers argue, is to enact measures, like term limits, that are central to the public's populist agenda.

It is my belief that term limits would not improve the public's opinion of Congress in the long run. Much public unrest stems from the belief that Congress creates conflict. The common notion is that agreement exists among the masses but that when special interests, parties, and ambitious politicians come together in Congress they manage to construct disagreement where it need not exist. But the truth of the matter is that, while interest groups, parties, and politicians sometimes create conflict, most of the time they only reflect the people's diverse views. Survey research indicates clearly that people are deeply divided over how to solve almost every major societal problem. This disagreement would exist whether or not term limits were enacted. In fact, I contend the public would be even more disillusioned than they are currently once they saw political conflict continuing unabated long after term limits were enacted.

The real solution is to educate people on the extent of their own disagreements and on the difficulties faced by elected officials in moving from these disagreements to responsible, brokered solutions to problems. People harbor beliefs that reforms such as term limits will be able to reduce conflict and the accompanying deliberation (bickering) and compromise (selling out) that they find so objectionable. Nothing could be further from the truth. Rather than pretending there is a magic solution to political conflict, we need to educate the people on the necessity of having learned, experienced legislators who can work their way through the challenging assignment of coming to agreement in the face of public ignorance and uncertainty.

THE CONTINUING DEBATE: Congressional Term Limits

What Is New

The 2004 elections demonstrated the relative safety of incumbents. Of the 34 senators whose terms were up, 26 sought new terms, and 25 were reelected. There was also scant turnover in the House, to which voters returned 99% of the 400 incumbents who ran again. For the 109th Congress (2005–2007), the average length of service in the House was 9.3 years and the average senator had been serving 12.1 years. If a term limit using the most often discussed parameters (12 years in either chamber) existed, it would mean 163 of 435 members of the House would be barred from seeking reelection in 2004, as would be 70 of 100 senators in their next election.

Since the late 1990s, term-limit advocates have had more defeats than victories. The "informed voter measures" favored by advocate Paul Jacobs did not withstand the test of constitutionality. Those in Missouri were challenged and ruled unconstitutional by the U.S. Supreme Court in *Cook v. Gralike* (2001). As for term limits as such, the Supreme Courts of Massachusetts, Oregon, and Washington struck them down as violating their respective state constitutions. Idaho's legislature repealed limits in 2002, and Utah's legislature followed suit in 2003. The last states to hold a referendum on term limits were Mississippi in 1999 and Nebraska in 2000. In Mississippi, 55% of the voters rejected term limits, making the state the first to do so by direct democracy. Taking the opposite stand, 56% of Nebraska's voters supported term limits. This leaves 16 states with limits in place. A final note is that the concept remains popular with the public. When a 2003 survey asked about term limits, 67% of the respondents said term limits were a "a good idea," 27% thought them a "bad idea," 3% replied "it depends," and 4% were unsure.

Where to Find More

A good new study that presents a series of empirical studies of the impact of term limits on state legislatures is Rick Farmer, John David Rausch, Jr., and John C. Green (eds.), *The Test of Time: Coping with Legislative Term Limits* (Lexington, 2003). U.S. Term Limits, the group represented by advocate Paul Jacob, has a helpful Web site at: www.termlimits.org/. You can also find good information on the site of the National Conference of State Legislators at www.ncsl.org/programs/legman/about/termlimit.htm.

What More to Do

Think about one or more members of Congress whom you admire or who, because of their seniority, are powerful advocates of positions you support but who, at the end of their current term, will have been in their chamber 12 years or longer. Would you want them to be forced to retire because of term limits?

Consider your two senators and one member of the House. How do they stand with the 12-year rule? Also figure out which of the several U.S. senators who are being mentioned as possible presidential candidates in 2008 would have already had to retire under the 12-year rule or would have to do so in 2006. Would term limits affect the quality of future presidents?

DEBATE 12

PRESIDENCY

CENSURE PRESIDENT BUSH FOR ABUSE OF POWER: Justified *or* Politically Motivated?

JUSTIFIED

ADVOCATE: John W. Dean, former Counsel to the President of the United States

SOURCE: Testimony during hearings on "Senate Resolution 398 Relating to the Censure of George W. Bush," U.S. Senate, Committee on the Judiciary, March 31, 2006

POLITICALLY MOTIVATED

ADVOCATE: Professor Robert Turner, Associate Director, Center for National Security Law, University of Virginia

SOURCE: Testimony during hearings on "An Examination of the Call to Censure the President," United States Senate, Committee on the Judiciary, March 31, 2006

A key characteristic of the Constitution is its brevity. Totaling only 7,525 words, it is shorter than any of the 50 state constitutions. This brevity often leaves the Constitution imprecise and open to interpretation. That can be a positive trait. One reason that the Constitution has survived so long with so few amendments is that it has been possible to interpret its provisions to meet contemporary views and needs. Yet this flexibility is also a negative trait, because it often leads to conflict over what the Constitution allows and does not.

To a significant degree, this debate over whether to censure President George W. Bush for allegedly abusing his power by authorizing the National Security Agency (NSA) to conduct electronic surveillance on communications between people in the United States and those overseas suspected of terrorism without first obtaining a court warrant. The part of the Constitution that most clearly says that the president would have to get a court is the Fourth Amendment. It provides that people have a right "to be secure in their persons, houses, papers against unreasonable searches..." and further specifies that no warrants (legal writs, or orders, by a court) for a search can be issued except for "probable cause." Unfortunately, it is not clear what constitutes either "unreasonable" or "probable cause." Moreover, the amendment does not say, or has not been interpreted by the courts as saying, that all searches must be supported by a warrant. Indeed, most searches conducted by police probably are done without a warrant. For instance, whenever a police office "frisks" a suspect for a weapon, a warrantless search has occurred. For the federal governments, such searches without warrants are generally carried out under the inherent executive power, including the police power, given to the president by Article 2: "The executive power shall be vested in a president of the United States of America."

A third part of the Constitution relevant to this debate is the language in Article 2 designating the president "commander in chief." Beyond making him civilian commander of the armed forces, it is unclear what else, if anything, that phrase might mean, especially when juxtaposed with the clause of Article 1 that gives to Congress the authority "to make rules for the government and the regulation of the land and naval forces." Whatever such language was meant to do, presidents have impetrated their authority as commander in chief broadly to authorize them to order the military into combat without a declaration of war or other authorization by Congress and take many other actions that the presidents have construed as protecting national security. Generally Congress and the citizenry have acquired to these claims of power. Occasionally, the courts have found against such assertions of power by the president. When during the Korean War, President Harry Truman reacted to a threatened strike by steelworkers by seizing the steel mills and ordering the workers to stay on the job, the Supreme Court disallowed his action in *Youngstown Sheet & Tube Co. v. Sawyer* (1952). More often, though, the Court has upheld executive assertions of authority. In *United States v. Curtiss-Wright Export Corp.* (1936), a case related to the ability of the president to halt the export of weapons to warring countries, the Court opined that the presidents was "the sole organ of the federal government in the field of international relations" and, therefore, the authority in foreign affairs did not rest on any express grant of authority in the Constitution or by Congress.

The more immediate setting to this debate is the terrorist attack on 9/11 and its aftermath. One immediate response was Congress authorizing the president by votes of 98 to 0 in the Senate and 420 to 1 in the House "to use all necessary and appropriate force…to prevent any future acts of international terrorism against the United States." One of the initiatives in the "war on terrorism" was to authorize the NSA to monitor communications suspected of being related to terrorism. The White House claims these have only involved messages coming into or out of the Untied States, and therefore involving a foreign source or destination. This monitoring program was disclosed in leaks to the *New York Times* in late 2005 and set off furious objections. Among other things, critics charged that the president's action violated the 1978 Foreign Intelligence Surveillance Act (FISA), which bars foreign intelligence agencies from monitoring Americans in the United States without a warrant issued by the especially created Foreign Intelligence Surveillance Court. Taking the criticism another step, Senator Russell Feingold (D-WI) introduced a resolution censuring of the president. John Dean supports it in the first reading. Robert Turner rejects the call for censure in the second reading, argues that the president was well within legal boundaries under his authority as commander in chief and the authority in the provision of the post 9/11 congressional support for the "war on terrorism, and implies that the calls for censure are no more that partisan grandstanding.

POINTS TO PONDER

- Read this debate with two contradictory thoughts in mind. One is that citizens in a democracy should be free of unwarranted, covert government intrusion. The other is the argument that preventing terrorism requires procedures that may not fit easily with existing rules under the Fourth Amendment.
- Separate in your mind what you think about the warrantless wire taps as such and whether the president had the legal authority to authorize them. It may be that he did have the legal authority but exercised it unwisely or, the reverse, that he acted understandably, but illegally, to wisely combat terrorism.

Censure President Bush for Abuse of Power: Justified

JOHN W. DEAN

I [will] set forth a brief overview of the testimonial subject where I feel I might be of assistance to the Senate Judiciary Committee's consideration of Senate Resolution 398 relating to the censure of President George W. Bush, for (1) unlawful electronic surveillance of Americans contrary to the provisions of the Foreign Intelligence Surveillance Act of 1978, as amended; (2) the failure of the President to inform the respective congressional committees of his actions as required by that law; and (3) the presidents conspicuously misleading statements to the American people about the nature of his actions along with his dubious legal arguments claimed as justification for his actions.

I assume...that no one disagrees with the Administrations desire to deal aggressively with terrorism. Rather the question is about ways and means not about desired results or hopeful outcomes.

QUALIFICATIONS TO TESTIFY

My qualifications for addressing the committee are more expertise than anyone might wish to have based on personal experience in how presidents can get themselves on the wrong side of the law. Obviously, I refer to my experiences at the Nixon White House during Watergate. That, as it happens, was the last time I testified before the Senate. As with my testimony today, that testimony was voluntarily given. I appear today because I believe, with good reason, that the situation is even more serious. In addition to my first-hand witnessing a president push his powers beyond the limits of the Constitution during my years as White House counsel from, 1970 to 1973, I have spent the past three plus decades studying presidents past and present.

No presidency that I can find in history has adopted a policy of expanding presidential powers merely for the sake of expanding presidential powers. Presidents in the past who have expanded their powers have done so when pursuing policy objectives. It has been the announced policy of the Bush/Cheney presidency, however, from its outset, to expand presidential power for its own sake, and it continually searched for avenues to do just that, while constantly testing to see how far it can push the limits. I must add that never before have I felt the slightest reason to fear our government. Nor do I frighten easily. But I do fear the Bush/Cheney government (and the precedents they are creating) because this administration is caught up in the rectitude of its own self-righteousness, and for all practical purposes this presidency has remained largely unchecked by its constitutional coequals.

MUST CENSURE BE A PURELY POLITICAL CONDEMNATION?

Members of this committee are quite familiar with the debate that arose during the Clinton impeachment proceedings regarding the propriety of censuring a president. That thirteen month debate involved members of the House and Senate, as well as political commentators and constitutional scholars. Some members thought it a viable alternative to impeachment or conviction of a president; other members believed it a threat to the separation of powers. For example, Senator John D. Rockefeller [Democrat] of West Virginia thought it an effective way "to say to myself and my people" that President Clinton had done something wrong. Senator [Republican] Larry Craig of Idaho viewed it as "a raw political cover" and "nothing more than a slap on the wrist." [Republican] Senator Phil Gramm of Texas thought it was too easy a way out of a difficult political decision that could "corrode" the constitutional structure of the separation of powers. Legal scholars fell on both sides of the question of whether it was a constitutionally permissible action, although the weight of the arguments clearly fell on the side of its constitutionality.

Michael Gerhardt [Professor of Law and Director of the Center on Legislative Studies, University of North Carolina Law School], whose work is very familiar to this committee, observed that there are several provisions in the Constitution authorizing both the House and the Senate to including the mention the First Amendment. As Gerhardt summed it up:

> One may plainly infer from these various textual provisions the authority of the House, the Senate, or both to pass a non-binding resolution expressing an opinion—pro or con—on some public matter, such as that a president's conduct has been reprehensible or worthy of condemnation.

One thing was clear from this protracted debate during the Clinton impeachment, and the same can be said of the debate so far that has been provoked by Senator [Russell] Feingold's [D-WI] proposed resolution, censure has long been viewed as a purely political action. That has been true historically as well. Historian Richard Shenkman assembled the precedents for censure during the Clinton proceeding, which he recently republished.

Shenkman found, "All four censures [John Adams, Andrew Jackson, John Tyler, and James Buchanan], however, have more in common than that they simply have been largely forgotten. All were the work of highly partisan politicians eager to score political points." He concluded, "censures must be bipartisan to carry weight with the American people. History suggests that a resolution passed along party lines would be a source of palpable political divisiveness."

I am hopeful that Congress for institutional reasons, not partisan gamesmanship, will act on Senator Feingold's resolution. If the term "censure" carries too much historical baggage, then the resolution should be amended, not defeated, because the president needs to be reminded that separation of powers does not mean an isolation of powers; he needs to be told he cannot simply ignore a law with no consequences.

INSTITUTIONAL REASON FOR CENSURE: PREVENTING WAIVER

[U.S. Supreme Court] Justice Felix Frankfuter's concurrence in *Youngstown* [*Sheet & Tube v. Sawyer*, 1952] recognized the power of "executive construction of the Constitution," citing *United States v. Midwest Oil Co.* (1915), as the basis for that authority, but finding it to exist only when there is a showing of "a systematic, unbroken, executive practice, long pursued to the knowledge of the Congress and never before questioned." [The *Midwest* case upheld the president authority to act with discretion under some laws, especially when the president's actions were known to Congress and it did nothing to counter them. The Youngstown case involved the authority of the president to take control of steel mills and striking workers during wartime. The Supreme Court rejected the president's assertion of authority]

Midwest Oil—the leading case on congressional acquiesce—is pretty old and times have changed. Nor is this a very precise body of law. What does it take for Congress to question presidential action? Does it mean a member of Congress, a committee, a single chamber, or both houses? And what if the president deliberately and knowingly ignores Congress, relying on his own construction of the Constitution, when both houses have questioned residential conduct and a law has been signed by a predecessor president? Is it a "political question" that the courts today will not touch? What if Congress does nothing about it? At some point will not a waiver occur when we are talking about constitutional co-equals? These, I suggest, are issues this committee must address. There are two ways to address them: legislation or a resolution expressing the sense of the Congress. Or, of course, doing nothing, and permitting the President to break the laws adopted by Congress.

Bush's on-going action with his NSA [National Security Agency] wiretapping (if not secrecy, torture, etc.) and congressional inaction (or acquiescence) must, sooner or later, intersect, and a point will be reached and crossed when the Congress has all but sanctioned the conduct and the president can violate the law with utter abandonment. No one can say that the Congress has not been put on notice. While there is vague law that says congressional inaction is not a license for executive action, Congress is now confronted with executive branch attorneys who take the most aggressive reading possible in all situations that favor executive power. It is only necessary to look at the Administration's interpretation of the September 18, 2001 Authorization for Use of Military Force which it reads as authorization for the NSA program, to appreciate how far it will push.

And that is what I believe will happen if [Committee] Chairman [Arlen] Specter's [R-PA] proposal to involve the Foreign Intelligence Surveillance Act court should become law. If past is prologue, President Bush will not bother to veto the bill, rather he will quietly issue a signing statement saying as Commander in Chief he disagrees with the bill, and he does not care what the FISA court says, and he will just keep doing what he has been doing. In short, should Congress pass Chairman Specter's bill, the Chairman should recall what happened to Senator John McCain's [R-AZ] torture amendment before he attends the photo op at the White House while Vice President [Richard] Cheney is off somewhere approving the signing statement—and gutting the law. If this committee does not believe this Administration is hell bent on expanding its powers with such in-your-face actions, you have been looking the other way for some five years of this presidency.

That is why censure might be the only way for the Senate to avoid acquiescing in what is clearly a blatant violation of the 1978 FISA stature, not to mention the Fourth Amendment. If "censure" is politically too strong for the Senate, then an appropriately worded Sense of the Senate resolution not acquiescing in the president's defiance of the law might be a fall back position to prevent a waiver, and preserve Congress's prerogatives.

In short, I implore the Senate to undertake not a partisan action, but a strong institutional action. I recall a morning—and it was just about this time in the morning and it was exactly this time of the year—March 21, 1973—that I tried to warn a president of the consequences of staying his course. I failed to convince President Nixon that morning, and the rest, as they say, is history. I certainly do not claim to be prescient. Then or now. But actions have consequences, and to ignore them is merely denial.

Today, it is very obvious that history is repeating itself. It is for that reason I have crossed the country to visit with you, and that I hope that the collective wisdom of this committee will prevail, and you will not place the president above the law by inaction. As I was gathering my thoughts yesterday to respond to the hasty invitation, it occurred to me that had the Senate or House, or both, censured or somehow warned Richard Nixon, the tragedy of Watergate might have been prevented. Hopefully the Senate will not sit by while even more serious abuses unfold before it.

Censure President Bush for Abuse of Power: Politically Motivated

ROBERT F. TURNER

I appear before you today with a great sense of sadness. Indeed, my emotions approach anger as I consider this outrageously partisan effort to divide our country without reason in the midst of not one but two congressionally-authorized wars.

Others have made the point that it is a cherished tradition of the rule of law that fact-finding be completed before the accused is hanged, but I realize that further delay in this case might lead members and the American voters to realize that you are going after the wrong "lawbreaker."

Let me highlight a few of the relevant facts in this matter:

◆ American wartime leaders have been authorizing the warrantless intercept of enemy communications into the United States since General George Washington authorized the surreptitious interception of mail from Great Britain during the American Revolution. Abraham Lincoln authorized the tapping of telegraph lines, Woodrow Wilson authorized monitoring all cable traffic between the United States and Europe, and Franklin D. Roosevelt authorized broad monitoring of international communications long before Congress authorized American participation in World War II.

◆ When FISA [Foreign Intelligence Surveillance Act] was before the Senate in 1978, President Carter's Attorney General, former Court of Appeals Judge Griffin Bell, testified. He noted that FISA did not include any recognition of the President's independent constitutional authority to authorize warrantless wiretaps for foreign intelligence purposes, as the 1968 Crime Control and Safe Streets Act had done. And Attorney General Bell observed that the FISA statute "does not take away the power of the President under the Constitution."

◆ When FISA was enacted, Congress established not only the Foreign Intelligence Surveillance Court, but also a Foreign Intelligence Surveillance Court of Review to hear appeals from the FISA Court. In its only case, decided on November 18, 2002, the unanimous FISA Court of Review observed that every court to have decided the issue has, and I quote, "held that the President did have inherent authority to conduct warrantless searches to obtain foreign intelligence information," and concluded: "We take for granted that the President does have that authority and, assuming that is so, FISA could not encroach on the President's constitutional power."

◆ It is not as if the Founding Fathers ignored the issue of Intelligence. As early as 1776, Benjamin Franklin and his colleagues on the Committee of Secret Correspondence in the Continental Congress unanimously agreed that they could not share sensitive secrets about a French covert operation to assist the American Revolution, because: "we find by fatal experience that Congress consists of too many members to keep secrets."

◆ On March 5, 1788, writing in *Federalist* No. 64, John Jay explained to the American people, while advocating ratification of the Constitution, that Congress could not be trusted to keep secrets. It is worth quoting his words:

There are cases where the most useful intelligence may be obtained, if the persons possessing it can be relieved from apprehensions of discovery. Those apprehensions will operate on those persons whether they are actuated by mercenary or friendly motives, and there doubtless are many of both descriptions, who would rely on the secrecy of the president, but who would not confide in that of the senate, and still less in that of a large popular assembly. The convention have done well therefore in so disposing of the power of making treaties, that although the president must in forming them act by the advice and consent of the senate, yet he will be able to manage the business of intelligence in such manner as prudence may suggest.

And from that time until the Vietnam War, both Congress and the judiciary were very deferential to the Executive when it came to managing "the business of intelligence"—whether in peace or war.

◆ The very first appropriation of Treasury funds for foreign affairs told President Washington to "account specifically" only for those expenditures "as in his judgment may be made public, and also for the amount of such expenditures as he may think it advisable not to specify...." That is to say, understanding that its members could not keep secrets, the Congress deferred to the President on matters of intelligence and foreign affairs. They didn't seek "classified reports" or "secret briefings."

Indeed, this was the consistent practice during the early years of our nation. In a February 19, 1804, letter to Treasury Secretary Albert Gallatin, President Thomas Jefferson explained:

The Constitution has made the Executive the organ for managing our intercourse with foreign nations....The Executive being thus charged with the foreign intercourse, no law has undertaken to prescribe its specific duties....From the origin of the present government to this day....it has been the uniform opinion and practice that the whole foreign fund was placed by the Legislature on the footing of a contingent fund, in which they undertake no specifications, but leave the whole to the discretion of the President.

◆ In 1818, the great Representative Henry Clay observed on the House floor that expenditures from the President's "secret service" account were not "a proper subject of inquiry" by Congress.

◆ And since the ninth Whereas Clause in the pending resolution makes a reference to a requirement in the "National Security Act of 1947" that Congress be kept informed about intelligence activities, I should point out that this reference really ought to say "as amended," because the original 1947 act did not include the slightest suggestion that Congress had any business looking into secret national security activities. And that was not an oversight.

◆ I would also add that I see no serious Fourth Amendment problem in this program (as it was described by the *New York Times* in the December 16 [2005] article that broke the story, and as it has been explained by the Attorney General and by Lt. Gen. Michael Hayden, who served as Director of the National Security Agency when the program began and until last year). Even Kate Martin, head of the Center for National Security Studies, has acknowledged that "surveillance of communications with al Qaeda...is manifestly reasonable"—which would seem to take care of any concern about "unreasonable" searches or seizures. During a Voice of America "Talk to America" show that I did some weeks ago paired against Morton Halperin, Mort challenged my description of the program as involving only communications in which one party was a foreign national outside our borders who was known or believed to be tied to al Qaeda—explaining that could not possibly be accurate, because such communications could obviously be legally intercepted without a warrant. Many bright scholars who have come down on the other side of the issue seem simply to have assumed that this program includes the intentional interception of communications that begin and end in this country, but that is not what the available data suggest. And I would add that, just as if the government has a lawful right to record and use my statements communicated to an American who is the target of an investigation for which a judge has issued a wiretap warrant, there should be no constitutional objection to intercepting communications during wartime involving known or suspected enemy agents outside (or, for that matter, inside) this country—even when Americans take part in the communication.

◆ Further, it is my impression from [various sources] that not a single member of this Committee believes that the United States should terminate the program (as described). That is to say, no serious person seems to be denying that America ought to be listening in when al Qaeda operatives in other countries communicate with people inside this country. (That, after all, is how 9/11 was planned.) The only issue is whether the President must get a warrant before that can be done. And, again, past presidents of both parties, and every court to have considered the issue, have taken the position that the Constitution gives the President the power to authorize warrantless national security foreign intelligence wiretaps....

◆ Finally, I would note that...the constitutional origins of the President's extraordinary authority in this field [national security] is found not merely in the Commander in Chief language of Article II, Section 2; but, more fundamentally, in the first sentence of Article II, Section 1, which vests the nation's "executive Power" in the President....

Chief Justice John Marshall...reaffirmed [that executive power in] perhaps the most famous of all Supreme Court cases, *Marbury v. Madison* (1803). Here is what Chief Justice Marshall wrote:

> By the constitution of the United States, the President is invested with certain important political powers, in the exercise of which he is to use his own discretion, and is accountable only to his country in his political character, and to his own conscience....[A]nd whatever opinion may be entertained of the manner in which executive discretion may be used, still there exists, and can exist, no power to control that discretion. The subjects are political. They respect the nation, not individual rights, and being entrusted to the executive, the decision of the executive is conclusive.

What John Marshall was explaining here is that not all powers vested in the President are "checked" by Congress or the courts. Some very important powers are given exclusively to the discretion of the President, and I submit at the core of those powers is his control over the gathering of foreign intelligence information—all the more so during periods of authorized war. Controlling intelligence collection is every bit as critically important during war as deciding where to deploy an infantry division or naval carrier battle group. (Indeed, these decisions are normally determined on the basis of the best available intelligence.)

Chief Justice Marshall's other key point from *Marbury* is equally important. He declared, and again I quote: "an act of the legislature, repugnant to the constitution, is void." This observation is fundamental to the widespread misunderstanding of the current dispute. It is true that President Bush is not "above the law," but in this country we have a hierarchy of laws in which the Constitution is supreme. And when Congress attempts to seize control of a power vested by the American people in their President through the Constitution, then Congress becomes a "lawbreaker" and the President is right and duty-bound to be guided by the Constitution.

For further evidence that certain presidential powers were not to be "checked" by Congress, we need look only at the most frequently cited of all foreign affairs cases, *Unites States v. Curtiss-Wright Export Corp.* [1936], where the Supreme Court said:

> Not only, as we have shown, is the federal power over external affairs in origin and essential character different from that over internal affairs, but participation in the exercise of the power is significantly limited. In this vast external realm, with its important, complicated, delicate and manifold problems, the President alone has the power to speak or listen as a representative of the nation. He makes treaties with the advice and consent of the Senate; but he alone negotiates. Into the field of negotiation the Senate cannot intrude, and Congress itself is powerless to invade it.

...The basic foreign affairs paradigm is that control over both the making and implementation of American foreign policy and international relations—including the conduct of war and the gathering of intelligence—is vested exclusively in the President except when Congress or the Senate are expressly given "checks" or "negatives" in the Constitution. And the unanimous view of the Framers, as far as my research over several decades has revealed, was that the "exceptions" vested in Congress or the Senate were to be "construed strictly...."

I honestly don't know where the idea for increased congressional involvement in "the business of intelligence" came from about the time of the Vietnam War. Obviously, the 1975 [Senator Frank] Church [D-ID] and [Representative Otis] Pike [D-NY] Committee hearings [to investigate alleged illegal activities by the Central Intelligence Agency] were a key factor, but I have traced it back at least to 1969. A radical leftist named Richard J. Barnet, who was instrumental in the founding of the Institute for Policy Studies (a group that was often involved in illegal contacts with the Castro regime and other Communist governments), proposed in a book entitled The Economy of Death:

> Congressmen should demand far greater access to information than they now have, and should regard it as their responsibility to pass information on to their constituents. Secrecy should be constantly challenged in Congress, for it is used more often to protect reputations than vital interests. There should be a standing Congressional committee to review the classification system and to monitor secret activities of the government such as the CIA. Unlike the present CIA review committee, there should be a rotating membership.

[However, whatever the origins,] what is clear is that the Founding Fathers understood that secrecy was important and that Congress could not keep secrets..., and prior to the Vietnam War it was widely understood by all three branches that the control of foreign intelligence gathering was the exclusive province of the Executive—subject, of course, to the requirements of the Constitution....[For example,] he may not violate the Bill of Rights....

SENATOR FEINGOLD'S RESOLUTION

Let me now make a few observations about Senator Feingold's resolution. The first one has to do with motive. I assure you that I am most reticent to speculate about the motives of strangers and prefer to give them the benefit of the doubt. My special outrage over this resolution comes almost entirely from an Associated Press story authored by Frederic J. Frommer that appeared in several papers on Monday of this week. If that story is factually inaccurate, then my comments about the motivation for this resolution have no greater credibility. I have no other information on the facts and no specific information about the Senator's character. (It is my impression that he is a very bright and well-educated individual.)

The article quotes the Senator as denying any political motivation for introducing his resolution, but then quotes him as declaring that it is also "good politics." According to the AP story, Senator Feingold explained: "'These Democratic pundits are all scared of the Republican base getting energized, but they're willing to pay the price of not energizing the Democratic base,' he said. 'It's an overly defensive and meek approach to politics.'"

I don't think I've ever had a partisan bumper sticker on my car endorsing any specific candidate for federal office. I don't think I'm registered as a member of any political party, and when Senator Chuck Robb [D-VA] was here I repeatedly gave him my vote. But I do have "political" bumper stickers on the back of my 2005 Toyota Prius, and it reads:

> "Politics stops at the water's edge.
> Stand UNITED in wartime."

....To the extent that Senator Feingold, or any other person—Republican or Democrat...views these issues as appropriate opportunities for "politics as usual," I would commend to you the February 10, 1949, remarks of the late Senator Arthur Vandenberg [R-MI], who said during a "Lincoln Day" address:

> It will be a sad hour for the Republic if we ever desert the fundamental concept that politics shall stop at the water's edge. It will be a triumphant day for those who would divide and conquer us if we abandon the quest for a united voice when America demands peace with honor in the world. In my view nothing has happened to absolve either Democrats or Republicans from continuing to put their country first. Those who don't will serve neither their party nor themselves.

Now let me turn specifically to some of Senator Feingold's "Whereas" clauses and make some brief comments:

◆ His first clause states that FISA "provided the executive branch with clear authority to wiretap suspected terrorists inside the United States." No President and no court has ever denied that the President has constitutional authority to engage in foreign intelligence wiretaps even during peacetime, and no Congress ever denied it prior to the Vietnam War. This is akin to arguing that a presidential pardon involved "lawbreaking" by the President because Congress had enacted a gratuitous statute "authorizing" the President to grant pardons, but then providing pardons would only be valid if issued between the hours of noon and 3 PM on Fridays, or only if first approved by the Speaker of the House. Congress can not usurp the independent power vested by the people in the President through the Constitution any more than it can usurp the power of Judicial Review by passing a mere statute....

◆ Whereas Clause Seven declares that "the President's inherent constitutional authority does not give him the power to violate the explicit statutory prohibition on warrantless wiretaps" in the FISA statute. I'm candidly not sure of the logic here—is it that statutes and the Constitution are of equal dignity, and thus the "later in time" controls? Surely, if as John Jay explained, the Constitution left the President free "to manage the business of intelligence as prudence might suggest,"...it follows that a mere statute that attempts to alter this constitutional distribution of power must be "void."

◆ Then we have Clause Nine, which attacks the President for not sharing sensitive national security secrets with the full membership of the intelligence committees. (The [committee's] leaders were informed.) The Founding Fathers would hardly have been shocked at this.

I've already cited Ben Franklin's observation that Congress (referring to a much smaller Continental Congress in 1776) consisted of "too many members to keep secrets." [In earlier] testimony I documented many other examples of the problems caused when Congress tried to manage foreign intercourse and failed to keep secrets. And I've already noted that the original National Security Act of 1949 did not provide for the slightest congressional oversight of intelligence.

◆ Then we come to Clause Ten, which denounces President Bush for having "repeatedly misled the public" about sensitive intelligence collection during wartime. Wow! One only wonders the job the good Senator would have done on President [Franklin] Roosevelt for failing to announce in advance to the world the planned D-Day invasion of June 6, 1944. Indeed, there was an active disinformation campaign involving General George Patton and a phantom army—including inflatable rubber tanks—to deceive the German High Command that the invasion was being planned for Pas de Calais rather than [Normandy]. Well, one might conceivably argue that it was a brilliant ploy that saved tens of thousands of American lives and perhaps even meant the difference between victory and defeat. But, hey—FDR "lied" to the American people, and he didn't brief Congress or the press either! Perhaps the Senate can consider a retroactive resolution to censure such an evil public official? If the good Senator can find a way for the President to inform Congress and the American people without in the process increasing the risk that our enemies will gain valuable intelligence in the process, that would be wonderful. Until then, I think most Americans are willing to forego knowledge of intelligence programs with the understanding that keeping them secret makes them more likely to be effective and may well save countless American lives.

◆ I was struck (but not surprised) by the absence of judicial authority for the legal assumptions underlying this resolution. On the other hand, I was impressed by the creativity reflected in Clause Twelve, where the Senator [Feingold] reasons that "no Federal court has evaluated whether the President has the inherent authority to authorize wiretaps inside the United States without complying with" FISA. He doesn't mention that every federal court that has addressed the issue has recognized inherent presidential authority for foreign intelligence wiretaps, or that the appeals court established by FISA itself declared in 2002 that FISA could not "take away" the President's independent constitutional power in this area. Let's go instead with the theory that, so long as a Federal court has not considered the issue, the President aught to be censured for anything Senators don't like. (Well, that doesn't really help here either, as I gather Senator Feingold does like what is being done—only that the President didn't ask permission to do it (injecting further elements of delay in our efforts to identify terrorist cells whose members are plotting to kill large numbers of Americans).... I strongly suspect it would be difficult to find a Federal court opinion declaring that the President may issue pardons on Friday mornings. But the absence of such an opinion would hardly be meaningful evidence that such behavior would be "illegal" or deserving of a Senate resolution of censure.

With all due respect, I would suggest that the Resolved clause in this resolution be modified as indicated below and then the resolution put on the fast-track for floor consideration by the full Senate:

> Resolved, That the United States Senate does hereby censure the United States Congress of 1978, and does condemn its unlawful usurpation of the constitutional powers granted to the President by the American people through the Constitution to manage the business of intelligence as prudence might suggest.

THE CONTINUING DEBATE
Censure President Bush for Abuse of Power:

What Is New

There have been occasional attempts in the House of the Senate to rebuke the president since John Adams served in the late 1790s. Only one has ever passed. That occurred in 1834 when the Senate censured President Andrew Jackson for allegedly abusing his power. Senator Feingold's charge in 2006 that President Bush had misused his power was less successful, and the resolution never came to a vote. That, however, halted neither debate over Bush's actions nor efforts to support or block the NSA program. Numerous bills were filed in Congress in 2006 to facilitate or end the NSA program, but none had moved to a floor vote as of September 2006.

There were also challenges to the NSA program in the courts. In a case brought by the American Civil Liberties Union, *ACLU v. NSA*, in the U.S. District Court in Detroit, Judge Anna Diggs Taylor ruled the program was unconstitutional. However, the administration quickly filed an appeal with the Court of Appeals' Sixth Circuit, and Judge Diggs agreed to a stay in her ruling (allowing the program to continue) pending appeal.

Where to Find More

The position of the American Civil Liberties Union on the NSA program is available at the ACLU's Website, www.aclu.org/safefree/nsaspying/. Judge Taylor's decision can be found at www.mied.uscourts.gov/eGov/taylorpdf/06%2010204.pdf. The position of the administration on the program is laid out in a January 22, 2006 White House press release at www.whitehouse.gov/news/releases/2006/01/20060122.html. A review of the interaction of Congress and the president on anti-terrorism policy is John E. Owens, "Presidential Power and Congressional Acquiescence in the 'War' on Terrorism: A New Constitutional Equilibrium?" *Politics & Policy* (2006). General background is also available in Seth F. Kreimer, "Watching the Watchers: Surveillance, Transparency, and Political Freedom in the War on Terror," *Journal of Constitutional Law* (2004).

What More to Do

Robert Turner points out correctly that few, even among Democrats, wanted the NSA to stop trying to intercept communications coming into or out of the country related to terrorism. Given the difficulty of obtaining a specific warrant for each possible source/recipient of suspect communications given their number and speed of transmittal, devise a plan that would satisfy both the complaints of civil libertarians and the goal of providing security from terrorism.

DEBATE

13 BUREAUCRACY

THE DEPARTMENT OF EDUCATION AND WOMEN IN SPORTS:

Undermining Progress *or* Regulating Reasonably?

UNDERMINING PROGRESS

ADVOCATE: Nancy Hogshead-Makar, Professor, Florida Coastal School of Law and U.S. Olympic triple goal medalist in swimming (1984)

SOURCE: Testimony during hearings on "The First Tee and Schools: Working to Build Character Education," U.S. House of Representatives, Committee on Education and the Workforce, June 28, 2006

REGULATING REASONABLY

ADVOCATE: Amanda Ross-Edwards, Lecturer, Department of Political Science, North Carolina State University

SOURCE: "Additional Clarification of Intercollegiate Athletics Policy: A Step in the Right Direction," an essay written especially for this volume, October 2006

We tend to think that elected representatives serving in Congress and, to a degree, the elected president, make federal rules. However, in terms of sheer volume, non-elected agency officials make most government rules. Off these functionaries, the president appoints about 600, with career civil servants making up the rest of the 2.8 million civilian federal employees.

One measure of the deluge of bureaucratic rules is the *Federal Register*, the annual compilation of new rules, rule changes, and other authoritative bureaucratic actions. Just for 2003, the *Federal Register* was an immense 75,795 pages of regulations addressing almost every conceivable subject. So great is the impact of the rule-making and implementation authority of the bureaucracy that some analysts refer to it as the fourth branch of government.

Administrators make binding rules in two ways. One is by issuing regulations that, in theory, simply add detail to the general intent of laws passed by Congress. In practice, many analysts say, agency-made rules take laws in a direction that Congress did not anticipate or even want. The second way that bureaucrats make rules is by how they implement the law. As with regulations, implementation is supposed to follow the intent of the law, but whether that is true is sometimes controversial. You will see presently that advocate Amanda Ross-Edwards charges that the Department of Education has both formulated rules and implemented them in a manner that has subverted Congress' original intent when it enacted Title IX of the Education Amendments (Act) in 1972. This legislation declared that no one "shall, on the basis of sex, be...subjected to discrimination under any education program or activity receiving Federal financial assistance." It is language that covers most activities at all levels of education, although here we will focus on athletics in higher education.

The legislation also, as most acts do, authorized and directed agencies "to effectuate the provisions of [this act]...by issuing rules, regulations, or orders of general applicability which shall be consistent with achievement of the objectives of the statute."

What is not in dispute here is the value of the basic law. It has ended overt discrimination against women in athletics and substantially reduced covert barriers, thus dramatically increasing the number of women participating in sports at every educational level. What is at issue here is how the Office of Civil Rights of the U.S. Department of Education judges compliance with Title IX. In 1979, the department established a three-prong test for colleges to do so. The three prongs are: (1) whether opportunities for participation by male and female students at a school are "substantially proportionate" to proportion of men and women who are full-time undergraduates at the school, (2) whether the school has a "history and continuing practice of program expansion" for the underrepresented sex, or (3) whether the institution is "fully and effectively" accommodating the interests and abilities of the underrepresented sex.

In 2002, the secretary of education created a commission to examine the implementation of Title IX. It made several recommendations, two of which drew furious dissent from various sources. One, which is at the heart of the debate here, was that the Department of Education establish "additional ways of demonstrating equity" by colleges. Critics fretted this might give rise to measurements that would diminish enforcement. The secretary announced that he would not act on the controversial recommendation, but in 2005 the department reversed itself and issued a new method for measuring compliance. It would permit a school to evaluate Prong Three by using an e-mail survey to measure the interest of undergraduate women in athletic participation. By implication, the fewer women who are interested, the fewer opportunities have to be afforded to them. In the following readings, the advocates differ on whether this action by the bureaucracy is an effort to undermine Title IX or is a reasonable adjustment to gauging compliance.

POINTS TO PONDER

- ➢ Amanda Ross-Edwards argues that Title IX has, in effect, reduced athletic opportunities for men. If true, is that relevant to evaluating Title IX?
- ➢ Currently only 45.5% of college students are men. Should this mean that 54.5% of all college athletic scholarships should go to women?
- ➢ Would it be advisable for colleges to rebalance their student bodies by undertaking an affirmative action program designed to ensure that more males are admitted and stay in school?

The Department of Education and Women in Sports: Undermining Progress

NANCY HOGSHEAD-MAKAR

The subject we are discussing today is important.... The subject we are discussing is also heavily researched. While we in athletics have long espoused the transformative nature of a sports experience, there is substantial empirical evidence to support that what we've known intuitively: Athletics are a vital part of education. Sports participation teaches young people critical lessons, including how to set goals and work to achieve them, how to win and lose gracefully, how to postpone short term gratification for long term rewards, how to perform under pressure, how to function as part of a team, and how to take criticism. Student-athletes develop self-confidence, perseverance and a desire to succeed.

Representing my country for eight years on the United States National Team was a tremendous source of pride. But the most valuable prizes from all those years are not my Olympic gold medals. Standing on the victory stand was an exceedingly proud moment, but the real value to me was in those life lessons. Success is a learned skill. World-class training in my sport at that time involved swimming an incredible 800 laps per day, plus lifting weights and running, 6 days a week. From seventh grade until I graduated from high school, I woke up at 4:45 to get ready for a 5:30–7:30am practice. I learned a lot by getting into that cold pool on days when every cell in my body wanted to be elsewhere. I did it because I was more committed to doing something significant with my life than I was to being in a good mood on any one particular day. Seeing what I could achieve became my own noble purpose. The lessons I took with me 22 years ago are the same ones available to every kid participating in athletics today.

WOMEN'S HEALTH AND ATHLETICS

I have provided to you copies of the Women's Sports Foundation's publication, "Her Life Depends on It," a compilation of the best research on the impact of sports participation on young children, but particularly young girls. The results of this large body of research show that sports participation and physical activity are fundamental solutions for many of the serious health and social problems faced by American girls.

For example, research confirms that participation in athletics is associated with academic success. Contrary to the "dumb jock" myth, interscholastic sports participation provides both boys and girls from diverse socioeconomic, race and ethnicity backgrounds measurable positive educational impacts, including improvements in self-concept, higher educational aspirations, improved school attendance, increased math and science enrollment, more time spent on homework, and higher enrollment in honors courses.

The educational benefits girls, in particular, derive from sports participation are stunning. For example, female student-athletes have higher grades and higher graduation rates than their non-athletic peers. NCAA graduation rates for women remain high—68% compared to 58% for the Division I female student body. In high school, both white and black female student-athletes graduated at rates higher than their student-body counterparts. A state-wide, three-year study by the North Carolina High School Athletic Association found that athletes had higher grade point averages (by almost a full grade point), lower dropout rates, and higher high school graduation rates, than their non-athletic peers.

These educational benefits appear to translate into business success. A recent study by the Oppenheimer Fund found that more than four out of five executive businesswomen (81%) played sports growing up—and the vast majority reported that the lessons they learned on the playing field have contributed to their success in business. A common gateway into a career in the sports industry is having significant sports experience on one's resume.

The life-long health benefits of an adolescent sports experience are as dramatic as the academic benefits. The risks for girls and women appear daunting.

- Obesity: In 1970, only one out of every 21 girls was obese or overweight; today that figure is one in six.
- Heart Disease: Cardiovascular disease is the number-one cause of death among American women (44.6% of all deaths), and the death rate is 69% higher for black women than for white women.
- Cancer: Breast cancer is the most common cancer among women, accounting for nearly one of every three cancers diagnosed in American women.
- Osteoporosis: Of the 10 million Americans estimated to have osteoporosis, eight million are women.
- Tobacco Use: In grades 9–12, 29.5% of female students report current tobacco use
- Drug Use: Thirty-eight percent of 12th-grade girls and 18% of eighth-grade girls have used an illicit drug at least once during the past year.
- Sexual Risk: About 1/4 of sexually active adolescents are infected with a sexually transmitted disease each year.
- Teen Pregnancy: The United States has the highest teen pregnancy and birth rates in the industrialized world. About 80% of teen pregnancies are unintended.
- Depression: By age 15, girls are twice as likely as boys to have experienced a major depressive episode. This gender gap continues for the next 35 to 40 years, until menopause.
- Suicide: In 2001, about one in four U.S. high school girls seriously considered suicide, and one in 10 actually attempted to kill herself.
- Pathogenic Weight Loss Behavior: Over 90% of victims of eating disorders are female, and 86% report onset by age 20.

These issues account for much of the more than $1 trillion spent on healthcare for treating these issues. The available research demonstrates that more physical activity and sports participation are fundamental solutions for many of these serious health and social problems faced by our nation's young girls. For example, women who participated in regular physical exercise during their reproductive years have up to a 60% reduced risk of breast cancer. Physical activity and sports participation in the school-age years have been shown to increase bone density to prevent osteoporosis. Higher levels of physical activity earlier in life may reduce the risk for Alzheimer's later in life. These results suggest that implementation of regular physical exercise programs as a critical component of a healthy lifestyle should be a high priority for adolescent and adult women.

Female athletes are also less likely to engage in risky behaviors. Female athletes are less likely to become pregnant as teenagers than their non-athlete counterparts. They are also less likely to smoke or use illicit drugs.

Additionally, athletic participation is also associated with heightened mental health benefits. Female high school athletes show a markedly lower incidence of considering or planning a suicide attempt, and women and girls who participate in regular exercise suffer lower rates of depression. Indeed, this research suggests that the failure to provide girls with athletic and fitness opportunities endangers the public health.

THE CONTRIBUTIONS OF AND DANGER TO TITLE IX

One law this legislative body passed more than 34 years ago last week—Title IX—is responsible for impressive gains in opportunities for girls and women in athletics. Gender equity in athletic departments is fueled by the longing for access to these life-long skills and benefits that sports participants reap, the same ones lauded here today. Before Title IX was enacted, fewer than 32,000 young women took part in collegiate sports. Now more than 150,000 take part. In high school, the number has gone from 300,000 girls to over 2.8 million. This law has proven to provide girls and women with sporting opportunities.

But even after 34 years, the playing field is still far from level. Women's athletic programs continue to lag behind men's athletic programs in every measurable criterion, including participation opportunities, athletic scholarships, operating budgets and recruiting expenditures. Much remains to be done. For example, although on average women are 54% of the students in colleges, they receive only 43% of the sports participation opportunities, 38% of athletic operating dollars and 33% of the money spent on recruitment. At the high school level, girls represent only 42% of varsity athletes.

Moreover, the gains that women have achieved through Title IX are in jeopardy. On March 17, 2005, the Department of Education announced its "Additional Clarification" of its policy for collegiate compliance with Title IX in athletic programs. It issued the "Clarification" without any public input or comment, merely posting it on its website on a Friday afternoon. The "clarification" is a terrible step backward that undermines the values of the mission of sports opportunities for both genders. In this regard, I am joined by more than 100 organizations who have called for the Department's "Clarification" to be rescinded. These organizations include the NCAA, the National Coalition for Women and Girls in Education, and many college presidents. Of all the things this Committee could do to promote today's agenda—to build character, leadership skills and health through athletics participation—none is more critical than to demand that the Department of Education rescind its recent "Additional Clarification", which undermines the provision of full and fair opportunities in athletics. Because the "Clarification" directly conflicts with the goals that this Committee is supporting today, I respectfully urge further action in this regard.

Over the 34-year life of Title IX, it has enjoyed tremendous bi-partisan support. The framers of the legislation (and later the guidelines governing athletics) understood that requiring equality in educational opportunities in sports programs could not happen overnight, and that is the reason why the current guidelines and the three-part participation test are crafted the way they are. The guidelines and the test are flexible and fair. But Title IX has also been under constant attack and scrutiny since it was enacted, and today is unfortunately no different. Despite the fact that sports for girls and women have proven to be so beneficial—and despite the fact that the evidence shows that girls' gains have not come at boys' expense—there is still a deeply destructive backlash against the promise of equality made in the law more than three decades ago.

In June 2002, a 15-member commission was appointed by Secretary of Education Roderick Paige to review opportunities in athletics. The Department spent a year and about $700,000 of taxpayers' money to come up with 23 recommendations. Although a USA Today/CNN/Gallup poll conducted during the Commission's tenure indicated that seven of ten adults who are familiar with Title IX think the federal law should be strengthened or left alone, many of the Commission's ultimate recommendations would have seriously weakened Title IX's protections and substantially reduced the opportunities to which women and girls are entitled under current law.

For this reason, and because the Commission's report failed to address key issues regarding the discrimination women and girls still face in obtaining equal opportunities in athletics, Co-Commissioners Julie Foudy and Donna DeVarona released a Minority Report because their positions were not included in the final report. The Minority Report pointed out that Title IX athletics policies have been critical in the effort to expand opportunities for women and girls, have been in place through Republican and Democratic Administrations, and have been upheld unanimously by the federal appellate courts. In addition, advances for women and girls have not resulted in an overall decrease in opportunities for men; in the cases where men's teams have been cut, moreover, budgetary decisions and the athletics "arms race" are the true culprits. Even Myles Brand, President of the NCAA, has testified that revenue-producing sports in big-time colleges are to blame for current budget problems in colleges. Based on these findings, the Minority Report recommended that the current Title IX athletics policies not be changed but enforced to eliminate the continuing discrimination against women and girls in athletics. It also recommended that schools and the public be educated about the flexible nature of the law, reminded that cutting men's teams to achieve compliance is not necessary or favored, and encouraged schools to rein in escalating athletics costs to give more female and male athletes chances to play.

Instead of implementing any of the 23 recommendations, the outcome of this lengthy and costly Opportunity in Athletics debate was that the Department of Education laudably rejected the Commission's proposals and strongly reaffirmed the longstanding Title IX athletics policies. In its July 11, 2003 "Further Clarification of Intercollegiate Athletics Policy Guidance Regarding Title IX Compliance," the Department of Education stated: "After eight months of discussion and an extensive and inclusive fact-finding process, the Commission found very broad support throughout the country for the goals and spirit of Title IX. With that in mind, OCR [the Department of Education's Office of Civil Rights] today issues this Further Clarification in order to strengthen Title IX's promise of non-discrimination in the athletic programs of our nation's schools." The document goes on to say that Title IX's three-part participation test provides schools with three separate ways to comply and that nothing in that test requires or encourages schools to cut men's teams; it also promised that OCR would aggressively enforce the longstanding Title IX standards, including implementing sanctions for institutions that do not comply.

However, less than two years after strongly reaffirming the longstanding Title IX athletics policies, and without any notice or public input, the Department of Education did an about-face and posted on its website, late in the afternoon of Friday, March 17, 2005, a new Title IX policy that threatens to reverse the enormous progress women and girls have made in sports since the enactment of Title IX. This new policy, called an "Additional Clarification," creates a major loophole through which schools can evade their obligation to provide equal sports opportunities to women and girls. The Clarification allows schools to gauge female students' interest in athletics by doing nothing more than conducting an e-mail survey and to claim—in these days of excessive e-mail spam—that a failure to respond to the survey shows a lack of interest in playing sports. It eliminates schools' obligation to look broadly and proactively at whether they are satisfying women's interests in sports, and will thereby perpetuate the cycle of discrimination to which women have been subjected. The new Clarification violates basic principles of equality, as I explain further below.

It is deeply troubling that the Department would change its 2003 stated position, in which it reaffirmed the longstanding Title IX policies and pledged to enforce them. Instead, the Department of Education has unilaterally adopted this dangerous new policy without public announcement or opportunity for public comment. To fully understand why this new Clarification is so dangerous, it is important to review the relevant longstanding Title IX athletics policies. Title IX requires schools to provide males and females with equal sports participation opportunities. A 1979 Policy Interpretation elaborates on this requirement by providing three independent ways that schools can meet it—by showing that:

- The percentages of male and female athletes are about the same as the percentages of male and female students enrolled in the school (the "proportionality" prong); or
- The school has a history and continuing practice of expanding opportunities for the underrepresented sex—usually women; or
- The school is fully and effectively meeting the athletic interests and abilities of the underrepresented sex.

The Department's new Clarification allows schools not meeting the first or second prongs—that is, schools that are not providing equal opportunities to their female students and that have not consistently improved opportunities for them—to show that they are nonetheless in compliance with Title IX by doing nothing more than sending a "model" e-mail survey to their female students asking about their interest in additional sports opportunities.

This new policy would dramatically weaken existing law and policy. First, it allows schools to use surveys alone to demonstrate compliance with the law. Under prior Department policies, schools had to consider many other factors besides surveys to show compliance with Prong Three, including: requests by students to add a particular sport; participation rates in club or intramural sports; participation rates in sports in high schools, amateur athletic associations, and community sports leagues in areas from which the school draws its students; and interviews with students, coaches, and administrators. The new Clarification eliminates the obligation to consider these important criteria.

Second, surveys are likely to measure only the current discrimination that has limited, and continues to limit, sports opportunities for women and girls. If surveys had been permissible when I graduated from college, in the late 1980s, "interest and ability" would have been capped the then-current rate of 25%, rather than the 41% collegiate women enjoy today. If a girl has never been given the opportunity to participate, she is unlikely to respond favorably to a survey. To quote the movie Field of Dreams, "If you build it, they will come." I know of no instance in which a high school or college started a varsity women's team, hired a coach and then had the coach return his or her paycheck because he or she could not find enough women to play. Courts, too, have recognized that interest cannot be measured apart from opportunity. The new Clarification is particularly damaging for students in high school, where female students are likely to have had even fewer sports opportunities to gain experience prior to being surveyed. Instead, like exposure to new academic topics, all students should be encouraged to try many different sports to take advantage of the many health, economic, academic and leadership opportunities that we are addressing today, and not have their opportunities limited by what they might have already experienced.

Third, by allowing schools to restrict surveys to enrolled and admitted students, the Clarification lets schools off the hook from having to measure interest broadly. The Clarification ignores the reality that most student athletes are recruited—or, at the very least, that students self-select based on what a school is offering. If Duke University had not had a swimming program, I would not have applied to attend. At the college level, athletes are only rarely recruited from the existing student body, but rather are recruited from the region or country at large. It is no accident that Duke has seven-foot tall basketball players walking the halls. It spends enormous resources to make sure that it attracts the top talent from all over the country. At the high school level, the coach finds students with and without experience or skill who are big enough or fast enough and urges them to come out for the team. Now, a college that goes out and recruits male athletes from all over the country can eliminate the obligation to do the same for female athletes if female students fail to receive or respond to an e-mail survey. Now, a high school is not obligated to encourage female athletes to come out for teams in the same way it encourages male athletes to come out for teams, so long as it administers an e-mail survey and does not generate sufficient response from the girls.

Fourth, the Clarification authorizes flawed survey methodology. As one example, schools may e-mail the survey to all female students and interpret a lack of response as evidence of lack of interest. The Clarification reads, "Although rates of nonresponse may be high with the e-mail procedure, under these conditions, OCR will interpret such nonresponse as a lack of interest." Experts in survey methodology confirm that inferring nonresponses as "no interest" turns survey empiricism on its ear. A general rule of thumb is that only a small percentage of persons who receive a survey respond to it. The results of the respondents are then generalized to the population of interest. If half of the respondents indicated they were interested in sports, then the school should assume that half of the female students are interested. For bias demonstrative purposes, reverse the OCR approach. A school would send out an e-mail survey and ask students if they have NO interest in a given sport. Nonresponses would then be interpreted as affirmative interest. Additionally, many high school and college athletes lack access to e-mail. The Clarification will allow schools to avoid adding new opportunities for women even where interest does in fact exist on campus.

Fifth, the new Clarification shifts the burden to female students to show that they are entitled to equal opportunity. The survey creates a presumption of compliance with Title IX, as long as the school has not recently dropped a women's team or had a recent request for elevation of women's club sport to varsity status. Once the survey is administered, the burden of demonstrating compliance shifts from the college or school to the athlete, a difficult legal hurdle for an athlete to surmount. It will be the rare student who will attend a school and then be prepared to surmount such a legal high hurdle.

Finally, the Department's new policy does not even require that the Office for Civil Rights monitor schools' use of the survey to ensure that they meet minimal requirements for survey use or interpret the results accurately.

In summary, the Clarification and "model survey" contravene the basic principles of Title IX and its long-standing jurisprudence. Every legal authority—including the department's own prior policies and interpretations—agrees that surveys of existing students are an inaccurate, biased, and invalid method of determining compliance under Title IX's third prong. Surveys ignore the effect of recruiting and the self-selection of athletes with existing desired sports programs. Yet the Department's letter and "model survey" contravene the law's very purpose by further disadvantaging women via a biased and rejected methodology.

Since then, a wide array of organizations, including athletic, civil rights, and academic organizations have continued to object to the Clarification on a number of grounds. Opposing organizations include the NCAA, the Women's Sports Foundation, the National Women's Law Center, the Leadership Conference on Civil Rights, the National Education Association, and the YMCA, to name a few.

In response to a Senate Appropriations Committee request, the Department prepared a report in March of 2006 that was to respond to the substantial negative public response to the Clarification. Unfortunately, the Department of Education's report does not change even the most glaring problems with the Clarification, such as allowing e-mail survey non-responses to be interpreted as lack of interest. The report only re-confirms that its controversial Clarification is a seismic change in course and that schools can shun their fundamental responsibility of offering equal athletic opportunities for women, in a manner never before permitted.

For example, the Department's new report concludes that for the 14 year study period, the Department's Office for Civil Rights (OCR) has never allowed a school or university to rely upon a survey alone to deny women additional sports opportunities. Moreover, the report found that most schools considered many factors other than surveys in determining the extent of women's interest in sports, such as participation in high school and community sports, coaches' opinions and participation in club or intramural sports. The report documents 54 cases where schools attempted to justify low numbers of athletic opportunities for women under Prong 3, which is an assertion that the school is providing all the interested women with opportunities to participate in athletics. These schools relied on surveys and other indicators, and when the previously-required factors were considered, the schools were ultimately required to add a total of 70 new women's athletic teams. Additionally, in each of the six cases where schools attempted to use interest surveys alone to assert compliance under Prong 3, the OCR rejected each claim of compliance. Again, when the OCR evaluated the previously-required additional factors, they found that women were interested in more participation opportunities at these schools.

In short, the new report supports the obvious conclusion that interest surveys alone are woefully inadequate at showing the extent of interest that truly exists on a campus. The report highlights the low response rates of surveys, and that the OCR's active intervention is necessary to ensure full Title IX compliance. The Clarification, of course, imposes no such requirement.

In summary, the overwhelming evidence—including the Department's own new report on the Clarification—demonstrates the Clarification's serious methodological flaws, which have been exposed by commentators, interest groups, and prior judicial decisions. As Neena Chaudhry, senior counsel at the National Women's Law Center said in response to the report, "The report confirms that the Department set too low a bar for Title IX compliance—and that that standard is unprecedented in OCR's enforcement efforts. The Department of Education should rescind the policy and instead focus on enforcing the law so that women can finally enjoy equal athletic opportunities at our nation's schools and colleges and universities."

For all these reasons, the Department's new Clarification represents a giant step backwards and thwarts the progress that women and girls have made in the past 34 years. If left in place and used by schools, the new Clarification will lead to a reduction in opportunities for our nation's daughters. We call on this Congress to do everything within its power to ensure that this does not happen. The most effective action this Committee can take to promote today's agenda—to build character, leadership skills and health through athletics participation—none would be more effective than to demand that the Department of Education rescind its recent "Additional Clarification."

Additional Clarification of Intercollegiate Athletics Policy: A Step in the Right Direction

AMANDA ROSS-EDWARDS

Nancy Hogshead-Makar's testimony highlights the potential problems with the most recent clarification of Title IX policy. In particular, she expresses concern that, as a basis for determining Title IX compliance, on-line interest surveys include many potential problems. This essay refutes several of her points and presents evidence that the most recent clarification by U.S. Department of Education's Office of Civil Rights (OCR) sufficiently addresses the potential problems associated with online surveys. The OCR used logical analysis in arriving at the most recent interpretation, and most importantly, the recent clarification is a positive step towards correcting the significant problems that resulted from the earlier 1996 clarification.

1. Hogshead-Makar provides a great deal of evidence about the benefits that Title IX has afforded women in sport. No one is arguing that Title IX has not been good for women in sport and no one is arguing for an end to Title IX. The issue of contention lies with Title IX's implementation since OCR issued its clarification in 1996. There is a great deal of documented evidence that Title IX as it has been implemented since 1996 has become reliant on quotas, which have subsequently hurt men's non-revenue producing sports.

There are ultimately 3 prongs that schools can use to comply with Title IX, but the 1996 clarification effectively established Prong One as a safe harbor. Prong One requires that the provision of athletic opportunities be substantially proportionate to the composition of the student body. For a school to be in compliance, therefore, the ratio of men to women participating in sports at a school should be proportionately the same as the ratio of men to women attending the school overall. Until the most recent clarification, only Prong One was objectively measurable means of complying with Title IX and therefore the only true "safe harbor." Historically, schools have chosen to comply with Prong One because it has been the clearest and safest way to comply with Title IX and thus avoid potentially expensive and time-consuming legal issues.

As a result, schools have chosen to use quotas to comply with Title IX. Unfortunately for men's sports, schools have created new women's sports and cut men's sports as a means of creating the proper ratios. As evidence, The College Sports Council lists these facts on its website (www.savingsports.org/about/facts.cfm):

- In 1979, there were 107 men's gymnastic teams at NCAA schools; there are now 20 men's college teams.
- In 1985 there were 253 male athletes per NCAA campus. In 2001 there were 199 male athletes per NCAA campus.
- Participants in collegiate intramural sports, which are totally interest-driven, are about 78% male.
- There are nearly 1000 more women's teams than men's teams in the NCAA. This is after a decade of proportionality has caused the loss of thousands of male athletes through forced squad size reductions and the dropping almost 400 men's teams.
- With males projected to be only 41% of college students by 2009 it is clear

that proportionality will mean that men will only have half as many NCAA teams as women—and that this will entail the elimination of anywhere from a third to a half of NCAA male athletes

Schools faced with the limits of a budget and the need to comply with Title IX legislation have chosen to eliminate men's sports as the preferred method to come into compliance. OCR's most recent clarification, however, provides schools with a clearly defined model for coming in to compliance under Prong Three, thereby, establishing Prong Three as an alternative "safe harbor". The incentive to favor Prong One is thus eliminated and schools are provided with an alternative to cutting men's sports.

2. Hogshead-Makar is incorrect in stating that the Bush administration put forth this clarification with no warning and without considering public input. This is not true. In 2003, OCR provided "Further Clarification of Intercollegiate Athletics Policy Guidance Regarding Title IX Compliance" in response to the report from the Secretary's Commission on Equal Opportunity in Athletics. In his introductory statement, Gerald Reynolds, the Assistant Secretary for Civil Rights, clearly indicated that additional guidance would be forthcoming. He stated that "In order to ensure that schools have a clear understanding of their options for compliance with Title IX, OCR will undertake an education campaign to help educational institutions appreciate the flexibility of the law, to explain that each prong of the test is a viable and separate means of compliance, to give practical examples of the ways in which schools can comply, and to provide schools with technical assistance as they try to comply with Title IX."

Furthermore, in the introduction to the Additional Clarification issued in 2005, James F. Manning, a representative of the OCR, reiterates that OCR is offering the clarification in response to an earlier commitment to provide clearer guidelines for compliance using prongs 2 and 3. He states, "OCR has pledged to provide further guidance on recipients' obligations under the three part test, which was described only in very general terms in the Policy interpretation...OCR believes that institutions may benefit from further specific guidance on part 3".

In "Open to All—Title IX at Thirty", the Secretary of Education's Commission on Opportunity in Athletics, in 2003, reported that it:

> "heard numerous complaints about the three-part test. Many have argued to the Commission that because the guidance concerning the second and third parts of the test is so ambiguous, the proportionality part is the only meaningful test....The Commission also concluded that the test for compliance can be revitalized if the Secretary of Education will provide new guidance, while also significantly increasing efforts to reach out with educational materials."

Many groups and individuals complained that there was a lack of guidance for schools to comply with Prong Three and the Commission had suggested that new guidelines be established and supported with educational materials. Under Prong Three, a school is in compliance with Title IX if, despite the underrepresentation of one sex in the intercollegiate athletics program, the institution is fully and effectively accommodating the athletic interests and abilities of its students who are underrepresented in its current varsity athletic program offerings. Clear guidelines were not firmly established about how schools could prove that the interests and abilities of the underrepresented population were being met. Contrary to Hogshead-Makar's argument, it is not at all surprising that three years after the Commission's report, the OCR provided the clarification that it promised in 2003.

3. Hogshead-Maker also expresses legitimate concern that non-responses to an email the survey would be interpreted by schools and accepted by the OCR as an indication of lack of interest. Although this is true to a certain extent, further examination of the guidelines indicates that the OCR provides guidelines for maximizing the number of response rates and includes measures that would prevent schools from relying solely on non-response to email surveys as an indication of non-interest.

As part of its clarification, the OCR prescribes the use of a census survey rather than a sample survey. A census survey would thus reach all students at an institution and thus avoid the potential problems associated with polling a representative sample of the population. Furthermore, the OCR suggests two specific methods for producing high response rates. The first method involves administering the interest survey as a required part of the school's registration process; thereby eliminating the non-response fact. The second method involves sending an email to the entire student population which includes a link to the survey. If a school chooses this method, there is legitimate concern that there would be a high non-response rate. OCR, however, clarifies that non-response will indicate non-interest only if "all students have been given an easy opportunity to respond to the census, the purpose of the census has been made clear, and that students have been informed that the school will take non-response as an indication of lack of interest." Furthermore, if a school chooses to use an email as the method of delivering the survey then OCR requires that "the school has accurate email addresses, the students have access to email, and the school take reasonable steps to follow-up with students who do not respond."

Although Hogshead-Makar brings up a legitimate concern, the OCR has taken sufficient steps to address the concern. If a school uses a voluntary email survey to poll student athletic interest and the response rates are low; then the school would be required to follow up with those students who did not respond. It is the school's responsibility to prove compliance; therefore, schools have an interest in finding the most efficient way to come into compliance. This is what led schools to choose proportionality; they wanted to avoid costly legal trouble and extended battles with OCR to prove compliance with guidelines that were unclear. Following this logic, schools should choose the option that includes a mandatory survey. Schools will want to avoid getting tangled up trying to prove that they have followed up with the high number of non-response rates that will result from voluntary email surveys.

4. Hogshead-Makar also argues that the use of surveys is unacceptable because it potentially limits the opportunity provided to women to current levels of discrimination. The survey method of compliance, however, does apply to high schools and it is required that it be repeated periodically. Hogsmead-makar states, "The new Clarification is particularly damaging for students in high school, where female students are likely to have had even fewer sports opportunities to gain experience prior to being surveyed. Instead, like exposure to new academic topics, all students should be encouraged to try many different sports to take advantage of the many health, economic, academic and leadership opportunities that we are addressing today, and not have their opportunities limited by what they might have already experienced."

Hogshead-Makar's seems to argue that it is the school or state's responsibility to create opportunity. The law is clear, however, that it is meant to provide equal opportunity, not create opportunity. Following Hogshead-Makar's logic, should schools be required to have ballet classes and field hockey teams for boys and men because they may have not had exposure to these opportunities prior to being surveyed?

5. Title IX has not been implemented correctly since the 1996 clarification and the establishment of Prong One as a safe harbor. For example, under the new implementation standard, schools may use the Model Survey to comply under Prong Three. This is an alternative objective measure to the proportionality rule for complying with Title IX. Schools should thus no longer be compelled to cut men's sports as a means of complying with Prong One; now they can use objective measure to comply under Prong Three.

Scholars also suggest that even those schools that comply under Prong One may benefit from using the model survey to comply under Prong Three. Writing in the Winter 2005 edition of *Vanderbilt Journal of Entertainment and Technology Law*, John J. Almond and Daniel A. Cohen state:

> "Even if a school's athletic program satisfies the proportionality test of Prong One, there are reasons to consider using the Model Survey. The demographics of college student populations continue to change, with women approaching sixty percent majority on campuses. As a result, schools that are proportional today might find themselves falling out of Prong One compliance in the near future. Schools that employ the Model Survey and can demonstrate compliance by way of Prong Three in addition to Prong One gain the additional assurance that changing demographics will not cause them to fall out of compliance. These schools would also gain flexibility to avoid the need to implement "roster caps" or to impose other limitations on men's athletic programs."

The Additional Clarification thus allows schools more flexibility in coming into compliance with Title IX; more flexibility should mean schools feel less compelled to cut sports to comply with Title IX under the proportionality rule.

In conclusion, there may in fact be problems with the Additional Clarification put forth by the OCR in 2005; however, it is still a step in the right direction. Policy formulation is an ongoing dialogue among all three branches of government. The most recent clarification is just another piece of the "conversation" that speaks in particular to the lack of guidance provided to schools who wish to comply using Prong Three. The proposed Model Survey is OCR's attempt to provide an objective measurement for compliance under Prong Three thereby allowing schools to use Prong Three, as well as Prong One, as a "safe-harbor". There may be problems with the current clarification; maybe the administration's precautionary measures will not be enough to prevent the use and abuse of online surveys. The most recent clarification is, however, a positive measure as it attempts to respond to the many complaints that have arisen under the 1996 clarification.

THE CONTINUING DEBATE: The Department of Education and Women in Sports

What Is New

The furious opposition to the new measurement approach authorized by the Department of Education brought widespread pressure on it. However, as of October 2006, the department was standing its ground, and the revised measurement approach remained in place. Only time will tell how many schools use a survey of their women's interest in athletics to try to change the proportion of opportunities available respectively to men and women, how the department's Office of Civil Rights will evaluate the approach, and, perhaps, whether it will be subject to court challenge. In the meanwhile, the issue demonstrates that the impact of laws are based not just one what they stipulate, but also partly on how they are interpreted and implemented by agencies.

Where to Find More

An overview of the controversy is Welch Suggs *A Place on the Team: The Triumph and Tragedy of Title IX* (Princeton University Press, 2005). The revised regulations which are the focus of this debate can be found by going to the Web page of the Office of Civil Rights, U.S. Department of Education at www.ed.gov/about/offices/list/ocr/index.html, and under "Reports and Resources," looking for "Additional Clarification of Intercollegiate Athletics Policy: Three-Part Test—Part Three" (March 17, 2005). A review of Title IX law is in a Congressional Research Service report, "Title IX, Sex Discrimination, and Intercollegiate Athletics: A Legal Overview" (April 28, 2005) at wwwc.house.gov/case/crs_reports/TitleIX.pdf. For a group that criticizes Title IX, go to the Web site of the Independent Women's Forum at www.iwf.org, where the "issues" hyperline will take you to Title IX under "education." A pro-Title IX stance is taken by the National Women's Law Center. On its Web site (www.nwlc.org/), look for "athletics" under issues.

What More to Do

One thing to do is to contact the office of your school's athletic department to get data for your college and to see how it measures compliance. In particular, check whether it will survey women's interest in being on a sports team. There are no Web site to join an anti-Title IX group, but to support it, and easy first step is to sign the electronic petition to reverse the evaluation change. Go to the Save Title IX page at www.titleix.info/petition.jsp?petition_KEY=301&t=save_title_IX.dwt. Also, you can help the Department of Education come up with Title IX enforcement standards and measurements. on which everyone can agree. Draft a department regulation detailing how compliance will be measured.

DEBATE 14

JUDICIARY

FILIBUSTERING FEDERAL COURT NOMINEES:
Frustrating the Majority *or* Protecting the Minority?

FRUSTRATING THE MAJORITY

ADVOCATE: Orrin G. Hatch, U.S. Senator (R-UT)

SOURCE: *Congressional Record*, May 10, 2005

PROTECTING THE MINORITY

ADVOCATE: Harry F. Byrd, U.S. Senator (D-WV)

SOURCE: *Congressional Record*, March 1, 2005

This debate has two related parts. One is the filibuster as such. It is a tactic legislators use to try to defeat a measure by "talking it to death," that is, continuing to speak on the subject to force the majority to compromise or even give way in order to resume normal operations. The second part of this debate is whether filibusters, even if sometimes reasonable, are appropriate to block nominees for the federal bench because of their judicial philosophy.

Filibusters: One of the often-cited adages of democratic governance is "majority rule with respect to minority rights." Today we tend to equate "minority" with groups that are disadvantaged based on race, ethnicity, sexual orientation, or some other inherent characteristic. To the framers of the Constitution, "minority" had a broader meaning. It included any group in the minority, such as property owners, and even minorities with a belief in a philosophical principle or even in an issue position. What is controversial is which should prevail when majority rule conflicts with minority rights. Taking one view, Thomas Jefferson held, "It is my principle that the will of the majority should always prevail." James Madison differed, contending that in democracies "the great danger is that the majority may not sufficiently respect the rights of the minority."

During their first 50 years or so, neither house of Congress limited debate, although there is no indication this process was consciously tied to protecting minorities. During this time, legislators tried occasionally to defeat legislation by using a filibuster, a word derived from the Spanish *filibustero* (freebooter or pirate). In response, the House in 1842 adopted procedures to close debates by majority vote. By contrast, the Senate continued unlimited debate until 1917, and then required a two-thirds vote of those senators "present and voting" to invoke "cloture" (halting debate). The cloture rule was modified in 1975 to permit stopping debate by three-fifths of all senators. This currently means 60 votes unless there is a vacancy.

Filibustering Judicial Nominees Because of their Judicial Philosophy: The second part of this debate involves the more modern use of filibusters to try to block the confirmation of judges based on their political/ideological/judicial outlook. Currently, this involves the question of whether it is acceptable for Democrats, who are a minority in the Senate, to use filibusters to try to block the conservative nominees for federal judgeships made by a Republican President George W. Bush.

It is the power of federal judges that make their nominations so important. As Supreme Court Chief Justice Charles Evans Hughes once put it, "We are under a Constitution, but the Constitution is what the judges say it is." This translates into the ability to make policy based on the courts' *power of interpretation*, their ability to find meaning in the words of the Constitution and legislative acts, and the courts' *power of judicial review*, their authority to decide whether laws passed by Congress and actions taken by officials are constitutional. Adding to the importance of judicial nominations is that most appointees continue to influence policy long after the president that appointed them and the senators that confirmed them have departed from the political stage.

Nevertheless, by most estimates it has only during the past half century or so that judicial nominations have become frequently and increasingly controversial. At least one reason is the contention that the courts have played a growing role in creating policy rather than merely interpreting the law. Some analysts also point to the growing partisanship in Congress and even in the country. Whatever the reason may be, all Supreme Court nominations now undergo intense scrutiny, with six Supreme Court nominees rejected since 1968. Especially during the terms of Bill Clinton and George W. Bush, resistance to appointments has also increasingly affected nominations to lower courts. Moreover, opposition to nominees has increasingly extended beyond their legal competence and judicial temperament to include their personal and political philosophy. More than any single issue, the question of where a nominee would uphold *Roe v. Wade* (1972), the abortion rights decision (see Debate 3) has become a "litmus test" for many senators.

The immediate debate here that pits Senator Orin Hatch against Senator Harry Reid resulted from Republican frustration with filibusters that blocked several nominations by President Bush for the U.S. Court of Appeals for the Federal Circuit. In response, the republican leadership in the Senate threatened to employ a complex parliamentary maneuver that would have allowed their party to bar filibusters of judicial nominations. Democrats characterized the threat to Senate tradition as so severe that it was a "nuclear option" and issued counter threats about using filibusters and other parliamentary tactics to halt Senate business if the Republicans went forward with their threat. This standoff, which imperiled the ability of the U.S. government to function normally, is the setting for the readings that follow.

POINTS TO PONDER

- ➢ Be consistent. For example, if you favor Democrats being able to filibuster the nominees of Republican president, then consistency dictates that you also agree to Republicans filibustering future nominees of Democratic presidents.
- ➢ Consistency would also arguably favor taking the same stand on whether senators should vote for or against judicial nominees based on their ideology alone and whether it is acceptable to filibuster on the basis of ideology. Should liberal legislators vote against conservative judges and vice versa?
- ➢ Consider having members of the Court of Appeals and Supreme Court serve set terms of, say, 10 years as a way to limit the impact of any one judge/justice and to ease the intensity of the conflict over judicial appointments.

Filibustering Federal Court Nominees: Frustrating the Majority

ORRIN G. HATCH

Yesterday [May 9, 2005] marked the fourth anniversary of President [George W.] Bush's first judicial nominations, a group of 11 highly qualified men and women nominated to the U.S. courts of appeals. As I said in the East Room at the White House on May 9, 2001: I hope the Senate will at least treat these nominees fairly. Many of our Democratic colleagues instead chose to follow their minority leader's order issued days after President Bush took office, to use "whatever means necessary" to defeat judicial nominees the minority does not like.

While the previous 3 presidents saw their first 11 appeals court nominees confirmed in an average of just 81 days, today, 1,461 days later, 3 of those original nominees have not even received a vote, let alone been confirmed. Three have withdrawn.

In 2003, the minority [the Democrats] opened a new front in the confirmation conflict by using filibusters to defeat majority-supported judicial nominees. This morning I will briefly address the top 10 most ridiculous judicial filibuster defenses. Time permits only brief treatment, but it was difficult to limit the list to 10.

No. 10 is the claim that these filibusters are part of Senate tradition. Calling something a filibuster, even if you repeat it over and over, does not make it so. These filibusters block confirmation of majority-supported judicial nominations by defeating votes to invoke cloture or end debate. Either these filibusters happened before or they did not.

Let me take the evidence offered by filibuster proponents at face value. [Let us examine the historical record of]...some representative examples of what Democrats repeatedly claim is filibuster precedence....Some examples are more ridiculous than others. Stephen Breyer is on the Democrats' list of filibusters, suggesting that the Senate treated his nomination the way Democrats are treating President Bush's nominations today. The two situations could not be more different. Even though President [Jimmy] Carter nominated now-Justice Breyer [since 1994] but then attorney Breyer, law professor Breyer, [for a seat on the U.S. Court of Appeals, First Circuit] in November 1980, after losing his bid for reelection—that is when he nominated him—and after Democrats lost control of the Senate, we voted to end debate and overwhelmingly confirmed Stephen Breyer just 26 days after his nomination. And I had a lot to do with that. The suggestion that confirming the Breyer nomination for the party losing its majority now justifies filibustering nominations for the party keeping its majority is, well, just plain ridiculous.

No. 9 on the list of the most ridiculous filibuster defenses is that they are necessary, they [the Democrats] say, to prevent one-party rule from stacking the Federal bench. Now, if you win elections, you say the country has chosen its leadership. If you lose, you complain about one-party rule. When your party controls the White House, the president appoints judges. When the other party controls the White House, the president stacks the bench—at least that seems to be the attitude.

Our Democratic colleagues say we should be guided by how the Democratic

Senate handled Franklin Roosevelt's attempt to pack the Supreme Court. It is true that FDR's legislative proposal [in 1937] to create new Supreme Court seats failed, and without a filibuster, I might add. But as it turned out, packing the Supreme Court required only filling the existing seats. President Roosevelt packed the Court all right, by appointing no less than eight Justices in 6 years—more than any president, except George Washington himself.

[With regard]...to FDR's court packing without a filibuster....let me just make some points. During the 75th, 76th, and 77th Congresses [1937–1943], when President Roosevelt made those nominations, Democrats outnumbered Republicans by an average of 70 Democrats to 20 Republicans. Now, that is one-party rule. Yet the Senate confirmed those Supreme Court nominees in an average of just 13 days, one of them on the very day it was made and six of them without even a roll-call vote. That is not because filibustering judicial nominations was difficult. In fact, our cloture rule did not then apply to nominations. A single member of that tiny, beleaguered Republican minority could have filibustered these nominations and attempted to stop President Roosevelt from packing the Supreme Court—just a single member could have. [Instead]...the number of filibusters against President Roosevelt's nominees [was] zero.

No. 8 on this list is the claim that without the filibuster the Senate would be a patsy, nothing but a rubberstamp for the president's judicial nominations. To paraphrase a great Supreme Court Justice: If simply stating this argument does not suffice to refute it, our debate about these issues has achieved terminal silliness. Being on the losing side does not make one a rubberstamp.

For all of these centuries of democratic government, have we seen only winners and rubberstamps? Was the famous tag line for ABC's Wide World of Sports "the thrill of victory and the agony of rubberstamping"? Democrats did not start filibustering judicial nominations until the 108th Congress. Imagine the history books describing the previous 107 Senates as the great rubberstamp Senates. Did Democrats rubberstamp the Supreme Court nomination of Clarence Thomas in 1991 since they did not use the filibuster? That conflict lasting several months and concluding with that 52-to-48 confirmation vote did not look like a rubberstamp to me.

Some modify this ridiculous argument by saying this applies when one party controls both the White House and the Senate. They make the stunning observation that senators of the president's party are likely to vote for his nominees. The assistant minority leader, Senator [Richard] Durbin [D-IL], recently said, for example, that Republican senators are nothing but "lapdogs" for President Bush.

Pointing at others can be dangerous because you have a few fingers pointing back at yourself. Counting both unanimous consent or roll-call votes, more than 37,500 votes were cast here on the Senate floor on President Clinton's judicial nominations. Only 11 of them, just a teeny, tiny, three one-hundredths of 1 percent, were "no" votes from Democrats—only 11 of 37,500. Were they just rubberstamping lapdogs in supporting President Clinton?

The Constitution assigns the same roles to the president and the Senate no matter which party the American people put in charge of which end of Pennsylvania Avenue.

In the 1960s, the Democrats were in charge, yet Minority Leader Everett Dirksen [R-IL] refused to filibuster judicial nominees of Presidents [John F.] Kennedy or [Lyndon B.] Johnson. Was he just a rubberstamp?

In the 1970s, the Democrats were in charge, yet Minority Leader Howard Baker [R-TN] refused to filibuster President Carter's judicial nominees. Was he just a rubberstamp?

In the 1980s, the Republicans were in charge, yet Minority Leader Robert Byrd [D-WV] did not filibuster President [Ronald] Reagan's judicial nominees. Was he just a rubberstamp?

And a decade ago, the Democrats were again in charge, yet Minority Leader Bob Dole [R-KS] refused to filibuster President [Bill] Clinton's judicial nominees. Was he a rubberstamp?

To avoid being a rubberstamp, one need only fight the good fight, win or lose.

No. 7 on the list of most ridiculous judicial filibuster defenses is that these filibusters are necessary to preserve our system of checks and balances. That is an argument we have heard from the other side. Any civics textbook explains that what we call "checks and balances" regulates the relationship between the branches of Government. The Senate's role of advice and consent checks the president's power to appoint judges, and we exercise that check when we vote on his judicial nominations.

The filibuster is about the relationship between the majority and minority in the Senate, not about the relationship between the Senate and the president. It actually interferes with being a check on the president's power by preventing the Senate from exercising its role of advice and consent at all. Former Majority Leader Mike Mansfield [D-MT] once explained that by filibustering judicial nominations, individual senators presume what he called "great personal privilege at the expense of the responsibilities of the Senate as a whole, and at the expense of the constitutional structure of the federal government." In September 1999, the [Democratic] senator from Massachusetts, [Ted] Kennedy, expressed the same view when he said:

> It is true that some senators have voiced concerns about these nominations. But that should not prevent a roll call vote which gives every senator the opportunity to vote "yes" or "no."

Those were the words of our colleague from Massachusetts, Senator Kennedy: Give every senator the opportunity to vote yes or no. That was then; this is now....

No. 6 on the list is that these filibusters are necessary to prevent appointment of extremists. What our Democratic colleagues call "extreme" the American Bar Association calls "qualified." In fact, all three of the appeals court nominees chosen 4 years ago who have been denied confirmation received the ABA's highest "well qualified" rating. Now, that was the gold standard under the Democrats when Clinton was president. The same Democrats who once called the ABA rating the gold standard for evaluating judicial nominees now disregard it and call these people extreme.

Did 76 percent of Californians vote to keep an extremist on their supreme court when they voted to retain Justice Janice Rogers Brown [one of President Bush's filibustered nominees for the Court of Appeals], an African-American woman, a sharecroppers' daughter, who fought her way all the way up to the Supreme Court of California?

Did 84 percent of all Texans and every major newspaper in the state support an extremist when they reelected Justice Priscilla Owen [another filibustered Bush nominee to the Court of Appeals] to the Texas Supreme Court—84 percent?

The Associated Press reported last Friday that the minority leader [Senator Harry Reid, D-NV] reserves the right to filibuster what he calls "extreme" Supreme Court nominees. Now, that is quite an escape hatch, if you will, since the minority already defines any nominee it does not like as "extreme." This is simply a repackaged status quo masquerading as reform.

If senators want to dismiss as an extremist any judicial nominee who does not think exactly as they do, that certainly is their right. That is, however, a reason for voting against a confirmation, not for refusing to vote at all. As our former colleague, Tom Daschle [D-SD], said, "I find it simply baffling that a senator would vote against even voting on a judicial nominee."

No. 5 on this list of most ridiculous judicial filibuster defenses is the claim that these filibusters are about free speech and debate. If senators cannot filibuster judicial nominations, some say, the Senate will cease to exist, and we will be literally unable to represent our constituents.

The same men who founded this republic designed this Senate without the ability to filibuster anything at all. A simple majority could proceed to vote on something after sufficient debate. Among those first senators were Oliver Ellsworth of Connecticut, who later served on the Supreme Court, as well as Charles Carroll of Maryland and Richard Henry Lee of Virginia, who had signed the Declaration of Independence. When they ran for office, did they know that they would be unable to represent their states because they would be unable to filibuster?

These filibusters are about defeating judicial nominations, not debating them. The minority rejects every proposal for debating and voting on nominations it targets for defeat. In April 2003, my colleague from Utah, Senator [Robert] Bennett [R], asked the minority leader, how many hours Democrats would need to debate a particular nomination. His response spoke volumes. [He commented,] "[T]here is not a number [of hours] in the universe that would be sufficient." Later that year, he said, "We would not agree to a time agreement...of any duration." Just 2 weeks ago, the minority leader summed up what really has been the Democrats' position all along: "This has never been about the length of the debate."

He is right about that. This has always been about defeating nominations, not debating them. If our Democratic colleagues want to debate, then let us debate. The majority leader said we will give 100 hours for each of these nominees. Let's debate them. Let us do what Democrats once said was the purpose of debating judicial nominations. As my colleague from California, Senator Barbara Boxer [D], put it in January 1998, "[L]et these names come up, let us have debate, let us vote."

No. 4 on the list is that returning to Senate tradition regarding floor votes on judicial nominations would amount to breaking the rules to change the rules. As any consultant worth even a little salt will tell you, that is a catchy little phrase. The problem is that neither of its catchy little parts is true. The constitutional option, which would change judicial confirmation procedure through the Senate voting to affirm a parliamentary ruling, would neither break nor change Senate rules. While the constitutional option has not been used to break our rules, it has been used to break filibusters. [The constitutional option refers to the Republican threat to have the president of the Senate, Vice President Richard Cheney, rule the filibuster of nominees to be unconstitutional and thus out of order. Under Senate rules, it would require a majority vote to overturn that ruling.]

On January 4, 1995, the senator from West Virginia, Senator Byrd, described how, in 1977, when he was majority leader, he used this procedure to break a filibuster on a natural gas bill. Now, I have genuine affection and great respect for the senator from West Virginia, and he knows that. But....since I would not want to describe his repeated use of the constitutional option in a pejorative way, let me use his own words. Here is what he said back in 1995:

> I have seen filibusters. I have helped to break them. There are few senators in this body who were here [in 1977] when I broke the filibuster on the natural gas bill....I asked Mr. [Walter] Mondale, the Vice president, to go please sit in the chair; I wanted to make some points of order and create some new precedents that would break these filibusters. And the filibuster was broken—back, neck, legs, and arms....So I know something about filibusters. I helped to set a great many of the precedents that are on the books here.

Well, he certainly did. I was here. And using the constitutional option today to return to Senate tradition regarding judicial nominations would simply use the precedents the distinguished senator from West Virginia put on the books.

No. 3 on the list of most ridiculous judicial filibuster defenses is that the constitutional option is unprecedented....In 1977, 1979, and 1987, the then majority leader, Senator Byrd, secured a favorable parliamentary ruling through a point of order and a majority of senators voted to affirm it. He did this even when the result he sought was inconsistent with the text of our written rules. In 1980, he used a version of the same procedure to limit nomination-related filibusters. Majority Leader Byrd made a motion for the Senate to vote to go into executive session and proceed to consider a specific nomination. At the time, the first step was not debatable but the second step was debatable. A majority of senators voted to overturn a parliamentary ruling disallowing the procedural change Majority Leader Byrd wanted. Seven of these [Democratic] senators serve with us today....They can explain for themselves how voting against restricting nomination-related filibusters today is consistent with voting to restrict them in 1980.

No. 2 on the list is that preventing judicial filibusters will doom legislative filibusters. As you know, there are two calendars in the Senate. One is the legislative calendar. I would fight to my death to keep the filibuster alive on the legislative calendar to protect the minority. But then there is the executive calendar, which is partly the president's in the sense that he has the power of appointment and nomination and sends these people up here and expects advice and consent from the Senate. Advice we give. Consent we have not given in the case of these nominees who have been filibustered, or so-called filibustered.

[The contention] that preventing judicial filibusters...will doom legislative filibusters....[is] pure bunk. Our own Senate history shows how ridiculous this argument really is. Filibusters became possible by dropping the rule allowing a simple majority to proceed to a vote. The legislative filibuster developed, the judicial filibuster did not. What we must today limit by rule or ruling we once limited by principle or self-restraint—for 214 years, that is. The filibuster is an inappropriate obstacle to the president's judicial appointment power but an appropriate tool for exercising our own legislative power. I cannot fathom how returning to our tradition regarding judicial nominations will somehow threaten our tradition regarding legislation. The only threat to the legislative filibuster and the only votes to abolish have come from the other side of the aisle. In 1995, 19 senators, all Democrats, voted against tabling an amendment to our cloture rule [to cut off debate] that would prohibit all filibusters of legislation as well as nominations. Nine of those senators still serve with us and their names are right here on this chart.

I voted then against the Democrats' proposal to eliminate the legislative filibuster, and I oppose eliminating it today. The majority leader, Senator [Bill] Frist [R-TN], also voted against the Democrats' proposal to eliminate the legislative filibuster. In fact, that was his first vote as a new member of this body. I joined him in recommitting ourselves to protecting the legislative filibuster. I urge...the Democrats to follow the example of our colleague from California, Senator [Barbara] Boxer [D], who recently said that she has changed her position, that she no longer wants to eliminate the legislative filibuster.

In 1995, *USA Today* condemned the filibuster as "a pedestrian tool of partisans and gridlock meisters." The *New York Times* said the filibuster is "the tool of the sore loser." I hope these papers will reconsider their position and support the legislative filibuster.

The No. 1 most ridiculous judicial filibuster defense is that those wanting to filibuster Republican nominees today opposed filibustering Democratic nominees only a few years ago. In a letter dated February 4, 1998, for example, the leftwing urged confirmation of Margaret Morrow to the U.S. District Court for the Central District of California. They urged us to "bring the nomination to the Senate, ensure that it received prompt, full and fair consideration, and that a final vote on her nomination is scheduled as soon as possible." Groups signing this letter included the Alliance for Justice, Leadership Conference on Civil Rights, and People for the American Way. As we all know, these leftwing groups today lead the grassroots campaign behind these filibusters that would deny this same treatment to President Bush's nominees. Their position has changed as the party controlling the White House has changed....

I opened the debate on the Morrow nomination by strongly urging my fellow senators to support it. We did, and she is, today, a sitting Federal judge, as I believe she should be. The same Democrats who today call for filibusters called for up-or-down votes when a Democrat was in the White House....

Let me...give some [other] illustrations [of the Democrats' changing position]. In 1999, Senator Diane Feinstein [D-CA], said of the Senate, "It is our job to confirm these judges. If we don't like them, we can vote against them." She [also] said, "A nominee is entitled to a vote. Vote them up, vote them down." Senator Charles Schumer [D-NY] properly said in March 2000, "The president nominates and we are charged with voting on the nominees." I have already quoted Senator Boxer once, but in 2000 she said that filibustering judicial nominees, "would be such a twisting of what cloture really means in these cases. It has never been done before for a judge, as far as we know—ever." And [Senator Herbert] Kohl [D-WI], said in 199, "Let's breathe life back into the confirmation process. Let's vote on the nominees...."

The same view comes from three former Judiciary Committee chairmen, members of the Democratic leadership. A former committee chairman, Senator [Joseph] Biden [D-DE], said in 1977 that every judicial nominee is entitled "to have a shot to be heard on the floor and have a vote on the floor." Former chairman [Ted] Kennedy [D-MA] said in 1998, "If senators don't like them, vote against them. But give them a vote." And my immediate predecessor as chairman, Senator [Patrick] Leahy [D-VT], said a year later, judicial nominees are "entitled to a vote, aye or nay." Finally, the minority leader, Senator Reid, expressed in March 2000 the standard that I hope we can reestablish: "Once they [nominations] get out of committee, bring them down here and vote up or down on them."

The majority leader, Senator Frist, recently proposed a plan to accomplish precisely this result. But the minority leader dismissed it as—I want to quote this accurately now—"a big fat wet kiss to the far right." I never thought voting on judicial nominations was a far-right thing to do.

These statements speak for themselves. Do you see a pattern here? The message at one time seems to be let us debate and let us vote. That should be the standard, no matter which party controls the White House or the Senate.

As I close, let me summarize these 10 top most ridiculous judicial filibusters in this way. Blocking confirmation of majority-supported judicial nominations by defeating cloture votes is unprecedented. In the words of the current Judiciary Committee chairman, Senator [Arlen] Specter [R-PA], "What Democrats are doing here is really seeking a constitutional revolution." We must turn back that revolution. No matter which party controls the White House or Senate, we should return to our tradition of giving judicial nominations reaching the Senate floor an up-or-down vote. Full, fair, and vigorous debate is one of the hallmarks of this body, and it should drive how we evaluate a president's judicial nominations.

Honoring the Constitution's separation of power, however, requires that our check on the president's appointment power not highjack that power altogether. This means debate must be a means to an end rather than an end in itself. Senators are free to vote against the nominees they feel extreme, but they should not be free to prevent other senators from expressing a contrary view or advising and consenting. In this body, we govern ourselves with parliamentary rulings as well as by unwritten rules. The procedure of a majority of senators voting to sustain a parliamentary ruling has been used repeatedly to change Senate procedure without changing Senate rules, even to limit nomination-related filibusters....

We confirmed, in 6 years of Republican control of the Senate, 377 judges for President Clinton. That was five less than the all-time confirmation champion Ronald Reagan. All of these people [judicial nominees of President Bush] who are up have well-qualified ratings from the ABA, all had a bipartisan majority to support them. What is wrong with giving them an up-or-down vote and retaining 214 years of Senate tradition? What is wrong with that? I think it is wrong to try and blow up that tradition the way it is being done.

Filibustering Federal Court Nominees: Protecting the Minority

HARRY F. BYRD

In1939, one of the most famous American movies of all time, *Mr. Smith Goes to Washington*, hit the box office. Initially received with a combination of lavish praise and angry blasts, the film went on to win numerous awards and to inspire millions around the globe. The director, the legendary Frank Capra, in his autobiography, *Frank Capra: The Name Above the Title*, cites this moving review of the film, appearing in the *Hollywood Reporter*, November 4, 1942:

> Frank Capra's *Mr. Smith Goes to Washington*, chosen by French Theaters as the final English language film to be shown before the recent Nazi-ordered countrywide ban on American and British films went into effect, was roundly cheered....Storms of spontaneous applause broke out at the sequence when, under the Abraham Lincoln monument in the Capital, the word, "Liberty," appeared on the screen and the Stars and Stripes began fluttering over the head of the great Emancipator in the cause of liberty. Similarly, cheers and acclamation punctuated the famous speech of the young senator on man's rights and dignity. "It was....as though the joys, suffering, love and hatred, the hopes and wishes of an entire people who value freedom above everything, found expression for the last time."

For those who may not have seen it, *Mr. Smith* is the fictional story of one young senator's crusade against forces of corruption and his lengthy filibuster—his lengthy filibuster—for the values he holds dear.

My, how things have changed. These days, Mr. Smith would be called an obstructionist. Rumor has it that there is a plot afoot to curtail the right of extended debate in this hallowed chamber, not in accordance with its rules, mind you, but by fiat from the chair [the presiding officer, the vice president, through] the so-called nuclear option....This morning I asked a man, "What does nuclear option mean to you?" He said: Oh, you mean with Iran? I was at the hospital a few days ago with my wife, and I asked a doctor, "What does the nuclear option mean to you?" He said, "That sounds like we're getting ready to drop some device, some atomic device on North Korea." Well, the so-called nuclear option purports to be directed solely at the Senate's advice and consent prerogatives regarding federal judges. But the claim that no right exists to filibuster judges aims an arrow straight at the heart of the Senate's long tradition of unlimited debate.

The Framers of the Constitution envisioned the Senate as a kind of executive council, a small body of legislators, featuring longer terms, designed to insulate members from the passions of the day. The Senate was to serve as a check on the executive branch, particularly in the areas of appointments and treaties, where, under the Constitution, the Senate passes judgment absent the House of Representatives.

James Madison wanted to grant the Senate the power to select judicial appointees with the [president] delegated to the sidelines. But a compromise brought the present arrangement: appointees selected by the [president], with the advice and consent of the Senate confirmed. Note that nowhere in the Constitution of the United States is a vote on appointments mandated.

When it comes to the Senate, numbers can deceive. The Senate was never intended to be a majoritarian body. That was the role of the House of Representatives, with its membership based on the populations of states. The Great Compromise of July 16, 1787, satisfied the need for smaller states to have equal status in one House of Congress, the Senate. The Senate, with its two members per state, regardless of population, is, then, the forum of the states.

Indeed, in the last Congress 52 members, a majority, representing the 26 smallest states, accounted for just 17.06 percent of the U.S. population. In other words, a majority in the Senate does not necessarily represent a majority of the population of the United States.

The Senate is intended for deliberation, not point scoring. The Senate is a place designed, from its inception, as expressive of minority views. Even 60 Senators, the number required under Senate rule XXII for cloture [closing debate], would represent just 24 percent of the population if they happened to all hail from the 30 smallest states.

So you can see what it means to the smallest states in these United States to be able to stand on this floor and debate, to their utmost, until their feet will no longer hold them, and their lungs of brass will no longer speak, in behalf of their states, in behalf of a minority, in behalf of an issue that affects vitally their constituents.

Unfettered debate, the right to be heard at length, is the means by which we perpetuate the equality of the states. In fact, it was 1917, before any curtailing of debate was [allowed], which means that from 1789 to 1917...the Senate rejected any limits to debate. Democracy flourished along with the filibuster. The first actual cloture rule in 1917 was enacted in response to a filibuster by those people who opposed the arming of merchant ships. Some might say they opposed U.S. intervention in World War I, but to narrow it down, they opposed the arming of merchant ships.

But even after its enactment, the Senate was slow to embrace cloture, understanding the pitfalls of muzzling debate. In 1949, the 1917 cloture rule was modified to make cloture more difficult to invoke, not less, mandating that the number needed to stop debate would be not two-thirds of those present and voting but two-thirds of all senators. Indeed, from 1919 to 1962, the Senate voted on cloture petitions only 27 times and invoked cloture just 4 times over those 43 years.

On January 4, 1957, Senator William Ezra Jenner of Indiana [R] spoke in opposition to invoking cloture by majority vote. He stated with great conviction:

> We may have a duty to legislate, but we also have a duty to inform and deliberate. In the past quarter century we have seen a phenomenal growth in the power of the executive branch. If this continues at such a fast pace, our system of checks and balances will be destroyed. One of the main bulwarks against this growing power is free debate in the Senate....So long as there is free debate, men of courage and understanding will rise to defend against potential dictators....The Senate today is one place where, no matter what else may exist, there is still a chance to be heard, an opportunity to speak, the duty to examine, and the obligation to protect. It is one of the few refuges of democracy.

> Minorities have an illustrious past, full of suffering, torture, smear, and even death. Jesus Christ was killed by a majority; Columbus was smeared; and Christians have been tortured. Had the United States Senate existed during those trying times, I am sure that these people would have found an advocate. Nowhere else can any political, social, or religious group, finding itself under sustained attack, receive a better refuge.

Senator Jenner was right. The Senate was deliberately conceived to be what he called "a better refuge," meaning one styled as guardian of the rights of the minority. The Senate is the "watchdog" because majorities can be wrong and filibusters can highlight injustices. History is full of examples.

In March 1911, Senator Robert Owen of Oklahoma [D] filibustered the New Mexico statehood bill, arguing that Arizona should also be allowed to become a state. President [William H.] Taft opposed the inclusion of Arizona's statehood in the bill because Arizona's state constitution allowed the recall of judges. Arizona attained statehood a year later, at least in part because Senator Owen and the minority took time to make their point the year before.

In 1914, a Republican minority led a 10-day filibuster of a bill that would have appropriated more than $50,000,000 for rivers and harbors. On an issue near and dear to the hearts of our current majority, Republican opponents spoke until members of the Commerce Committee agreed to cut the appropriations by more than half.

Perhaps more directly relevant to our discussion of the "nuclear option" are the 7 days in 1937, from July 6 to 13 of that year, when the Senate blocked Franklin Roosevelt's Supreme Court–packing plan.

Earlier that year, in February 1937, FDR sent the Congress a bill drastically reorganizing the judiciary. The Senate Judiciary Committee rejected the bill, calling it "an invasion of judicial power such as has never before been attempted in this country" and finding it "essential to the continuance of our constitutional democracy that the judiciary be completely independent of both the executive and legislative branches of the Government." The committee recommended the rejection of the court-packing bill, calling it "a needless, futile, and utterly dangerous abandonment of constitutional principle...without precedent and without justification."

What followed was an extended debate on the Senate floor lasting for 7 days until the majority leader, Joseph T. Robinson of Arkansas [D], a supporter of the plan, suffered a heart attack and died on July 14. Eight days later, by a vote of 70 to 20, the Senate sent the judicial reform bill back to committee, where FDR's controversial, court-packing language was finally stripped. A determined, vocal group of senators properly prevented a powerful president from corrupting our nation's judiciary.

Free and open debate on the Senate floor ensures citizens a say in their government. The American people are heard, through their senator, before their money is spent, before their civil liberties are curtailed, or before a judicial nominee is confirmed for a lifetime appointment. We are the guardians, the stewards, the protectors of the people who send us here. Our voices are their voices. If we restrain debate on judges today, what will be next: the rights of the elderly to receive social security; the rights of the handicapped to be treated fairly; the rights of the poor to obtain a decent education? Will all debate soon fall before majority rule?

Will the majority someday trample on the rights of lumber companies to harvest timber or the rights of mining companies to mine silver, coal, or iron ore? What about the rights of energy companies to drill for new sources of oil and gas? How will the insurance, banking, and securities industries fare when a majority can move against their interests and prevail by a simple majority vote? What about farmers who can be forced to lose their subsidies, or western senators who will no longer be able to stop a majority determined to wrest control of ranchers' precious water or grazing rights? With no right of debate, what will forestall plain muscle and mob rule?

Many times in our history we have taken up arms to protect a minority against the tyrannical majority in other lands. We, unlike Nazi Germany or Mussolini's Italy, have never stopped being a nation of laws, not of men. But witness how men with motives and a majority can manipulate law to cruel and unjust ends. Historian Alan Bullock writes that Hitler's dictatorship rested on the constitutional foundation of a single law, the Enabling Law. Hitler needed a two-thirds vote to pass that law, and he cajoled his opposition in the Reichstag [Germany's legislature] to support it. Bullock writes that "Hitler was prepared to promise anything to get his bill through, with the appearances of legality preserved intact." And he succeeded.

Hitler's originality lay in his realization that effective revolutions, in modern conditions, are carried out with, and not against, the power of the state: the correct order of events was first to secure access to that power and then begin his revolution. Hitler never abandoned the cloak of legality; he recognized the enormous psychological value of having the law on his side. Instead, he turned the law inside out and made illegality legal.

That is what the nuclear option seeks to do to rule XXII of the Standing Rules of the Senate. The nuclear option seeks to alter the rules by sidestepping the rules, thus making the impermissible the rule, employing the nuclear option, engaging a pernicious, procedural maneuver to serve immediate partisan goals, risks violating our nation's core democratic values and poisoning the Senate's deliberative process.

For the temporary gain of a handful of out-of-the-mainstream judges, some in the Senate are ready to callously incinerate each and every senator's right of extended debate. Note that I said every senator. For the damage will devastate not just the minority party;...it will cripple the ability of each member, every member, to do what each member was sent here to do—namely, represent the people of his or her state. Without the filibuster—it has a bad name, old man filibuster out there. Most people would be happy to say let's do away with him. We ought to get rid of that fellow; he has been around too long. But someday that old man filibuster is going to help me, you, and every senator in here at some time or other, when the rights of the people he or she represents are being violated or threatened. That senator is then going to want to filibuster. He or she is going to want to stand on his or her feet as long as their...lungs will carry their voice.

If the nuclear option is successful here, no longer will each Senator have that weapon with which to protect the people who sent him or her here. And the people finally are going to wake up to who did it. They are going to wake up to it sooner or later and ask: "Who did this to us?"

Without the filibuster or the threat of extended debate, there exists no leverage with which to bargain for the offering of an amendment. All force to effect compromise between the parties will be lost. Demands for hearings will languish. The President of the United States can simply rule by executive order, if his party controls both Houses of Congress and majority rule reigns supreme. In such a world, the minority will be crushed, the power of dissenting views will be diminished, and freedom of speech will be attenuated. The uniquely American concept of the independent individual asserting his or her own views, proclaiming personal dignity through the courage of free speech will forever have been blighted. This is a question of freedom of speech....And the American spirit, that stubborn, feisty, contrarian, and glorious urge to loudly disagree, and proclaim, despite all opposition, what is honest, what is true, will be sorely manacled.

Yes, we believe in majority rule, but we thrive because the minority can challenge, agitate, and ask questions. We must never become a nation cowed by fear, sheeplike in our submission to the power of any majority demanding absolute control. Generations of men and women have lived, fought, and died for the right to map their own destiny, think their own thoughts, speak their own minds. If we start here, in this Senate, to chip away at that essential mark of freedom—here of all places, in a body designed to guarantee the power of even a single individual through the device of extended debate—we are on the road to refuting the principles upon which that Constitution rests. In the eloquent, homespun words of that illustrious, obstructionist, Senator Smith, in *Mr. Smith Goes to Washington*, "Liberty is too precious to get buried in books. Men ought to hold it up in front of them every day of their lives and say, 'I am free—to think—to speak. My ancestors couldn't. I can. My children will.'"

THE CONTINUING DEBATE: Filibustering Federal Court Nominees

What Is New

The confrontation between Democrats and Republicans that sparked this debate was defused in late May 2005 when a group of seven Democratic senators and seven Republicans agreed to a deal. It allowed three of President Bush's stalled nominees proceed to a vote and confirmation, while two others remained subject to filibuster and, thus, in effect, blocked. More importantly, the seven Democrats pledged not to filibuster future Bush nominees except under "extraordinary circumstances." In turn, the Republicans promised to oppose the nuclear option. Although there was and remains considerable uncertainty about what constitutes "extraordinary circumstances," the leadership of the two parties eventually agreed and a legislative crisis was averted.

That set the stage for what many observers were anticipating: one or more vacancies on the Supreme Court. These soon came when Associate Justice Sandra Day O'Conner retired and Chief Justice William Rehnquist died. Many observers anticipated a pitched battle over their replacements, but President Bush's nominees, John G. Roberts, Jr. for chief justice and Samuel Alito for associate justice, both had exceptional qualifications and winning personalities. Despite heated opposition from liberal, Senate Democrats did not try to mount a filibuster and both Roberts and Alito were confirmed. How the Democrats will react to other conservative nominees is unclear however. Joseph Lieberman, one of the seven Democrats sponsoring the compromise, was denied his party's nomination in Connecticut in a 2006 primary. Lieberman's support of the war in Iraq was the major issue, but his opponent also pointed to the senator's unwillingness to filibuster Bush's judicial nominees as unforgivable. Other Democratic senators may take heed of Lieberman's fate and take a harder line in the future.

Where to Find More

Two good studies of the appointment process are David Yalof, *Pursuit of Justices: Presidential Politics and the Selection of Supreme Court Nominees* (University of Chicago Press, 1999) and Joyce A. Baugh, *Supreme Court Justices in the Post-Bork Era: Confirmation Politics and Judicial Performance* (Peter Lang, 2002). For a group that would support the opposition to conservative judges, go to www.pfaw.org/pfaw/general/, the site of the liberal group, People for the American Way. The opposite view is held by the Committee for Justice at www.committeeforjustice.org/.

What More to Do

Begin by asking yourself whether the nomination and confirmation process for judges works well. Particularly think about whether it is possible to select non-ideological judges and justices through what is inherently a political process. If the process is wanting, what would you do to fix it?

DEBATE 15

STATE AND LOCAL GOVERNMENT

TAKING PROPERTY BY EMINENT DOMAIN FOR ECONOMIC DEVELOPMENT:

Serving the Public Good *or* Abusing Government Power?

SERVING THE PUBLIC GOOD

ADVOCATE: Jeffrey Finkle, President And Chief Executive Office, International Economic Development Council

SOURCE: Testimony during hearings on "Protecting Property Rights After *Kelo,*" before the U.S. House of Representatives, Committee on Energy And Commerce Committee, Subcommittee on Commerce, Trade, and Consumer Protection, October 19, 2005

ABUSING GOVERNMENT POWER

ADVOCATE: Michael D. Ramsey, Professor, School of Law, University of San Diego

SOURCE: Testimony during hearings on "Protecting Property Rights After *Kelo,*" before the U.S. House of Representatives, Committee on Energy And Commerce Committee, Subcommittee on Commerce, Trade, and Consumer Protection, October 19, 2005

Private property has something of an air of sanctified ground in the United States. Signs reading, No Trespassing, Keep Out, No Entry, or simply Private Property are ubiquitous. Sayings like "A man's home is his castle" are often heard. There is also a long line of political theory that supports property rights. One of the great democratic philosophers, John Locke, theorized in his *Second Treatise on Civil Government* (1690) that people carried with them into society certain rights that could not be taken away. He believed that natural law, inherent laws of nature, created rights and mandated that "no one ought to harm another in his life, health, liberty or possessions." Locke was not an absolutist. While he believed that the community could not take away an individual's rights, he made an exception if the individual transgressed, for example, by taking another life, restricting someone else's liberty, or "hord[ing] up more [property] than he could make use of" for "whatever is beyond this is more than his share and belongs to others."

Other political theorists have thoroughly disagreed about the near inviolability of private property. Jean Jacques Rousseau argued in *The Social Contract* (1762) that the concept of private property was divisive and that strife among people had intensified after "the first man...enclosed a piece of ground, [proclaimed]...'This is mine,' and found people simple enough to believe him."

In between those two extremes, the United States and other democratic countries have tried to craft laws that protect private property but allow the government to take that property provided that the purpose is for the public good and owners are paid for it. This is expressed by the Fifth Amendment to the Constitution, which, closely paraphrasing Locke, reads in part: "No person shall...be deprived of life, liberty, or property, without due process of law; or shall private property be taken for the public use, without just compensation." In the United States the right of the government to require the compulsory sale of land is called "eminent domain," a phrase that relates to the right of the monarch (an eminence) to acquire land within his/her realm (domain). The word "condemnation" describes the act of a government designating property it will acquire under its authority of eminent domain.

Although the legality of condemning property under eminent domain is well established, what is uncertain is what "public good" means in the Fifth Amendment. The meaning of those two words is at the heart of this debate. In the mid-1990s the city of New London, Connecticut, began to seek ways to improve its deteriorating downtown and waterfront areas. To assist it, the city hired the New London Development Corporation (NLDC), a private nonprofit organization. In 2000, the city accepted the NLDC's recommendations, which included condemning under eminent domain over 100 pieces of private property, including private homes, in the waterfront area and turning the land over to private developers. They, in turn, would build hotels, office complexes, and other structures according to broad plans approved by the city. New London believed this would help revitalize the city. Most of the homes and other buildings in the area were old, but they were not rundown.

Most of those with homes or other property in the area, known as Fort Trumbull, soon agreed to terms with the city. But Susette Kelo and a few others did not. They valued their homes more than their monetary worth and sued the New London. The plaintiffs claimed that transferring their property to private developers did not constitute "public use" and thus violated the doctrine of eminent domain. The city argued that its economic development constituted public use because the town and its tax base would be improved by upgraded use of the area and by the tearing down what were old, but not woefully rundown, homes and other buildings. A Superior Court in Connecticut found for the petitioners, but the Connecticut Supreme Court overturned that decision. Kelso and the others then appealed to the U.S. Supreme Court. In June 2005, it decided by 6 to 3 in favor of New London. Writing for the majority, Associate Justice John Paul Stevens held that "public use" can be equated with "public purpose," and that the city had acted legally because, "There is no basis for exempting economic development from our traditionally broad understanding of public purpose." The decision set the stage for this debate. Jeffrey Finkle argues in the first reading that the *Kelo* decision wisely supported the use of eminent domain as a tool for local governments in the redevelopment and revitalization of economically distressed areas. Michael Ramsey disagrees in the second reading. He contends that Kelo was legally unsound and also greatly reduced the protection for private property.

POINTS TO PONDER

- Before reading the debate, think about what "public use" means to you. Then see if you change your mind after reading the debate.
- Given that the condemned property was not blighted, think about whether economic development could include, say, demolishing an well-cared for middle class neighborhood to build a privately owned multi-billion dollar theme park?
- To a degree this debate involved a clash between individualism (the good of individuals) versus communitarianism (the good of the community). Where should the line be between protecting individual rights and promoting the general welfare?

Taking Property by Eminent Domain for Economic Development: Serving the Public Good

JEFFREY FINKLE

I have been in the economic development field for nearly 25 years and am the former U.S. Department of Housing and Urban Development (HUD) Deputy Assistant Secretary of Community Planning and Development during the Reagan Administration. Since then I have been leading our professional association [The International Economic Development Council, IECD] as our members build vibrant local economies.

For our profession, eminent domain is an economic development tool that allows local communities to acquire and assemble land for new development projects that generate new jobs, investment and taxes. The Supreme Court's 5-4 decision in *Kelo v. New London* [2005] leaves eminent domain in the hands of states and affirms eminent domain as an important tool for local governments in the redevelopment and revitalization of economically distressed areas.

The court stated in its opinion that the pursuit of economic development is a "public use" within the meaning of the Fifth Amendment's Takings Clause ["nor shall private property be taken for public use without just compensation"]. The New London economic development project at issue in the [*Kelo*] case is similar to projects across the country aimed at revitalizing depressed communities. It is IEDC's understanding, based on conversations with attorneys familiar with the decision, that the Supreme Court decision did not in any way expand the power of eminent domain. Rather, the Court simply upheld the longstanding inclusion of economic development as a 'public use.'

It is therefore unlikely that the Supreme Court's decision will result in city officials exercising eminent domain randomly or without balanced consideration. The Court's decision affirmed years of interpretations allowing the use of eminent domain to redevelop our nations' communities and to protect our local economies. Judiciously used eminent domain is critical to the economic growth and development of cities and towns throughout the country. Assembling land for redevelopment can be an important element in the process of revitalizing local economies, creating much-needed jobs, and generating revenues that enable cities to provide essential services. When used prudently and in the sunshine of public scrutiny, eminent domain helps achieve a greater public good that benefits the entire community.

There are many examples of the public benefit of the judicious use of eminent domain. One example can be seen in the return of retail to our urban cores. Eminent domain has been crucial in encouraging retailers, particularly anchor tenant supermarkets, to locate in the heart of inner cities rather than on the periphery where they have traditionally positioned themselves. A combination of educational efforts, land assembly, and economic development incentives are encouraging the supermarkets that abandoned inner cities in the 1970s to return. For example, South Los Angeles, CA, a densely populated urban area that is critically underserved by retail, will soon have a vibrant shopping area thanks to the successful employment of eminent domain. The Slauson Central

Shopping Center will be the first retail shopping center in the community in over 20 years. The supermarket-anchored shopping center will include a state-of-the-art grocery store along with small shop space, two freestanding commercial areas and a community Educational Training Center. The project will create approximately 150 new permanent jobs in the community and will bring grocery services close to thousands of low-income residents.

Successful redevelopment projects facilitated by eminent domain are proving that there are underserved populations/markets, and that perceived or actual higher costs of doing business in inner cities can be absorbed by sales volume. Without the ability to exercise the power of eminent domain for redevelopment purposes, the public would be unable to support many inner-city retail projects, and those neighborhoods would continue to decline.

Eminent domain has also strengthened suburban economies. In the early 1990's the city of Lakewood, CO was a Denver suburb at an economic crossroads due to a struggling shopping mall. Then, the Lakewood Reinvestment Authority and a developer decided to redevelop the mall into a mixed-use town center. The result is Belmar, 22 city blocks of stores, entertainment, office space, and residences that have emerged as the symbolic heart of the community and center of Denver's Metro West Side.

Eminent domain has also helped our struggling rural communities. In March 2002, Shawnee County, Kansas exercised its power of eminent domain to acquire the last few remaining parcels of a 432-acre site intended in part for a new Target Corporation distribution center. Although two property owners fought the condemnation proceedings primarily on the grounds that the distribution center did not satisfy a "public use," the Kansas Supreme Court ultimately ruled that the taking of private property for industrial and economic development was in fact a valid public purpose. The $80 million, 1.3 million square-foot warehouse distribution center opened in June 2004 to the tune of over 600 new jobs, with the expectation of adding an additional 400 jobs within the next three years.

Whether you represent an urban, suburban or rural area, the use of eminent domain is never the first choice of any community. The eminent domain process is time consuming and expensive; it is therefore the last resort pursued during a land assembly process. Many local authorities rarely exercise their power of eminent domain, particularly when it deals with occupied housing. Public officials who do use eminent domain comply with existing rules protecting individual property owners, and they have the ultimate accountability to the citizens and voters.

There is no question that eminent domain is a power that, like any government power, must be used prudently, and there are many built in checks. One such check is the public nature of the takings process. Probing questions should be raised about any complex undertaking financed by taxpayers, and nothing in local government attracts more scrutiny or more criticism than eminent domain. In their majority opinion in Kelo, the Supreme Court refers favorably to New London's long engagement in an open and comprehensive planning process. There are many other examples of public officials engaging their constituents. When Lakewood, CO began the process of redeveloping their failing mall, the city underwent an extensive public process that over the course of one year established a citizens advisory committee and invited members of the community to comment on potential redevelopment options.

Each of your states and localities legislates the use of eminent domain, and a public purpose or benefit needs to be clearly demonstrated. Authorities that abuse this privilege risk creating volatile political situations. Few government or elected officials are willing to risk their position and political stability in pursuit of a project overwhelmingly opposed by the community.

In another check on abuse, the Fifth Amendment requires that anyone whose property is taken for a public use be fairly compensated, and in practice, most takings are compensated generously. In case after case, the majority of property owners willingly accept just compensation for their property. According to our research, some are compensated as much as 25% above market value for their property. Just compensation allows property owners to relocate with an equal or improved quality of life.

Critics of the *Kelo* decision have said that it authorizes seizing the property of one person merely to give it to another. While it is true that once the public entity acquires title to the property, it is conveyed to a developer or end user to carry out the project, the public sector intervenes so that the private sector can bring much needed investment to a distressed area. Government agencies are not and should not be in the private real estate development business; therefore, the assembled land is typically leased or sold to the private sector for redevelopment. As a matter of policy, cities should not be in the long-discredited practice of building redevelopment projects; rather they should facilitate the use of private capital and private management to achieve the same end.

The use of eminent domain has evolved over the years from a 'bulldozer' technique to today's careful surgical approach. In the 1960s the federal government gave cities resources under the Urban Renewal Act to plow down hundreds of acres of land and thousands of homes and commercial buildings. That left many cities with land vacant for years. This policy has since been attacked by many as an inefficient use of resources. Today, economic development professionals wait until there is a specific market opportunity before we use eminent domain to acquire distressed properties. If your district's officials have to wait for land assembly holdouts, your communities will see jobs and market opportunities disappear.

In closing, I would like to comment on pending eminent domain legislation. In response to the Kelo decision, Congress is offering legislation that would prohibit the use of federal funds for economic development projects that involve the exercise of eminent domain. Should Congress act to prohibit the use of eminent domain for economic development purposes, the economies of many Congressional districts will suffer. No municipality in America could use eminent domain to carry out an economic development project.

Communities impacted by hurricanes Katrina and Rita are of special concern to us all. While IEDC members in the region are grateful for the billions of dollars the federal government has pledged to support economic and infrastructure redevelopment, gulf coast communities impacted by the hurricanes will face incredibly complicated and expensive redevelopment challenges. In order to redevelop devastated communities, states and localities will first need to raze crumbling homes and businesses.

We are very concerned that proposed Congressional legislation limiting the use of federal funds for eminent domain would allow one landowner to veto the redevelopment of an entire distressed area. This would have the practical effect of thwarting the ability of communities to demolish ruined infrastructure and begin successful redevelopment plans, further distressing an already devastated area. In IEDC's opinion, Congress should not preempt or displace existing state and municipal laws that govern the local application of eminent domain. The Supreme Court's decision keeps the economic health of communities in the hands of local leaders who are not out to destroy communities, but rather who work for the best interests of their communities at large. State or federal bills prohibiting the use of eminent domain for economic development are job-killing pieces of legislation. Assembling land for redevelopment helps revitalize local economies, create much needed jobs, and generate revenues that enable your communities to provide essential services. Exemplified by New London, eminent domain is used to breathe new life and give new hope to residents.

EMINENT DOMAIN GUIDING PRINCIPLES

1. When a public agency engages in land assembly, the process should be open to community stakeholders such as residents and local businesses.
2. Eminent domain should be employed as a last resort in the land assembly process and only when a property owner, after attempted negotiations, refuses to sell at a fair market value. To protect landowners, independent appraisals should be conducted.
3. All reasonable efforts should be made to avoid taking occupied residences and active businesses. A community must carefully weigh the benefits of redevelopment against the hardship associated with displacement.
4. When eminent domain is used in the taking of occupied property, relocation costs should be covered for the property owner. This may also include providing assistance to homeowners in finding a new home.
5. Before initiating the eminent domain process, municipalities should carefully review the legal parameters of the process as provided in their local charter. The process should be fully documented and completely transparent.
6. States that only allow the use of eminent domain for blighted land and property need to establish a clear definition of blight. This will reduce ambiguity for municipalities initiating the eminent domain process. Municipalities should establish a standardized approach in land assembly and eminent domain to provide consistent expectations amongst stakeholders.

EMINENT DOMAIN: MYTH VS. REALITY

Myth 1: Eminent domain is a quick and low cost means of acquiring land.

Reality: Eminent domain is more expensive and time consuming than the traditional method of land acquisition through negotiated purchase. Land acquired through eminent domain is often acquired at a price above fair market value. Unfortunately, the related legal fees frequently nullify any sales price premium benefits for the landowner. The acquiring agency is often affected even more by the premium price and legal costs associated with eminent domain.

Myth 2: Eminent domain is typically used as the first option in the land assembly process.

Reality: The eminent domain process is time consuming and expensive; it is therefore the last resort pursued during a land assembly process. Many local authorities rarely exercise their power of eminent domain.

Myth 3: State and local authorities promote urban redevelopment for the sole purpose of increasing the tax base.

Reality: Eminent domain is an important tool in revitalizing declining areas. Redevelopment projects remove blight, create jobs, and increase private investment in an area. Tax base growth is only one potential benefit.

Myth 4: The use of eminent domain violates private property rights.

Reality: Local and state authorities have the constitutional power to acquire property through eminent domain on the condition of just compensation.

Myth 5: Eminent domain is a government tool used to strip individuals of their private property rights.

Reality: Each state legislates its use of eminent domain. A public purpose or benefit generally needs to be clearly demonstrated. Authorities that abuse this privilege risk creating volatile political situations. Few government or elected officials are willing to risk their position and political stability in pursuit of a project overwhelmingly opposed by the community.

Myth 6: Local authorities and private developers undertake land assembly and eminent domain without involving the community.

Reality: Most local governments or redevelopment agencies incorporate community participation early on in a redevelopment initiative. There are many cases that demonstrate successful collaboration between community, private sector, and government representatives in the revitalization of distressed areas.

Myth 7: The government employs eminent domain to take property from one owner and give it to another owner that is financially or politically stronger. State and local governments use eminent domain as part of corporate incentive packages that benefit specific businesses.

Reality: Eminent domain is part of the land assembly process for redevelopment with the intent to remove blight and/or create jobs and/or create housing. The public sector intervenes so that the private sector can bring in much needed investment in a distressed area. Government agencies are not in the private real estate development business, therefore, the assembled land is typically leased or sold to the private sector for redevelopment. Often the prices and terms of the deals are very favorable because 1) the location and characteristics of the property are otherwise very unfavorable, and/or 2) the private party can create or retain much-needed jobs.

Myth 8: The flexible definition of blight facilitates the state's power in repossessing land.

Reality: Each state has its own definition of blight. Some have a strict test for blight, requiring physical or economic decline. Others have a more flexible definition. A few states do not have a blight requirement as a condition of eminent domain, but require that the project lead to job creation. There have been some highly publicized cases of local governments who have abused the blight designation to justify government repossession of land. These negative cases highlight the need for states to clarify their intentions and incorporate community involvement in defining eminent domain regulations.

Myth 9: The public money spent on assembling land for private use is tax money that will forever be lost to the community.

Reality: Initial public money invested is recaptured through increased tax revenue generated by the increase in property values and retail sales. In a well-planned project, the return on investment usually exceeds the initial cost. Furthermore, the benefits of redevelopment go beyond tax recovery to include job creation and area revitalization.

Myth 10: Land assembly and condemnation activities position a municipality as a real estate broker and developer in what has traditionally been private land deals. The free market can and will allow for redevelopment of older areas without any government intervention.

Reality: In many cases, a large, blighted area is comprised of numerous small properties. Private developers are reluctant to spend the time and money necessary to acquire each property with no assurance that they will ever assemble a large enough site to develop. Without land assembly assistance in urban areas, developers are likely to choose large tracts of undeveloped land on the suburban/city fringe. Such actions promote sprawl. Urban land assembly curtails sprawl and encourages smart growth.

Myth 11: Eminent Domain is an unnecessary tool for economic development.

Reality: Eminent domain is an important tool for economic development. Eminent domain gives communities a last resort option to help ensure that significant development opportunities are not hindered when reluctant landowners refuse to negotiate fair sale of their property. Without this valuable tool, local economic development professionals would not be able to sufficiently assemble land for beneficial redevelopment and public gain.

Taking Property by Eminent Domain for Economic Development: Abusing Government Power

MICHAEL D. RAMSEY

I [am testifying] to express my views of the protection of private property rights after the Supreme Court's decision in *Kelo v. City of New London*. My views are, in sum, as follows.

(1) The plain text of the Constitution, and its undisputed historical understanding, is that the government's power to take private property by eminent domain is limited by the Fifth Amendment to situations in which the property will be put to "public use." This means situations in which the property will be used by the government itself to fulfill one of the traditional public functions of government, such as providing a park or a highway, or situations in which the property is operated by a "common carrier," such as a railroad, with an obligation to serve the public.

(2) In *Kelo v. City of New London*, the U.S. Supreme Court greatly reduced this protection for private property. It ruled that the city could seize and demolish private homes to make way for private office buildings and other private development that the city believed would increase its tax revenues and create new jobs, even though the land would be privately owed and not open to the public.

(3) The Court did not pretend to base its conclusion up on the text and historical understanding of the Constitution. Instead, it said that the evolving modern needs of society required that it substitute the phrase "public purpose" for the Constitution's phrase "public use"—so that the government could seize private land any time that seizure would facilitate "economic development." As Justice [Sandra Day] O'Connor pointed out in dissent, this effectively removes all constitutional limits on the eminent domain power.

(4) The *Kelo* decision is an attack, not only upon private property rights, but upon the whole idea of constitutional rights. If a right written into the text of the Constitution can be altered by five members of the Supreme Court simply because they believe that the evolving modern needs of government require it to give way, then we have no fixed rights, but only those rights the Court is willing to accept at any given time.

(5) Congress can remedy the Court's error in several ways. It cannot directly overrule the Court. However, it can, for example, use its spending power to insist that no federal money be spent in any project that takes private property for private use. It can use its commerce power to prohibit the operation in interstate commerce of any project that take private property for private use. Using these powers, it can largely restore the rights denied in *Kelo*.

I. The Constitution's Protection for Private Property

The plain text of the Constitution, and its undisputed historical understanding, is that the government's power to take private property by eminent domain is limited to situations in which the property will be put to "public use." The Fifth Amendment, made applicable to states and local governments by the Fourteenth Amendment, provides: "[N]or shall private property be taken for public use, without just compensation." The most obvious meaning of this provision is that if the government wants to take private property for "public use," it must pay "just compensation"—thus assuring that the public as a whole, not just the property owner, bears the cost.

Although the text does not say so in exactly these words, the clear and undisputed indication is that private property may *not* be taken, *other* than for "public use," under any circumstances. Otherwise, the clause would be incoherent: it would mean that the government could take private property for private use without paying any compensation at all. No court or commentator reads the clause in that way. Rather, everyone agrees that the Fifth Amendment, as historically understood, imposes two restrictions on the eminent domain power: the property must be taken "for public use" and the government must pay "just compensation."

The question here, then, is the meaning of "public use." As a historical matter, that phrase meant exactly what it appears to mean. Most obviously, it refers to situations in which the property will be used by the government itself to fulfill one of the traditional public functions of government, such as providing a park or a highway. Additionally, it may refer to situations in which the property will be operated by a "common carrier," such as a railroad, with an obligation to serve the public. It emphatically did not include situations in which the government transferred property from one private owner to another. Under no possible meaning of the phrase could that be considered taking land "for *public* use."

II. The Decision in *Kelo v. City of New London*

In *Kelo v. City of New London* (2005), the U.S. Supreme Court greatly reduced the Fifth Amendment's protection for private property. It ruled that the city could take private homes to make way for private office buildings and other private development that the city believed would increase its tax revenues and create new jobs, even though, after the taking, the land would be privately owed and not open to the public. As the Court explained: "The city has carefully formulated an economic development plan that it believes will provide appreciable benefits to the community, including—but by no means limited to—new jobs and increased tax revenue." In particular, the Court concluded, the plaintiffs' private homes could be seized and demolished, and replaced by private "research and office space" that would "complement" an adjacent facility planned by Pfizer, Inc., the multinational pharmaceuticals company.

The Court specifically held that "promoting economic development" qualifies as a "public use" of property under the Fifth Amendment. As it concluded, "[p]romoting economic development is a traditional and long accepted function of government," and "the city's interest in the economic benefits to be derived from the development" on the land taken from the plaintiffs—by which the Court principally meant increased tax revenue from the expected new commercial use—had enough of a "public character" to satisfy the Amendment.

The Court added that it would not second-guess the city's determination that the re-development would, in fact, boost economic development and hence tax revenues. As Justice [Anthony M.] Kennedy acknowledged in concurrence, the Court would uphold a taking "as long as it is rationally related to a conceivable public purpose" Under this very low standard, it is hard to imagine any seizure of private property being unconstitutional under the "public use" requirement. As Justice O'Connor stated in dissent:

> Under the banner of economic development, all private property is now vulnerable to being taken and

transferred to another private owner, so long as it might be upgraded—i.e., given to an owner who will use it in a way that the legislature deems more beneficial.…[The Court] holds that the sovereign may take private property currently put to ordinary private use, and give it over for new, ordinary private use, so long as the new use is predicted to generate some secondary benefit for the public—such as increased tax revenue, more jobs, maybe even aesthetic pleasure. But nearly any lawful use of real private property can be said to generate some incidental benefits to the public. Thus, if predicted (or even guaranteed) positive side effects are enough to render transfer from one private party to another constitutional, then the words "for public use" do not realistically exclude *any* takings, and thus do not exert any constraint on the eminent domain power.)

III. The Basis of the Court's Decision

The *Kelo* Court did not pretend to base its conclusion upon the words and historical understanding of the Constitution. Instead, it effectively admitted that it was re-writing the key phrase in the Fifth Amendment to produce what it thought was a better outcome. According to the Court, modern needs required it to substitute the phrase "public purpose" for the Constitution's phrase "public use." This would allow the government to seize private land and transfer it to other private parties any time that such transfer would facilitate "economic development," even though neither the government nor the public would end up owning or using the land.

Indeed, in a move of Orwellian proportions, the Court specifically rejected "'use by the public' as the proper definition of public use." Instead, it declared that "the diverse and always evolving needs of society" required it to "embrace the broader and more natural interpretation of public use as 'public purpose.'" Only this re-definition allowed the Court to reach its conclusion that "economic development" in the sense of (supposedly) higher tax revenues satisfied the Fifth Amendment. It is at least plausible to say, as the Court did, that the New London development plan has a "public purpose," but no possible stretch of language would allow one to say that the city's plan allowed "public use" of the property.

The Court purported to be following prior precedent in reaching these conclusions. It is true that at least two prior decisions [*Hawaii Housing Authority v. Midkiff* (1984) and *Berman v. Parker* (1954)] had allowed a transfer of property from one private owner to another, without any guarantee of public use. These decisions were themselves in some tension with the plain language of the Constitution, and illustrate the danger of bending constitutional rules even for the best of purposes.

But as Justice O'Connor pointed out in her *Kelo* dissent (p. 2674–75), *Midkiff* and *Berman* only created a limited exception to the general rule of "public use." In both cases, prior to the taking, the property had been used in a way that was harmful to the public interest. *Kelo* abandoned any such limitation. No one argued that there was anything injurious about the plaintiffs' use of their property in *Kelo* (these are "well-maintained homes") [according to Justice O'Conner]. Instead, *Kelo* allows seizure whenever the government thinks some *better* use (not a non-injurious use) could be made of the property. As Justice O'Connor concluded, this effectively eliminates any constitutional limit on the eminent domain power.

IV. The Effect on Constitutional Law

The *Kelo* decision is an attack, not only upon private property rights, but upon the whole idea of constitutional rights. If a right written into the text of the Constitution can be eliminated by five members of the Supreme Court simply because they believe that "the diverse and always evolving needs of society" require it to give way, then we have no fixed rights, nor, for that matter, any fixed structure of government. Everything depends upon what the Court thinks most useful at any particular moment.

Such an approach is contrary to the basic function of a written Constitution. The reason a phrase such as "public use" is written into the Constitution is so that it—and not some other standard, such as "public purpose"—is the measure of our rights. This approach is also contrary to the basic function of a constitutional court. As Alexander Hamilton argued in *Federalist* 78, "A constitution is, in fact, and must be regarded by the judges as, a fundamental law"; thus he referred to "that inflexible and uniform adherence to the rights of the Constitution, and of individuals, which we perceive to be indispensable in the courts of justice." Just as courts exceed their authority by inventing new limits on government that do *not* exist in the written Constitution, they shirk their duty when they fail to enforce rights that *do* exist in the written Constitution.

V. How Congress May Restore Private Property Rights

Congress can remedy the Court's attack upon property rights in several ways. It cannot directly overrule the Court on a matter of constitutional law. In parallel circumstances, the Supreme Court held that Congress lacked power to overturn a constitutional holding by statute, even though Congress sincerely believed that the Court had failed to enforce individual rights guaranteed by the plain text of the Constitution. [The case was] *Boerne v. Flores* (1997) (invalidating part of the Religious Freedom Restoration Act, which sought to correct the Court's perceived misinterpretation of the First Amendment's Free Exercise Clause).

However, Congress has a number of constitutional options available. First, it can declare that, with respect to the exercise of eminent domain power by the U.S. government, the constitutional rule of "public use" remains in force. There is precedent for this approach: the Religious Freedom Restoration Act directed that federal laws would remain subject to the constitutional rule of the Free Exercise Clause, as Congress understood it, despite the Court's contrary holding. No one doubts that this part of the Act is constitutional, and remains in effect: Congress can always limit the scope of federal action.

Congress also has several options for limiting the scope of state and local government exercise of eminent domain power. Under current law, Congress may use its spending power to insist that no federal money be spent in any state or local project that takes private property for private use. If the limitation is strictly linked to state and local projects that themselves use federal money, the limitation would not be at all constitutionally problematic.... A more aggressive approach would ban any state or local entity that takes private property for private use from receiving any federal money for *any* redevelopment project (or, even more controversially, from receiving any federal money for any purpose). The less direct the link between the federal money and the state or local taking, the more constitutionally suspect the law would become.

Finally, under current law, Congress can use its commerce power to prohibit any project that takes private property for private use, if the project operates in or substantially affects interstate commerce. Because current law defines Congress' interstate commerce power quite broadly, this would likely reach most "economic development" projects such as the one proposed in New London....It is worth noting, though, that this broad reading of Congress' interstate commerce power (that is, that it reaches all economic activity) remains controversial in some circles, and it is possible that some (though probably not many) redevelopment project could be considered so localized as to be beyond Congress' power.

The Continuing Debate: Taking Property by Eminent Domain for Economic Development

What Is New

The Supreme Court's decision in *Kelo v. City of New London* caused a sensation, with most of the commentary in Congress, state legislatures, editorials, and elsewhere highly critical of the ruling. During the following year, 25 states have enacted legislation tightening the use of eminent domain. South Dakota passed the strictest standard, barring the use of eminent domain "for transfer to any private person, nongovernmental entity, or other public-private business entity." At the other end of the continuum, Kentucky made "public use" stricter but expanded the definition of "blight," making it both harder and easier to utilize eminent domain. A few states moved in the opposite direction. Delaware, for one, amended its law to bring it closer to the *Kelo* standard.

At the federal level, the House passed a bill by 376 to 38 withholding prohibiting the federal government from using eminent domain for economic development and denying federal development funds to states that allow private property to be taken in circumstances similar to those in *Kelo*. However, the Senate had not acted by late in the 109th Congress, and it appeared that the house bill would die with adjournment. As for Susette Kelo, she finally came to terms with New London in a deal in which the city bought the land and will move her pink cottage to another location in town by June 2007.

Where to Find More

For an overview of eminent domain, read Richard Epstein, *Takings: Private Property and the Power of Eminent Domai*n (Harvard University Press, 1989). You can read the Supreme Court's decision in *Kelo v. New London* and the concurring and dissenting opinions on the Web site of Cornell University Law School at www.law.cornell.edu/supct/html/04-108.ZO.html. Commentary on eminent domain from the Institute for Justice, an organization that supported Susette Kelo, is available at www.ij.org/. For an opposing view, visit the site of the National League of Cities at www.nlc.org.

What More to Do

It is easy to take the side of the "little guy" battling "bid, bad" government, but consider this case in the abstract. A struggling small city tries to improve itself and benefit the vast majority of its residents through an ambitious redevelopment project that will bring jobs and new municipal revenue. It his blocked, however, by a handful of intransient people who won't sell their property for a fair price. The project is lost, and the city continues to struggle to provide decent municipal service to its residents, a large part of whom, as in most cities, are poor. Are the holdout individualistic heroes or communitarian hardheads?

BUDGETARY POLICY

A LINE-ITEM VETO FOR THE PRESIDENT:
Prudent Way to Restrain Spending *or* Unwise Grant of Power?

PRUDENT WAY TO RESTRAIN SPENDING

ADVOCATE: Paul Ryan, U.S. Representative (R-WI)

SOURCE: Testimony during hearings on "The Constitution and the Line-Item Veto," U.S. House of Representatives, Committee on the Judiciary, Subcommittee on the Constitution, April 27, 2006

UNWISE GRANT OF POWER

ADVOCATE: Cristina Martin Firvida, Senior Counsel, National Women's Law Center

SOURCE: Testimony during hearings on "The Constitution and the Line Item Veto," U.S. House of Representatives, Judiciary Committee, Subcommittee on the Constitution, April 27, 2006

"Take it or leave it" is a familiar phrase most of us have used, and it is also implicitly the reality of every bill passed by Congress and sent to the president. Once a bill arrives in the Oval Office, the president has three options: (1) Sign it into law. (2) Veto the bill by returning it to Congress. In this case it requires a two-thirds vote in both houses to override the veto and to make the measure law. (3) Do nothing, figuratively put the measure in his pocket, in which case there are two possible outcomes. If Congress has adjourned, then the bill dies after 10 days by what is called a pocket veto. If, however, Congress remains in session, then after 10 days the bill becomes law in what might be called a pocket passage. What presidents cannot do is "line out" specific provisions of a measure presented to them. They must accept or reject it as a whole.

The president's ability to reject legislation gives him considerable influence in the legislative process. By threatening to veto an act, presidents gain leverage to have it shaped at least in part according to their wishes. But Congress also has it ways and means of avoiding vetoes. One is to build provisions that a president might dislike into important legislation that the president would be reluctant to veto. If, for instance, a member manages to get a provision to build a veterans hospital slipped into the Defense Department budget, the president can either accept a hospital he had not wanted or veto the entire defense appropriations act. Sometimes, especially in the Senate, such unwanted provisions are attached to bills that are not related. These are called riders and would apply to a veterans hospital inserted into a bill about food stamps.

From the very beginnings of the Republic, presidents have been frustrated with their take-it-or-leave-it position. "From the nature of the Constitution," George Washington grumbled, "I must approve all the parts of a bill, or reject it in toto." And as far back as Ulysses S. Grant, presidents of both parties have sought the authority to line item veto. In a literal sense the term line item veto could apply to any provision of any legislation, but in practice it has come to apply mostly to spending and taxation measures. Advocates of a line item veto argue it is particularly important to combat "pork barrel" provisions, or just "pork, a designation that stems from the pre-Civil War practice of providing barrels of salt pork to be divided among slaves. These are expenditures like the hypothetical veterans hospital above, which benefit the district of a member of Congress and which are added on to spending bills because of a member's power, to secure a member's vote, or to help a member get reelected.

The pressure to give the president a line item veto has increased in recent years, and is very much related to budget deficits that the federal government has had during all but three years since 1970. This line item veto drive reached its high point when in 1996 the Republican-dominated Congress and Democratic President Bill Clinton found it was something they could agree on. From the Republicans' perspective, the Line Item Veto Act seemed to be a way to restrain spending. From the president's point of view, it added to his powers. The act permitted the president to line out specific spending provisions and those taxing provisions that affected fewer than 100 taxpayers before signing the legislation. Any lined out provision had to be sent back to Congress, which could once again approve the item by a majority in each house. In this case, the re-approved provisions went back to the president, who could sign or reject them, subject to the normal override procedures.

During the first two years after the Line Item Veto act became law, President Clinton lined out very few items, a record that can be reviewed in the section Where To Find More that follows. Then, however, the act was ruled unconstitutional by a 6 to 3 vote in the Supreme Court case of *Clinton v. City of New York* (1998). The court found that eliminating some items created a law different from the one passed by Congress. In the majority opinion, Justice John Paul Stevens wrote, "If the Line Item Veto Act were valid, it would authorize the President to create a different law—one whose text was not voted on by either House of Congress or presented to the President for signature. [Such a law] may or may not be desirable, but it is surely not [valid] pursuant to the procedures designed by the Framers of...of the Constitution." The Court's decision led to proposals in Congress to amend the Constitution to permit a line item veto and others to try to craft a line-item veto that would pass the Court's scrutiny. It was during those hearings on such a proposal that the two advocates in this debate gave testimony.

POINTS TO PONDER

➢ Notice that like many debates in this volume, the controversy over the line item veto has ramifications beyond the immediate issue. In this case, giving the new authority to the president would enhance the power of the presidency relative to Congress.

➢ Consider whether it would be better for Congress to control its own pork barrel spending rather than give a new grant of power to the president.

➢ Think about whether the budget does or should reflect the interests of the whole versus the disaggregated interests of the many. Since every budget inherently collect revenue and distributes benefits, what is the line between what is laudable and what is pork?

A Line-Item Veto for the President: Prudent Way to Restrain Spending

PAUL RYAN

[I am here] to testify...on H.R. 4890, the Legislative Line-Item Veto Act of 2006. This legislation would help the President and Congress work together to reduce our budget deficit by providing the President with the authority to single out wasteful spending items and narrow special-interest tax breaks included in legislation that he signs into law and send these specific items back to Congress for a timely vote. Unlike the line-item veto authority provided to President [Bill] Clinton in 1996, H.R. 4890 is constitutional because it requires an up-or-down vote in both chambers of Congress under an expedited process in order to effectuate the President's proposed rescissions. It is important that Congress act now to give the President this tool to bring greater transparency, accountability and a dose of common sense to the federal budget process.

THE PROBLEM

The amount of pork-barrel spending included in the federal budget continues to increase every year. According to Citizens Against Government Waste (CAGW), the federal government spent $29 billion on 9,963 pork-barrel projects in Fiscal Year 2006 (FY 2006), an increase of 6.3% from 2005, and an increase of over 900% since 1991. [Pork barrel spending refers to budget allocations favored by one or another member of Congress but are of questionable national concern.] Overall, the federal government has spent $241 billion on pork-barrel projects between 1991 and 2005, an amount greater than two-thirds of our entire deficit in FY 2005. This includes irresponsible spending on items such as the $50 million Rain Forest Museum in Iowa; $13.5 million to pay for a program that helped finance the World Toilet Summit; and $1 million for the Waterfree Urinal Conservation Initiative.

Many of these pork-barrel spending projects are quietly inserted into the conference reports of appropriations bills where Congress is unable to eliminate them using the amendment process. In fact, the only time that Congress actually votes on these items is during an up-or-down vote on the entire conference report, which includes spending for many essential government programs in addition to the pork-barrel earmarks. In this situation, it is very difficult for any member to vote against an appropriations bill that, as an overall package, may be quite meritorious, despite the inclusion of wasteful spending items.

Unfortunately, the current tools at the President's disposal do not enable him to easily combat these wasteful spending items either. Even if the President identifies numerous pork-barrel projects in an appropriations bill, he is unlikely to use his veto power because it must be applied to the bill as a whole and cannot be used to target individual items. This places the President in the same dilemma as members of Congress. Does he veto an entire spending bill because of a few items of pork when this action may jeopardize funding for our troops, for our homeland security or for the education of our children?

The President's ability to propose the rescission of wasteful spending items under the Impoundment Control Act of 1974 has been equally ineffective at eliminating wasteful spending items. The problem with the current authority is that it does not include any mechanism to guarantee congressional consideration of a rescission request and many Presidential rescissions are ignored by the Congress. In fact, during the 1980's, Congress routinely ignored President Reagan's rescission requests, failing to act on over $25 billion in requests that were made by the administration. The historic ineffectiveness of this tool has deterred Presidents from using it with any regularity.

SUMMARY OF H.R. 4890, THE LEGISLATIVE LINE-ITEM VETO ACT OF 2006

I introduced H.R. 4890, the Legislative Line-Item Veto Act of 2006, on March 7, 2006. This legislation, which currently has the support of 101 bipartisan cosponsors in the House, is based on the administration's proposal to provide line-item veto authority to the President and is the product of discussions that I and my congressional colleagues have had with the White House since the President announced his intent to seek line-item veto authority in the State of the Union Address on January 31, 2006.

The Legislative Line-Item Veto Act is very similar to an expedited rescissions amendment that I offered during the consideration of H.R. 4663 on June 24, 2004, with my former colleague Representative Charlie Stenholm, a Democrat from Texas. Like H.R. 4890, this amendment would also have allowed the President to propose the elimination of wasteful spending items subject to congressional approval under an expedited process. Although this amendment failed to pass the House, it attracted the support of 174 members of Congress, including 45 Democrats. A similar provision is also included in Section 311 of the Family Budget Protection Act, legislation that I introduced along with Congressman Jeb Hensarling of Texas [R], Congressman Chris Chocola of Indiana [R], and former Congressman Christopher Cox of California [R] during 2004 and again in 2005.

If passed, H.R. 4890 would give the President the ability to put on hold wasteful discretionary spending, wasteful new mandatory spending, or new special-interest tax breaks (those that affect less than 100 beneficiaries) after signing a bill into law. The President could then ask Congress to rescind these specific items. The requirement that both the House and Senate approve all proposed rescissions means that Congress will continue to control the power of the purse and will have the final word when it comes to spending matters. However, unlike the current rescission authority vested in the President under the Impoundment Control Act of 1974, the bill also includes a mechanism that would virtually guarantee congressional action in an expedited time frame.

Using the Legislative Line-Item Veto, the President and Congress will be able to work together to combat wasteful spending and add transparency and accountability to the budget process. This tool will shed light on the earmarking process and allow Congress to vote up or down on the merits of specific projects added to legislation or to conference reports. Not only will this allow the President and Congress to eliminate wasteful pork-barrel projects, but it will also act as a strong deterrent to the addition of questionable projects in the first place. On the other hand, members who make legitimate appropriations requests should have no problem defending them in front of their colleagues if they are targeted by the President. With H.R. 4890, we can help protect the American taxpayer from being forced to finance wasteful pork-barrel spending and ensure that taxpayer dollars are only directed toward projects of the highest merit.

The process under H.R. 4890 would begin with the President identifying an item of wasteful spending or a special-interest tax break in legislation that is being signed into law. The President would then submit a special message to Congress, asking for Congress to rescind this wasteful item or items. House and Senate leadership would have the opportunity to introduce the President's rescission requests within two days following receipt of the President's message. After that time period, any member of Congress would be able to introduce the President's rescission proposal, virtually guaranteeing congressional action. Once the bill is introduced, it would be referred to the appropriate committee, which would then have five days to report the bill without substantive revision. If the committee fails to act within that time period, the bill would be automatically discharged to the floor. The bill would have to be voted on by the full House and Senate within 10 legislative days of its introduction, with a simple majority required for passage.

Since introducing H.R. 4890, I have received substantial feedback from interested Members of Congress on ways to improve the legislation to ensure that it best meets its intent of controlling federal spending while keeping the power of the purse squarely in the legislative branch. Among the changes that I think may improve the legislation are the following: limiting the time period available to the President to make a rescission request after signing a bill into law; limiting the number of rescission requests that can be made for each piece of legislation signed into law; allowing for the bundling of rescission requests; explicitly prohibiting duplicative requests; and tightening the language that allows the administration to defer spending while a rescission request is being considered by Congress. These changes will strengthen the bill and better ensure that the legislative branch retains all of the powers delegated to it by our founding fathers. I am committed to continuing to work with my colleagues in Congress and the administration throughout the legislative process to make sure that H.R. 4890 is narrowly drafted in order to best achieve its goals.

CONSTITUTIONAL ISSUES

H.R. 4890 passes constitutional muster because it requires both the House and Senate to pass rescission legislation and send it to the President for his signature before the rescissions become law. In *Clinton v. City of New York* [1998], the U.S. Supreme Court held that the line-item veto authority provided to President Clinton in 1996 violated the Presentment Clause of the U.S. Constitution (Article I, Section 7, Clause 2), which requires that "every bill which shall have passed the House of Representatives and the Senate, shall, before it become a Law, be presented to the President of the United States." The problem with this version of the line-item veto was that the President's requested rescissions would become law by default if either the House or Senate failed to enact a motion of disapproval to stop them from taking effect. The lower court in *Clinton v. City of New York* also held that this version of the line-item veto upset the balance of power between the executive and legislative branches. Unlike the 1996 line-item veto legislation, H.R. 4890 leaves Congress in the middle of the process where it belongs and follows the procedure and balance of power outlined in our Constitution.

H.R. 4890 also withstands constitutional scrutiny under the U.S. Supreme

Court's holding in *I.N.S. v. Chadha* [1983]. In *I.N.S. v. Chadha*, the Supreme Court invalidated part of the Immigration and Nationality Act that allowed a single house of Congress to override immigration decisions made by the Attorney General. The Legislative Line-Item Veto Act of 2006 is consistent with this holding because the President's authority to defer funds would not explicitly be terminated by the disapproval of a proposed rescission by one of the houses of Congress.

I agree with the Supreme Court's rulings in *Clinton v. City of New York* and *I.N.S. v. Chadha*. It is extremely important that Congress does not cede its law-making power to the President. I believe that this violates the Separation of Powers in addition to the Presentment Clause. In contrast, H.R. 4890 would withstand constitutional scrutiny because it requires both houses of Congress to act on any rescission request and for this legislation to be sent back to the President for his signature.

CONCLUSION

In 2006, the federal government will once again rack up an annual budget deficit of over $300 billion, and our debt is expected to surpass $9 trillion. Meanwhile, the retirement of the baby boom generation looms on the horizon, threatening to severely exacerbate this problem. Given these dire circumstances, it is essential that we act now to give the President all of the necessary tools to help us get our fiscal house in order. By providing the President with the scalpel he needs to pinpoint and propose the elimination of wasteful spending, H.R. 4890 takes an important first step toward achieving this goal.

A Line-Item Veto for the President: Unwise Grant of Power

Cristina Martin Firvida

[I am here] to testify on behalf of the National Women's Law Center on H.R. 4890, the Legislative Line Item Veto Act of 2006. The bill would dramatically expand the powers of the President in relation to Congress, presenting serious policy and constitutional questions while doing little, if anything, to control growing deficits.

The bill has sometimes been described as a means of eliminating unnecessary earmarks, but its scope is far broader. H.R. 4890 would give the President unprecedented power to suspend, and effectively cancel, provisions of law enacted by Congress, even after Congress has rejected the President's rescission proposal. The expanded rescission power would apply not only to appropriations, currently subject to a more limited rescission authority, but also to direct spending for programs upon which millions of Americans rely, and, on its face, some targeted tax benefits. In addition, the bill would enable the President to control the legislative agenda of Congress, because the President would have the ability to control the timing and number of rescission bills sent to Congress, and the expedited rescission process would require that Congress respond. These sweeping new provisions raise significant policy issues and effectively confer upon the President the power to amend or repeal duly enacted legislation, in violation of the separation of powers doctrine and the presentment and bicameralism clauses of Article I, Section 7 of the Constitution of the United States.

In addition, empirical evidence suggests that the proposed Legislative Line Item Veto Act would not result in substantial savings that would reduce our nation's record deficits. Indeed, the potential for Congress to agree to fund the President's priorities in exchange for the President's promise not to exercise the veto suggests that spending may increase as a result of this legislation.

H.R. 4890 GRANTS THE PRESIDENT SWEEPING POWERS TO SUSPEND—AND EFFECTIVELY CANCEL—COVERED SPENDING AND TAX PROVISIONS

This bill would give the President the unilateral power to suspend, and in some cases, effectively cancel, spending and tax provisions enacted by Congress. This Presidential power to essentially amend or repeal duly enacted legislation is bad public policy and presents the clearest constitutional violation in H.R. 4890.

H.R. 4890 would give the President sweeping new authority to suspend covered spending and tax provisions even after Congress had rejected the proposed rescission. The bill would allow the President to suspend funding for a period of 180 days (and possibly more) after sending a special message to Congress seeking legislative approval of the rescission, even if Congress explicitly rejects it. This is a dramatic departure from current rescission authority. Current law gives the President authority to withhold appropriated funds for up to 45 session days while Congress considers a proposed rescission, but explicitly requires that the President's suspension of funding immediately end if one legislative house rejects the President's rescission request (or at the end of the 45-day period if no action is taken) and that budget authority be made available for obligation immediately. The Line Item Veto Act of 1996 likewise required the President to immediately reinstate canceled funding if Congress adopted a joint resolution of disapproval. Giving the President the power to ignore the expressed will of Congress as H.R. 4890 would do is unprecedented.

In addition, H.R. 4890 grants the President extremely broad discretion to determine when, in what fashion, and how often to rescind covered provisions of law. While H.R. 4890 requires Congress to act upon a rescission request sent by the President within 13 session days, the bill permits the President to send his proposed rescissions to Congress up to one year after enacting a spending or tax bill. In addition, the bill allows the President to send rescissions from one spending or tax law in numerous rescission bills to Congress, or to send rescissions from several spending or tax laws in one rescission bill. Finally, in contrast to current law, the bill does not appear to prohibit the President from resubmitting the rejected rescission in a different rescission request, and continuing to suspend the operation of the provision.

The powers granted to the President under H.R. 4890, taken together, would effectively grant the President the ability not merely to delay, but to cancel provisions of law unilaterally. For example, the President could submit a package of rescissions to Congress in the spring and withhold funding until the end of the fiscal year, when spending authority would cease for many items, terminating the program even if Congress explicitly rejected the rescission. As a result of the broad new powers granted to the President in H.R. 4890, federal agencies, state and local governments, and individuals who administer or receive federal funding through a variety of programs and benefits, would be unable to rely on funding approved by Congress.

H.R. 4890 WOULD ALLOW THE PRESIDENT TO RESCIND DIRECT SPENDING AS WELL AS APPROPRIATIONS, BUT DO LITTLE TO CONTROL SPECIAL INTEREST TAX BREAKS

The breadth of the cancellation power granted to the President under H.R. 4890 is matched by the breadth of the spending items to which it can apply, compounding the constitutional and policy concerns raised by the new power. Despite the fact that H.R. 4890 has been justified as a mechanism for controlling earmarks and tax benefits for powerful special interests, the bill also would apply to broad-based items of direct spending, and render low-income recipients of mandatory spending programs especially vulnerable to program cuts.

The expanded rescission powers authorized by H.R. 4890 would apply not only to appropriations, to which more limited rescission authority currently applies, but also to new items of mandatory spending, allowing the President to override individual entitlements enacted into law. The expansion of the President's rescission authority to apply to direct spending items is especially troubling because the broad definition of "direct spending" in the bill may be claimed to allow the cancellation of existing entitlement spending in reauthorizations, rather than only new spending. For example, if H.R. 4890 were to be enacted, it is possible that a significant number of provisions in the reauthorizations next year of the State Children's Health Insurance Program and the Farm Bill (which authorizes Food Stamps) could be subject to rescission even if those provisions were not new and did not add to the costs of the legislation.

Conversely, the definition of targeted tax benefit in the bill is so narrowly constructed as to virtually guarantee that no carefully drafted tax benefit will be subject to the new cancellation power. The definition used in the bill would apply to tax provisions that benefit 100 or fewer beneficiaries, except that it would not apply if the provision treats all persons engaged in the same industry or activity or owning the same type of property similarly. The Joint Committee on Taxation [of Congress] analyzed this definition (which was included as part of the Line Item Veto Act of 1996), and concluded that the exceptions were vague and poorly defined. As a result, this creates the potential to altogether exempt tax breaks from the line item veto. For example, had the Legislative Line Item Veto Act of 2006 been in effect when the 2004 corporate tax bill was passed, the President might have been powerless to cancel special interest tax breaks for ceiling fan importers and tackle-box manufacturers, among others, which were criticized by many observers as pork, and which presumably would be the type of targeted tax benefit H.R. 4890 is supposed to eliminate.

While some justify limiting the definition of "targeted tax benefits" to ensure that only special interest tax breaks and not broad-based tax policies are subject to cancellation, no similar limitation exists to ensure that broad-based direct spending policies are also not subject to cancellation. In fact, the only broad-based tax policies that may be subject to the Legislative Line Item Veto are those that include items of direct spending. The two most prominent tax credits that trigger direct spending are the Earned Income Credit and the Additional Child Tax Credit. Both of these credits assist low-income families. Should H.R. 4890 be adopted, the President may be authorized to cancel portions of these credits should Congress, for example, vote to extend improvements to the credits passed in 2001 and 2003. There is no justification for giving the President the authority to suspend tax provisions that help millions of poor children but not tax provisions that benefit a few thousand multi-millionaires.

H.R. 4890 ALLOWS THE PRESIDENT TO CONTROL THE CONGRESSIONAL AGENDA

The process for Congress to respond to the President's proposed rescissions set forth by H.R. 4890 creates the potential for the President to exercise considerable control over the congressional schedule and agenda, above and beyond budget and spending bills. This ability to reorder congressional legislative priorities in and of itself will result in a bad policy outcome, and when combined with the broad authority to cancel spending granted by H.R. 4890, exacerbates the constitutional breach contained in this proposal.

Under current law, if Congress fails to approve the President's rescission proposal within 45 session days, including by inaction, spending authority must be restored. Given that Congress has the power of the purse under our constitutional structure of separation of powers, it is appropriate to leave to Congress the discretion to act on the President's suggested rescissions, to act instead on its own package of rescissions, or to do nothing at all. However, H.R. 4890 would strip Congress of this discretion and would amend House and Senate rules to provide for fast-track consideration of presidential rescission messages.

Under the new fast-track rules in H.R. 4890, a bill encompassing the President's rescission package must be introduced by congressional leadership no later than two session days after the President sends a special message to Congress proposing the rescissions. If no bill is introduced by the second session day, any member may introduce the bill thereafter. Once the rescission bill is introduced, the appropriate committees are required to approve the bill without any change no later than the fifth session day, or, if the appropriate committees fail to do so by that day, the bill is automatically discharged from the committees. Both the House and Senate must have an up or down vote on the rescission bill, without amendment, by the end of the tenth session day after introduction of the bill. In summary, if the procedures are adhered to and are not waived by rule or otherwise ignored, Congress would be compelled to complete action on the President's rescissions within 13 session days of the President's sending the proposal to Congress.

In combination with the broad discretionary authority granted to the President to send rescission messages at any time and in any manner that the President sees fit, these fast-track procedures are an invitation to allow the President to control the entire Congressional legislative agenda. For example, a President could exercise the rescission authority as a parliamentary tool to tie up the Congressional schedule indefinitely or until the President receives the concessions he or she seeks. The President could send over a series of bills that rescind spending items from bills that were passed and signed at different times, bundling the rescission of spending items that are popular in Congress with those that are unpopular with the public, in order to compel Congress to turn away from other work and dispose of the rescissions. This would enable the President to control the timing of votes in Congress on other pending legislation. If deployed during the second half of a second session of any given Congress, the tactic could run out the clock on other pending legislation. It is important to note that H.R. 4890 could affect consideration of all pending legislation in this way, not just legislation related to spending items.

THE EXPANSIVE POWERS GRANTED TO THE PRESIDENT BY H.R. 4890 RAISE SERIOUS CONSTITUTIONAL PROBLEMS

The extraordinary new powers that H.R. 4890 would confer upon the President raise serious constitutional problems under the separation of powers doctrine, as well as the presentment and bicameralism requirements of Article 1, section 7 of the Constitution of the United States.

The separation of powers is a fundamental feature of our Constitution and our system of government. It was designed to and does play a crucial role in safeguarding the liberties and freedoms that the Constitution created and which the founding fathers endeavored to protect. As Justice [Anthony M.] Kennedy so succinctly put it in his concurrence in *Clinton v. City of New York* [1998]:

> Liberty is always at stake when one or more of the branches seek to transgress the separation of powers. Separation of powers was designed to implement a fundamental insight: Concentration of power in the hands of a single branch is a threat to liberty. The Federalist states the axiom in these explicit terms: "The accumulation of all powers, legislative, executive, and judiciary, in the same hands...may justly be pronounced the very definition of tyranny."

The Supreme Court has historically taken a strict approach to analyzing potential violations of the separation of powers doctrine. A long line of cases demonstrates that the Court is extremely skeptical of any encroachment on the power of each branch and consequently will apply a strict formal analysis frequently resulting in the invalidation of the Congressional act. As the court stated in *Mistretta v. United States* [1989]:

> Accordingly, we have not hesitated to strike down provisions of law that either accrete to a single Branch powers more appropriately diffused among separate Branches or that undermine the authority and independence of one or another coordinate Branch. For example, just as the Framers recognized the particular danger of the Legislative Branch's accreting to itself judicial or executive power, so too have we invalidated attempts by Congress to exercise the responsibilities of other Branches or to reassign powers vested by the Constitution in either the Judicial Branch or Executive Branch.

In *Clinton v. City of New York*, the Court emphasized that while some lawmaking responsibilities are assigned to the President in Articles I and II of the Constitution, "there is no provision in the Constitution that authorizes the President to enact, to amend, or to repeal statutes." In addition, the lack of a constitutional provision assigning the President such a role was interpreted to be the equivalent of an express prohibition. The Court ruled in Clinton that allowing the President to cancel spending unilaterally amounted to an impermissible exercise of the power to amend or repeal statutes, a power that is explicitly reserved for the Congress under the Constitution.

Like the power to cancel items of spending struck down by the Court in Clinton, the powers granted to the President by H.R. 4890 constitute an amendment or repeal of a statute by the President. Under H.R. 4890, the President can suspend the operation of provisions of law for 180 days even if Congress rejects the proposed rescission. H.R. 4890 gives the President the power to decide when to submit a rescission request, and, depending when the rescission is submitted, the "suspension" could result in the permanent elimination of spending authority. H.R. 4890 also would allow the President to resubmit proposed rescissions that Congress had previously rejected, which likewise could effectively terminate spending authority. Because the broad powers granted to the President by H.R. 4890 could end, as a practical matter, programs funded by discretionary spending, direct spending programs, or tax benefits previously approved by Congress, "[i]n both legal and practical effect, the President [would have] amended...Acts of Congress by repealing a portion of each." As the Congressional Research Service concluded, these provisions may reach "far enough to be considered an effective grant of authority to cancel provisions of law...," and that was proscribed by the Supreme Court in *Clinton v. City of New York*.

In addition, because the cancellation authority the President is granted by H.R. 4890 is legislative in nature, it also violates the provisions of Article I, Section 7 of the Constitution of the United States, namely, the presentment and bicameralism clauses. These clauses provide that no law can take effect without the approval of both Houses of Congress and that all legislation must be presented to the President before becoming law. As *INS v. Chadha* [1983] makes clear, the amendment and repeal of statutes, no less than their enactment, must conform with Article I. Pursuant to H.R. 4890, the President would have the ability to create a different law from one duly enacted by Congress and signed by the President, temporarily and possibly permanently, without Congressional approval and despite Congressional disapproval.

The fact that Congress is considering granting the President such extraordinary power does not resolve the constitutional issues. The Constitution does not authorize Congress to cede to the executive that power which is properly its own. As Justice Kennedy stated in his concurrence in Clinton:

> That a congressional cession of power is voluntary does not make it innocuous. The Constitution is a compact enduring for more than our time, and one Congress cannot yield up its own powers, much less those of other Congresses to follow. ...Abdication of responsibility is not part of the constitutional design.

H.R. 4890 IS UNLIKELY TO REDUCE AND COULD EVEN INCREASE SPENDING

The experience with line item vetoes at the federal and state level does not suggest that enacting H.R. 4890 will significantly reduce the deficit. Moreover, by significantly increasing the President's ability to negotiate for the Administration's own budget priorities, the line item veto may actually increase spending. While no amount of savings or deficit reduction could justify a violation of the Constitution, the very poor track record of the line item veto as a tool to control spending should alone be grounds to reject the proposal.

The President's current rescission authority has not produced significant savings over time. In fact, the current administration (in contrast to other administrations) has never used current rescission authority (nor the constitutional veto power) to curtail spending. Nonetheless, frustration with current rescission authority has suggested to some that a line item veto is needed to give the President the power to control spending.

However, the evidence on the effect of a more aggressive—and unconstitutional—rescission authority, the Line Item Veto Act of 1996, shows minimal impact on budget savings. According to the Congressional Research Service, the implementation of the 1996 Act produced modest savings. In one year, the President successfully vetoed $355 million in spending out of a $1.7 trillion budget. The total savings produced by President Clinton's line item vetoes amounted to less than $600 million over five years. The savings would have been greater had Congress approved all of the President's request to cancel funding—but even if each and every cancellation had been accepted, the amount would still have come to well under $1 billion over five years.

The picture from the states also provides little evidence that the line item veto is an effective means of controlling spending. Currently, 43 states have line item veto authority for their governors. State budget practices are fundamentally different from federal budgeting practices, in part because the constitutions of most states provide very explicit details on how budgets are to be enacted, and most give the executive branch of government a much stronger role in budgeting than is constitutionally permissible at the federal level. However, even governors with significant line item veto power are unable to secure significant savings through it. Douglas Holtz-Eakin, former director of the Congressional Budget Office [CBO], in a survey of evidence from the states concluded "that long run budgetary behavior is not significantly affected by the power of an item veto." In testimony last month before the House Rules Committee, the CBO renewed the observation that in some states the line item veto has not decreased spending, as the result of governors and legislatures negotiating to include a governor's spending priorities in a state's budget in exchange for a promise that the governor will not exercise line item veto authority. The CBO expressed concern that a similar dynamic at the federal level would result in higher spending.

Indeed, the concerns expressed by the CBO have been echoed and expanded upon by other observers. George Will, in an insightful column examining the line item veto, stated that, "knowing the president can veto line items, legislators might feel even freer to pack them into legislation, thereby earning constituents' gratitude for at least trying to deliver." He went on to describe how the President could buy the support of members of Congress on his legislative priorities in exchange for a promise that he would not veto the spending priorities of the members. The Congressional Research Service came to a similar conclusion in a 2005 report. Warning that savings would be very limited under a line item veto, the Congressional Research Service went on to state, "Under some circumstances, the availability of an item of veto could increase spending. The Administration might agree to withhold the use of an item veto for a particular program if Members of Congress agreed to support a spending program initiated by the President." The concern that the Legislative Line Item Veto will not only fail to decrease spending but may exacerbate the record deficits that we face is one that must be taken seriously.

CONCLUSION

The separation of powers is fundamental to our Constitution and system of government. Our Constitution does not authorize the President to enact, amend, or repeal statutes. Granting the President that authority—as H.R. 4890 would effectively do—would be unwise as well as unconstitutional.

THE CONTINUING DEBATE: A Line-Item Veto for the President

What Is New

The bill under discussion in this debate, H.R. 4890 passed the House of Representatives by a vote of 247 to 172. Almost all those voting aye were Republicans; almost all those voting nay were Democrats. A similar bill sponsored by majority leader Bill Frist (R-TN) was pending in the Senate, but it was not clear in September 2006 whether the press of business in an election year would leave enough time for the Senate to consider the bill. In the mean time, the pork barrel kept rolling along in Congress. According the Citizens Against Government Waste, Congress appropriate $29 billion for almost 10,000 pork barrel projects in Fiscal Year 2006. Some of the alleged pork include, $1 million to develop alternative salmon products, $750,000 for multiflora rose control research, $234,000 to support the National Wild Turkey Federation, $500,000 for the Arctic Winter Games in Alaska, $250,000 for a Mojave Desert bird study, 150,000 for the Bulgarian-Macedonian National Education and Cultural Center in Pittsburgh, $100,000 for the Richard Steele Boxing Club in Henderson, Nevada, and $5,880,000 to upgrade the Zora and Main Street intersection in Joplin, Missouri.

Where to Find More

A group favoring a line-item veto is the Citizens Against Government Waste at www.cagw.org/. Among other things, you will find a hyperlink to the annual *Pig Book* detailing what the group considers pork barrel legislation. How the Line-Item Veto Act of 1996 was used before it was ruled unconstitutional is at the National Archives and Records Administration, "History of Line Item Veto Notices," at www.access.gpo.gov/nara/nara004.html. The site also links to a copy of the legislation. Additional information can be found in a Congressional Research Service issue brief for Congress, "Item Veto and Expanded Impoundment Proposals," September 15, 2000 at: www.senate.gov/~budget/democratic/crsbackground/itemveto.pdf. The National Conference of State Legislatures reviews the use of line item veto authority in the states in, "Gubernatorial Veto Authority with Respect to Major Budget Bill(s)" at www.ncsl.org/programs/fiscal/lbptabls/lbpc6t3.htm.

What More to Do

Pork exists in the eye of the beholder. What to some may seem like outrageously wasteful spending may seem to others to be a prudent allocation of budget dollars. One way to evaluate this is to go the Web site of Citizens Against Government Waste and to the last annual *Pig Book*, which lists the spending that group considers pork barrel appropriations. Think about the items. Do you agree all are wasteful? You can even divide the class up. One person or a team could be the "pork prosecutors" advocating rejection of all these spending items. Others in the class could be senators from the states receiving the alleged pork. They would defend the appropriations for their state. The rest of the class could be the collective president, assuming you have a line-item veto and lining out or leaving in each item presented by the pork prosecutors and defended by the indignant senators.

DEBATE 17

CRIMINAL JUSTICE POLICY

THE DEATH PENALTY: Fatally Flawed *or* Defensible?

FATALLY FLAWED

Advocate: Stephen B. Bright, Director, Southern Center for Human Rights, Atlanta, Georgia; Visiting Lecturer in Law, Harvard and Yale Law Schools

Source: Testimony during hearings on "An Examination of the Death Penalty in the United States" before the U.S. Senate, Committee on the Judiciary, Subcommittee on the Constitution, February 1, 2006

DEFENSIBLE

Advocate: John McAdams, Professor of Political Science, Marquette University

Source: Testimony during hearings on "An Examination of the Death Penalty in the United States" before the U.S. Senate, Committee on the Judiciary, Subcommittee on the Constitution, February 1, 2006

Murder and capital punishment share four elements. They are: (1) a planned act (2) to kill (3) a specific person who (4) is not immediately attacking anyone. Should then murder and capital punishment be judged just or unjust by the same standard?

The first question is whether killing is ever justified. The doctrine of most religions contain some variation of the commandment, "Thou shalt not kill." For moral absolutists and pacifists, this prohibition is unbendable. They would not kill another person under any circumstances. Most people, however, are moral relativists who evaluate good and evil within a context. They do not condemn as immoral killing in such circumstances as self-defense and military combat.

What about premeditated acts by individuals? Most societies condemn these as murder even if the other person has harmed you. To see this, assume that a murderer has killed a member of your family. You witnessed it and thus are sure who is guilty. If you track down the murderer and execute him or her, by law now you are also a murderer. Yet 67% of Americans favor capital punishment, which is the state carrying out roughly the same act.

Arguably the difference is the willingness of most people to apply different moral standards to individuals acting privately and society acting through its government. This distinction is an ancient one. For example, God may have commanded "Thou shalt not kill" for individuals (Exodus 20:13), but in the very next chapter God details "ordinances" to Moses, including, "Whosoever strikes a man so that he dies shall be put to death" (Exodus 21:12). The point here is not whether you want to accept the words that Exodus attributes to a deity. After all, just two verses later, God also decrees death to "whoever curses his father or his mother." This would leave few teenagers alive today. Instead, the issue to wrestle with is whether and why it is just or unjust for a government, but not an individual, to commit an act with the four elements noted in the first paragraph. For those who see no moral distinction between actions by individuals and a society, capital punishment is wrong no matter how heinous the crime is, how fair the legal system is, or what the claimed benefits of executing criminals are.

There are others, though, who do not argue that capital punishment is inherently immoral. Instead they make a pragmatic case. They begin with the reasonable proposition that executing someone is a drastic step, then argue that there is no evidence of positive effect that would warrant such an extreme act. To think about this point, you have to first decide what it is you want capital punishment to accomplish. One possibility is to deter others from committing similar crimes. The other possibility is punishment as a way of expressing the society's outrage at the act. A great deal of the debate at his level is about whether capital punishment is a deterrent. It is beyond the limited space here to take up that debate, but to a degree it misses the point of why most Americans who favor capital punishment do so. When asked in one poll why they support it, 70% replied it is "a fitting punishment for convicted murders, while only 25% thought, "the death penalty deters crime," and 4% were unsure.

Yet another line of attack on capital punishment is the argument that the system is flawed. Some contend that mistakes get made, and innocent people are sometimes convicted and executed. This view is well represented by Stephen B. Bright in the first reading and disputed by John McAdams in the second reading.

Then there is the argument that, as conducted in the United States, the process from investigation, through trial and sentencing to the carrying out of the death penalty is racially tainted. As evidence, those making this argument point to the fact that the demographic characteristics of those executed are not in proportion to their group's percentage of the society. African Americans (about 12% of the population) made up 36% of those executed in 2005. Among other groups, Latinos, 14% of the population accounted for only 5% of those executed, and Asian Americans, at 4% of the population, made up only 0.2% of those put to death. It is worth noting that 59 of the 60 prisoners executed in 2005 were men.

POINTS TO PONDER

➢ Before beginning, make a note to yourself about whether or not you favor the death penalty and the most important reason you take that view.

➢ Since no judicial system is perfect, it is safe to assume that at least some of those executed have been wrongly convicted. If you believe that the error rate does not have to be zero to continue capital punishment, then what is the highest acceptable error rate?

➢ What, if anything, would make you change your view on capital punishment?

The Death Penalty: Fatally Flawed

STEPHEN B. BRIGHT

This is a most appropriate time to assess the costs and benefits of the death penalty. Thirty years ago, in 1976, the Supreme Court allowed the resumption of capital punishment after declaring it unconstitutional four years earlier in *Furman v. Georgia*. Laws passed in response to Furman were supposed to correct the constitutional defects identified in 1972.

However, 30 years of experience has demonstrated that those laws have failed to do so. The death penalty is still arbitrary. It's still discriminatory. It is still imposed almost exclusively upon poor people represented by court-appointed lawyers. In many cases the capabilities of the lawyer have more to do with whether the death penalty is imposed than the crime. The system is still fallible in deciding both guilt and punishment. In addition, the death penalty is costly and is not accomplishing anything. And it is beneath a society that has a reverence for life and recognizes that no human being is beyond redemption. Many supporters of capital punishment, after years of struggling to make the system work, have had sober second thoughts it. Justice Sandra Day O'Connor, who leaves the Supreme Court after 25 years of distinguished service, has observed that "serious questions are being raised about whether the death penalty is being fairly administered in this country" and that "the system may well be allowing some innocent defendants to be executed."

Justices Lewis Powell and Harry Blackmun also voted to uphold death sentences as members of the court, but eventually came to the conclusion, as Justice Blackmun put it, that "the death penalty experiment has failed."

The *Birmingham News* announced in November that after years of supporting the death penalty it could no longer do so "[b]ecause we have come to believe Alabama's capital punishment system is broken. And because, first and foremost, this newspaper's editorial board is committed to a culture of life."

The death penalty is not imposed to avenge every murder and—as some contend—to bring "closure" to the family of every victim. There were over 20,000 murders in 14 of the last 30 years and 15,000 to 20,000 in the others. During that time, there have been just over 1,000 executions—an average of about 33 a year. Sixteen states carried out 60 executions last year. Twelve states carried out 59 executions in 2004, and 12 states put 65 people to death in 2003.

Moreover, the death penalty is not evenly distributed around the country. Most executions take place in the South, just as they did before *Furman*. Between 1935 and 1972, the South carried out 1887 executions; no other region had as many as 500. Since 1976, the Southern states have carried out 822 of 1000 executions; states in the Midwest have carried out 116; states in the west 64 and the Northeastern states have carried out only four. The federal government, which has had the death penalty since 1988, has executed three people. Only one state, Texas, has executed over 100 people since 1976. It has executed over 350.

Further experimentation with a lethal punishment after centuries of failure has no place in a conservative society that is wary of too much government power and skeptical of government's ability to do things well. We are paying an enormous cost in money and the credibility of the system in order to execute people who committed less than one percent of the murders that occur each year. The death penalty is not imposed for all murders, for most murders, or even for the most heinous murders. It is imposed upon a random handful of people convicted of murder—often because of factors such as the political interests and predilections of prosecutors, the quality of the lawyer appointed to defend the accused, and the race of the victim and the defendant. A fairer system would be to have a lottery of all people convicted of murder; draw 60 names and execute them. Further experimentation might be justified if it served some purpose. But capital punishment is not needed to protect society or to punish offenders. We have not only maximum security prisons, but "super maximum" prisons where prisoners are completely isolated from guards and other inmates, as well as society.

THE DEATH PENALTY IS ARBITRARY AND UNFAIR

Justice Potter Stewart said in 1972 that the death penalty was so arbitrary and capricious that being sentenced to death was like being struck by lightning. It still is. As was the case in 1972, there is no way to distinguish the small number of offenders who get death each year from the thousands who do not. This is because prosecutorial practices vary widely with regard to the death penalty; the lawyers appointed to defend those accused are often not up to the task of providing an adequate defense; differences between regions and communities and the resulting differences in the composition of juries; and other factors.

PROSECUTORIAL DISCRETION AND PLEA BARGAINING

Whether death is sought or imposed is based on the discretion and proclivities of the thousands of people who occupy the offices of prosecutor in judicial districts throughout the nation. (Texas, for example, has 155 elected prosecutors, Virginia 120, Missouri 115, Illinois 102, Georgia 49, and Alabama 40). Each prosecutor is independent of all the others in the state.

The vast majority of all criminal cases—including capital cases—are decided not by juries, but through plea bargains. The two most important decisions in any capital case are the prosecutor's—first, whether to seek the death penalty and, second, if death is sought, whether to agree to a lesser punishment, usually life imprisonment without any possibility of parole, instead of the death penalty as part of a plea bargain.

The practices of prosecutors vary widely. They are never required to seek the death penalty. Some never seek it; some seek it from time to time; and some seek it at every opportunity. Some who seek it initially will nevertheless agree to a plea bargain and a life sentence in almost all cases; others will refuse a plea disposition and go to trial. In some communities, particularly predominantly white suburban ones, the prosecutor may get a death sentence from a jury almost any time a case goes to trial. In other communities—usually those with more diverse racial populations—the prosecutors often find it much more difficult, if not impossible, to obtain a death sentence. Those prosecutors may eventually stop seeking the death penalty because of they get it so seldom. And regardless of the community and the crime, juries may not agree to a death sentence.

Timothy McVeigh's codefendant, Terry Nichols, was not sentenced to death by either a federal or state jury for his role in the bombing of the federal building in Oklahoma City that caused 168 deaths. Without being critical of any person or community and without questioning the motives of any of them, it is clear that there is not going to be consistent application of the death penalty when prosecutors operate completely independent of one another.

Because of different practices by prosecutors, there are geographical disparities with regard to where death is imposed within states. Prosecutors in Houston and Philadelphia have sought the death penalty in virtually every case where it can be imposed. As a result of aggressive prosecutors and inept court-appointed lawyers, Houston and Philadelphia have each condemned over 100 people to death—more than most states. Harris County, which includes Houston, has had more executions in the last 30 years than any state except Texas and Virginia.

Whether death is sought may depend upon which side of the county line the crime was committed. A murder was committed in a parking lot on the boundary between Lexington County, South Carolina, which, at the time, had sentenced 12 people to death, and Richland County, which had sent only one person to death row. The murder was determined to have occurred a few feet on the Lexington County side of the line. The defendant was tried in Lexington County and sentenced to death. Had the crime occurred a few feet in the other direction, death penalty almost certainly would not have been imposed.

There may be different practices even within the same office. For example, an Illinois prosecutor announced that he had decided not to seek the death penalty for Girvies Davis after Davis' case was reversed by the state supreme court. However, while the case was pending, a new prosecutor took office and decided to seek the death penalty for Davis. He was successful and Davis was executed in 1995.

As a result of a plea bargain, Ted Kaczynski, the Unabomber, who killed three, injured many others, and terrified even more by mailing bombs to people, avoided the death penalty. Serial killers Gary Leon Ridgway, who pleaded guilty to killing 48 women and girls in the Seattle area, and Charles Cullen, a nurse who pleaded guilty to murdering 29 patients in hospitals in New Jersey and Pennsylvania, also avoided the death penalty through plea bargains, as did Eric Rudolph, who killed a security guard in Birmingham and set off a bomb that killed one and injured many more at the 1996 Olympics. Rudolph was allowed to plead and avoid the death penalty in exchange for telling the authorities where he hid some dynamite in North Carolina. Others avoid the death penalty by agreeing to testify for the prosecution against the other(s) involved in the crime.

Although some serial killers are sentenced to death, most of the men and women on death rows are there for crimes that, while tragic and fully deserving of punishment, are less heinous that the examples mentioned above as well as many other cases in which death was not imposed.

REPRESENTATION FOR THE ACCUSED

Once a prosecutor decides to seek death, the quality of legal representation for the defendant can be the difference between life and death. A person facing the death penalty usually cannot afford to hire a attorney and is at the mercy of the system to provide a court appointed lawyer. While many receive adequate representation (and often are not sentenced to death as a result), many others are assigned lawyers who lack the knowledge, skill, resources—and sometime even the inclination—to handle a serious criminal case. People who would not be sentenced to death if properly represented are sentenced to death because of the incompetent court-appointed lawyers.

For example, Dennis Williams was convicted twice of the 1978 murders of a couple from Chicago's south suburbs and sentenced to death. He was represented at his first trial by an attorney who was later disbarred, and at his second trial by a different attorney who was later suspended. Williams was later exonerated by DNA evidence. Four other men sentenced to death in Illinois were represented by a convicted felon who was the only lawyer in Illinois history to be disbarred twice.

A dramatic example of how bad representation can be is provided by this description from the *Houston Chronicle* of a capital trial:

> Seated beside his client—a convicted capital murderer—defense attorney John Benn spent much of Thursday afternoon's trial in apparent deep sleep. His mouth kept falling open and his head lolled back on his shoulders, and then he awakened just long enough to catch himself and sit upright. Then it happened again. And again. And again.
>
> Every time he opened his eyes, a different prosecution witness was on the stand describing another aspect of the Nov. 19, 1991, arrest of George McFarland in the robbery-killing of grocer Kenneth Kwan.
>
> When state District Judge Doug Shaver finally called a recess, Benn was asked if he truly had fallen asleep during a capital murder trial. "It's boring," the 72-year-old longtime Houston lawyer explained....

Court observers said Benn seems to have slept his way through virtually the entire trial. This sleeping did not violate the right to a lawyer guaranteed by the United States Constitution, the trial judge explained, because, "[t]he Constitution doesn't say the lawyer has to be awake." On appeal, the Texas Court of Criminal Appeals rejected McFarland's claim that he was denied his right to counsel over the dissent of two judges who pointed out that "[a] sleeping counsel is unprepared to present evidence, to cross-examine witnesses, and to present any coordinated effort to evaluate evidence and present a defense." Last year, the Court reaffirmed its opinion.

George McFarland was one of at least three people sentenced to death in Houston at trials where their lawyers slept. Two others were represented by Joe Frank Cannon. One of them, Carl Johnson, has been executed. Cannon was appointed by Houston judges for forty years to represent people accused of crimes in part because of his reputation for hurrying through trials like "greased lightening," and despite his tendency to doze off during trial.

Ten of Cannon's clients were sentenced to death, one of the largest numbers among Texas attorneys. Another notorious lawyer appointed to defend capital cases in Houston had 14 clients sentenced to death.

The list of lawyers eligible to handle capital cases in Tennessee in 2001, circulated to trial judges by the state Supreme Court, included a lawyer convicted of bank fraud, a lawyer convicted of perjury, and a lawyer whose failure to order a blood test let an innocent man languish in jail for four years on a rape charge. Courts in other states have upheld death sentences in cases in which lawyers were not aware of the governing law, were not sober, and failed to present any evidence regarding either guilt-innocence or penalty. One federal judge, in reluctantly upholding a death sentence, observed that the Constitution, as interpreted by the U.S. Supreme Court, "does not require that the accused, even in capital cases, be represented by able or effective counsel."

The Supreme Court has said that the death penalty should be imposed "with reasonable consistency, or not at all." That is simply not happening.

THE COURTS ARE FALLIBLE

Innocent people have been wrongfully convicted because of poor legal representation, mistaken identifications, the unreliable testimony of people who swap their testimony for lenient treatment, police and prosecutorial misconduct and other reasons. Unfortunately, DNA testing reveals only a few wrongful convictions. In most cases, there is no biological evidence that can be tested. In those cases, we must rely on a properly working adversary system—in which the defense lawyer scrutinizes the prosecution's case, consults with the client, conducts a thorough and independent investigation, consults with experts, and subjects the prosecution case to adversarial testing—to bring out all the facts and help the courts find the truth. But even with a properly working adversary system, there will still be convictions of the innocent. The best we can do is minimize the risk of wrongful convictions. And the most critical way to do that is to provide the accused with competent counsel and the resources needed to mount a defense.

The innocence of some of those condemned to die has been discovered by sheer happenstance and good luck. For example, Ray Krone, was convicted and sentenced to death in Arizona based on the testimony of an expert witness that his teeth matched bite marks on the victim. During the ten years that Krone spent on death row, scientists developed the ability to compare biological evidence recovered at crime scenes with the DNA of suspects. DNA testing established that Krone was innocent.

The governor of Virginia commuted the death sentence of Earl Washington to life imprisonment without parole in 1994 because of questions regarding his guilt. Were it not for that, Washington would not have been alive six years later, when DNA evidence—not available at the time of Washington's trial or the commutation—established that Washington was innocent and he was released.

Poor legal representation led to a death sentence for Gary Drinkard, who spent five years on Alabama's death row for a crime he did not commit. At his trial, he was represented by one lawyer who did collections and commercial work and another who represented creditors in foreclosures and bankruptcy cases. The case was reversed on appeal for reasons having nothing to do with the quality of his representation. Our office joined with an experienced criminal defense lawyer from Birmingham and represented him at his retrial. After all the evidence was presented, including the testimony of the doctor, the jury acquitted Drinkard in less than two hours.

Evidence of innocence has surfaced at the last minute and only because of volunteers who found it. Anthony Porter, sentenced to death in Illinois, went through all of the appeals and review that are available for one sentenced to death. Every court upheld his conviction and sentence. As Illinois prepared to put him to death, a question arose as to whether Porter, who was brain damaged and mentally retarded, understood what was happening to him. Just two days before he was to be executed, a court stayed his execution for a mental examination.

After the stay was granted, a journalism class at Northwestern University and a private investigator examined the case and proved that Porter was innocent. They obtained a confession from the person who committed the crime. Porter was released, becoming the third person released from Illinois's death row after being proven innocent by a journalism class at Northwestern.

There has been some argument over how many innocent people have been sentenced to death and whether any have been executed. We do not know and we cannot know. If DNA evidence had not been available to prove Ray Krone's innocent, if Earl Washington had been executed instead of commuted to life, if Gary Drinkard had not received a new trial, and if Anthony Porter was not mentally impaired and the journalism class had not come to his rescue, all would have been executed and we would never know to this day of their innocence. Those who proclaim that no innocent person has ever been executed would continue to do so, secure in their ignorance.

With regard to the quibbling over how many people released from death rows have actually been innocent, even one innocent person being convicted of a crime and sentenced to death or a prison term is one too many. "Close enough for government work" is simply not acceptable when life and liberty are at stake. Regardless of how one counts and what one counts, we know that an unacceptable number of innocent people have been convicted in both capital and non-capital cases.

There is nothing wrong with looking at the system as it really is and with a little humility about what it is capable of. There are cases—many of them—in which the criminal courts have correctly determined that a person is guilty. There are others where it is clear the system was wrong because the innocence of those convicted has been conclusively established though DNA evidence or other compelling proof. There are also cases in which it is virtually impossible to tell for sure whether a person is guilty or innocent. There is no DNA evidence or other conclusive proof. The case depends upon which witness the jury believes. Or new facts come to light after the trial. It is impossible to know what the jury's verdict would have been if it had considered those facts. We want to believe that our judges and juries are capable of doing the impossible—determining the truth in every instance. And in most instances, they can determine the truth.

But cases that depend upon eyewitness identification, forensic evidence from a crime laboratory with shoddy practices like those that have come to light in Houston and Oklahoma City, the testimony of a co-defendant, who claims the defendant was the primary person, or the cellmate who claims the defendant admitted committing the crime to him, or there is inadequate defense for the accused, there is a serious possibility of an error. Just last week, a judge who presided over a capital case in California in which death was imposed wrote to the governor urging clemency for the defendant because the judge believes the sentence was based on false testimony from a jailhouse informant.

Often overlooked is the jury's verdict with regard to sentence—whether to condemn the person to die or sentence him to a long prison sentence—which is as important as its verdict on guilt. The decision of the legal system to bring about the deliberate, institutionalized taking of a person's life is surely a determination that the person is so beyond redemption that he or she should be eliminated from the human community. But that determination is quite often erroneous.

I have seen many people who were once condemned to die but are now useful and productive members of society. One of them, Shareef Cousin, works in our office. He was sentenced to death when he was 16 years old. However, it turned out that he was not guilty of the murder for which he was sentenced to death. We are tremendously impressed with him. He is a hard worker; someone we have found we can count on. He is applying to colleges. He is very serious about getting in to college and will be a very serious student.

But it is not just the innocent. William Neal Moore spent 16½ years on Georgia's death row for a murder he committed in the course of a robbery. He had eight execution dates and came within seven hours of execution on one occasion. His death sentence was commuted to life imprisonment in 1990 and a year later he was paroled. He comes to the law schools and speaks to my classes every year. He was very religious while in prison, and he is has remained every bit as religious in the 15 years he has been out. He met and married someone with two daughters and has been a good father. Both girls are in college. He has judgment and maturity now that he did not have when he committed the crime.

I can give you many more examples like these of people who were condemned to die but who have clearly demonstrated that they were more than the worst thing they ever did.

PEOPLE WHO KILL ARE NOT DETERRED

The scholars will address whether a punishment that is imposed in less than one percent of murder cases serves as a deterrent to murder. I offer no statistics, only a few observations from over 30 years of dealing with the people who are supposedly being deterred.

In my experience, these are not people who assess risks, plan ahead and make good judgments. They would not have committed their crimes if they thought they were going to be caught, regardless of the punishment. But they don't expect to get caught so they d don't even get to the question of what punishment will be inflicted. Why would anyone commit a crime—for example, murder and robbery to get money to buy drugs—if they thought that instead of enjoying the drugs in the free world they would be spending the rest of their life in prison or even years in prison?

Even if they get to the issue of punishment—I cannot imagine how they process the information. A large portion of the people who end up on death rows are people with very poor reading skills. They don't read the newspaper or watch the news or listen to public radio. When they are assessing the risk of getting executed, are they supposed to consider that nationally they have a one percent chance of getting the death penalty if they are caught and convicted? Or are they to consider whether they are in one of the 12 to 16 states that has carried out a death sentence in the last three years? How much of a deterrent can it be in the states that have two or three people on their death rows and have carried out one or two executions over 30 years? Are they deterred if they are in New Hampshire, which has a death penalty law but has never imposed it? How do they learn that New Hampshire has a death penalty law? Do states that have not carried out any executions or have carried out just a few need to carry out more in order to deter, or can they benefit from executions in other states?

The more routine executions become, the less media coverage they get. How are people supposed to find out about executions and be deterred if they are not getting any media coverage?

Beyond that, is the potential murderer going to take into account the likelihood of being assigned a bad court-appointed lawyer, of being tried before an all-white jury instead of a racially diverse jury, and other factors which will increase his chances of getting the death penalty?

The people I have encountered who committed murder do not have the information and many are not capable of going through a reasonable consideration of it if they had it. Many people who commit murder suffer from schizophrenia, bipolar disorder, major brain damage or other severe mental impairments. They may have a very distorted sense of reality or may not even be in touch with reality.

Finally, if death were a deterrent, it would surely deter gang members and drug dealers. They see death up close. Killings over turf and in retaliation for other killings make death very real. It is summary and there are no appeals. They see brothers and friends killed; go to funerals. They have much greater likelihood of getting death on the streets than in the courts. But, it does not change their behavior.

THE COST IS NOT JUSTIFIED

There is a growing recognition that it is just not worth it. A Florida prosecutor let a defendant plead guilty to killing five people because a sentence of life imprisonment without parole would bring finality. The Palm Beach Post observed "The State saves not only the cost of a trial; the victims' relatives—who supported the deal—do not have to relive the horror. The state will save more by avoiding years of appeals;...Most important, [the defendant] never again will threaten the public."

New York spent more than $170 million on its death penalty over a ten year period, from 1995 to 2005, before its Court of Appeals declared its death penalty law unconstitutional. During that time, the state did not carry out a single execution. Only seven persons have been sentenced to death—an average of less than one a year—and the first four of those sentences were struck down by the New York Court of Appeals on various grounds. The speaker of the state's assembly remarked, "I have some doubt whether we need a death penalty....We are spending tens of millions of dollars [that] may be better spent on educating children." He also pointed out that the state now has a statute providing for life imprisonment without parole that ensures those convicted of murder cannot go free. Similarly, Kansas did not carry out any executions between 1994, when it reinstated the death penalty, and 2004 when the state supreme court ruled it unconstitutional. Kansas had eight people under sentence of death, six from one county. New Jersey, which just declared a moratorium on executions, has spent $253 million on its death penalty since 1983. It has yet to carry out an execution and has only ten people on its death row. In other words, the state has spent a quarter of a billion dollars over 23 years and has not carried out a single execution. Michael Murphy, a former prosecutor for Morris County, remarked, "If you were to ask me how $11 million a year could best protect the people of New Jersey, I would tell you by giving the law enforcement community more resources. I'm not interested in hypotheticals or abstractions, I want the tools for law enforcement to do their job, and $11 million can buy a lot of tools."

These are states which made every effort to do it right. It is also possible to have death on the cheap. A number of states have done this. Capital cases may last as little as a day and a half. Georgia recently executed a man who was assigned a lawyer—a busy public defender—just 37 days before his trial and denied any funds for investigation or expert witnesses. But this completely undermines confidence in the courts and devalues life.

CONCLUSION

Supreme Court Justice Arthur Goldberg said that the deliberate institutionalized taking of human life by the state is the greatest degradation of the human personality imaginable. It is not just degrading to the individual who is tied down and put down. It is degrading to the society that carries it out. It coarsens the society, takes risks with the lives of the poor, and diminishes its respect for life and its belief in the possible redemption of every person. It is a relic of another era. Careful examination will show that the death penalty is not serving any purpose in our society and is not worth the cost.

The Death Penalty: Defensible

JOHN MCADAMS

There are a huge number of issues that relate to the merits of the death penalty as a punishment, including deterrence, the moral justice of the punishment, the cost of the imposition of the sanction, and even (implausibly) what policies European nations have. But I'm going to concentrate, given the limited time I have, on two issues that I think are key: the issue of "innocents" convicted and sent to death row, and the issue of racial disparity in the application of the punishment.

HOW MANY INNOCENTS ON DEATH ROW?

One of the most compelling arguments against the death penalty, at least one that accepts the claims of the death penalty opponents at face value, is the claim that a great many innocent people have been convicted of murder and put on death row. Liberal Supreme Court Justice John Paul Stevens, just to pick one case out of hundreds, told the American Bar Association's Thurgood Marshall Award dinner that "That evidence is profoundly significant, not only because of its relevance to the debate about the wisdom of continuing to administer capital punishment, but also because it indicates that there must be serious flaws in our administration of criminal justice."

The most widely publicized list of "innocents" is that of the Death Penalty Information Center (DPIC). As of January 2003, it listed 122 people. That sounds like an appallingly large number, but even a casual examination of the list shows that many of the people on it got off for reasons entirely unrelated to being innocent. Back in 2001, I analyzed the list when it had ninety-five people on it. By the admission of the Death Penalty Information Center, thirty-five inmates on their list got off on procedural grounds. Another fourteen got off because a higher court believed the evidence against them was insufficient. If the higher court was right, this would be an excellent reason to release them, but it's far from proof of innocence.

Interestingly, prosecutors retried thirty-two of the inmates designated as "innocent." Apparently prosecutors believed these thirty-two were guilty. But many whom prosecutors felt to be guilty were not tried again for a variety of reasons, including the fact that key evidence had been suppressed, witnesses had died, a plea bargain was thought to be a better use of scarce resources, or the person in question had been convicted and imprisoned under another charge.

More detailed assessments of the "Innocents List" have shown that it radically overstates the number of innocent people who have been on death row. For example, the state of Florida had put on death row 24 inmates claimed, as of August 5, 2002, to be innocent by the DPIC. The resulting publicity led to a thorough examination of the twenty-four cases by the Florida Commission on Capital Crimes, which concluded that in only four of the twenty-four cases was the factual guilt of these inmates in doubt.

Examinations of the entire list have been no more favorable. For example, [in

2002] a liberal federal district judge in New York ruled, in *United States v. Quinones*, that the federal death penalty is unconstitutional. In this case, the court admitted that the DPIC list "may be over-inclusive" and, following its own analysis, asserted that for thirty-two of the people on the list there was evidence of "factual innocence." This hardly represents a ringing endorsement of the work of the Death Penalty Information Center. In academia, being right about a third of the time will seldom result in a passing grade.

Other assessments have been equally negative. Ward A. Campbell, Supervising Deputy Attorney General of the State of California reviewed the list in detail, and concluded that:...it is arguable that at least 68 of the 102 defendants on the List should not be on the list at all—leaving only 34 released defendants with claims of actual innocence—less than ½ of 1% of the 6,930 defendants sentenced to death between 1973 and 2000.

There is, of course, a degree of subjectivity in all such assessments. The presence of "reasonable doubt" does not make a person factually innocent (although it's an excellent reason to acquit them), and circumstances might conspire to make a factually innocent person appear to even an objective observer to be guilty "beyond a reasonable doubt." The key thing to remember is that the numbers produced by DPIC are "outliers"—grossly inflated. Indeed, staffers of this very committee have pretty much dismantled the DPIC list. Taking at face value the claims of the activists is about as bad as taking at face value the claims of the National Rifle Association about the number of Americans who save themselves from bodily harm because they own and carry guns, or the claims of NARAL [National Abortion & Reproductive Rights Action League] about how many "back alley abortions" would result from overturning *Roe v. Wade* [1973].

HAVE ANY INNOCENTS BEEN EXECUTED?

Worse than putting an innocent person on death row (only to have him later exonerated) would be to actually execute an innocent person. But death penalty opponents can't point to a single innocent person known to have been executed for the last 35 years. They do make claims, however.

In the 1980s, two academics who strongly opposed the death penalty (Hugo Adam Bedau and Michael Radelet) claimed that of 7,000 people executed in the United States in the 20th century, 23 were innocent. This doesn't seem like a large number, especially when we remember that most of the cases they claimed were from an era when defendants had many fewer due process rights than they do today, when police forces and prosecutors were much less well-trained and professional than they are today, and when the media was less inclined to take an "advocacy" role in claimed cases of injustice.

Indeed, Bedau and Radelet produced only one case since the early 1960s where they claimed an innocent man had been executed—that of one James Adams. But even this one case was quite weak. Steven J. Markman and Paul G. Cassell, in a *Stanford Law Review* article, took Bedau and Radelet to task for "disregard of the evidence," and for putting a spin on the evidence that supported their thesis of Adams' innocence. Markman and Cassell concluded that there is, "no persuasive evidence that any innocent person has been put to death in more than twenty-five years." In response, Bedau and Radelet admitted to the *Chronicle of Higher Education* that (in the words of the *Chronicle's* reporter) "some cases require subjective analysis simply because the evidence is incomplete or tainted." They admitted this was true of all 23 cases that they reported.

The most sober death penalty opponents have apparently given up claiming solid evidence of any innocent person executed in the modern era. Indeed Barry Scheck, cofounder of the Innocence Project, was featured speaker at the Wrongfully Convicted on Death Row Conference in Chicago (November 13–15, 1998), and was interviewed by the "Today Show."

Schenk was asked by Matt Lauer, "Since 1976, 486 people have been executed in this country. Any doubt in your mind that we've put to death innocent people?" Scheck responded "Well, you know, I—I think that we must have put to death innocent people, but if you're saying to me to prove it right now, I can't."

Nothing stops death penalty opponents from making all sorts of claims about innocent people being executed. But in the rare cases when their claims can actually be tested, they turn out to be false. Consider, for example, the case of Roger Keith Coleman, who was tried for a rape/murder, and finally executed by the State of Virginia in 1992. An essay still on the site of the Death Penalty Information Center discusses the case at considerable length, and clearly leaves the impression that Coleman must be innocent. After attacking all the evidence against Coleman, the essay claims that "official misconduct that has left the case against Roger Coleman in shreds" and goes on to claim:

> ...there is dramatic evidence that another person, Donney Ramey, committed the murder. For one thing, a growing number of women in the neighborhood have reported being sexually assaulted by Ramey in ways strikingly similar to the attack on Wanda McCoy. For another, one of these rape victims, Teresa Horn, has courageously signed an affidavit stating that Ramey told her he had killed Mrs. McCoy. He threatened to do the same to Ms. Horn.

Someone reading the Death Penalty Information Center website, and lacking due skepticism toward the assertions there, would doubtless conclude that Coleman was innocent. Unfortunately, the State of Virginia allowed DNA testing of key evidence in 2005, using technology unavailable in 1992, and proved decisively that Coleman was in fact guilty as charged. The credibility of anti-death penalty activists when making claims of innocence—whether for those on death row or those who have been executed—is tenuous at best.

HOW MANY INNOCENTS ON DEATH ROW ARE ACCEPTABLE?

At this point, death penalty opponents will argue that it doesn't matter if their numbers are inflated. Even if only 20 or 30 innocent people have been put on death row, they will say, that is "too many" and calls for the abolition of the death penalty. If even one innocent person is executed, they claim, that would make the death penalty morally unacceptable.

This kind of rhetoric allows the speaker to feel very self-righteous, but it's not the sort of thinking that underlies sound policy analysis. Most policies have some negative consequences, and indeed often these involve the death of innocent people—something that can't be shown to have happened with the death penalty in the modern era. Just wars kill a certain number of innocent noncombatants. When the FDA approves a new drug, some people will quite likely be killed by arcane and infrequent reactions. Indeed, the FDA kills people with its laggard drug approval process. The magnitude of these consequences matters.

Death penalty opponents usually implicitly assume (but don't say so, since it would be patently absurd) that we have a choice between a flawed death penalty and a perfect system of punishment where other sanctions are concerned.

Death penalty opponents might be asked why it's acceptable to imprison people, when innocent people most certainly have been imprisoned. They will often respond that wrongfully imprisoned people can be released, but wrongfully executed people cannot be brought back to life. Unfortunately, wrongfully imprisoned people cannot be given back the years of their life that were taken from them, even though they may walk out of prison.

Perhaps more importantly, its cold comfort to say that wrongfully imprisoned people can be released, when there isn't much likelihood that that will happen. Wrongful imprisonment receives vastly less attention than wrongful death sentences, but Barry Scheck's book Actual Innocence lists 10 supposedly innocent defendants, of whom only 3 were sent to death row.

Currently, the Innocence Project website lists 174 persons who have been exonerated on the basis of hard DNA evidence. But the vast majority was not sentenced to death. In fact, only 15 death row inmates have been exonerated due to DNA evidence.

There is every reason to believe that the rate of error is much lower for the death penalty than for imprisonment. There is much more extensive review by higher courts, much more intensive media scrutiny, cadres of activists trying to prove innocence, and better quality counsel at the appeals level (and increasingly at the trial level) if a case might result in execution.

Consider the following quote from an article about how prosecutors in Indiana are tending more and more to ask for life imprisonment and not the death penalty because of the cost of getting an execution:

> Criminal rules require a capital defendant to have two death penalty certified attorneys, which, if the defendant is indigent, are paid for on the public dime. Other costs that might be passed onto taxpayers are requirements that the accused have access to all the tools needed to mount a fair defense, including mitigation experts, investigators, and DNA experts. Because the stakes are so high in a death penalty case, the courts believe a defendant is entitled to a super due process. The cost of getting a death penalty is too high in some ways (seemingly endless appeals). But in other ways lesser penalties are too cheap (lacking good lawyers, DNA testing, etc.). The system, in fact, it quite unbalanced, with it being relatively cheap and easy to sentence someone to life imprisonment but excessively expensive to have them executed. But until some balance is restored, the death penalty will remain the fairest penalty we have.

Balance will be achieved by ending "dead weight loss" in administering the death penalty (further limiting the number of appeals), while working for more substantive justice where lesser sanctions are at issue.

Playing the Race Card Death penalty opponents tend to inhabit sectors of society where claiming "racial disparity" is an effective tactic for getting what you want. In academia, the media, the ranks of activist organizations, etc. claiming "racial disparity" is an excellent strategy for getting anybody who has qualms about what you are proposing to shut up, cave in, and get out of the way.

Unfortunately, this has created a hothouse culture where arguments thrive that carry little weight elsewhere in society, and carry little weight for good reasons.

Consider the notion that, because there is racial disparity in the administration of the death penalty, it must be abolished. Applying this principle in a consistent way would be unthinkable. Suppose we find that black robbers are treated more harshly than white robbers?

Does it follow that we want to stop punishing robbers? Or does it follow that we want to properly punish white robbers also? Nobody would argue that racial inequity in punishing robbers means we have to stop punishing robbers. Nobody would claim that, if we find that white neighborhoods have better police protection than black neighborhoods that we address the inequity by withdrawing police protection from all neighborhoods. Or that racial disparity in mortgage lending requires that mortgage lending be ended. Yet people make arguments exactly like this where capital punishment is concerned.

A further problem with the "racial disparity" argument—and one underlining the fundamental incoherence of the abolitionist's thinking—is the fact that there are two versions of it, both widely bandied around, and they are flatly contradictory. I have elsewhere described these as the "mass market" and the "specialist" versions of the racial disparity thesis.

The mass market version is the easiest to understand, since it relies on the notion that racist cops, racist prosecutors, racist judges, and racist juries will be particularly tough on black defendants. Jessie Jackson, never one to pass up an opportunity to nurse a racial grievance, has expressed this view as follows:

> Numerous researchers have shown conclusively that African American defendants are far more likely to receive the death penalty than are white defendants charged with the same crime. For instance, African Americans make up 25 percent of Alabama's population, yet of Alabama's 117 death row inmates, 43 percent are black. Indeed, 71 percent of the people executed there since the resumption of capital punishment have been black.

In a more scholarly vein, Leigh B. Bienen [of Northwestern University Law School] has claimed:

> There is a whole other dimension with regard to arguments that the death penalty is "racist." The death penalty and the criminal justice system is an institutional system controlled by and dominated by whites, although the recipients of punishment, including the recipients of the death penalty, are disproportionately black. The death penalty is a symbol of state control and it is a symbol of white control over blacks, in fact and in its popular and sensationalist presentations. Black males who present a threatening personae and a defiant personae are the favorites of those administering the punishment, including the overwhelmingly middle-aged white male prosecutors who are running for election or retention or re-election and find nothing gets them more votes than demonizing young black men. By portraying themselves as punishers and avengers of whites who are the "victims" of blacks, prosecutors get a lot of political support.

Thus Bienen adds another element to the mix: a racist public whose bias is translated by those paragons of political incorrectness, middle-aged white males, into harsh punishments for blacks. The problems of this view are numerous, but I'll discuss only the most important one: it's empirically just flat wrong. A whole raft of relatively sophisticated studies of the death penalty have been done, and findings of bias against black defendants are rare. Indeed, they are so few that they seem to illustrate the point that if you run a huge number of statistical "coefficients," a few will turn up as "significant" when in fact nothing is there.

What the studies do show is a huge bias against black victims. Offenders who murder black people get off much more lightly than those who murder whites. Since the vast majority of murders are intraracial and not interracial, this translates into a system that lets black murderers off far more easily than white murderers.

This is clearly unjust, but it leaves open the question of whether the injustice should be remedied by executing nobody at all, or rather executing more offenders who have murdered black people.

Even more relevant is the question: would doing away with the death penalty improve the situation? Here, as elsewhere, death penalty opponents assume that the choices are a flawed death penalty and a pristine system of criminal justice for every other punishment. But the data don't support that.

Scholars who study the death penalty often study several decisions in the process that might theoretically lead to execution. What they almost invariably find is large-scale bias in these earlier decisions, including decisions that would continue to be made if the death penalty were abolished. One particularly interesting study (although pre-Furman)…dealt with 245 persons arrested for homicide in Philadelphia in 1970.

Of these, 170 were eventually convicted of some charge. Sixty-five percent of defendants who killed a white got either life imprisonment or a death sentence, while only 25 percent of those who killed a black did. Since these murders produced only three death sentences (all imposed on blacks who killed whites), most of the apparent racial unfairness involved life imprisonment, not execution. Blumstein, in a study of the racial disproportionality of prison populations, found that in 1991 blacks were underrepresented among prisoners convicted of murder. There were many limitations to Blumstein's study, including failure to control for aggravating circumstances, and a research design what leaves possible racial discrimination in arrests entirely out of account. But his results strongly imply that the system does for imprisonment what it does with regard to executions: under punish those who kill blacks.

William J. Bowers [also at Northwestern University]…found that defendants who killed whites were more likely to be indicted for first degree murder—rather than a lesser charge—and more likely to be convicted for first degree murder than defendants who killed blacks. Along similar lines…a study of indictments for murder in Florida found that 85 percent of the killers of white victims were indicted for first-degree murder, while only 53.6 percent of the killers of black victims were.

Leigh Bienen and her colleagues, in their study of New Jersey homicides examined the issue of whether a particular case is plea bargained, or whether it goes to trial. Cases involving white victims were found to go to trial more often than cases involving either black or Hispanic victims.

One particularly interesting study involved prosecutors' decisions to "upgrade" or "downgrade" a homicide. An "upgrade" involved a prosecutor making a charge of a felony connected with the homicide when no such felony was mentioned in the police report. On the other hand, cases were said to be "downgraded" when the police report indicated the commission of a felony, but the prosecutor's charge did not mention it. A statistical model which controlled for the circumstances of the crime and of the offender showed that white victim murders were more likely to be upgraded than black victim murders.

In sum, the system is relatively lenient toward those who kill blacks, and that leniency extends to decisions that would continue to advantage those defendants who have killed blacks even in the absence of the death penalty. All of this makes perfect sense. If the system is biased toward punishing those who murder whites, it is implausible indeed that decisions leading up to sentencing are made with strict racial fairness, and only the imposition of a death sentence is racially biased. If people want to punish those who murder whites more harshly than those who murder blacks, this is likely to be reflected in prosecutors' decisions to move ahead with a case, in decisions about whether to plea-bargain, in the allocation of staff to a particular case, in the decision to indict on more or less serious charges, and in jury verdicts. Even in sentencing, abolition of the death penalty only narrows the range of possible punishments, rather than eliminating it. While not all decision points have been studied equally well, theoretically the pervasive undervaluing of the lives of black victims ought to be reflected everywhere there is discretion.

CONCLUSION

It cannot be stressed too strongly that we do not face the choice of a defective system on capital punishment and a pristine system of imprisonment. Rather, nothing about the criminal justice system works perfectly. Death penalty opponents give the impression that the death penalty is uniquely flawed by the simple expedient of dwelling on the defects of capital punishment (real and imagined) and largely ignoring the defects in the way lesser punishments are meted out.

The death penalty meets the expectations we can reasonably place on any public policy. But it can't meet the absurdly inflated standards imposed by those who are culturally hostile to it. But then, no other policy can either.

THE CONTINUING DEBATE: The Death Penalty

What Is New

Globally, almost two-thirds of the world's countries have abolished the death penalty, and most of those that retain it seldom use it. Indeed, just ten countries carried out 98% of all the legal (judicially authorized) executions in 2005. The United States is the fourth most likely country to execute prisoners. According to Amnesty International, there were 2,145 known legal executions in 22 countries in 2005. China had by far the most (1,770), followed by Iran (94), Saudia Arabia (86), the United States (60), and Pakistan (31). The number of death row inmates in U.S. prisons has grown from 692 in 1980, to 2,246 in 1990, to 3,415 in 2005. In another U.S. development, the Supreme Court ruled in *Roper v. Simmons* (2005) that executing prisoners for crimes committed as juveniles (under age 18) was unconstitutional. Whatever the arguments about the death penalty or the data may or may not indicate, Americans continue to strongly support capital punishment. A poll in 2006 found that even though that 63% of its respondents thought it probable that at least one innocent person had been executed in the previous 5 years, 65% still favored the death penalty. Furthermore, among those who favored the death penalty 51% said it was not applied often enough, compared to 25% who were satisfied with the way it was being applied, 21% who said it was being too often, and 3% who were unsure.

Where to Find More

A pro-death penalty position is taken by Joshua Marquis, "The Myth of Innocence," *Journal of Criminal Law & Criminology* (Winter 2005), and the opposite view is taken by Eliza Steelwater, *The Hangman's Knot: Lynching, Legal Execution, and America's Struggle with the Death Penalty* (Westview Press, 2003). For a group on each side of the issue, visit the Web sites of Pro-Death Penalty.com at www.prodeathpenalty.com/ and the Death Penalty Information Center at www.deathpenaltyinfo.org/. A site worth visiting is that of the Texas Department of Criminal Justice at www.tdcj.state.tx.us/stat/deathrow.htm. You can hyperlink from the name of each of the more than 300 people executed since 1982 to a picture, personal information, a description of the crime each committed, and their last statement. It puts a "face" on the data about both those convicted of murders and the victims.

What More to Do

Discuss all the various permutations of the death penalty debate, including whether it is ever justified under any circumstances and, if so, under what circumstances; whether it is only justified by utilitarianism (it deters later murders) and/or as punishment per se, and whether the fact that executions are not proportionate among various demographic groups is evidence that capital punishment should be abolished. Also, get active. The federal government and 38 states have death penalty laws on the books; 12 states and the District of Columbia do not. Find out the law in your state and support or oppose it.

DEBATE 18

EDUCATION POLICY

AFFIRMATIVE ACTION ADMISSIONS:
Promoting Equality *or* Unfair Advantage?

PROMOTING EQUALITY

ADVOCATES: 41 College Students and 3 Student Coalitions

SOURCE: Amicus Curiae brief to the U.S. Supreme Court in *Grutter v. Bollinger* (2003)

UNFAIR ADVANTAGE

ADVOCATES: 21 Law Professors

SOURCE: Amicus Curiae brief to the U.S. Supreme Court in *Grutter v. Bollinger* (2003)

Surveys show that nearly all Americans support the idea of equal opportunity, but the data on the circumstances of various groups casts doubt on whether the country has yet to achieve it. Economically, for example, the average household income of whites is 63% greater than that of African Americans and 69% greater than that of Hispanics. The 24% poverty rate among black and Latino households is triple that for white households. There are also income gaps for the employed. For every dollar made by the average white worker, blacks make 72 cents, and Latinos make 65 cents. As for unemployment, the spring 2004 rate of white unemployment was about 4.3%, compared to 9.8% for blacks and 5.8% for Latinos. Moreover, significant disparities in poverty, income, and unemployment have persisted as far back as the data goes.

To address such gaps, the federal government began to promote affirmative action in 1961 when President John F. Kennedy issued Executive Order 10925 requiring that federally financed projects "take affirmative action to ensure that hiring and employment practices are free of racial bias."

Later, state and local governments also adopted affirmative action programs, and they and the federal government extended them to education and other areas. Title IX, featured in Debate 16, was part of that effort. Whether because of these policies or more general social changes, the position of women and minorities in education has improved somewhat. Women now make up a majority of college undergraduates and 44% of graduate students. Asian Americans are a greater percentage of both undergraduate and graduate students than they are in the general population. However, improvement for blacks and Latinos has been slower. Between 1980 and 2000, African Americans rose from 9.9% to 13.4% of undergraduates, and Latino enrollment went from 3.7% to 8.6%. This enrollment gap has created a large disparity in college graduates, with 28% of whites over age 25 having a bachelor's degree, compared to 16.5% of African Americans, and 10.6% of Hispanics. At the professional school level, white enrollment between 1980 and 2000 dropped from 81% to 73.9%, while black enrollment grew from 5.8% to 7.2%, and Latino enrollment climbed from 3.9% to 4.7%. This leaves minorities particularly underrepresented in law, medicine, and other professions. Among lawyers, 5.4% are black, and 3.9% are Latino. African Americans are 6.3% of the physicians, and Hispanics are 3.4%. As a reference point, the population in 2000 was 69% white, 12.3% African American, 12.5% Hispanic, and 3.3% Asian American, with other groups making up the balance. Women were 51.9% of the population.

While Americans strongly support the theory of equal opportunity, many have disagreed with the application of affirmative action programs in education and other areas. As a result, there have been a number of court challenges alleging unconstitutional "reverse discrimination." The first significant education case was *Regents of the University of California v. Bakke* (1978), which involved the rejection of a white applicant to medical school that reserved 16% of its places for minority students. In a 5–4 decision, the Supreme Court ruled somewhat confusingly that (a) numerical quotas were not constitutional but that (b) race could legitimately be considered during the admissions process. The following articles trace the legal background more, but the ambiguities in the *Bakke* ruling created disagreements among various Circuit Courts of Appeals over what could and could not be done with respect to affirmative action admissions. This set the groundwork for two "companion" cases involving the University of Michigan. One, *Gratz v. Bollinger*, focused on undergraduate admission and involved the university giving minority students 20 points on a 150-point admissions score. The second, *Grutter v. Bollinger*, related to law school admissions but did not involve a stated quota or a point scheme, only the goal of achieving a "critical mass" of minority students.

The articles below relate to *Grutter*, although most of its underlying rationale also applied to *Gratz*. The two articles are *amicus curiae* (friend of the court) briefs filed by those who were not direct parties to the case but who the court agreed had an important concern. The first, supporting the university's affirmative action program, was filed by a coalition of three student groups and 41 individual students. The second, opposing the university, was written by 21 law professors.

POINTS TO PONDER

- Read the briefs as a Supreme Court justice. What is your decision in *Grutter v. Bollinger* and why?
- Assuming the only difference *Gratz v. Bollinger* is the explicit use of a point system, would you make the same decision as in *Grutter* and why?
- What should affirmative action mean as a policy directive?

Affirmative Action Admissions: Promoting Equality

41 College Students and 3 Student Coalitions

STATEMENT OF THE CASE

When plaintiff filed suit in *Grutter v. Bollinger* in 1997, 41 individually named black, Latino, Native American, Arab American, Asian Pacific American, other minority and white students and three coalitions—United for Equality and Affirmative Action (UEAA), Law Students for Affirmative Action, and the Coalition to Defend Affirmative Action and Integration & Fight for Equality By Any Means Necessary (BAMN), sought and eventually won the right to present our defense of the Law School's affirmative action plan.

Beginning on the 16th of January 2001, a day after the Martin Luther King holiday, the *Grutter v. Bollinger* case went to trial. One month later, after 15 days of trial, and 24 witnesses, the case concluded. The student intervenors fought for the district court trial in order to disprove the plaintiff's claim of "reverse discrimination" and to lift the profound stigma that the attack on affirmative action has placed on the shoulders of minority students. We presented the overwhelming majority of evidence at trial: 15 of the 24 witnesses were called by us, and we used 28 hours and 48 minutes of the 30-hour limit imposed by the district court.

As the student intervenors will show, the plaintiff has not proved that she has been a victim of discrimination—and the United States has not offered a viable alternative to affirmative action. The facts show that if the plaintiff prevails in this Court, the Law School will quickly and inevitably resegregate. That conclusion is confirmed by the resegregation of the universities that has resulted from the end of affirmative action in California, Texas, and Florida. If the plaintiff prevails, gains toward integration will be reversed and replaced by a massive return to segregation starting in the most selective universities and spreading throughout higher education and into the society as a whole.

I. RACE AND THE LAW SCHOOL APPLICATION POOL

For two-thirds of black students and 70 percent of Latino students, the path to the future leads through segregated elementary and secondary schools. The worst segregation, which was once in the South, is now in the major industrial states of the Northeast and Midwest. Michigan [has] 83 percent of its black students attending segregated schools. For Latinos, segregation by race and ethnicity is compounded by segregation by language, with 50 percent of the Latinos in California speaking Spanish at home. For Native Americans, over half live in cities where they face segregation like that faced by blacks and Latinos, while just under half remain in impoverished government-run reservations and boarding schools.

The segregation concentrates and compounds the effects of poverty. While poverty disadvantages the poor of all races, poor whites are more dispersed residentially, and their children are far more likely to enroll in schools that have a substantial number of middle-class students. That is far less likely for black, Latino, and Native American students.

Even for black students from middle- and upper-middle-class families, substantial disadvantage exists. For equivalent incomes, black families have less wealth, less education, and fewer relatives who can provide financial and other assistance in times of trouble. Even when middle-class black people or Latinos move to nearby suburbs, the suburbs are, or quickly become, segregated and the school systems quickly decline. Even for the very few black families who move to stable white, upper-middle-class suburbs with good school systems, there remain racial isolation, stereotyping, tracking, and stigma.

In testimony at trial [in the Federal District Court] on behalf of the student defendants, Professor Gary Orfield of the Harvard University School of Education summarized the impact of segregation:

> There never was a separate but equal school system. That's because of many things. It's because the poverty levels in segregated schools are much higher.... [T]here are fewer minorities in teacher training. There are many fewer teachers who choose to go to work in schools of this sort. Most teachers who start in segregated schools leave faster. The curriculum that is offered is more limited. The probability that the teacher will be trained in their field is much more limited. The level of competition is less. The respect for the institution in the outside world is less. The connections to colleges are less. There are more children with health problems....The population is much more unstable....The kids don't have books....There [are] no facilities....[I]t is like a different planet, a different society.

Segregation—separate and unequal schools—means that there are far fewer black, Latino, and Native American students who graduate from college. The national pool of students who could apply to a school like Michigan is disproportionately white—and many of the comparatively small number of black, Latino, and Native American students in that pool attended segregated elementary and secondary schools.

II. BIAS IN MICHIGAN'S ADMISSIONS SYSTEM WITHOUT AFFIRMATIVE ACTION

A. A Segregated School in a Segregated Profession

Before the advent of affirmative action, there were very few black students who graduated from college, fewer still who applied to law school, and almost none who were admitted to law school.

In the 1950s and early 1960s, except for the law schools at the historically black colleges and universities, the nation's law schools were essentially all white and all male. In 1960, the nation had 286,000 lawyers, of whom 2180 were black and not more than 25 were Native American. The number of Latinos was not recorded but was unquestionably minuscule. Before 1968, each year there were about 200 black law graduates in the nation.

From 1960 through 1968, the Law School graduated 2687 law students, of whom four were black and none were Latino or Native American.

B. The LSAT

In the early 1960s, the University of Michigan Law School admitted students based on a rigid index that combined undergraduate grades with an LSAT score. At that time, the School was not nearly as selective as it would become. But as more students went to college—and as affirmative action began to open the doors to minorities and to women of all races—the number of applicants to all law schools expanded dramatically. The schools became more selective and the LSAT became far more important.

The plaintiff and the United States call the LSAT "objective"—but they offer no proof to support the claim that it is an "objective" measure of anything important or that it is "race-neutral" in any way. In fact, all the evidence at trial showed the reverse.

The uncontested evidence presented at trial by the student defendants also demonstrated that test scores had little predictive value. In an uncontested study, Professor Richard Lempert, a member of the committee that drafted the 1992 policy, testifying for the students at trial, established that an applicant's LSAT score did not correlate with later success as a lawyer, measured by income, stated satisfaction, or political and community leadership.

C. Undergraduate Grades

The other major "objective" criterion in the traditional Law School admissions system is the undergraduate grade point average (UGPA). While the racial gap on that average is much smaller than the LSAT gap, the gap is still significant when admissions are very competitive, as they have been at the Law School for many years.

The racial segregation in K–12 education causes part of the racial gap in UGPAs; but the conditions on the nation's campuses also contribute to the gap. Black, Latino, and Native American students feel and are isolated; and the cumulative effect of a daily run of slights and profiling takes its toll on black and other minority students. As the district court conceded, while the effect cannot be quantified for each student, racial prejudice depresses the undergraduate grades and overall academic performance of minority students who apply to Law Schools.

The grids prepared by the plaintiff's chief witness, Dr. Kinley Larntz, reflect the gap in test scores and grades and stand as a measure of the cumulative effect of discriminatory tests, segregated education, social inequality, and the depressing effect of racial prejudice on the undergraduate grades and overall academic performance of minority students.

III. THE LAW SCHOOL AFFIRMATIVE ACTION PROGRAM

Under pressure from students on the campus and the civil rights movement, the law faculty began an intense series of debates that stretched from the 1960s through the current date about how to deal with the realities outlined above.

In the course of those debates, faculty members repeatedly recognized that numerical credentials discriminated against black and other minority applicants, "caus[ing] [their] actual potential…to be underestimated, especially when gauged by standard testing procedures…thought to be 'culturally biased.'"

In 1973, the [University of Michigan] Law School graduated 41 black students and its first Latino student. In 1975, it graduated its first two Asian-Americans, followed by its first Native American in 1976. The increasing number of black and other minority students cleared the way for the admission of increasing numbers of women of all races.

After this Court handed down its decision in *Bakke* in June 1978, the faculty formulated a policy to comply with the decision.

In 1992, the faculty adopted the plan that is now in effect. The plan calls for consideration of each applicant as an individual; attempts to seek many forms of diversity; and states the School's commitment to enrolling a "critical mass" of black, Latino, and Native American students, who would not be admitted to the Law School in significant numbers without that commitment.

IV. WHAT ENDING AFFIRMATIVE ACTION WOULD MEAN

In ruling for the plaintiff, the district court conceded that the elimination of affirmative action at the Law School would result in an immediate reduction in underrepresented minority enrollment of over 73 percent. But this would only be the start. The end of affirmative action at selective colleges would dramatically reduce the pool of minority applicants to the Law School, driving the number of minority law students down still further. Within a few years at most, the Law School would again be nearly as segregated as it was in the 1960s.

In 1997, the ban on affirmative action announced by the University of California (UC) Board of Regents went into effect. The following year, only one black student enrolled at Boalt Hall. Minority enrollment at the UCLA School of Law dropped dramatically.

The few black and other minority students who remain at California's most selective campuses have faced increased racism caused by the elimination of affirmative action.

Dr. Eugene Garcia, the Dean of the Graduate School of Education at Berkeley, testified that black, Latino, and Native American students have been forced from the flagship campuses of the UC system onto its two least selective campuses. As the state's population continues to grow, the "cascade" will continue until the vast majority of black, Latino, and Native American students are forced out of the UC system altogether.

The UC faculty and administrations opposed the ban and sought to undo its effects. At Berkeley, the school downplayed the importance of grades and test scores; at UCLA, the school attempted to substitute the consideration of socio-economic status for the consideration of race. Because neither approach could serve as a substitute for affirmative action, both schools found it impossible to enroll a class including more than token numbers of black and other minority students.

SUMMARY OF THE ARGUMENT

In this case, the plaintiff is asking the Court to reinterpret the American Constitution to the dramatic detriment of black, Latino, and other minority people and women of all races. If the Court does what [the] plaintiff asks, it will resegregate, divide, and polarize our country. The authority of the Court would be compromised.

Segregation and inequality are increasing in education. Irrespective of the legal forms used to enforce, to maintain, or passively to justify the separate and unequal condition of education at virtually every level, the fact stands as a profound insult and provocation to the minority youth of America and to the best of the nation's legal and political traditions. Minority children are, in their increasing majority, relegated to second-class, segregated schools—today's version of the back of the bus. The very small handful of black, Mexican American, and Native American students who have made it to the front of America's education bus—institutions like the University of Michigan Law School—are now being told by the plaintiff to get out of their seat and move to the back of the bus.

The demographic fabric of America is changing. By the middle of this century, no racial grouping will be in the majority. America will be a more diverse society; it must not become a more segregated society. We must strive to make equality more, not less, of a reality, or we will surely face renewed social convulsions.

The movement to defend affirmative action and integration has awakened and stirred into action every sector of this society. What unites these many peoples in defense of affirmative action is the conviction that the Constitution's pledge of equality should have meaning and currency in our collective American future. Our progress as a nation depends on the realization of this prospect.

Affirmative Action Admissions: Unfair Advantage

21 LAW PROFESSORS

INTEREST OF *AMICI CURIAE*

Amici curiae are law professors with a professional interest in promoting learning environments free from the taint of racial discrimination. *Amici* are committed to the principles of equality under law embodied in the Constitution, and oppose invidious racial discrimination of any kind. In particular, *amici* oppose as unconstitutional the race-based admissions policies employed by the University of Michigan School of Law and many other institutions of higher learning. A list of the *amici* and their institutional affiliations is provided as an appendix to this brief. The institutional affiliations are for identification purposes only. The views expressed in this brief are those of the individual *amici* and do not necessarily reflect the views of the institutions at which they teach.

SUMMARY OF ARGUMENT

This Court should hold that "diversity" is not a compelling state interest sufficient to justify race-based discrimination. First, "diversity" is employed by universities as a shorthand term for discrimination on the basis of race, is indistinguishable from the use of quotas, and is not a remedial interest. Second, racial "diversity" in the classroom does not constitute academic diversity; to the contrary, it is based on racial stereotyping and fosters stigmatization and hostility. Furthermore, even stereotypically assuming it resulted in a greater diversity of views and information, such a result is not a compelling interest that would outweigh constitutional rights in this or other contexts. Finally, "diversity" is a race-balancing interest that would, by its own terms, require race discrimination for eternity.

ARGUMENT

The Court has held repeatedly that racial classifications are "*presumptively invalid* and can be upheld only upon an extraordinary justification" (*Shaw v. Reno*, 1993). Race-based classifications can survive strict scrutiny only if they are narrowly tailored to serve a compelling state interest.

The University of Michigan School of Law ("Michigan") employs race-based classifications in its admissions policies, and race often is the deciding factor between the admission of one applicant and the rejection of another with equal or better qualifications. The questions for this Court, therefore, are whether Michigan's asserted interest is constitutionally "compelling" and whether its admissions program is narrowly tailored to serve that interest.

Amici [we] respectfully submit that this Court should state in words so clear that they cannot be misunderstood by university administrators that the use of racial preferences, classifications, or "pluses" for the purpose of achieving a racially diverse student body is prohibited by the Fourteenth Amendment. The failure of the Court to address the "diversity" question head-on could have devastating consequences for the rights of individuals of all races who participate in the admissions process. Since *Bakke* [*University of California v. Bakke*, 1978], the "diversity" principle in practice has been used to create a loophole through which universities continue to discriminate broadly and openly on the basis of race.

I. MICHIGAN'S DIRECT PURSUIT OF RACIAL DIVERSITY NECESSARILY ENTAILS RACIAL CLASSIFICATIONS

The pursuit of "diversity" in general is a broad and potentially varied exercise that can turn on any number of characteristics or traits. Universities can seek geographic diversity, intellectual diversity, athletic and artistic diversity, and even socio-economic diversity. Those qualities are directly relevant to the educational mission and are not themselves constitutionally suspect. But the direct pursuit of *racial* diversity as an end unto itself, and as a supposed means of creating other types of diversity, is quite different. That pursuit involves taking a single characteristic—race—that the Constitution and this Court have declared unrelated to legitimate bases for distinguishing among individuals, and relying upon it not withstanding such admonitions.

A. Pursuit of "Diversity" Is a Euphemism for Race-Based Decisionmaking

Making disingenuous use of Justice Powell's lone dictum regarding "diversity," [in the *Bakke* decision], universities such as Michigan have adopted the seemingly benign language of pursuing diversity in general as a misleading euphemism for decision-making processes and goals based overtly on race. It is the view and experience of *amici* here that whatever nods of the head universities make toward more general notions of diversity, their affirmative action programs, such as the one in this case, remain targeted at a narrow vision of *racial* diversity *regardless* of the consequences of such programs for other types of diversity.

Numerous experienced law professors, including even those who support racial preferences in admissions, have recognized and acknowledged that the language of educational diversity in the admissions context is generally used as a cover for direct racial decision-making. Such professors speak not merely as academics who have studied the issue, but as first-hand observers within law school communities and administrations, and often as direct participants of the very admissions processes they describe. Professor Alan Dershowitz of Harvard has been forthright about the deceptive use of the "diversity" label in connection with race-driven admissions programs:

> The *raison d'être* for race-specific affirmative action programs has simply never been diversity for the sake of education. The checkered history of "diversity" demonstrates that it was designed largely as a cover to achieve other legally, morally, and politically controversial goals. In recent years, it has been invoked—especially by professional schools—as a clever post facto justification for increasing the number of minority group students in the student body.

Professor Samuel Issacharoff, of Columbia and formerly of Texas, makes a similar point. One of the attorneys who defended the University of Texas School of Law's racedriven admissions policy, has nonetheless acknowledged that "diversity" is the current jargon for racial discrimination: "[O]ne of the clear legacies of *Bakke* has been to enshrine the term 'diversity' within the legal lexicon to cover everything from curricular enrichments to thinly-veiled set-asides."

Other experienced law professors with diverse views of the affirmative action issue in general have recognized the same truth.

Professor Jed Rubenfeld of Yale, who defends "affirmative action" on non-diversity grounds not advanced by Michigan in this case, notes the disingenuousness of the claim that race-driven admissions advance true "diversity" measured by any criteria *other than* race. "[T]he pro-affirmative action crowd needs to own up to the weaknesses of 'diversity' as a defense of most affirmative action plans. Everyone knows that in most cases a true diversity of perspectives and backgrounds is not really being pursued."

In the end, even the proponents of affirmative action, if they are being candid, recognize that the "diversity" pursued by programs such as Michigan's is directly race-based in both its means and its ends, favoring or disfavoring particular races for their own sake without concern for diversity of qualities other than race. While such programs may pay lip-service to intellectual or experiential qualities other than race, they invariably collapse back to using race for its own sake, or as a proxy for other, pertinent, qualities without regard to whether such racial stereotyping is true or permissible.

B. Direct Pursuit of Racial Diversity Is Functionally Indistinguishable from Racial Quotas

"Diversity"-based admissions policies such as the one at Michigan necessarily begin and end with some perceived level of optimal diversity among the characteristics—in this case race—that they use to classify candidates. In order to achieve its claimed interest in diversity, Michigan must have at least some sense of what constitutes the proper representation of each race before it can decide that certain racial groups are "under-represented" and the student body thereby insufficiently diverse. Professor Issacharoff candidly acknowledges the point:

> The problem with diversity as a justification for a challenged affirmative action program is that it is an almost incoherent concept to operationalize, unless diversity means a predetermined number of admittees from a desired group....[S]elective institutions must approach the applicant pool with predetermined notions of what an appropriately balanced incoming class should look like.

The only way to ensure adequate "representation" among the races at the end of the admissions process is to begin with an institutional definition of "diversity" that necessarily produces the desired proportions of racial representation in a class of admitted students. Michigan's "diversity" policy is symbolic of the numbers game that has become synonymous with admissions policies that employ racial preferences. For example, members of Michigan's admissions staff receive "daily reports," which track applicants by race. Dennis Shields, the former director of admissions at Michigan, has acknowledged that "as an admissions season progressed, he would consult the daily reports more and more frequently in order to keep track of the racial and ethnic composition of the class." Mr. Shields said that he did this to ensure that a "critical mass" of minority students were enrolled. "Diversity in education" through race-driven admissions is meaningless without quotas or something constituting the functional equivalent of a quota system.

The district court determined after careful consideration of all of the facts that the "critical mass" concept is functionally equivalent to a quota system. The district court explained:

> [O]ver the years, [critical mass] has meant in practice that the law school attempts to enroll an entering class 10% to 17% of which consists of underrepresented minority students. The 10% figure, as a target, has historical roots going back to the late 1960s. Beginning in the 1970s,

> the law school documents begin referring to 10–12% as the desired percentage. Professor Lempert testified that critical mass lies in the range of 11–17%. Indeed this percentage range appeared in a draft of the 1992 admissions policy, and it was omitted from the final version despite Professor Regan's suggestion that it remain for the sake of "candor."

"Diversity" policies must be described as what they are—means of implementing racial quotas. That such quotas might be informal or hidden under a cloak of rhetoric does not change that essential fact.

C. "Diversity" Is Not a Remedial Interest

Thus far, the only constitutionally compelling interest recognized by this Court as satisfying strict scrutiny for racial classifications is the remediation of the effects of past race discrimination.

Michigan's "diversity" policy is not, and does not purport to be, remedial. The question for this Court then is whether "diversity" should be added as a "compelling," not merely valid or permissible, state interest that can be used to justify direct and intentional racial discrimination.

Because the Court has "strictly" limited the use of racial classifications to the remedial context, respondents must demonstrate that there is something so special, so *compelling*, about marginal differences in the educational experiences of post-secondary students that universities, alone among our government-sponsored institutions, should be allowed to practice what the Constitution prohibit[s]—naked race discrimination. Although the question properly posed seems to answer itself, an examination of the realities of "diversity" in the classroom also leads to the conclusion that this so-called justification for discrimination does not pass constitutional muster.

II. RACIAL "DIVERSITY" IS NOT A COMPELLING INTEREST

Because the pursuit of racial diversity for its own sake is an affront to the Fourteenth Amendment, the defenders of "diversity" ultimately resort to some version of the argument that bringing together persons of different "backgrounds"—as defined by their skin color or national origin—will "enhance" the educational experience of students by creating academic or viewpoint diversity. But Michigan's admissions policy, and other "diversity" policies like it, cannot be defended on the ground that racial diversity promotes academic diversity. The defense of "diversity" programs on the ground that they expose people of different races to one another, thereby facilitating learning, respect and appreciation among the races, does not relate to a true "interest in intellectual diversity—diversity of 'experiences, outlooks and ideas' that would otherwise be left out—but specifically in racial and ethnic diversity as such."

A. Interests in "Diversity" That Assume Stereotyping Cannot Have Compelling Weight

The "diversity" rationale suggests that it is permissible to use race as a proxy for experiences, outlooks or ideas, and that the use of race as a proxy will ensure that different viewpoints are brought to the classroom. But however desirable a diversity of *ideas* may be, there is no basis for categorizing it as "compelling," rather than merely acceptable or substantial for purposes of analyses *other than* strict scrutiny. The abhorrent essential predicate to the interest—governmental stereotyping of different races as to their views—also assures that the interest in racial diversity for its secondary viewpoint effects cannot count as compelling.

Common sense and classroom experiences demonstrate that "viewpoint diversity" and "academic diversity" in the classroom are not affected by the racial composition of a student body. Dean and long-time professor at Michigan, Professor Terrance Sandalow, wrote in the *Michigan Law Review*:

> My own experience and that of colleagues with whom I have discussed the question, experience that concededly is limited to the classroom setting, is that racial diversity is not responsible for generating ideas unfamiliar to some members of the class. Students do, of course, quite frequently express and develop ideas that others in the class have not previously encountered, but even though the subjects I teach deal extensively with racial issues, I cannot recall an instance in which, for example, ideas were expressed by a black student that have not also been expressed by white students. Black students do, at times, call attention to the racial implications of issues that are not facially concerned with race, but white and Asian-American students are in my experience no less likely to do so.

Racial diversity is not required to foster a full discussion of issues and viewpoints in the classroom. If a white applicant and a black applicant each have the same view on an issue, and their respective race is ignored as it must be under the Constitution, there is no true "intellectual" or "academic" reason for admitting one of the students over the other.

Any "diversity" policy that is premised on the notion that people of different races bring particular viewpoints to the classroom solely because of their race should be struck down. If schools truly think that viewpoint diversity enhances education, they can pursue it directly rather than using race as a proxy.

Apparently realizing the difficulty of defending its admissions policy on the ground that race defines viewpoint, Michigan attempts an alternative claim that racial diversity in the classroom is required to *dismantle* stereotypes.

[The University of] Michigan argues in essence that, because it assumes individuals generally believe that members of a "minority" race all share the same viewpoint on all issues, the educational experiences of members of the benighted majority will be "enhanced" by interaction with a "critical mass" of minority students. This argument merely shifts the stereotyped assumptions over to the majority racial group, but is no less offensive therefore.

Moreover, Michigan hardly needs racial preferences to teach the obvious—that not all members of any given minority think alike. If, miraculously, something more were needed to make this point to students, surely a sufficiently diverse *reading list* would suffice. Michigan's self-contradictory treatment of individuals as members of groups, purportedly in order to demonstrate that individuals are *not* members of groups, is closer to being incredible than it is to being compelling.

B. Discrimination Resulting from Racial Stereotyping Results in Stigmatization and Hostility

Even if one were to hypothesize that a compelled increase in racial diversity would increase educationally valuable viewpoint diversity to some degree, it would also generate educationally detrimental stigma and hostility based on precisely the same type of stereotyping regarding race employed by the University. Indeed, policies that seek diversity through race are [according to one scholar] a "statement by government that certain persons identified by race are in fact being placed in positions they may be presumed not likely to hold but for their race."

"Diversity" admissions programs, such as Michigan's, foster rather than minimize the focus on race. The policy treats preferred minorities as a group, rather than as individuals. Although Michigan purports to consider other types of diversity—such as unusual employment experiences and extracurricular activities—race is the most identifiable diversity factor that separates one applicant from another.

Amici's collective experiences support the conclusion that both students who are admitted, and those who are not admitted, recognize that race indisputably plays an important role in admissions. Applicants from races that do not benefit from Michigan's preferences, who have high LSAT scores and GPAs, but who nonetheless are denied admission, will likely conclude that race determined their fate in the admissions process. Similarly, members of all races who gain admission may believe that their minority classmates would not be their classmates but for their race. Because of the lowered expectations that accompany racial preferences in admissions, members of minority groups are and will be stigmatized—sometimes self-stigmatized—as inferior.

The racial hostility and stigmatization that is bred in universities as a result of racial preferences is felt both in our classrooms and throughout all of society. If not stopped now, the hostility and scarring that can result from racial preferences based on "diversity" could take generations to heal. At a minimum, however, such consequences cut against any claimed benefits and render Michigan's asserted interest in the educational benefits of racial diversity necessarily less than compelling.

C. Government-Defined Viewpoint Diversity Is Not a Compelling Interest

Regardless whether racial classifications generate viewpoint diversity and accepting that viewpoint diversity is, in general, a valuable thing in an educational environment, that does not even remotely satisfy the requirement that it must be a "compelling" interest sufficient to justify otherwise unconstitutional conduct. The difficulty in too-easy a transition from merely desirable to constitutionally compelling seems apparent: We would not authorize state universities to violate students' right to free speech or free exercise of religion on the ground that doing so would, in the view of academics, create a better educational environment or a greater "diversity" of views.

But if it is a compelling interest to discriminate on the basis of race in order to promote an educational atmosphere with a supposedly more diverse set of student views, then it is unavoidably a compelling interest for all other constitutional purposes. The notion that the government might impose a myriad of speech restrictions and compulsions in the name of "diversity" demonstrates the absurd premise that marginal differences in educational diversity rise to the level of "compelling" state interests.

D. The "Diversity" Rationale Is Limitless

"Diversity" also fails as a "compelling interest" because it has no logical stopping point. The Court has repeatedly rejected alleged "compelling interests" that extend indefinitely into the future.

By definition, a "diversity" interest supports indefinite discrimination on the basis of race in university admissions because there will always be a need to engage in race-based decisionmaking to ensure a "properly diverse" student body. "Diversity"—with its concomitant quotas and careful monitoring of racial admissions—indeed would *require* unending use of race in admissions.

For this reason, and for all of the other reasons set forth above, "diversity" does not constitute an extraordinary justification sufficient to overcome the presumptive invalidity of government-sponsored race discrimination.

THE CONTINUING DEBATE: Affirmative Action Admissions

What Is New

In 2003, the Supreme Court upheld the University of Michigan's position in *Grutter v. Bollinger* and rejected it in *Gratz v. Bollinger*. By a 5 to 4 vote in *Grutter*, the Court permitted the law school's use of race as one factor in determining admissions on the grounds that a "compelling state interest" existed in promoting diversity at all levels of society. But by 6 to 3 in *Gratz*, the justices rejected the undergraduate admission process that gave automatic points to minorities on the admissions scale. These decisions reconfirmed *Bakke*, but thereby also left some of that decision's uncertainties in place about how to judge an affirmative action program without resorting to numbers when establishing goals or monitoring progress.

Perhaps reflecting the fine line the Court walked in the two decisions, public opinion about affirmative actions varies with the way the question is asked. For example, consider the wording and results of three polls taken in 2003. The first asked Americans if they "generally favor or oppose affirmative action programs for racial minorities?" A plurality (49%) replied, "favor," 43% said "oppose," and 8% were unsure. The second poll introduced a reason for affirmative action, asking, "In order to overcome past discrimination, do you favor or oppose affirmative action programs...[for minorities]?" With that prompt, support for affirmative action was much higher (63% in favor, 29% opposed, 8% unsure). By contrast, support declined to 38% (with 51% opposed, and 10% unsure) in a poll whose question included the word "preferences" ("Do you favor or oppose affirmative action programs that give preferences to...minorities?").

Where to Find More

For a history of affirmative action, read Terry H. Anderson, *The Pursuit of Fairness: A History of Affirmative Action* (Oxford University Press, 2005). You can read the decisions and the dissents for both *Grutter v. Bollinger* and *Gratz v. Bollinger* by going to the Supreme Court Collection Web page of Cornell University's Legal Information Institute at supct.law.cornell.edu/supct/ and entering the case names in the search function. The Web site of the Coalition to Defend Affirmative Action and Integration & Fight for Equality **B**y **A**ny **M**eans **N**ecessary (BAMN), one of the student groups who filed an amicus curiae brief in *Grutter*, is at www.bamn.com/. An organization with an opposing point of view is American Civil Rights Institute at www.ACRI.org/.

What More to Do

Write an admission policy for your university that addresses the demographic component. Then find out what your school's written policy is (if any) and interview admissions officials to find out how they implement affirmative action. How does the school's policy compare with your views?

DEBATE 19

FOREIGN POLICY

U.S. MILITARY FORCES IN IRAQ: Stay the Course *or* Withdraw Quickly?

STAY THE COURSE

ADVOCATE: George W. Bush, President of the United States

SOURCE: "This Is Going To Be Freedom's Century," address delivered at the Freedom House, Washington, D.C., March 29, 2006

WITHDRAW QUICKLY

ADVOCATES: Wesley B. Renfro and Brian Urlacher, doctoral students, Department of Political Science, University of Connecticut

SOURCE: "With Terrorism Growing and Civil War Looming the United States Must Withdraw from Iraq," an essay written especially for this volume, October 2006

Since 1990, U.S. foreign policy related to Iraq can be summarized as shifting but unbroken levels of violence and tension. In August 1990, Iraq overran Kuwait. Four months later, President George H. W. Bush sent U.S. troops to war to liberate Kuwiat and to "defang" Iraq. The United Nations-authorized invasion soon defeated Iraq's military later uncovered huge stocks of Iraqi chemical weapons. The peace terms spelled out by the UN Security Council barred Iraq seeking or having any biological, chemical, or nuclear weapons of mass destruction (WMDs) and required that UN arms inspectors have unrestricted access to ensure compliance.

In the ensuing years, U.S.-Iraqi tensions remained high. President Bill Clinton twice launched major aerial attacks against Iraq. The first came in 1993 after Iraq plotted to assassinate former President Bush. The second was in 1998 after Iraq's repeated refusal to cooperate with UN inspectors persuaded Clinton "to attack Iraq's nuclear, chemical and biological weapons programs and its military capacity to threaten its neighbors."

The U.S. posture hardened further under President George W. Bush, who believed that the threat from Saddam Hussein could only be eliminated by toppling him from power. Even though UN inspectors in Iraq had found no hard evidence of WMDs, and even though the UN Security Council refused to authorize action, Bush acted anyway. In March 2003, U.S. troops, supported by smaller contingents from several other countries, once again invaded Iraq. Bush justified the war based on Iraq's alleged WMD program, its supposed ties to terrorist groups, and his determination to democratize Iraq.

The invading forces routed Iraq's military, but the travails of Americans and Iraqis were not over. Instead they had just begun. Terrorist-style operations soon broke out. Saddam loyalists directed some. Others were the work of outside Muslim extremists, some of them with ties to al Qaeda. American casualties soon exceeded the number of killed and wounded during invasion, and by mid 2006 more than 2,300 U.S. and coalition troops had been killed in combat and another 20,000 wounded.

The violence assailing the Iraqis was even worse, with about 40,000 Iraqis civilians dead and another 1,000 a month dying in 2006 in attacks that increasingly resembled a civil war. The U.S. goal was to found a democratic, unified Iraq, but that effort was in grave doubt by 2006. An Iraqi government came into being in 2005, but it was struggling to gain authority. The core issue was the division of Iraq into three competing groups: Shiite Muslims, who are a majority (±60%) of the population, are mostly Arab, and live mostly in the south; Sunni Muslims, who were in control under Saddam, are ±25% of the population, dominate the central part of the country, and are mostly Arabs; and Kurds, who are non-Arabs (more closely related Persians/Iranians), live in the north, are ±15% of the population, and have aspirations of joining with Kurds in Turkey, Iran, and elsewhere to form an independent Kurdistan. There is deep enmity among the three, and these divisions left the Kurds nurturing their traditional dream of an independent Kurdistan and Shiites and Sunni death squads slaughtering each other's populations.

Most Americans supported the invasion of Iraq in 2003, and that support held for a substantial time. By July 2005, however, a public opinion was evenly divided. Support continued to fall, and 53% of Americans thought invading Iraq had been a mistake when in March 2006 President Bush took to the airwaves and in the first reading explained to Americans why he believed that they should stay the course in Iraq. Others disagree, with some wanting the president to establish a long-term timetable for U.S. withdrawal from Iraq, and others, including Wesley Renfro and Brian Urlacher in the second reading, urging a much more rapid U.S. departure from Iraq.

POINTS TO PONDER

- ➢ What will be the consequences for Iraq and the region if the United States withdraws without ensuring a stable government? Are those better or worse for the United States than the consequences of remaining in Iraq?
- ➢ President's Bush argues progress is being made in Iraq, but most news focus on the violence. Is the president deluding himself or is press coverage imbalanced?
- ➢ Who makes the better case: those who say the occupation of Iraq is fomenting new terrorism or those who argue that failing in Iraq will provide the terrorists with a victory that will embolden them?

U.S. Military Forces in Iraq: Stay the Course

GEORGE W. BUSH

I appreciate very much the men and women of Freedom House [the organization to which President Bush was speaking]. For more than 60 years, this organization has been a tireless champion for liberty. You've been a clear voice for the oppressed across the world. At Freedom House you understand that the only path to lasting peace is the expansion of freedom and liberty.

Free societies are peaceful societies. When governments are accountable to their own citizens, when people are free to speak and assemble, when minorities are protected, then justice prevails. And so does the cause of peace.

Freedom House was founded on the principle that no nation is exempt from the demands of human dignity. And you're carrying that message across the world, from Africa to China to Belarus and beyond. At Freedom House, you also understand free societies do not take root overnight, especially in countries that suffer from decades of tyranny and repression. You understand that free elections are an instrument of change; yet they're only the first step. So as you press for democratic change across the world you're helping new democracies build free institutions they need to overcome the legacies of tyranny and dictatorship....

We meet at a time of war, but also at a moment of great hope. In our world, and due in part to our efforts, freedom is taking root in places where liberty was unimaginable a couple of years ago. Just 25 years ago, at the start of the 1980s, there were only 45 democracies on the face of the Earth. Today, Freedom House reports there are 122 democracies, and more people now live in liberty than ever before.

The advance of freedom is the story of our time, and we're seeing new chapters written before our eyes. Since the beginning of 2005, we've witnessed remarkable democratic changes across the globe. The people of Afghanistan have elected their first democratic parliament in more than a generation. The people of Lebanon have recovered their independence and chosen their leaders in free elections. The people of Kyrgyzstan have driven a corrupt regime from power and voted for democratic change. The people of Liberia have overcome decades of violence and are now led by the first woman elected as a head of state in any African nation. And the courageous people of Iraq have gone to the polls not once, not twice, but three times, choosing a transitional government, a democratic constitution, and a new government under that constitution.

Each of these countries still faces enormous challenges that will take patience and the support of the international community to overcome. Yet, Freedom House has declared the year 2005 was one of the most successful years for freedom since the Freedom House began measuring world freedom more than 30 years ago. From Kabul to Baghdad to Beirut and beyond, freedom's tide is rising, and we should not rest, and we must not rest, until the promise of liberty reaches every people and every nation.

In our history, most democratic progress has come with the end of a war. After the defeat of the Axis powers in World War II and the collapse of communism in the

Cold War, scores of nations cleared away the rubble of tyranny and laid the foundations of freedom and democracy.

Today, the situation is very different. Liberty is advancing not in a time of peace, but in the midst of a war, at a moment when a global movement of great brutality and ambition is fighting freedom's progress with all the hateful violence they can muster. In this new century, the advance of freedom is a vital element of our strategy to protect the American people, and to secure the peace for generations to come. We're fighting the terrorists across the world because we know that if America were not fighting this enemy in other lands, we'd be facing them here in our own land.

On September the 11th, 2001, we saw the violence and the hatred of a vicious enemy, and the future that they intend for us. That day I made a decision: America will not wait to be attacked again. We will confront this mortal danger. We will stay on the offensive. America will defend our freedom.

We're pursuing the terrorists on many battlefronts. Today, the central front in the war on terror is Iraq. This month I've given a series of speeches on recent events in Iraq and how we're adapting our approach to deal with the events on the ground. At George Washington University I reported on the progress we have made in training the Iraqi security forces, the growing number of Iraqi units that are taking the lead in the fight, the territory we're handing over to them, and the performance they turned in after the bombing of the Golden Mosque in Samarra.

Last week in Cleveland, I told the American people about the northern Iraqi city of Tal Afar, which was once a key base of operations for al Qaeda and is now a free city that gives us reason to hope for a free Iraq. I explained how the story of Tal Afar gives me confidence in our strategy, because in that city we see the outlines of the Iraq we've been fighting for, a free and secure people who are getting back on their feet, who are participating in government and civic life, and are becoming allies in the fight against the terrorists.

Today, I'm going to discuss the stakes in Iraq and our efforts to help the Iraqi people overcome past divisions and form a lasting democracy, and why it is vital to the security of the American people that we help them succeed.

In the wake of recent violence in Iraq, many Americans are asking legitimate questions: Why are Iraqis so divided? And did America cause the instability by removing Saddam Hussein from power? They ask, after three elections, why are the Iraqi people having such a hard time coming together? And can a country with so many divisions ever build a stable democracy? They ask why we can't bring our troops home now and let the Iraqis sort out their differences on their own.

These are fair questions, and today, I'll do my best to answer them. I'll discuss some of the reasons for the instability we're seeing in Iraq, why democracy is the only force that can overcome these divisions, why I believe the vast majority of Iraqis want to live in freedom and peace, and why the security of our nation depends on the success of a free Iraq.

Today, some Americans ask whether removing Saddam caused the divisions and instability we're now seeing. In fact, much of the animosity and violence we now see is the legacy of Saddam Hussein. He is a tyrant who exacerbated sectarian divisions to keep himself in power. Iraq is a nation with many ethnic and religious and sectarian and regional and tribal divisions. Before Saddam Hussein, Iraqis from different communities managed to live together. Even today, many Iraqi tribes have both Sunni and Shia [or Shiite] branches. And in many small towns with mixed populations, there's often only one mosque where Sunni and Shia worship together. Intermarriage is also common with mixed families that include Arabs and Kurds and Sunnis and Shia and Turkmen, Assyrians, and Chaldeans.

To prevent these different groups from coming to challenge his regime, Saddam Hussein undertook a deliberate strategy of maintaining control by dividing the Iraqi people. He stayed on top by brutally repressing different Iraqi communities and pitting them one against the other. He forced hundreds of thousands of Iraqis out of their homes using expulsion as a weapon to subdue and punish any group that resisted his rule. By displacing Iraqi communities and dividing the Iraqi people, he sought to establish himself as the only force that could hold the country together.

In Saddam's campaign of repression and division, no Iraqi group was spared. In the late 1980s, Saddam Hussein unleashed a brutal ethnic cleansing operation against Kurds in northern Iraq. Kurdish towns and villages were destroyed. Tens of thousands of Kurds disappeared or were killed. In his effort to terrorize the Kurds into submission, Saddam dropped chemical weapons on scores of Kurdish villages. In one village alone, a town called Halabja, his regime killed thousands of innocent men and women and children, using mustard gas and nerve agents. Saddam also forcibly removed hundreds of thousands of Kurds from their homes, and then he moved Arabs into those homes and onto the properties of the people who were forced to leave. As a result of this strategy deep tensions persist to this day.

Saddam also waged a brutal campaign of suppression and genocide against the Shia in the south of Iraq. He targeted prominent Shia clerics for assassination. He destroyed Shia mosques and holy sites. He killed thousands of innocent men, women and children. He piled their bodies into mass graves. After the 1991 Persian Gulf War, Saddam brutally crushed a Shia uprising. Many Shia fled to the marshes of southern Iraq. They hid in the wetlands that could not be easily reached by Saddam's army.

The wetlands, by the way, were also home to the Marsh Arabs, an ancient civilization that traces its roots back 5,000 years. So Saddam destroyed the Marsh Arabs, and those who hid in the marshes, by draining the marshes where they lived. In less than a decade, the majority of these lush wetlands were turned into barren desert, and most of the Marsh Arabs were driven from their ancestral home. It is no wonder that deep divisions and scars exist in much of the Shia population.

Saddam also oppressed his fellow Sunnis. One of the great misperceptions about Iraq is that every Sunni enjoyed a privileged status under Saddam's regime. In truth, Saddam trusted few outside his family and his tribe. He installed his sons and his brothers and his cousins in key positions. Almost everyone was considered suspect, and often those suspicions led to brutal violence.

In one instance, Saddam's security services tortured to death a pilot from a prominent Sunni tribe, and then dumped his headless body in front of his family's house. It caused riots that he then brutally suppressed. In the mid-1990s, Saddam rounded up scores of prominent Sunni economists and lawyers and retired army officers and former government officials. Many were never heard from again.

It is hard to overstate the effects of Saddam's brutality on the Iraqi nation. Here's what one Marine recalls when he was on the streets of the Iraqi capital. He said, quote, "I had an Iraqi citizen come up to me. She opened her mouth and she had no tongue. She was pointing at the statue.

There were people with no fingers waving at the statue of Saddam, telling us he tortured them. People were showing us scars on their back." Iraq is a nation that is physically and emotionally scarred by three decades of Saddam's tyranny, and these wounds will take time to heal. As one Marsh Arab put it, "Saddam did everything he could to kill us. You cannot recover from that right away."

These are the kinds of tensions Iraqis are dealing with today. They are the divisions that Saddam aggravated through deliberate policies of ethnic cleansing and sectarian violence. As one Middle East scholar has put it, Iraq under Saddam Hussein was "a society slowly and systematically poisoned by political terror. The toxic atmosphere in today's Iraq bears witness to his terrible handiwork."

The argument that Iraq was stable under Saddam and that stability is now in danger because we removed him is wrong. While liberation has brought its own set of challenges, Saddam Hussein's removal from power was the necessary first step in restoring stability and freedom to the people of Iraq.

Today some Americans are asking why the Iraqi people are having such a hard time building a democracy. The reason is that the terrorists and former regime elements are exploiting the wounds inflicted under Saddam's tyranny. The enemies of a free Iraq are employing the same tactics Saddam used—killing and terrorizing the Iraqi people in an effort to foment sectarian division.

For the Saddamists, provoking sectarian strife is business as usual. And we know from the terrorists' own words that they're using the same tactics with the goal of inciting a civil war. Two years ago, we intercepted a letter to Osama bin Laden from the terrorist [Abu Musab al-] Zarqawi, in which he explains his plan to stop the advance of democracy in Iraq. Zarqawi wrote:

> "If we succeed in dragging the Shia into the arena of sectarian war, it will become possible to waken the inattentive Sunnis as they feel imminent danger. The only solution is for us to strike the religious and military and other cadres among the Shia with blow after blow."

The terrorists and Saddamists have been brutal in the pursuit of this strategy. They target innocent civilians; they blow up police officers; they attack mosques; and they commit other acts of horrific violence for the cameras. Their objective is to stop Iraq's democratic progress. They tried to stop the transfer of sovereignty. They tried to stop millions of Iraqis from voting in the January 2005 elections. They tried to stop Sunnis from participating in the October referendum on the constitution. And they tried to stop millions from voting in the December elections to form a government under that constitution.

And in each case, they failed. With every election, participation was larger and broader than the one that came before. And in December, almost 12 million people—more than 75 percent of eligible voters—defied the terrorists to cast their ballots. With their votes, the Iraqi people have spoken and made their intentions clear: They want to live in liberty and unity, and they're determined to chart their own destiny.

Now the elements of a free Iraq are trying to stop the—the enemies of a free Iraq are trying to stop the formation of unity government. They've learned they cannot succeed by facing coalition and Iraqi forces on the battlefield, so they've taken their violence to a new level, by attacking one of Shia Islam's holiest sites. They blew up the Golden Mosque in Samarra in the hope that this outrageous act would provoke the Shia masses into widespread reprisals which would provoke Sunnis to retaliate and drag the nation into a civil war.

Yet, despite massive provocations, Iraq has not descended into civil war. Most

Iraqis have not turned to violence. The Iraqi security forces have not broken up into sectarian groups waging war against each other. Instead, Sunni, Shia, and Kurdish soldiers stood together to protect religious sites, enforce a curfew, and restore civil order.

In recent weeks, these forces passed another important test when they successfully protected millions of Shia pilgrims who marched to the cities of Karbala and Najaf for an annual religious holiday. In 2004, the terrorists launched coordinated strikes against the pilgrims, killing scores of innocent worshipers. This year, the pilgrimage was largely peaceful, thanks to the courage and the unity of the Iraqi security forces. In the midst of today's sectarian tension, the ability of Iraqis to hold a peaceful gathering by millions of people is a hopeful sign for the future of Iraq.

In these last few weeks, we've also seen terrible acts of violence. The kidnappings and brutal executions and beheadings are very disturbing. There's no place in a free and democratic Iraq for armed groups operating outside the law. It's vital to the security of a free Iraq that the police are free of militia influence. And so we're working with Iraqi leaders to find and remove leaders from the national police who show evidence of loyalties to militias. We're partnering U.S. battalions with Iraqi national police to teach them about the role of a professional police force in a democratic society. We're making clear to Iraqi leaders that reining in the illegal militias must be a top priority of Iraq's new government when it takes office.

The violence we're seeing is showing the Iraqi leaders the danger of sectarian division, and underscoring the urgency of forming a national unity government. Today, Iraqi leaders from every major ethnic and religious community are working to construct the path forward. Our Ambassador to Iraq, Zal Khalilzad, is helping Iraq's leaders reach out across political and religious and sectarian lines, so they can form a government that will earn the trust and the confidence of all Iraqis.

Putting aside differences to build a democracy that reflects the country's diversity is a difficult thing to do. It's even more difficult when enemies are working daily to stop your progress and divide your nation. Yet Iraqis are rising to the moment. They deserve enormous credit for their courage, and their determination to succeed.

Iraqi leaders are coming to grips with an important truth: The only practical way to overcome the divisions of three decades of tyranny is through democracy. Democracy is the only form of government where every person has a say in the governance of a country. It's the only form of government that will yield to a peaceful Middle East. So Iraqis are working to overcome past divisions and build a free society that protects the rights of all its citizens. They're undertaking this progress with just a year's experience in democratic politics.

Many of the institutions and traditions we take for granted here in America—from party structures to centuries' experience with peaceful transitions of power—are new to Iraq, so we should not be surprised if Iraqis make mistakes or face setbacks in their efforts to build a government that unites the Iraqi people.

We're beginning to see the signs of progress. Earlier this month, Iraqi leaders announced they had reached an agreement on the need to address critical issues such as de-Baathification in the operation of security ministries, and the distribution of oil revenues in the spirit of national unity. They agreed to form a new national security council that will improve coordination within the government on these and other difficult issues. This council will include representatives from all major political groups, as well as leaders from Iraq's executive, judicial and legislative branches. As a result of this council's considered advice, the Iraqi government that emerges will be more effective and more unified.

Another important sign of progress is that Saddam Hussein is now being called to account for his crimes by the free citizens of a free Iraq. Millions of Iraqis are seeing their independent judiciary in action. At the former dictator's trial, Iraqis recently saw something that's got to be truly amazing to them. When Saddam Hussein stood up and began to give a political speech, the presiding judge gaveled him down. Saddam growled at the judge, declaring, "I'm the head of state." The judge replied, "You used to be the head of the state. And now you're a defendant."

Three years ago any Iraqi who addressed Saddam in this way would have been killed on the spot. Now the former dictator is answering to a judge, instead of meting out arbitrary justice, and Iraqis are replacing the rule of a tyrant with the rule of law.

Finally, some Americans are asking if it's time to pull out our troops and leave the Iraqis to settle their own differences. I know the work in Iraq is really difficult, but I strongly feel it's vital to the security of our country. The terrorists are killing and maiming and fighting desperately to stop the formation of a unity government because they understand what a free Iraq in the heart of the Middle East means for them and their ideology. They know that when freedom sets root in Iraq, it will be a mortal blow to their aspirations to dominate the region and advance their hateful vision. So they're determined to stop the advance of a free Iraq, and we must be equally determined to stop them.

The irony is that the enemy seems to have a much clearer sense of what's at stake than some of the politicians here in Washington, D.C. One member of Congress who has proposed an immediate withdrawal of American forces in Iraq recently explained that what would happen after American forces pulled out was this: He said, "They'll fight each other, somebody will win, they'll settle it for themselves." While it might sound attractive to some, it would have disastrous consequences for American security. The Iraqi government is still in transition, and the Iraqi security forces are still gathering capacity. If we leave Iraq before they're capable of defending their own democracy, the terrorists will win. They will achieve their stated goal. This is what the terrorists have told us they want to achieve. They will turn Iraq into a safe haven. They will seek to arm themselves with weapons of mass destruction. They will use Iraq as a base to overthrow moderate governments in the Middle East. They will use Iraq as a base from which to launch further attacks against the United States of America.

Mindful of recent history, I ask you to think about what happened in Afghanistan. In the 1980s, the United States helped Afghan freedom fighters drive the Soviet Red Army from Kabul, and once the Soviets withdrew, we decided our work was finished and left the Afghans to defend [sic] for themselves. Soon the terrorists moved in to fill the vacuum. They took over the country; they turned it into a safe haven from which they planned and launched the attacks of September the 11th.

If we leave Iraq before the job is done, the terrorists will move in and fill the vacuum, and they will use that failed state to bring murder and destruction to freedom-loving nations.

I know some in our country disagree with my decision to liberate Iraq. Whatever one thought about the decision to remove Saddam from power, I hope we should all agree that pulling our troops out prematurely would be a disaster. If we were to let the terrorists drive us out of Iraq, we would signal to the world that America cannot be trusted to keep its word. We would undermine the morale of our troops by betraying the cause for which they have sacrificed. We would cause the tyrants in the Middle East to laugh at our failed resolve and tighten their repressive grip. The global terrorist movement would be emboldened and more dangerous than ever. For the security of our citizens and the peace of the world, we will not turn the future of Iraq over to the followers of a failed dictator, or to evil men like bin Laden and Zarqawi.

America will leave Iraq, but we will not retreat from Iraq. We will leave because Iraqi forces have gained in strength, not because America's will has weakened. We will complete the mission in Iraq because the security of the American people is linked to the success in Iraq.

We're pursuing a clear strategy for victory. Victory requires an integrated strategy: political, economic and security. These three elements depend on and reinforce one another. By working with Iraqi leaders to build the foundations of a strong democracy, we will ensure they have the popular support they need to defeat the terrorists. By going after the terrorists, coalition and Iraqi forces are creating the conditions that allow the Iraqi people to begin rebuilding their lives and their country. By helping Iraqis with economic reconstruction, we're giving every citizen a real stake in the success of a free Iraq. And as all this happens, the terrorists, those who offer nothing but death and destruction, are becoming isolated from the population.

I wish I could tell you the violence in Iraq is waning and that all the tough days in the struggle are behind us. They're not. There will be more tough fighting ahead with difficult days that test the patience and the resolve of our country. Yet, we can have faith in the final outcome because we've seen freedom overcome the darkness of tyranny and terror and secure the peace before. And in this century, freedom is going to prevail again.

In 1941, the year the Freedom House began its work, the future of freedom seemed bleak. There were about a dozen lonely democracies in the world. The Soviet Union was led by the tyrant Stalin who massacred millions. Hitler was leading Nazi Germany in a campaign to dominate Europe and eliminate the Jewish people from the face of the Earth. An imperial Japan launched a brutal surprise attack on America. Today, six decades later, the Soviet empire is no more; Germany and Japan are free nations, and they are allies in the cause of peace; and the majority of the world's governments are democracies.

There were doubters six decades ago who said that freedom could not prevail. History has proved them wrong. In this young century, the doubters are still with us; but so is the unstoppable power of freedom. In Afghanistan and Iraq and other nations, that power is replacing tyranny with hope, and no one should bet against it.

One of the greatest forces for freedom in the history of the world is the United States Armed Forces. In the past four-and-a-half years, our troops have liberated more people than at any time since World War II. Because of the men and women who wear our nation's uniform, 50 million people in Iraq and Afghanistan have tasted freedom, and their liberation has inspired millions more across the broader Middle East to believe that freedom is theirs, as well.

U.S. Military Forces in Iraq: Withdraw Quickly

WESLEY B. RENFRO AND BRIAN R. URLACHER

Since September 11, 2001, President George W. Bush and his advisors have sought to link their Iraq policy with the international terrorism. In March 2003, the United States invaded Iraq because Saddam Hussein's regime was allegedly developing covert nuclear, biological, and chemical weapons programs that posed an imminent threat to the United States. Congress and most Americans approved of the president's preferred policy solution—war—despite international protests and a distinct lack of conclusive evidence. Following the invasion, it became clear that there was little merit behind the original justifications for war. The costs of war and occupation, however, are mounting as victory seems increasingly improbable, if not impossible.

As the fourth anniversary of the war looms Iraq, despite the administration's predictions to the contrary, continues to grow less stable. Although recent U.S. multilateral cooperation on a range of international issues including the festering Iranian nuclear program has helped repair some relations with key European allies, including Germany and France; evidence strongly suggests that we have become less popular within Iraq and the rest of the Middle East. Most alarming are reports indicating that the American invasion and botched occupation have created hordes of anti-American Islamic radicals. In short, in addition to driving Iraq into civil war, U.S. policy has bred a new generation of would be terrorists. The climate of fear, violence, and reprisal fostered by Washington's Iraq policy is generating increasing amounts of anti-Americanism while drawing insurgents and extremists from all over the Middle East. Given the grim situation and the lack of a viable policy option capable of peacefully resolving the violence and anti-Americanism in Iraq, this essay argues that the U.S. has only one option—withdrawal from Iraq before the situation becomes worse.

This essay aims to rebut the president's justifications for a continued American presence in Iraq. To do this we attempt to demonstrate that much of the reasoning that the president uses to justify the Iraq conflict is as flawed as the reasoning behind the initial invasion of Iraq. Moreover, we argue that a prompt withdrawal, although not an optimum solution, is America's best available option. Based on a review of the president's continuing justifications for the war, the original context of the war, and the implications of the Iraq war on American homeland security, we conclude a quick withdrawal is American's best policy solution.

WINNING THE PEACE? WHAT PEACE?

In his speech to an audience at Freedom House on March 29, 2006, the president provided no solid claim regarding how much progress has actually been made Iraq. His rhetoric was and is overly confident, and we believe, inconsistent with the reality. When the president confidently exclaims, "Today, Iraqi leaders from every major ethnic and religious community are working to construct the path forward," he argues that things in Iraq are improving. But they are not. His optimistic appraisal, moreover, seems out of touch with keen Iraq watchers, including high-ranking members of the U.S. military, who have concluded that little, if any progress has occurred. Forty months after American forces toppled Saddam Hussein, the Iraq economy remains in shambles, unemployment is higher than before, oil exports are down, and most tellingly, the level of intrafactional and anti-American attacks continues to mount. There are no signs that Iraqi leaders are attempting to, "construct the path forward."

As long as the United States military remains in Iraq, American troops will carry out operations against insurgents, and thus will continue to generate intense anti-Americanism throughout the Arab and Muslim world. This anti-Americanism will result in more terrorist attacks, not less, as the president suggests. His position makes sense only if the number of terrorists in the world is fixed. It is not. The American presence in Iraq is itself increasingly responsible for the growing numbers of young men and women willing to participate in the insurgency. As a recent and well-publicized National Intelligence Estimate, produced in a cooperating process by the nation's 16 professional intelligence agencies, notes, "The Iraq conflict has become the 'cause celebre' for jihadists, breeding a deep resentment of U.S. involvement in the Muslim world and cultivating supporters the global jidadist movement."

Since 2002, the Bush administration has sought to link Iraq to the events of September 11, 2001 and the subsequent Global War on Terror, in spite evidence and analysis concluding just the opposite. The president tells us, "Today, the central front in the War on Terror is Iraq." We agree but only because the continued presence of unwelcome American troops has generated so many Iraqi radicals. The president's plan seems to hinge on the notion that if we pursue a policy of killing terrorists and insurgents in Iraq, the United States will not have to fight terrorism in its own territory. This line of reasoning suffers from several serious flaws, however. Recent history in Iraq demonstrates with chilling accuracy that for every insurgent killed by U.S. forces in Iraq another rises to take his or her place. These insurgents are unlikely to easily forget the suffering and pain caused by the U.S. occupation of Iraq, and we are thus more likely, not less, to be victims of terrorism, at home or aboard, at their hands. Furthermore, it is increasingly clear that the United States cannot impose peace on Iraq's quarrelsome factions. Iraq is exceedingly fragile, and it is doubtful that anything can be done to avert civil war much less win the peace. Consequently, with success hard to find and the number of terrorists increasing, the only viable policy option is a quick exit.

The U.S. invasion of Iraq, the abuses of Iraqi prisoners by American guards at Abu Ghraib, and the internment camps for suspected terrorists at the U.S. naval base at Guantánamo Bay in Cuba have incensed many in the Arab and Muslim worlds. Young men who previously may have regarded the United States as a land of opportunity now see it as a force of occupation and oppression. Although difficult to measure, we can gauge support for the insurgency by the escalating levels of violence in Iraq. There is little to suggest that support for the insurgency is doing anything but increasing.

Usama bin-Laden has called Iraq the central front in his war against the United States precisely because the American presence in Iraq is a rallying cry for disaffected youth throughout the region. Consequently, foreign fighters continue streaming into Iraq. It is naïve to think that these fighters have been lying in wait for years waiting for an opportunity to fight the United States. Foreign fighters in Iraq are responding to the call of bin-Laden, not because they are loyal al-Qaeda members with longstanding ties to the organization, but because they want the United States out of Iraq. They have chosen to participate in the insurgency in Iraq because they believe the U.S. occupation is unjust.

This is precisely why bin-Laden has designated Iraq and not Afghanistan the central front in his fight against the United States. The U.S. campaign against Afghanistan was in response to the 9/11 attacks masterminded by al-Qaeda. During 2001 and 2002, American forces in Afghanistan were reportedly close to capturing Usama bin-Laden. Working with the assistance of local Afghani leaders and neighboring states, many believed that the United States had created a vice to squeeze al-Qaeda and capture its leaders, including bin-Laden. Instead, the Bush team shifted focus and resources away from Afghanistan in favor of a new confrontation with Iraq.

Bin-Laden has declared Iraq the central front because al-Qaeda can fight and win in Iraq. Iraq's neighbors have made an already bad situation worse. Iran and Syria have, for example, facilitated the passage of foreign fighters into Iraq, specifically with the goal of undermining the U.S. position. The president has attempted to draw the false dichotomy of fighting terrorism in Iraq or in the United States. What President Bush and his advisors neglect to mention is that the United States had the option of fighting terrorism abroad before pursuing regime change in Iraq. Washington continues to fight al-Qaeda and a resurgent Taliban in Afghanistan. However, the United States must now divide its resources, human and material, between Afghanistan and Iraq.

Bin-Laden welcomes the American presence in Iraq because it confirms many Arab's worst suspicions about U.S. motivations, thereby generating increasing numbers of al-Qaeda sympathizers. It seems clear though that bin-Laden prefers Iraq because he is strong there and the United States weak. The United States has killed thousands of insurgents in Iraq, but the Bush administration cannot provide an estimate of how many of these insurgents were affiliated with al-Qaeda before the U.S. invasion and how many joined the insurgency because of the invasion. If the United States wants to crush bin-Laden's terrorist organization, it needs to deprive al-Qaeda of its newest and largest recruiting pool—young Muslims who are frustrated by the U.S. presence in Iraq and the abuse of detainees and prisoners at the hands of Americans. It seems unlikely that the United States can deprive the Iraqi insurgency of its most potent weapon, men willing to give their lives for the perceived liberation of their country, while maintaining an occupation force. Unless Washington drafts a clever strategy to win the hearts and minds of Muslim men throughout the region, it seems the only plausible way to diffuse the situation is the withdrawal of American troops from Iraq.

The president argued fervently that setting a timetable for leaving Iraq would play into the hands of terrorists in Iraq by emboldening the insurgents to wait out the U.S. withdrawal. Senator Russ Feingold (D-WI) and others reject the logic of this assertion. Finegold's rejection of the president's reasoning starts with the premise that there is a sense among Iraqis and across the broader Middle East that the United States has no plans to ever leave Iraq. Furthermore, may Arabs believe that deposing of Saddam Hussein for his alleged weapons of mass destruction (WMDs) was only a cover for a larger policy of colonization that has placed the United States in the heart of the Arab world.

The president is aware of this sentiment yet chooses to believe that democracy, American style, will be a panacea for Iraq's ills. This emphasis on the rehabilitive effects of democracy ignores the deeply divided nature of Iraqi society. Nationalism is a potent force, and the continued presence of the United States has allowed terrorist groups to used patriotism as a recruiting tool. It is also worth noting that the current justification for the continued presence of American troops in Iraq is a highly deceptive bait and switch. When it became clear that Iraq had not harbored WMDs, the president and his advisors began to justify the invasion and continued occupation of Iraq for nobler reasons, including the spread of liberal democracy to a region rife with authoritarian regimes.

FROM ROGUE STATE TO MODEL DEMOCRACY—WISHFUL THINKING FOR MR. BUSH

Following September 11, 2001, Bush began asserting that the Iraqi threat was too great to ignore and that America's only option was to invade Iraq and prevent a dictatorial and homicidal Saddam Hussein from acquiring WMDs. In March 2003, the United States did invade and toppled the unsavory Iraqi regime. The United States has been unable to locate any weapons of mass destruction in Iraq. As weeks turned into months and it became increasingly clear that there were no Iraqi WMDs, the president and his advisors began to justify the Iraqi invasion in others terms, most notably the need to spread peace via democracy in the Middle East and not to allow terrorism a new breeding ground in a failed state. President Bush was correct in his claim that failed states are breeding grounds for terrorism. However, the current Iraq strategy turned a stable, though unsavory, Iraq under Saddam Hussein into a failed state under American supervision. The Bush team now asserts that the United States can remake Iraq into a stable democracy and that this will, in turn, encourage other states in the region to democratize. This argument, while perhaps reasonable on the surface, collapses on closer examination and reveals several implicit and questionable assumptions.

The Bush team remains adamant in their claim that the United States can create a stable democracy in Iraq. The president articulates his position when he says, "By going after the terrorists, coalition and Iraqi forces are creating the conditions that allow the Iraqi people to begin rebuilding their lives and their country. By helping Iraqis with economic reconstruction, we're giving every citizen a real stake in the success of a free Iraq." These claims seem highly dubious given the ethnic and religious divisions that permeate Iraqi society. The United States, as the president notes, was able to foster democracy in Japan and German after World War II. However, in each of these situations the United States was dealing with a homogenous country exhausted by war and somewhat receptive to the American state-building enterprise. The situation in Iraq fundamentally differs in several respects. Most Iraqis, contrary to the president's assumptions, do not identify as Iraqi. Rather, they identify themselves on religious and ethnic lines, for example, as Shiites, Sunni, or Kurd.

Iraq, though an overwhelmingly Muslin nation, is not religiously or ethnically homogenous. The Kurds are the predominant ethnic group in the north and are ethnically distinct from most Iraqis, who are Arabs. Differences in history, culture, and language combined with their brutal repression by the Saddam Hussein regime have made the Kurds wary of their fellow Iraqis. The Shiites are Arab Muslims that practice a form on Islam common in Iran but rare in most of the rest of the Middle East. The Shiites, moreover, comprise about 60% of Iraq's population and like the Kurds they were systematically brutalized by the Sunni-dominated government of Saddam. Finally, the Sunnis are Arab Muslims who subscribe to the major variant of Islam in the Middle East. Although a minority it Iraq, the Sunni received preferential treatment by Saddam Hussein, a Sunni himself, often at the expense of non-Sunni Iraqis.

These groups have long and acrimonious histories of internecine strife. Nearly two years after the American invasion, the insurgency seems to be growing in strength, and Iraq is in the first stages of a civil war. President Bush has told Americans that, "Despite massive provocations, Iraq have not descended into civil war." This conclusion seems incorrect given the rising levels of violence in Iraq. It is likely that without the presence of American troops in the country, civil war would have occurred months ago. U.S. soldiers are providing a temporary bandage to a deeply rooted historical reality, namely that Iraq is unlikely to hold together as a coherent nation state absent massive American military pressure or a forceful dictator.

Second, even if the United States can help establish a democratic Iraq, there is no guarantee that this democratic state will not be radical and opposed to American interests in the region. President Bush would do well to recall the old adage, "be careful what you wish for." The Middle East is increasingly a radicalized region, and U.S. popularity within the Arab and Muslim world is at an all time low. Recent public opinion data from Iraq reflects a growing disenchantment with American occupation and an increasing desire for Washington to set a time-table to withdrawal. A democratic process in Iraq could yield a government with goals inimical to U.S. preferences for the region, including plentiful access to oil and a peaceful settlement to the Palestinian-Israeli conflict. A democratic Iraq dominated by a pro-Iranian Shiite majority would likely adopt Iran's strong pro-Palestinian stance in opposition to Washington's pro-Israeli position. Put simply, a reconstituted Iraq that seeks to stymie Washington's regional agenda is not in American's best interest.

THE DUBIOUS LINK BETWEEN IRAQ AND TERRORISM

American losses at the hands of Iraqi insurgents demonstrate that small groups of radical extremists can inflict severe damage, even to the world's most powerful state. This is a lesson that the United States should not have to learn again after the devastating 9/11 attacks illustrated American vulnerability to strikes from terrorists. In one horrific morning, 19 terrorists working on a slim budget managed to take thousands of lives, both American and foreign. In response, President Bush oversaw the most sweeping redesign on U.S. security policy since the end of the Cold War. Articulated in the *September 2002 National Security Strategy of the United States* (NSS 2002), President Bush claimed, "Enemies in the past needed great armies and great industrial capabilities to endanger America. Now, shadowy networks of individuals can bring great chaos and suffering to our shores for less than it costs to purchase a single tank."

The president's assertion is undoubtedly true. What is less clear, however, is the link between rogue states (such as Iraq, Iran, North Korea, and Libya) and international terrorism. In NSS 2002, the president repeatedly made the case that rogue states and international terrorists are two facets of one problem facing the international community. His solution to the growing menace, perceived or otherwise, of rogue states and international terrorism is a strategy of preemption and prevention. The argument is simple—in an age of weapons of mass destruction, the United States cannot afford to absorb the first blow. It must attempt to preserve U.S. security by preventing terrorists and their presumed rogue-state backers from obtaining the ability to strike the United States. Throughout 2002, the president, his cabinet, and his advisors repeatedly made the case before domestic and international audiences that Iraq was a state on the verge of obtaining nuclear, chemical, or biological weapons. Their argument assumed that once Iraq had these weapons, they would aggressively use them to bring harm to the United States. Although there was ultimately no evidence linking Saddam Hussein to either WMD or al-Qaeda, it stuck many as unusual that the president exercised selective judgment in focusing his efforts on Iraq while refusing to investigate alleged Saudi Arabian links to extremist groups.

If the United States is serious about fighting a "Global War on Terror," it seems strange that Saudi Arabia, the home of Usama bin-Laden and 15 other terrorists whose actions resulted in the death of thousands on September 11, 2001, has remained largely un-scrutinized. The president claims, "Many terrorists who kill innocent men, women, and children on the streets of Baghdad are followers of the same murderous ideology that took the lives of our citizens in New York, in Washington, and Pennsylvania." This argument is less than compelling as there is scant evidence linking Iraq to al-Qaeda before the invasion and occupation. What is clear, however, is that the Bush administration targeted Iraq while ignoring known Saudi links to al-Qaeda.

IRAQ VS. HOMELAND SECURITY

Recent history shows that the world is a dangerous place even for a superpower. The United States may be the wealthiest country in the world, but even the U.S. government must contend with issues of finite resources. Every policy requires hard decisions about what to fund and what not to fund. It is not enough to argue about whether the mushrooming cost of the Iraq war is a necessary expense; rather, American's should consider what they are not funding by staying in Iraq.

The president has funded the Iraq war through record deficits. This has stripped money from the private sector as surely as a tax would and has been a strain on the U.S. economy. American's appear more than willing to bear this burden to defeat terrorism, yet it is unclear if spending massive sums in Iraq is doing anything but generating more terrorism.

Instead of staying in Iraq and making a dangerous situation even worse, the United States should leave Iraq and concentrate its resources on homeland security. Furthermore, if the president seeks to spread democracy throughout the Middle East, then a national program to reduce dependency on petroleum would force oil-producing nations, which have been able to buy off their populations with petro-dollars, to make reforms to their economies and political systems. The United States likely has to power to affect political and economic change in the Middle East. However, we argue that war and occupation are unlikely to result in positive economic or political change in the region.

The ongoing cost of the Iraq war is not an expense that must be paid. Instead, it is a deliberate choice to use the resources of the American people to open a second, and increasingly dubious, front in the War on Terrorism. Funding and supporting the war in Iraq is an ongoing choice, one taken in lieu of dedicating more resources to homeland security, battling terrorism in Afghanistan, the first front, or affecting change in the Middle East through domestic energy independence.

The president says, "We're pursuing a clear strategy for victory." However, is seems increasingly clear that the fight in Iraq cannot be won. The longer we stay the greater the insurgency will become. The president asserts, "If we were to let the terrorists drive us out of Iraq, we would signal to the world that America cannot be trusted to keep its word." This type of reasoning will not enhance American security and will continue to drain resources that could be invested in more fruitful policies, like homeland security. The president is asking the American people to sacrifice much in pursuit of his failing policy in Iraq. The costs, already high, continue to mount and there is little chance of a positive return on this investment.

CONCLUSION

We have now considered Bush's continuing justification for the war, the original context of the war, and the implications of the Iraq war on the global security environment. We conclude that the United States has two policy options. Washington can either continue to pour resources, both human and material, into a failing project ad infinitum in the hopes the situation will somehow change. Alternatively, the United States can recognize that short of a permanent military occupation, Iraq is beyond democratic rehabilitation, at least in its proposed form, and that it is in America's best interest to leave the country as soon as possible.

The president and others claim that an immediate withdrawal would embolden terrorists and insurgents and demonstrate that the United States lacks resolve. Furthermore, the president opines that, "America will leave Iraq, but we will not retreat from Iraq. We will leave because Iraqi forces have gained in strength, not because America's will has weakened." Many argue that although the war may have been unnecessary in the first place, a sudden withdrawal would only make a bad situation worse. They believe that if we simply stay long enough we can help establish a stable Iraq that will be break apart in a civil war. This essay argues that the damage to Iraq is already done and no matter when the United States chooses to leave, civil war will occur. If civil war is inevitable, as most evidence suggests, it does not make sense for the United States to continue to sacrifice resources in an enterprise doomed to failure. Although an unpleasant reality, there is little hope of salvaging Iraq and avoiding civil war.

In recent months, the United States has made a serious commitment to training and equipping an Iraqi army capable of defeating the insurgency without American assistance. The U.S. military is widely recognized as the most professional and efficient in the world. If the world's most capable military is foundering trying to defeat a virulent insurgency, why is there reason to believe that a recently established Iraqi army will be able to do better? Furthermore, training and arming an Iraqi army seems a poor policy choice given inevitability of a civil war.

The president and his supporters are quick to point out that Iraq's military forces are growing in strength and capability. We disagree with this claim, and more importantly we find it troublesome that the internal composition of Iraq's embryonic security forces reflect the larger sectarian divisions present in society. When the Bush administration claims that it is training and arming Iraqi security forces aimed at preserving stability, it is evading the truth—that it is actually training and arms a military dominated by the Shiites. With the country in the early stags of civil war, it seems like a bad idea to arms one group, especially when that group is likely to use those arms to fight other groups in Iraq. We argue that today's Iraqi soldiers and officers are likely to become tomorrow's warlords and guerillas. The United States is not preparing the Iraqi military to defeat the insurgents; it is training and equipping it for a civil war that is sure to come.

While no easy option has presented itself to the Bush Administration, withdrawal seems to be more consistent with America's long-term objectives. As argued earlier, the American occupation is not a productive strategy in the "Global War on Terror." The continued occupation is only fostering greater resentment of the United States and creating more potential terrorists. While President Bush remains optimistic about creating a stable Iraq and avoiding a civil war, this seems unwarranted in light of the facts. If civil war will eventually come to Iraq, why stay and waste precious resources fighting a losing battle, while continuing to create enemies at every turn? Moreover, the United States can use a tactical withdrawal as an opportunity to regain the credibility and allies it lost during the past few years. Some argue that if the United States were to leave Iraq, it would be a sign of American weakness and would carry grave consequences for the United States. This, however, is simplistic interpretation. American credibility is not based on its willingness to invade and occupy foreign lands. Rather is based on economic prowess, practices of mutual respect, and a multilateral approach to foreign policy, based on consent, that helps foster a stable, peaceful, and prosperous international system. America can best start to rectify its recent deviation from these principles by making a strategic withdrawal from its poorly conceived and failing Iraq adventure.

THE CONTINUING DEBATE: U.S. Military Forces In Iraq

What Is New

Americans became even more discouraged about the war in the months following President Bush's address. Polls in October 2006 found 64% saying that the United States was losing ground in its effort to achieve democracy and stability in Iraq. However, these attitudes did not necessarily mean that Americans wanted to abandon the effort. When asked in one poll, "Do you think the United States should keep military troops in Iraq until the situation has stabilized, or do you think the U.S. should bring its troops home as soon as possible? " the replies were evenly divided, with 47% favoring each option and 6% unsure. Also disheartening for Americans was a poll among Iraqis in September 2006 that found 37% of them wanting foreign troops out within 6 months, 34% supporting a one-year deadline, 20% favoring a two-year timetable, and only 9% taking the position that foreign troops should stay as long as necessary to assure stability. Especially troubling was the finding that 61% of Iraqis approved of insurgent's attacks on U.S. and other foreign troops.

Where to Find More

A good place to begin is with a understanding of Iraq available in William R. Polk, *Understanding Iraq: The Whole Sweep of Iraqi History, from Genghis Khan's Mongols to the Ottoman Turks to the British Mandate to the American Occupation* (Perennial, 2006). Up-to-date information on the struggle in Iraq, including casualties, is available from CNN at www.cnn.com/SPECIALS/2003/iraq/forces/casualties/. The National Priorities Project has a counter for its up-to-the-minute estimate of the monetary cost of the war is at nationalpriorities.org/index.php?option=com_wrapper&Itemid=182.

What More to Do

One key to the future of Iraq is the ability of the troubled Iraqi government to provide stability for the country, thereby allowing a U.S. withdrawal with some sense of success. Analyze the prospects that Iraq with U.S. support will be able to establish a united, relatively peaceful, democratic country. Also consider the consequences of an rapid U.S. withdrawal. Many predict that would permit a vicious civil war killing countless Iraqis, an even greater destruction to Iraq's oil industry and higher world fuel prices, and even the dismemberment of Iraq and increased Middle East instability. What would be the consequences of a U.S. withdrawal and how do those measure up against the burden of a continued U.S. presence?

CREDITS

Amicus Curiae brief to the United States Supreme Court in *Grutter v. Bollinger* (2003).

Bright, Stephen B. Testimony during hearings on "An Examination of the Death Penalty in the United States" before the U.S. Senate, Committee on the Judiciary, Subcommittee on the Constitution, February 1, 2006.

Bush, George W. "This Is Going to Be Freedom's Century" address delivered at the Freedom House, Washington, D.C., March 29, 2006.

Byrd, Harry F. From *Congressional Record*, March 1, 2005.

Cannon, Carl. "She Can Win the White House," *Washington Monthly*, July/August 2005. Reprinted with permission from *The Washington Monthly*. Copyright by Washington Monthly Publishing, LLC, 733 15th St. NW, Suite 520, Washington, DC 20005. 202-393-5155. Web site: www.washingtonmonthly.com.

Charo, R. Alta. Testimony during hearings on "The Consequences of *Roe v. Wade* and *Doe v. Bolton*," before the U.S. Senate Committee on the Judiciary, Subcommittee on the Constitution, Civil Rights and Property Rights, June 23, 2005.

Chen, Christine. Testimony during hearings on "Non-citizen Voting," before the House of Representatives, Committee on House Administration, June 22, 2006.

Collett, Teresa. Testimony during hearings on "The Consequences of *Roe v. Wade* and *Doe v. Bolton*," before the U.S. Senate Committee on the Judiciary, Subcommittee on the Constitution, Civil Rights and Property Rights, June 23, 2005.

Comey, James B. Testimony during hearings on "Reporters' Shield Legislation: Issues and Implications," before the U.S. Senate Committee on the Judiciary, July 20, 2005.

Dean, John W. Testimony during hearings on "Senate Resolution 398 Relating to the Censure of George W. Bush," U.S. Senate, Committee on the Judiciary, March 31, 2006.

Dershowitz, Alan. "Debunking the Newest – and Oldest – Jewish Conspiracy: A Reply to the Mearsheimer-Walt 'Working Paper,'" Faculty Research Working Papers, Kennedy School of Government, Harvard University.

Edwards, James R. Jr. Testimony during hearings on "Should We Embrace the Senate's Grant of Amnesty to Millions of Illegal Aliens and Repeat the Mistakes of the Immigration Reform and Control Act of 1986?" U.S. House of Representatives, Committee on the Judiciary, Subcommittee on Immigration, Border Security, and Claims, July 18, 2006.

Farber, Daniel A. From "Disarmed by Time: The Second Amendment and the Failure of Originalism," *Chicago-Kent Law Review*, Vol. 76, No. 1 (2000). Reprinted by permission of the author.

Finkle, Jeffrey. Testimony during hearings on "Protecting Property Rights After *Kelo,"* before the U.S. House of Representatives, Committee on Energy and Commerce Committee, Subcommittee on Commerce, Trade, and Consumer Protection, October 19, 2005.

Firvida, Cristina Martin. Testimony during hearings on "The Constitution and the Line-Item Veto," U.S. House of Representatives, Committee on the Judiciary, Subcommittee on the Constitution, April 27, 2006.

Harkin, Tom. *Congressional Record,* March 29, 2006

Hatch, Orrin G. *Congressional Record,* May 10, 2005.

Hibbing, John R. Testimony during hearings on "Limiting Terms of Office for Members of the U.S. Senate and U.S. House of Representatives," U.S. House of Representatives, Committee on the Judiciary, Subcommittee on the Constitution, January 22, 1997.

Hogshead-Makar, Nancy. Testimony during hearings on "The First Tee and Schools: Working to Build Character Education," U.S. House of Representatives, Committee on Education and the Workforce, June 28, 2006.

Jacob, Paul. Testimony during hearings on "Limiting Terms of Office for Members of the U.S. Senate and U.S. House of Representatives," U.S. House of Representatives, Committee on the Judiciary, Subcommittee on the Constitution, January 22, 1997.

Laycock, Douglas. From a discussion of the topic "Under God? Pledge of Allegiance Constitutionality," sponsored by the Pew Forum on Religion & Public Life, March 19, 2004. Reprinted with the permission of the Pew Forum on Religion & Public Life. For more information on this issue, please visit www.pewforum.org. Copyright 2006 Pew Research Center.

Levy, Robert A. Testimony during hearings on "Oversight Hearing on the District of Columbia's Gun Control Laws," before the U.S. House of Representatives, Committee on Government Reform, June 28, 2005.

McAdams, John. Testimony during hearings on "An Examination of the Death Penalty in the United States" before the U.S. Senate, Committee on the Judiciary, Subcommittee on the Constitution, February 1, 2006.

Mearsheimer, John. "The Israel Lobby," *London Review of Books,* March 23, 2006. www.lrb.co.uk. Reprinted by permission.

O'Connor, Sandra Day. Opinion in *Gonzales v. Raich,* U.S. Supreme Court, June 6, 2005.

Pearlstine, Norman. Testimony during hearings on "Reporters' Shield Legislation: Issues and Implications," before the U.S. Senate Committee on the Judiciary, July 20, 2005.

Ramsey, Michael D. Testimony during hearings on "Protecting Property Rights After *Kelo,"* before the U.S. House of Representatives, Committee on Energy and Commerce Committee, Subcommittee on Commerce, Trade, and Consumer Protection, October 19, 2005.

Renfro, Wesley B., and Brian Urlacher. "With Terrorism Growing and Civil War Looming the United States Must Withdraw from Iraq," an essay written for this volume, September 2006.

Rogers, Patrick J. Testimony during hearings on "Non-citizen Voting," before the House of Representatives, Committee on House Administration, June 22, 2006.

Ross-Edwards, Amanda. "Additional Clarification of Intercollegiate Athletics Policy: A Step in the Right Direction," an essay written for this volume, October 2006.

Ryan, Paul. Testimony during hearings on "The Constitution and the Line-Item Veto," U.S. House of Representatives, Committee on the Judiciary, Subcommittee on the Constitution, April 27, 2006.

Sekulow, Jay Alan. From a discussion of the topic "Under God? Pledge of Allegiance Constitutionality," sponsored by the Pew Forum on Religion & Public Life, March 19, 2004. Reprinted with the permission of the Pew Forum on Religion & Public Life. For more information on this issue, please visit www.pewforum.org. Copyright 2006 Pew Research Center.

Siddique, Asheesh. "The New Nativism," *Campus Progress News*, Spring 2005. www.campusprogress.org. By permission of Campus Progress, Center for American Progress.

Simcox, Chris. Testimony during hearings on "Securing Our Borders: What We Have Learned From Government Initiatives and Citizen Patrols," before the U.S. House of Representatives Committee on Government Reform, May 12, 2005.

Stevens, John Paul III. Opinion in *Gonzales v. Raich*, U.S. Supreme Court, June 6, 2005.

Sullivan, Amy. "Hillary in 2008? Not So Fast," *Washington Monthly*, July/August 2005. Reprinted with permission from *The Washington Monthly*. Copyright by Washington Monthly Publishing, LLC, 733 15th St. NW, Suite 520, Washington, DC 20005. 202-393-5155. Web site: www.washingtonmonthly.com.

Turner, Robert. Testimony during hearings on "An Examination of the Call to Censure the President," United States Senate, Committee on the Judiciary, March 31, 2006.